Beyond Domination

NEW FEMINIST PERSPECTIVES
edited by Mary Vetterling-Braggin

WOMEN AND SPIRITUALITY
Carol Ochs

WOMEN, SEX, AND THE LAW
Rosemarie Tong

MOTHERING
Essays in Feminist Theory
Joyce Trebilcot, editor

BEYOND DOMINATION
New Perspectives on Women and Philosophy

Edited by
CAROL C. GOULD

ROWMAN & ALLANHELD
PUBLISHERS

ROWMAN & ALLANHELD

Published in the United States of America in 1984
by Rowman & Allanheld, Publishers
(A division of Littlefield, Adams & Company)
81 Adams Drive, Totowa, New Jersey 07512

Library of Congress Cataloging in Publication Data
Main entry under title:

Beyond domination.

(New feminist perspectives series)
Includes papers given at the Annette Walters Memorial
Conference on the Philosophy of Women's Liberation,
May 15-17, 1981, Milwaukee, Wis.
Bibliography: p.
Includes index.
1. Feminism—Philosophy—Congresses. I. Gould,
Carol C. II. Series: New feminist perspectives.
HQ1106.B49   1983   305.4'2   83-10894
ISBN 0-8476-7202-6
ISBN 0-8476-7236-0 (pbk.)

83 84 85/ 10 9 8 7 6 5 4 3 2 1

Printed in the United States of America

Contents

Preface

The Philosophy of Women's Liberation has never been systematically articulated. The national conference on this subject, and this book which resulted from it, represent a major contribution to this task. That there has been no well-defined philosophy may be one of the reasons why the women's movement crests and recedes in every century, for a social movement must have a philosophy in order to abide in every era of history.

The Institute of Women Today, seeking to address this need, contacted Dr. Carol Gould, whose pioneer effort in the field was established by her *Women and Philosophy: Toward a Theory of Liberation,** which she edited and to which she contributed. Carol accepted the invitation and responsibility to head the national convocation on the Philosophy of Women's Liberation. Under her leadership and the prestige of her reputation, some of the most eminent women philosophers were recruited to design the meeting, and with this purpose in mind met at the University of Chicago in the spring of 1980 to plan the program for one year later, May 15–17, 1981, in Milwaukee, Wisconsin, because Illinois was not an ERA–ratified state. The meeting was attended by an interdisciplinary participation of ninety members from 31 states. This book includes many of the papers given at that meeting, as well as papers contributed by others after the conference.

A special title was given to this first-of-its-kind conference: The Annette Walters Memorial Conference on the Philosophy of Women's Liberation. The late Annette Walters was perhaps the first nun to win a discrimination suit against a Catholic college, St. Ambrose College in Davenport, Iowa. The suit was found in her favor, but the real judgment was historic in its precedence.

As codirector with Sister Ritamary Bradley of the Sister Formation Conference in the 1950s and early 1960s, Sister Annette set the foundation for the education and the socialization of U.S. nuns. She pioneered efforts to see that all nuns were educated to the limit of each individual's ability. Thus, when Vatican II convened and called for renewal of religious communities, an educated and articulate

*New York: G. P. Putnam's, 1976.

group of American women was ready and rapidly set a pace within the Church and indeed within the women's movement itself.

Annette later recalled the 1975 national women's convention in Houston for which she had been an Iowa delegate. She wrote, "This is one of the greatest events in American history. For a few brief days the barriers were down, as women interacted with women, sister to sister, in unbelievable unity of purpose." Defending herself against irrational accusations of the Roman curia during the early 1960s, she wrote, "Yes, indeed, I said and believe that to yield one's conscience to the control of another is to risk the destruction and breakdown of personality." This is a theme in one of her several unfinished manuscripts on the psychology of conscience and moral development. Annette, a reknowned clinical psychologist, was praised by the psychologist B. F. Skinner of Harvard University as being "one of the most astute psychologists of her time." Thus, this conference on the Philosophy of Women's Liberation was properly dedicated to the memory of Annette Walters.

Convener of the conference was the Institute of Women Today, an organization founded in 1974 to "search for the religious and historical roots of women's liberation." Sponsored by Jewish, Protestant, and Catholic women's organizations, the Institute has 150 professional women who represent the four disciplines of law, psychology, theology, and history. Some of the national sponsors are such groups as Church Women United, the National Federation of Temple Sisterhoods, the American Jewish Committee, the National Coalition of American Nuns, the Leadership Conference of Women Religious, and the Presbyterian Women. Because the benchmark of the Institute is "we are our sisters' keeper," the group sponsors programs for women in four prisons and one jail by bringing to them legal services, classes in all the fine arts, and courses in the building trades of electrical wiring, carpentry, plumbing, and wall-restoration.

This book expresses, in essence, the thought-lines of the conference. In addition to those who contributed papers and discussion, numerous others helped with the program. Some of these were Dr. Kaye Rockwood, Dr. Margaret Carroll, Sister Irenaeus Checkouras, Ph.D., Sister Nancy Fineran, and Attorney Ralla Klepak, who is president of the board of the Institute. The following also served, together with many of those in this book, on the program: Sylvia De 'Jesus, Dr. Sonja Quitslund, Ann Van Dyke, and Sister Ann Mary Dooley, Ph.D. Sister Ritamary Bradley served as cochair and coplanner. Sister Barbara Valuckas, Ph.D., was the facilitator, and Ann Wolf of the American Jewish Committee, a cofounder of the Institute, was presiding chairperson.

The medal and citation of the Institute were given on this occasion to Drs. Dolores Frese and Carol Gould. The former was cited for her successful suit against the University of Notre Dame in a class action case concerning job discrimination on grounds of sex. This case, in which Dr. Frese was chief plaintiff, was settled by Notre Dame, whose officials realized their many years of error and came to an agreement with all litigants concerned. Dr. Gould was recognized for her brilliance and leadership in directing the conference.

The Institute of Women Today looks forward to a second such meeting to be held on the subject of philosophy as that philosophy develops and enlarges the dimensions for thinking about women's liberation. The enlargement of that concept takes place day by day; we hope that with the aid of ideas in this book, that concept will be ever-deepening and all-encompassing. The women's movement has been called the greatest social revolution of this century because it has changed human relationships. If this is true, it would be well that we reflect on the continuing articulation of the philosophy undergirding the movement with abiding embrace.

Sister Margaret Ellen Traxler, SSND
Director, *the Institute of Women Today*

Introduction

In a century marked by major social movements, the women's movement has undoubtedly been one of the most important. In addition to its practical accomplishments, the movement for women's equality and for the overcoming of domination provided the stimulus for the development of women's studies and for the rethinking of basic categories and theoretical frameworks concerning the nature of human beings. Within the field of philosophy, feminist theory made important advances, e.g. in criticizing and reclaiming the history of philosophy, in constructing new approaches to the question of women's "nature" and its relation to the human, in elaborating the values of equality and liberation, and in the analysis of such specific moral issues as abortion and affirmative action.

Recently, however, there has been a political reaction against the women's movement which has been accompanied by attacks on feminist theory as well. These theoretical criticisms have derived from an emphasis on the alleged biological or genetic basis for women's distinctive nature and roles (e.g., as in sociobiology), or from sociological, psychological, and ethical arguments that assert the need to return to the traditional family and to women's traditional role in it. In the face of such criticisms, some theorists, including former feminists, have proposed to take a second look at feminism and to revise it in order to accommodate these criticisms. It seems to me that this is a mistaken direction for theory concerning women. Instead of adopting such so-called "postfeminist" stances, it is important to develop the philosophy of feminism beyond its earlier formulations. The philosophical and normative frameworks of feminism need to be made deeper and more systematic, and new problems need to be addressed.

The present collection of essays attempts to advance feminist theory in these ways. A number of the essays rethink some of the earlier philosophical issues concerning women, such as the analysis of sex differences and women's identity, the relation of the public and private realms, and the critique of women's work. Other essays focus on new problems or on issues that have not yet received much attention in the literature. These include considerations of women and spirituality in both religious and philosophical contexts, the legal questions of women's privacy and of the relation of feminism to human rights, and such specific issues as pornography and sex preselection. The attempt to develop a more systematic framework for feminist theory in terms of values and ontology is also represented in some of the chapters.

The contributions to this volume do not represent a unified approach to feminism. Indeed, they represent a variety of approaches and philosophical orientations, as well as diverse disciplinary perspectives. Yet there is a common agreement among all the authors concerning the need to go beyond domination and the need to develop a feminist theory adequate to this task. Also, in my view, a level of sophistication in these discussions suggests that there has already been progress within feminist theory. This is certainly due in part to the wide-ranging discussion in philosophical and feminist journals over the past several years and at numerous symposia and conferences, such as those of the Society for Women in Philosophy and those sponsored by the Institute of Women Today.

The essays in this collection thus show vigor, range, and sophistication. Yet this is not to say that I, as editor, agree with all or even with many of them. But the diversity of their analyses I hope will provoke new thought and will contribute to the further development of feminist theory.

The essays are organized in six sections. The volume begins with a general consideration of a systematic value framework for feminism. It proceeds to two other major issues in the philosophy of women: the first concerns theories of women's nature in relation to biology, the social and natural sciences, ontology, and psychoanalytic theory; the second concerns the relation of women and spirituality in the contexts of theology and metaphysics. The next two groups of essays focus on the nature of women's oppression in society. They consider, first, the nature of domination and, second, the criticism of women's work and the relation of the domain of work and politics to personal life. The final group of essays deals with contemporary moral issues in public policy, specifically relating to law, medicine, and higher education.

I would like to express my thanks to Sister Margaret Traxler and the Institute of Women Today for their initiation and support of the Annette Walters Memorial Conference on the Philosophy of Women's Liberation, at which most of the papers in this volume were originally presented. Sister Traxler's enthusiasm and devotion to the cause of women are a continuing inspiration. I would also like to thank Mary Vetterling-Braggin, general editor of the New Feminist Perspectives Series, for her encouragement and editorial assistance.

C. C. G.

PART I

A Proposed Value Framework for Feminism

1

Private Rights and Public Virtues: Women, the Family, and Democracy

CAROL C. GOULD

Introduction

The most obvious and distressing fact about the feminist movement today is that it is under severe and sustained attack, both with respect to the gains women have made in the last decade and with respect to the feminist vision itself. A reactionary backlash has arisen against the movement for equal rights for women, including affirmative action and the ERA, and against abortion rights and other reproductive rights. A similar, active campaign advocates a return to the restrictive conception of the traditional family and marriage and even a return to traditional and supremacist conceptions of women's "essential" characteristics and roles. This reaction is widely evident in the mass media, in religious institutions, and in the contexts of political life, including legislatures and the courts. In the face of attacks on many fronts, an embattled feminist movement has had to engage in separate skirmishes and *ad hoc* responses. What is needed to meet these attacks is a unified and sustained strategy that would itself rest on a unified theoretical understanding of the values and philosophical presuppositions that underlie the women's movement. In this chapter, I hope to make a contribution to such an understanding by sketching a value framework for feminism and by showing its applications to some leading problems concerning women.

The first problem concerns the proper relation between the private and the public spheres, that is, between the domain of personal relations and the domain of political and other forms of public life;

second is the problem of the right to abortion and of the principles on which it is based; and third, the question of androgyny, that is, the desirability of synthesizing in one individual those characteristics which have historically been associated separately with either males *or* females. This third problem includes the possibility of introducing into political life those characteristics historically associated with women. In this essay, I will begin by presenting the proposed framework of values and philosophical principles within which these problems may be clarified, and then will take up each problem in turn. I will focus on the relation between the private and the public spheres, both because it has received less attention than the other two problems, and because the proper relation of the public and the private is involved in the issues of abortion and androgyny.

In presenting my views on these questions, I am reminded of Socrates' trepidation in Plato's *Republic* when he is about to present three of his more problematic proposals concerning the ideal state. He speaks of three waves that threaten to engulf the swimmer who plunges into this sea of problems. For him, these waves represent the proposals, first, for the equality of women, second, for the abolition of the family and of private property for the guardians of the state, and third, for the institution of philosopher-kings. Although my proposals are different, I have some of the same hesitation in approaching my three topics, for these proposals are at some distance from much of the popular view on these matters.

Value Framework and Philosophical Presuppositions

I think the preeminent value that ought to underlie the feminist movement is freedom, that is, self-development. This arises through the exercise of agency, that is, through the exercise of the human capacity for free choice, in forms of activity undertaken to realize one's purposes and to satisfy one's needs. Such activity is manifested both in social interaction and in human work as a transformation of the natural world. On this view, each human being is regarded as an agent with a capacity for free choice and self-development. In this respect, all individuals are equal. Since they are all equal in this way, there is no reason for one individual or for any class of individuals to have more of a right to exercise this capacity for self-realization than any other. Thus, there are no grounds for making differences in gender the basis for differential rights to self-realization. The equal rights of women and men are thus grounded in the nature of human agency itself.

Nevertheless, free choice as the characteristic of human agency is not in itself sufficient for freedom as self-development, although it is necessary. For this free choice to be effective, both material and social conditions must be available through which agents can achieve their purposes. Among the material conditions for self-development are means of subsistence, access to work, and the means of activity. Among the social conditions are forms of cooperation or of social interaction, and access to social institutions, such as education, which are necessary for the realization of one's purposes. Conversely, the denial of these conditions for agency by others or the constraint upon agency by others constitutes domination and thus violates the requirement for equal agency. Thus freedom from domination constitutes a social condition for self-development.

Thus there is an equal right to self-development, and such self-development requires the availability of conditions. It may be seen to follow that there is an equal right to these conditions of agency. Where some individuals control the conditions for the activity of others, those others lack control over the conditions of their agency and are therefore not free to set their own purposes.

The implications of these considerations for the situation of women are that for their full freedom they require control over, or participation in the control of, the economic and social conditions of their lives, as well as freedom from discrimination and domination. This involves not only the usual requirements of equality of opportunity, equal pay for equal work, and freedom from male domination, but also the requirement of equal responsibility for housework and childraising, as well as equal time and opportunities for self-development.

On the view proposed here, although it is only individual human beings that exercise agency and not institutions or society as a whole, yet these individuals are social beings who act in and through their social relations. They engage in joint or common agency in which they seek to realize common goals; or, in pursuit of their individual goals, they require the respect, recognition, or forbearance of others, and their individual acts bear on others in various ways. When individuals act with respect to each other, their relations take the form either of domination and subordination or of reciprocity. As noted earlier, domination involves the control by some agents over others by controlling the conditions that these others require for their activity. By contrast, reciprocity is that form of social relations in which the action of each agent with respect to the other is taken to be equivalent, on the basis of a shared understanding and a free agreement. In the most highly developed form of such reciprocal relations, which I call mutuality, each agent consciously endeavors to act in such a way as to enhance the agency of the other. Reciprocity thus presupposes equality, since each agent recognizes the other as equally free and equally entitled to the conditions of agency. But reciprocity goes beyond equality in that it involves the recognition by each agent of the differences of the other, in terms of the other's own projects and goals.

The import of this conception of reciprocity for feminism is that it poses a requirement for reciprocal and nondominating social relations among all individuals, male and female. Such reciprocity is required as the form which the recognition of equal agency takes in social relations. But since many social relations take on institutional forms in economic life, in politics, in marriage, etc., the transformation of contemporary forms of dominating social relations into reciprocal forms would require the transformation of the institutions themselves.

From the values of equal freedom and reciprocity, we may derive the value of democracy. By democracy, I mean the equal right to participate in decisions concerning the social activities which affect one and the conditions for such activities. This equal right to participate in decisions follows from equal freedom which entails the equal right to control the conditions of one's own activity, where this is a common or social activity. The right to participate in such decision-making has usually been conceived as a political right, that is, as a right to participate in decisions of government, most commonly through voting. On the view proposed here, the right to participate in decision-making would also extend to decisions in the economic, social, and cultural domains, for example, in self-management at the workplace. Furthermore, the value of reciprocity in these contexts suggests that the form of decision-making should be participatory to the greatest extent possible, since the requirement for reciprocal relations among individuals, in which each takes the other into account, is most fully realized in such participatory decision-making.

The development of democracy in all these spheres of social life would help effect a radical change in the status of women, for it would undermine the basis of domination by the few, predominantly men, who have the decision-making power over the conditions of the life and activity of women.

The Public and the Private Spheres

The value framework I have just proposed is intended to help clarify several problems confronting feminism today. The first problem, and the one which constitutes the major part of my analysis, is the proper relation of the public and the private realms. The public domain may be characterized as that in which institutionalized rules and practices, which define appropriate modes of action and interaction, prevail, including political, legal, economic, cultural, and social institutions, such as legislative bodies, firms, schools, and hospitals. It also includes the range of actions and practices covered by the law. The private domain, by contrast, consists of individual actions and interpersonal relations where these actions or relations are not institutionally prescribed or defined, but are in principle matters of the individual's own free choice. (On this interpretation, the private domain also includes roles where these are not institutionally prescribed.)

This interpretation of the distinction between the public and the private has come to replace an older distinction that rested on the difference between the domain of law and government, as the public domain, and the domain of the economic, cultural, and personal or family life, as the private domain. In the older interpretation, government or legislation had no role to play in the private sphere, which proceeded according to its own autonomous rules or principles, such as laws of the market or religious or moral principles. This interpretation of the public-private distinction still plays some role in discussions of the proper relation between government and the economic sphere, between government and the family, and in the question of the separation of church and state. It has often been replaced, however, by my first-mentioned interpretation of the distinction, in general, and also in feminist discussion. And the older divisions of public and private have in some respects been superseded in practice. For example, the government now plays a major role in the regulation of the economy. Indeed, in the case of the family, one might say that the division between public and private was not as sharp as theory made it out to be, inasmuch as governments acknowledged the male as the proper head of the household, at least with regard to property and political rights.

My main concern here is with the first interpretation of the public-private distinction, which roughly corresponds to the distinction between institutionalized and noninstitutionalized contexts of activity. What *is* the proper relation between these domains? On the basis of the earlier sketch of the value framework, one may propose some general points. First, to achieve full democracy in the public sphere, freedom and reciprocity are required in the personal relations of the private sphere, for what we might call a democratic character comes to be formed partly in the experience of interpersonal reciprocity. A person with such a character recognizes the agency and the equality of others and is thus able to take their interests rationally into account in making decisions together with them.

The ability to consider situations from the standpoint of others is particularly important for participatory democracy, for here personal interaction is central and it is desirable to come to common agreement or to respect differences in opinions. Someone who is accustomed either to dominate or to be subordinated in personal life is unlikely to be able to treat others as equals in the context of democratic decision-making. Even representative democracy requires the appreciation of the interests and needs of others and of their equal rights which is involved in reciprocity, for otherwise democracy becomes simply a contest of wills and powers and tends toward tyranny of the majority. Likewise, democracy in institutional contexts rests on the general exercise of free agency, not only in public life but in the context of personal life as well. For the cultivation of free choice in personal life contributes to an active character, which is required for participation in public life. Conversely, the practice of democracy in public life encourages the development of those values and traits of character that support reciprocity and freedom in personal relations.

It is clear from my earlier account that the same values of freedom and reciprocity that are operative in personal relations also apply in the public domain of social, political, and economic life, where these values are realized in democracy. Furthermore, freedom as the self-development of individuals requires both public and private domains and can be achieved by activity in both.

This view may be distinguished from that of the political philosopher Hannah Arendt, who has written at some length about the relation between the public and the private realms in *The Human Condition*.[1] On her view, the ancient Greek distinction between the public and the private is a distinction between the public life of the *polis* (the political community) and the private sphere of the household, which is a sphere of necessity, understood as the production and management of means of subsistence. She claims that, in the modern world, these activities of householding are shifted to the public spheres of the economy and society, and the distinctively public sphere of politics is greatly reduced in significance; moreover, the family becomes a residual domain of privacy or intimacy. Her claim seems to be that only the public sphere of politics affords the opportunity for freedom for, she argues, only in that context can individuals be fully active, achieve full recognition of their distinctiveness, and express their sociality by deliberating with others about the common good. By contrast, she believes that the sphere of personal relations does not offer the possibility of freedom.

I would take exception to such a view of the exclusion of the possibilities of freedom and sociality from the domain of privacy or of personal relations (as well as from the domain of the economy or of social life generally). Regardless of whether such freedom is in fact achieved at present in private life, any argument that it cannot in principle be achieved there seems to me to be mistaken. I have argued that freedom as self-development and sociality in the form of reciprocity and common activity find their place in both the public and the private domains and that where such freedom and sociality are lacking, this requires a transformation of prevailing social relations.

An alternative account of the relation between the public and the private is provided by the radical feminist view that "the personal is political." This somewhat vague slogan has several interpretations, some of which seem to me plainly true. The first sense of this phrase is that general political ideals, such as equality and the overcoming of domination, should not merely be upheld in the abstract, but should be manifested concretely in one's own personal relations. In this sense the slogan is unobjectionable, since it amounts to the requirement that one should practice what one preaches. A second sense in which the personal is political is that personal relations support political institutions for good or ill. For example, it may be argued that relations of male domination in personal life support authoritarianism and capitalism as modes of domination in political or economic life. In this sense, the slogan also seems correct. A third sense, which is the converse of the second, is that the structures of domination and exploitation within the public domain of political and economic life are carried over into the domain of personal life and thus come to be expressed in everyday forms of interpersonal relations. The view of the personal as political in this sense also has considerable plausibility. However, there is a fourth interpretation of the slogan, in which it is taken as a model for the future. On this reading, the slogan proposes to break down the distinction between the public and the private realms and to construct society and the state from personal relations of equality and mutuality. On this view, a good society depends entirely on the achievement of harmonious personal relations among individuals. This view stands in contrast with that of Hannah Arendt who claimed that the political sphere is the only domain of freedom.

Although I hold that the achievement of full democracy in the public sphere rests on reciprocity within the private sphere of personal relations, I do not agree that the public realm can be constructed simply as a composite of personal relations. Rather, the political, social, and economic domains require rules and practices beyond the moral rules that obtain in private interpersonal relations. Such established procedures of public life are required for the coordination of the activities of large groups of people. Moreover, I disagree with the proposal to fuse the personal and political realms, because a separation between them is necessary to preserve the privacy of individuals and their freedom to arrange their personal relations without the interference of institutions or of the state.

Again the question arises: what is the appropriate relation between the public and the private domains? A further question is: how is the private domain of personal relations to be conceived so that the opportunities for freedom and mutuality in such relations are enhanced? Both questions bear directly on the situation of women in several major respects. These include the status of marriage and the family, the modes of childraising and the responsibilities for it, and the question of work, both inside and outside the home. It also bears on the question of the nature of personal relations between men and women.

Contrary to the claim that the personal is political, in one sense the separation between the public and the private spheres should be drawn more sharply than it is at present. To be specific, I would argue for the deinstitutionalization of personal relations. At present there is considerable intrusion by the state in matters of personal life, which ought to be free of such control or regulation. Here, at the point of introducing my own criticism and my proposal for reform, Socrates' metaphor concerning the waves that threaten to engulf him in public disapproval of his idea suggests itself. In my case, the first wave concerns what I see as the problematic nature of the institution of marriage and the need for its abolition as an institution constituted and certified by the state. First, I should emphasize that to discuss marriage in this sense is to make no claims about love, monogamy, or cohabitation, all of which are separable from the institution of marriage and which are not my topic here. Second, the abolition of marriage as a state and legally defined institution does not rule out the possibilities of religious marriages, contract agreements between individuals or informal, personal, marriagelike agreements. Third, to propose the deinstitutionalization of marriage in the sense of a state-certified institution is not to propose that childraising should be completely left to the private domain. Rather, I would hold that legal protections for children are required in which responsibilities for childraising are specified.

There are two major grounds for this proposal concerning marriage. The first concerns the value of freedom of choice and self-development, which has several aspects. For one thing, privacy and the free choice of actions and of personal relations are conditions for full freedom. The problem with the institution of marriage in this respect is that it intrudes on privacy, contrary to the standard claims made for it as preserving the domain of private relations. It legally prescribes a particular form of personal relations as the appropriate one for the foundation of society, and it stipulates gender-based and -differentiated legal obligations and powers for husband and wife. In addition, full freedom of choice would require a diversity of alternative forms of childraising. Marriage is problematic in this respect in that it specifies a particular mode of relation and of childraising as the only legitimate one. Further, freedom for individual self-development requires that institutionalization of forms of activity should be limited to large-scale contexts of group action and decision, which require the coordination provided by established rules or procedures. The extension of such institutionalization into the domain of personal interaction between individuals is an unwarranted constraint on the freedom of their activity.

The second ground for the proposal concerning marriage is the criticism one may make of the present form of marriage and its relation to the family. The range of such criticism, which has been well developed in the literature, centers around the male domination and the unequal position of women, which characterize the marriage institution in its legal and social structure. Although recent court decisions have mitigated some of the more blatant inequalities, the marriage contract is legally still being interpreted primarily on the traditional model of roles and responsibilities, in which duties are divided by sex and in which the wife is subordinated to the husband. Similarly, women in marriages in general have less power than men and less ability to determine the course of events. Moreover, the woman's typical position in marriage and the family is such as to support the continuation of male domination in the economy at large. First of all, the woman performs the housework and childraising as unpaid labor which benefits and reinforces the already established male-dominant economy. In addition, the expectation that women will centrally perform these functions in the home contributes to the devaluation of women's work in the economy at large, such that their types of work and the pay available are lower than that for men. This situation also means that the working woman has the burden of two jobs, with the concomitant constraints on her freedom and time.

The alternative view that I propose distinguishes between marriage and childraising and advocates legal and institutional protections only for childraising. It also advocates a diversity of acceptable forms of childraising and of personal relations between men and women. On this view, such personal relations and forms of living together are deinstitutionalized and remain completely within the private sphere. Household management and duties are not to be regarded as based on sex differences and therefore as not devolving upon the woman alone or primarily. With respect to childraising, there must be clear responsibilities which are legally established. In this respect, there is a need for public protection of the rights of children. This follows from the fact that children are dependent and need the support and guidance of responsible and caring adults. Yet within this requirement I would favor the recognition of a variety of childraising arrangements as fully legitimate. Among these alternatives would be parental responsibility shared between mother and father on the one hand, as well as single parenting and communal childraising (for example in the kibbutz model) on the other. I would stress also that in none of these models should there be a presumption that the task of parenting falls primarily on women. Furthermore, whatever model of childraising individuals may choose, I would argue that there is need for a greater contribution from the community for childcare in order to give parents the opportunity for self-development at work and in leisure.

The traditional function of marriage in guaranteeing the disposition of private property seems to me to be replaceable either by individual ownership of property or by the sharing of property by contract in which individuals legally agree to joint ownership. The marriage contract would then no longer bear the burden of being an instrument of economic control or of legal jurisdiction by the state. Such a replacement of the property functions of marriage by either individual ownership or shared ownership through contract is facilitated in a situation where both men and women have independent incomes in virtue of their both working. Furthermore, it seems to me that having an independent income is in general desirable for women on other grounds as well, in that it provides material and psychological conditions for their freedom.

The Problem of Abortion

I will briefly consider the two other problems of which I spoke at the outset, namely, abortion and androgyny. In each case, I will indicate how the value framework which I proposed bears on these questions.

Abortion has become the most publicly discussed question concerning women, especially in the last few years. It became a major issue in the 1980 national election and has become an international question of morality and politics. Despite the various headings under which the problem of abortion has been raised, it seems clear that the fundamental motive force behind the anti-abortion campaign is sexism, and in particular a backlash against the women's movement and whatever gains it has made in the last decade. This sexism has taken the form of the attempt to repress women by depriving them of their reproductive rights which are fundamental to their freedom. Despite the fact that the motivation of those who argue against the right to abortion is often sexist, nonetheless moral, theological, and scientific arguments have also been advanced to support this view. It is therefore important for philosophers to examine and criticize such arguments and to clarify the basis for the feminist viewpoint of a right to abortion. My earlier discussion of the value framework and the philosophical presuppositions for feminism, as well as my analysis of the relation between public and private, both provide a background for a consideration of the abortion question, which I shall sketch briefly.

The right to abortion follows from the right to freedom of choice which individuals have with respect to their own persons, including their own bodies, and with respect to determining the course of their own lives. This right over one's own person, which follows from the conception of agency that I presented earlier, has been interpreted as the right to privacy. This right to privacy was recognized as the foundation of the right to abortion in the 1973 Supreme Court decision of *Roe v. Wade*. It is also clearly related to the distinction I drew earlier between the private and the public domains. In that context, I argued for the preservation of freedom of choice in the private domain and its protection against interference by public agencies, and especially the state. Action within the private domain was seen as a necessary condition for full freedom of individuals; any interference with what is appropriate in this domain constitutes an unjustified invasion of privacy and is thus coercive or constraining. But, as I have suggested, decisions about abortions are just such matters of privacy, inasmuch as they concern the woman's own person, body, and future. Thus they are appropriate matters to be included within this domain of privacy, matters of the woman's individual free choice.

The only condition under which this freedom could be superseded is if some preeminent value were at stake. The only such preeminent value is human life itself. If abortion did involve the destruction of the life of a human being, this would justify limitations on a woman's freedom to decide on an abortion (in the case that her own life were not at stake). Such a priority of human life over freedom would apply only with respect to actual human beings and not to potential human beings. Indeed, the anti-abortion arguments have focused on just this question of the so-called "right to life," by claiming that the fetus is an actual human being from the moment of conception. On this point, therefore, philosophical clarification is most needed.

I shall briefly sketch some of the arguments which may be offered against the conception of the fetus as a human being. This conception often turns on a presumed biological definition of the origin of human life at the moment of fertilization. However, this is a confusion between two essentially different categories, namely, that of a biologically human embryo and that of a human being. The determination of the point at which an embryo becomes a human being is not a biological or scientific question, but rather a moral and philosophical one. This determination presupposes a conception of being human that essentially involves social and moral characteristics beyond biological or natural ones.

It is sometimes argued that the fetus is a human being because it looks human. But this is an obviously fallacious form of argument because, as has been pointed out (by Jane English, for example), the fetus also looks very much *unlike* a human being. For the longest period of its existence, it resembles the fetuses of other species more than it resembles actual human beings; for example, it has gills and a tail for much of its existence.[2]

A further argument against the notion of the fetus as a human being specifies what constitutes something as a human being and shows that the fetus does not possess the required characteristics. On the basis of the philosophical framework I sketched earlier, I would propose that human beings are fundamentally characterized by being agents, that is, as being able to make choices. This ability has as its condition the independent existence of the human being. However, fetuses have neither independent existence nor the ability to choose, whereas babies have these abilities from the moment of birth.

By the ability to choose, I do not mean simply goal-oriented behavior, such as is found among animals. Rather, I mean the capacity for forming conscious purposes and for performing those actions which themselves constitute the process of self-development of the individual. From birth, the infant is involved in self-activity which constitutes the way in which self-development of the individual proceeds. Although conscious purposes cannot be attributed to neonate human infants, their self-activity is such as to generate such conscious purposes. The ground for this is the extraordinary openness and plasticity that characterizes infant activity.

Such self-activity and self-development have as their condition the independent existence of the individual, since such independence is necessary for the action to be its own. Without such independent existence, the behavior of the organism is simply a function of its biological determinants, whether environmental or genetic, and thus cannot be considered an action of the individual.

In this sense, the biological and topological separation of the infant from its mother at birth marks the beginning of distinctively human activity. For it is only such separation which permits the activity and development of the individual to be *self*-activity and *self*-development, and which permits the interaction and communication of the individual with others and with the environment which goes beyond the biological or biochemical. The fetus does not meet this condition of independent existence.

The view that the life of a human being begins at birth is in fact in agreement with traditional common sense. I suggest that the commonsense view is based on the recognition that independent existence and agency are the minimal hallmarks of a human being. It is surprising that most of the arguments for and against abortion disregard this perception; instead they either make the requirements for the human so strict (e.g., rationality, self-consciousness, etc.) that only children of two or older could conceivably meet them, or else, they biologize the conception of the human so that a human individual is said to exist before birth. I argue that both these positions are wrong. Common sense displays greater wisdom here in its practice of naming children only when they are born. Similarly, that a human being begins at birth is correctly perceived in the legal tradition, which recognizes that personhood begins at this time. I have attempted here to suggest what the philosophical foundations for such a view are.

Androgyny

Having just swum through the second wave, I am ready to take a quick plunge through the third and final wave. This third problem concerning women has to do with the question of overcoming the limitations of gender characteristics in personal life and in political life. On the basis of the earlier value framework, I would claim that freedom for women requires among its subjective conditions a conscious awareness of the manifold alternative possibilities available to them as modes of their self-development. With respect to the formation of character, the awareness is needed that the whole range of character traits which have hitherto been identified as either exclusively male or exclusively female are in fact human traits which have only contingently and historically been identified with some gender. Such an awareness makes possible the appropriation of any of these traits for one's own self-development, depending on one's free choice. Thus such traits as independence, rationality, enterprise, and vigor, which have historically been identified as male traits, should be understood as characterological options as much for women as for men. Similarly, such traits as supportiveness, intuitiveness, sensitivity, and emotionality, historically identified as female traits, should also be seen equally as options for men or for women. Needless to say, it would be important to be critical of those negative traits that have been historically identified with either sex. The awareness of the full range of human traits as available for the development of one's own character makes androgyny or the mixture of what are presently regarded as male or female characteristics a fully acceptable character form.

There is a further sense of androgyny beyond the context of the formation of personal character. This concerns what we may call political androgyny, that is, the overcoming of the domination of politics by those gender-based characteristics that are historically male. Androgyny of this sort consists of introducing into the political sphere and public life generally some of those characteristics historically identified as feminine, and further, of effecting some synthesis which utilizes those features of each tradition that contribute to the enhancement of freedom in political life and in society generally. In this discussion, as in the previous one, it is important to stress not only that gender characteristics are historical and not natural, but also that some men exhibit more of the traditionally identified feminine traits, such as supportiveness, communality, etc., than do some women, and vice versa. Thus, my argument here is only a suggestive and heuristic one and is not based on any hard and fast distinctions.

We may develop the idea of political androgyny by beginning from the conception of freedom presented earlier. This conception involves the free choice and self-development of individuals, as well as the social conditions required for their development. These social conditions include reciprocity in social and personal relations and specific forms of social organization. This conception of freedom may thus be analyzed as involving the two dimensions of individuality and community.

The concern with individuality has traditionally been primarily associated with men, and the concern with community or sociality has traditionally been primarily a woman's concern. In modern times, the public sphere of work and politics has been characterized by egoism, that is, an ideology of individual self-interest, and individual achievement and recognition. This public sphere has been one in which men have historically predominated, and so this ideology has been primarily associated with men. On the other hand, women have historically been mainly consigned to the private sphere of the family and personal relations. The ideology and concerns characteristic of this sphere have been those of supportiveness and compassion for others and the importance of the family or the community as a social whole—in general, the priority of social relations. One may therefore say that the concerns with individuality and community have been separately associated with men or with women. I am talking here only about the historical difference in the concerns of men and women; I claim neither that men have in fact achieved more communality than women nor that women have achieved more communality than men, only that there has been a historical differentiation in the predominant concerns of each sex in this regard.

But freedom as we have seen requires the full development of both individuality and community. Thus, full self-realization for both men and women requires the development of both of these dimensions. Specifically, the concern with community, which in modern times has been principally a woman's concern in regard to private life, needs to be brought more fully into the public sphere. The values of cooperativeness, reciprocity, and mutuality need to be introduced more fully into the social relations of the public sphere of work and politics and should be among the criteria for changes in the forms of social organization. Conversely, the values of individual achievement and self-esteem, which traditionally have been primarily male concerns in the context of public life, need to be more fully introduced into personal relations in the private sphere. A synthesis of these two emphases in social life is needed to bring about full human freedom. The specific contribution that the women's movement can make on the basis of women's historic experience is to bring the emphasis on community more fully into the public sphere, that is, into political, cultural, and economic life.

In addition to this concern with community or sociality, there are other distinctive concerns arising from women's experience which need to be taken more seriously in public life and which would in this way contribute to the development of human freedom. These are the concerns with peace, with life, and with the material conditions of human existence. Women have historically been concerned with the health and well-being of their families and so have focused on the conditions necessary to secure life and well-being and to enhance them. Decisive among these conditions are peace and the provision of material sustenance and health care. These stand opposed to war and the squandering of material resources.

All these concerns of women must not be understood as stemming from "women's nature" in any essentialist sense, but rather as deriving from the contingent and historical experiences of women. Thus they are not fixed characteristics of women's nature and can be appropriated as much by men as by women. It is evident that to a large extent these have also been concerns of men, but they need to be more fully shared as human rather than gendered concerns.

In this essay I have considered a range of what may be called private rights and public virtues. On the one hand, I have argued for the separation of the public from the private: with respect to the issues of marriage and abortion, the private realm should be kept free from excesses of public virtuousness—privacy and personal relations require the noninterference of public agencies. On the other hand, I have argued for a strong connection between the public and the private in other cases: I have proposed an androgynous character for the body politic which bases public virtues on those which developed historically in the private sphere. So, too, there must be public protection of the private rights of the child. Finally, I have also argued for a richer relation of mutual support between the public and the private in the domain of democracy. Here, democracy as a public virtue maintains a certain autonomy while yet being founded on the personal virtues and private rights of reciprocity and freedom. Further analysis of the relations between the private and public domains seems to be an important task for feminist social and political theory.

Notes

1. Hannah Arendt, *The Human Condition* (Chicago: The University of Chicago Press, 1958), esp. Chapter 2.
2. Jane English, "Abortion and the Concept of a Person," in *Feminism and Philosophy,* ed. M. Vetterling-Braggin, F. Elliston, and J. English (Totowa, N.J.: Littlefield, Adams, 1977), p. 420.

PART II

Sex, Gender, and Women's Identity

2

Human Biology in Feminist Theory: Sexual Equality Reconsidered

ALISON M. JAGGAR

The theme of human biology recurs continuously in both feminist and anti-feminist literature. Reflection on human biology has always seemed to promise answers to the urgent questions of why women everywhere are subordinated and whether and how that subordination can be ended. Invariably, anti-feminists have justified women's subordination in terms of perceived biological differences between the sexes, and feminists have responded to their claims in a variety of ways. Some feminists have challenged the existence of certain alleged biological differences; others have accepted that some biological differences do exist but have denied the social implications drawn by the anti-feminists. In this essay, I will look critically at some of the ways in which contemporary feminists have responded to the biologically based challenges of anti-feminism, and will examine the ways in which contemporary feminists have conceptualized the relation between human biology and the social status of women.

Two ways of conceptualizing this relation are especially popular. One is to suppose that human biology sets certain fixed limits to social possibility. This is the biological determinist approach and, although it is used ordinarily by anti-feminists, it also has some feminist adherents. The second popular option is to deny that human biology has any special relevance to the social status of women and to claim that women's subordination is to be understood entirely in terms of "culture" or economics. I shall argue that neither of these approaches is correct. As an alternative, I shall present a model that conceptualizes the relation between human biology and social structure as a dialectical relation. By itself, this model provides no substantive answers to the questions of why women are subordinated and how their subordination may be ended. Yet the model does provide a conceptual framework and a methodology in terms of which these perennial questions finally may be given more satisfactory answers.

The Western Philosophical Background

Feminists have always been suspicious of talk about biology—and their suspicion has good historical grounds. The Western philosophical tradition, which was the intellectual background against which modern feminism emerged, has always been marked by what E. V. Spelman calls a "notable lack of enthusiasm for the human body."[1] Within that tradition, Spelman reminds us, bodies have been seen as the source of epistemological uncertainty, mortality, and lack of freedom, whereas minds have been seen as offering the possibility of certainty, immortality, and freedom. On this view, our bodies are what humans share with the "lesser" creatures, whereas our minds are supposedly what elevate us above them.

Of course, men as well as women have bodies, but women have been seen consistently as being connected with (or entangled in) their bodies in a more intimate way than men are with theirs. Even in the twentieth century, we find a pioneering feminist like Simone de Beauvoir accepting the view that "the female, to a greater extent than the male, is the prey of the species." Elaborating on de Beauvoir's view, Sherry Ortner points out that many of the areas and processes of the female body serve no apparent function for the health of the individual, but instead, in the performance of their specific organic functions, are sources of discomfort, pain, and even danger.[2] Breasts are irrelevant to personal health; menstruation may be uncomfortable or painful and always involves bothersome procedures of cleansing and disposal; pregnancy and lactation involve depletion of women's own physical reserves for the sake of the offspring; and childbirth is painful and dangerous. Thus, women's bodies are thought to commit them to the biological reproduction of the species, and they are seen as closer to "nature." Men, on the other hand, are thought to express their creativity through the creation of "culture." The traditional Western view, therefore, is that women are more closely associated with nature and men with culture, women with the body and men with the mind. This identification of men with the mind (and especially with reason, which holds a particularly exalted place in the Western philosophical tradition) has been used to justify male political dominance over women. Simultaneously, the identification of women with the body has been used as evidence that women are deficient in their ability to reason and consequently are not worthy of social and political equality with men.

Liberal Feminism

Organized feminism (as opposed to isolated acts of resistance by individual women) began in England in the seventeenth century. Women began to demand that the new liberal ideals of liberty, equality, and democracy be extended to them as well as to men. Since it was generally accepted that men were entitled to these rights on the basis of their capacity to reason, feminists felt bound to show that women's capacity to reason was equal to that of men. This argument was pursued by Mary Wollstonecraft in the eighteenth century, by Harriet Taylor and J. S. Mill in the nineteenth century, and by Betty Friedan and many others in the twentieth century.

All these feminists accept the political theory and the underlying conception of human nature that constitute the basic conceptual framework of classical liberalism. According to the liberal conception of human nature, the essence of humanity consists in humans' special capacity for rationality. This is the specifically human capacity that constitutes the ground of the special moral worth of human beings and of their political rights. According to liberal theory, the physical or biological base of the human capacity to reason is theoretically and politically irrelevant. If Martians had a capacity to reason similar to our own, they would deserve to be treated with the same respect that we now accord to humans. Similarly with robots: whether they are made of "hard" or "soft" stuff is irrelevant to their moral and political status.[3] Of course, the same also applies to human beings: whether individuals are male or female is irrelevant to their equal rights to liberty and self-determination.

The liberal emphasis on "mental" capacities to the exclusion of "physical" ones may be called "normative dualism." It generates for political theory problems that are analogous to the epistemological problems generated by metaphysical dualism. In other words, normative dualism encourages political scepticism and political solipsism.

By political solipsism I mean the liberal assumption that human individuals are essentially solitary, with needs and interests that are separate from, if not in opposition to, those of other individuals. This assumption is the starting point of liberal theory. It generates what liberals take to be the fundamental questions of political philosophy: what are the circumstances in which essentially solitary individuals might agree to come together in civil society, what would justify them in doing so, and how might conflict be prevented when they do? Liberals typically have answered these questions with various versions of social contract theory. These specify the interests individuals have in civil association and limit the legitimate powers of association to fulfilling those interests. Central to the interests postulated is always the assumed interest in the protection of life, civil liberties, and property.

Much of the credibility of social contract theory derives, of course, from the plausibility of the questions it is designed to answer. But these questions are plausible only if one begins with the assumption of political solipsism, the assumption that human individuals are essentially self-sufficient entities. Individual self-sufficiency, however, is an unrealistic assumption even if one conceives of all human beings as healthy adults, which most social contract theorists have done. As soon as one takes into account the facts of human biology, especially reproductive biology, it becomes obvious that the assumption of individual self-sufficiency is impossible. Human infants resemble the young of many species in being born helpless, but they differ from all other species in requiring a long period of dependence on adult care. This care could not be provided by a single adult; in order to raise enough children to continue the species, humans must live in social groups where individuals share resources with the young and the temporarily disabled. Human interdependence is thus necessitated by human biology, and the assumption of individual self-sufficiency is plausible only if one ignores human biology.[4] Normative dualism, however, encourages liberal theorists to ignore human biology, and we can now see how it generates a political solipsism that fundamentally shapes liberal theory. If liberals were to stop viewing human individuals as essentially rational agents and were to take theoretical account of the facts of human biology—especially, although not only, the facts of reproductive biology—the liberal problematic would be transformed. Instead of community and cooperation being taken as phenomena whose existence and even possibility is puzzling, and sometimes even regarded as impossible, the existence of egoism, competitiveness and conflict, phenomena which liberalism takes as endemic to the human condition, would themselves become puzzling and problematic.

Liberal political theory expresses a kind of scepticism as well as a kind of solipsism. This is scepticism about the justifiability of establishing political institutions that are designed to promote any specific conception of human well-being and fulfillment. There are two sources of this scepticism: one is the liberal value of individual autonomy, which requires that each individual have the maximum freedom to make her or his individual determination of what is true and what is good. The other source is the instrumental interpretation of rationality, which holds that an individual can make a rational choice between a variety of means to a given end, but cannot give a rational justification for any particular rank ordering of ends. On this interpretation of rationality, it is because each individual is the ultimate authority on her or his own needs and desires that political society must allow maximum freedom for individuals to define their own needs. For both these reasons, liberals claim, political institutions must be as neutral as possible about the ends of human life. Ronald Dworkin, a contemporary liberal theorist, expresses what I call liberal scepticism in this way:

> political decisions must be, so far as is possible, independent of any particular conception of the good life, or of what gives value to life. Since the citizens of a society differ in their conceptions, the government does not treat them as equals if it prefers one conception to another.[5]

Mary Gibson, in a discussion of Rawls's political philosophy, makes explicit some of the problems that are implicit in the scepticism promoted by the liberal conception of rationality.[6] She constructs the hypothetical examples of a voluntary M-S (master-slave) and a voluntary S-M (sadist-masochist) society and points out that the liberal conception of rationality has no grounds for condemning either of these societies, no matter how "inegalitarian, exploitative or otherwise morally repugnant." In opposition to liberal scepticism, Gibson argues that it is impossible to develop any useful account of rationality that is value-neutral. Instead, she argues that a politically useful conception of human rationality must refer to such normative notions as personhood, human good, and harm to persons and inevitably, therefore, must incorporate value judgments. If Gibson's argument is correct, then liberal scepticism, the insistence on what Rawls calls the thinnest possible theory of the good, itself begins to seem irrational. For it demands a perpetual scepticism with regard to the fundamental questions of political philosophy, namely, what are real human needs and what are the objective criteria of their fulfillment.

In my view, the scepticism of liberal political theory results, at least in part, from its normative dualism. By ignoring the fact that humans are a biological species, liberals deprive themselves of one important route for identifying human needs. This is not to say that there exist purely biological criteria for the identification of human needs. People want and need far more than physical survival. Moreover, even the notion of physical survival itself is problematic, for it raises all kinds of questions about how long and under what conditions humans can and should survive. But I do think that our common biological constitution provides part of the groundwork for determining objective criteria of human need. No adequate philosophical theory of human need can ignore the facts of human biology: our common need for air, water, food, warmth, etc. Far from being irrelevant to political philosophy, these facts must form its starting point.

The liberal insistence on viewing people as "abstract individuals," of no determinate age, race, sex, or economic class, was extremely progressive in its time—and is progressive in many contexts even today. But it has its drawbacks. Its main drawback, of course, is that real human beings are not abstract individuals, but people who have lived different histories, who have different social relations with each other, and who have different capacities and different needs. Some, though probably not most, of these differences are linked with biological differences. To take an obvious example, the needs of physically disabled people are different from the needs of those who are not so disabled. We may say, if we like, that both groups have the same need for transportation, but this obscures the special arrangements that have to be made for physically different people. Similarly, I think it is also true that the special features of women's biology, as we currently experience them, may mean that occasionally women's needs are different from men's. Most evidently, women's reproductive function may mean that women have special needs for pregnancy leave, maternity services, and arrangements for easy access to their nursing babies.

On a commonsense level, of course, everyone knows that women (and other groups) have these special needs. But the liberal insistence on "formal" equality, which comes from viewing people as abstract individuals, makes it easy not only to ignore these special needs, but even to claim that satisfying them would amount to "reverse discrimination" or giving special privileges to women. A good example of this is the 1976 U.S. Supreme Court decision in the case of *Gilbert v. General Electric Co.* In this case, female employees of General Electric charged that the exclusion of pregnancy-related disabilities from their employer's disability plan constituted sex discrimination. The Supreme Court ruled that this was not so, in part because it argued that the exclusion of pregnancy was not in itself a gender-based discrimination but instead merely removed one physical condition from coverage. The justices counted as irrelevant the biological fact that this was a physical condition to which only women were subject!

In bringing up this example, I'm not suggesting that it poses a problem that cannot be resolved within the liberal tradition. The U.S. Congress reversed the *Gilbert* decision in 1978, and even in the original judgment there were dissenting justices (namely, Brennan and Stevens) who took a more commonsense point of view. Nor am I saying that all or even most of women's social inequalities should be attributed to a neglect of certain features of female biology. But I do think that the assumption that the human essence consists entirely in its capacity for rationality diverts our attention away from the facts of human biology and in this way makes possible such absurdities.

Many people today see that it is absurd to refuse to take account of existing biological and other differences between women and men. Unfortunately, they often identify this ridiculous view as feminism, pure and simple.[7] As Iris Young has pointed out, however, feminism in fact is the conviction that women in our society constitute an oppressed group and that this oppression ought to be ended. It is not a defining tenet of feminism that everyone should be treated exactly alike. There are in fact many views on how social equality between the sexes ought to be achieved, and none of them requires that we should ignore existing differences between women and men.[8]

I turn now to a consideration of another feminist tradition that is in many ways opposed to the tradition of liberal feminism, especially in its treatment of human biology. This is the Marxist tradition.

Traditional Marxism

For Marxists, humans are social animals, and our sociability is necessarily connected with our animality. For this reason, Marxists view human biology as an integral part of human nature, and they view reflection on human biology as fundamental to political theory. Marxists recognize that every society must satisfy the needs that are generated originally by the human biological constitution—needs for food, shelter, clothing, etc.—and they assert that these needs can be fulfilled only by cooperative activity. In the Marxist view, this cooperative activity is basic to all societies, so basic, in fact, that it ultimately determines the characteristic form of every other aspect of a given society: its legal system, its culture, its religion, etc. Fundamental and lasting change in any society can come about only through a change in the organization of this productive activity, through a change, that is, in what Marxists call the mode of production.

In acknowledging that human biology has social and political implications, Marxism is not presupposing biological determinism. That is to say, it is not asserting that human biology alone is capable of determining specific forms of social organization. On the contrary, it claims that human needs may be met, at least in part, through a variety of different ways of organizing production. In addition, Marxism views human needs themselves as a product, at least in part, of the prevailing mode of production. Thus Marxism argues that human biology and human social organization are related dialectically, or in such a way that each partially constitutes the other. Human biology is seen as having permitted the development of certain types of social organization at the same time as that social organization permitted and encouraged a certain direction in biological evolution. For instance, tool use is seen as a cause as well as an effect of bipedal locomotion. In our prehuman ancestors, limited bipedalism left the hands sufficiently free to pick up sticks and stones. Use of these objects gave their users an evolutionary advantage that led both to more bipedalism and more-developed tool use. So Engels writes: "The hand is not only the organ of labor, it is also the product of that labor."[9] On the Marxist view, therefore, a dialectical interrelation exists between human biology and the forms of human social organization.

How do Marxists apply this conception of human biology to the issue of sex equality? In my view, there is an inconsistency in Marxist reflections on this question, an inconsistency caused by a failure to utilize consistently a dialectical model in thinking about certain physical differences between men and women.

The dominant tendency in Marxist reflections on women has been to deny that women's subordination is in any way connected with female biology. One of Marxism's major contributions to feminism, especially in the context of the nineteenth century, was to deny that women's subordination was biologically determined and hence in any sense natural. Instead, Marxists have argued emphatically that women's subordination was a form of oppression, resulting originally from the institution of class society and maintained into the present because it served the interests of capital. From this, Marxists have concluded that women's oppression can be ended only by overthrowing the capitalist mode of production. Even within the capitalist mode of production, however, traditional Marxists believe that the first steps toward women's emancipation are being taken by the undermining of the sexual division of labor which is the "material base" of women's subordination. Thus, in a much-quoted sentence Engels wrote that "the first condition for the liberation of the wife is to bring the whole female sex back into public industry."[10] This side of Marxist theory may be summed up in the following well-known quotation from *Capital:*

> However terrible and disgusting the dissolution, under the capitalistic system, of the old family ties may appear, nevertheless modern industry, by assigning as it does an important part in the process of production outside the domestic sphere to women, to young persons, and to children of both sexes, creates a new economic foundation for a higher form of the family and of the relationship between the sexes. . . . Moreover, it is obvious that the fact of the collective working group being composed of individuals of both sexes and all ages, must necessarily, under suitable conditions, become a source of human development.[11]

In the context of the biological justifications of women's subordination that were prevalent in the nineteenth century, the Marxist denial that women's subordination was determined biologically was a significant contribution to feminism, and so was the Marxist emphasis on integrating women fully within the paid labor force. Even today, these claims appear radical in many quarters. Unfortunately, however, Marx's and Engels's radical views about women were not carried to their logical conclusion.

Although it argued that the sexual division of labor should be abolished within "public industry," traditional Marxism did not challenge the sexual division of labor within the home. Because the home was conceived as falling outside the scope of modern political economy, its organization received little direct attention from the classical Marxist theorists. Nevertheless, in a number of scattered passages in *Capital* Marx seems to suggest that there is a certain sexual division of labor within the family which is "natural." For instance, he writes: "Within a family . . . there springs up naturally a division of labour, caused by differences of sex and age, a division that is consequently based on a purely physiological foundation."[12] This passage, and others like it, obviously suggest that women's biological constitution does have social implications, after all. Yet Marx never explores those implications. He explains neither exactly what is the so-called "natural" division of labor in the family nor exactly how it emerges. Moreover, as Lorenne Clark points out,[13] Marx's suggestion that a sexual division of labor develops "spontaneously" in the household is not at all Marxian nor dialectical. Unlike other divisions of labor, the domestic division of labor is not treated in relation to the material substructure of relations, productive or otherwise, and is seen as equally characteristic of precapitalist and capitalist families. From Marx's writings, the most reasonable conclusion to draw is that he assumes that within the family there exists a sexual division of labor which is biologically determined and therefore ineliminable.

Is this a fair conclusion to draw from these passages? My own view is that it is wrong to try to squeeze out of them a full-fledged theory of the social implications of the biological differences between women, men, and children. Instead, what I think these passages indicate is precisely that Marxist thinkers have failed to reflect systematically on the reproductive aspects of human biology.

The Marxist neglect of human reproductive biology has serious consequences for women. Most obviously, it devalues women's traditional work by ignoring it. Marxist political economy accepts uncritically the capitalist division of society into the "public" sphere of the market and the "private" sphere of the family. For Marxist political economy, the market is the main stage of history, and class struggle is its main action. Women play a very limited part on this stage; mostly they stay at home, behind the scenes. The traditional Marxist strategy for sex equality is to invite women up onto the stage, even to invite them to take starring roles. But what traditional Marxism hardly considers is who is to do the continuing work behind the scenes. Who is to give birth to the actors, to feed and clothe them, to teach them their lines and how to play their parts? Theorists since Marx have talked about "industrializing" the sort of production that goes on in the home: about public cafeterias, laundries, and nurseries. But these suggestions have never been fully developed, either theoretically or in practice. This lack of development has been politically disastrous for women and theoretically disastrous for Marxism.

For women, the failure to fully "industrialize" childbearing and housework means that most women, even in the so-called socialist countries, are still stuck with two jobs. They have far less leisure time than men and of course are handicapped severely in their "public" job: in China, for instance, they average 59 percent of men's work points and are seriously underrepresented in top decision-making and prestige positions. Moreover, the lack of theoretical attention to domestic work enables Marxists to ignore the fact that there is in actuality a sexual division of labor that cuts across class lines, that there are significant commonalities in the experience of bourgeois and working-class women, and that women have shared interests which go beyond defeating capitalism. By focusing only on "public" production and then by analyzing it in terms of categories that cut across the lines of gender, traditional Marxist theory obscures the interests that women share with women and men share with men. Its gender-blind categories obscure the fact that social reality, far from being gender-blind, is structured in every aspect by gender. Thus Marxist theory delegitimizes gender conflict by claiming that it is apparent rather than real. From the Marxist perspective, the special needs and interests of women are invisible. And, by concealing those special needs and interests, traditional Marxist theory mystifies social reality and therefore constitutes yet another ideology of male domination.

One conceptual root of this shortcoming in Marxist theory and practice is the nondialectical treatment given to human reproductive biology and to the biological differences between the sexes. In general, Marxist theorists have taken reproduction as a biological given, lying beneath the levels of society on which political theory reflects. Most of the time they have assumed, as Sartre puts it, that an individual is born at the time of applying for "his" first paid job. They have ignored the facts both that an enormous amount of labor goes into bringing a human being up to this point and that the social formation of the individual character occurs largely before this time. As a result, the Marxist historical materialist analysis is seriously incomplete. It cannot explain the origins of women's subordination, because it begins by assuming a sexual division of labor that remains quite unexplained. And it fails to raise a number of crucial questions about the political implications of contemporary child-rearing practices. These include questions about the psychological, sexual, and economic significance of the fact that children in all societies are reared by women—some of which questions have been explored recently by Chodorow and Dinnerstein.[14] Traditional Marxist theory contains no systematic discussion of child-rearing practices nor of the other work currently done in the home: who should do this work and who should make the decisions about how the work should be done? Because sexuality, childbearing, and childrearing are thought to be more rigidly determined by biology and therefore "closer to nature" than other aspects of human social life, they are exempted from critical examination.

Radical Feminism

In the 1960s, with the emergence of the contemporary women's liberation movement, traditional political theory came under attack. Neither the liberal nor the Marxist tradition was seen as taking seriously the problem of women's subordination, let alone as giving an adequate account of its deep causes. The new and self-described radical feminists, by contrast, took the oppression of women as their central political and theoretical problem. They began to clarify the ways in which norms of gender, often invisible because so familiar, structure every aspect of contemporary society and subordinate women to men. Taking as their slogan "The personal is political," they began to develop a new political practice that included attempts to transform the family and sexual relations. Simultaneously, they began to develop a new political theory to provide an adequate description and explanation of women's subordination. The theoretical work of radical feminism contained a number of diverse strands, but two are especially interesting because of the way they conceptualize human biology.

WOMEN'S BIOLOGY AS THE PROBLEM

In the late 1960s and early 1970s, several radical feminist theories located the source of women's subordination in female biology. There are several variants of this view, including those of Sherfey and Brownmiller, but the most interesting and plausible was put forward by Shulamith Firestone in *The Dialectic of Sex*.

Firestone argues that the sexual division of labor has a biological basis. She claims that human reproductive biology has dictated a form of social organization that she calls "the biological family." This family is characterized by a child dependent on the mother and a woman dependent on a man. In Firestone's view, this "biological family" is the basic reproductive unit that has persisted in every society and throughout every transformation of what Marxists call the mode of production. The persistence of this unit is the result of two universal features of the human biological constitution: that women are physically weaker than men as a result of their reproductive physiology, and that infants are physically helpless relative to adults. These biological relationships necessitate certain social relationships if women and infants are to survive. Women must depend on men for physical survival, and infants must depend on adults, primarily on women, since human milk or a close substitute is one of an infant's basic needs. Although Firestone recognizes that biological imperatives are overlaid by social institutions that reinforce male dominance, she believes that the ultimate foundation of male dominance is human reproductive biology. Consequently, she argues that women can be liberated only by conquering human biology. In her view, this requires the development of, on the one hand, reliable contraceptive technology and, on the other hand, extrauterine gestation or what is popularly called test-tube babies. Only these will make possible

> *The freeing of women from the tyranny of their reproductive biology by every means available, and the diffusion of the childbearing and child-rearing role to the society as a whole, men as well as women.*[15]

In Firestone's view, these technological developments would constitute the imposition of a set of consciously designed and deliberately chosen cultural practices onto a sphere of human life where the practices until now had been determined by human biology. Thus, they would be a victory over "the Kingdom of Nature."

> (T)he "natural" is not necessarily a "human" value. Humanity has begun to outgrow nature: we can no longer justify the maintenance of a discriminatory sex class system on grounds of its origins in Nature.[16]

In spite of the power and originality of Firestone's theory, it was never taken up by grass-roots American radical feminism. One of the several reasons for this undoubtedly lies in the fact that Firestone does not hold men responsible for the system of male dominance. Instead, in her theory it is female biology that is at fault and men appear as being ultimately women's protectors. Consequently, Firestone does not stress the need for a political struggle against male power, and her vision of the good society, as the full integration of women, men, and children into all areas of life, is clearly a version of the androgynous ideal. This ideal has been under increasing attack by contemporary radical feminists and does not fit at all comfortably with the increasingly militant and separatist tendencies of the grass-roots radical feminist movement.

WOMEN'S BIOLOGY AS THE SOLUTION

Since the early 1970s, radical feminists have become increasingly reluctant to locate the cause of women's subordination in anything about women themselves. For radical feminism, accounts which see the problem as lying either in women's psychology or in their biology are simply blaming the victim. They are further expressions of the misogyny that pervades contemporary society. In consequence, many recent radical feminist writings have tended to see the fault as lying in some flaw in *male* biology.

The belief that male biology is somehow to blame for women's subordination has been strengthened by feminist research during the 1970s, which has revealed that physical force plays a far larger part in controlling women than previously had been acknowledged. For instance, 50 percent of marriages involve some physical abuse of the wife, and half of all women in the United States suffer beating at least once—and usually more than once. Rape is another form of physical assault, and it is estimated that a rape occurs every two minutes in the US. One out of every three US women either has been or will be sexually assaulted in her life. These figures are staggering, but their significance lies not only in their gross effects on the lives of those who are direct victims, but also in their more subtle effects on the lives of those who are lucky enough to avoid being actually beaten or raped. Whether or not she actually is assaulted, the knowledge that assault is a permanent possibility influences the life of every woman. Women are afraid to hitchhike, to take walks in the moonlight, to travel at night by bus or subway, to frequent certain areas of the city or campus. This fear restricts women's areas of residence, their social and political activities and, of course, their study and work possibilities. If they live with a potentially abusive man, much of their attention has to be given to avoiding "provoking" asault. Women live so constantly with the fear of physical violence that they may not notice it until it is removed, often at a women-only feminist event. The recognition that women live continually under the threat of physical violence from men has led many radical feminists to the conviction that men are dangerously different from women and that this difference is grounded in male biology.

For some radical feminists, the main problem with male biology is simply that it is not female. At its most obvious, this has meant that men lack the special life-giving power that women possess in virtue of their capacity to become mothers. Except for a very few privileged women, however, being a mother has always involved caring for a child as well as giving birth to it; motherhood is associated conventionally with certain psychological qualities such as nurturance, warmth, emotional expressiveness, endurance, and practical common sense. Most feminists have been at pains to argue that this association results simply from the social fact that mothers have always done child care. For some radical feminists, however, there is a biological as well as a social connection between women's manifestation of these psychological qualities and their biological ability to become mothers. In the early 1970s Jane Alpert, a member of the Weather Underground, wrote the following:

> It seems to me that the power of the new feminist culture, the powers which were attributed to the ancient matriarchies (considered either as historical fact or as mythic archetypes), and the inner power with which many women are beginning to feel in touch and which is the soul of feminist art, may all arise from the same source. That source is none other than female biology: the capacity to bear and nurture children. It is conceivable that the intrinsic *biological* connection between mother and embryo or mother and infant gives rise to those *psychological* qualities which have always been linked with women, both in ancient lore and in modern behavioural science. Motherhood must be understood here as a potential which is imprinted in the genes of every woman: as such it makes no difference to this analysis of femaleness whether a woman ever has borne, or ever will bear, a child.[17]

Contemporary radical feminist writings abound with references to "the power inherent in female biology," "the creative power that is associated with female biology," and the "native talent and superiority of women."[18] None of the radical feminist authors attempts to provide a systematic account of just what are women's special powers, other than their capacity to give birth, nor of their relation to female biology. Moreover, their style of writing is invariably poetic and allusive rather than literal and exact. But there is a repeated suggestion that women's special powers lie in women's special closeness to nonhuman nature. Susan Griffin, for instance, draws parallels between men's attitudes toward women and their attitudes toward nonhuman nature. Of course, such parallels are capable of a number of interpretations, but Griffin herself suggests that women and nonhuman nature are inseparable from each other.

> We know ourselves to be made from the earth. We know this earth is made from our bodies. For we see ourselves. And we are nature. We are nature seeing nature. We are nature with a concept of nature. Nature weeping. Nature speaking of nature to nature.[19]

PROBLEMS WITH THESE VERSIONS OF RADICAL FEMINISM.

Neither of these versions of radical feminism offers an optimistic prospect for women's liberation. Firestone's version requires a technological solution to alter the biological basis of women's subordination; currently, however, control of technology is firmly in male hands, and radical feminism gives us no reason to suppose that men will voluntarily use this control to abolish rather than to increase their power over women. As for the view that women are superior biologically to men, this implies that if women are not to be dominated by men, they must either build societies entirely separate from those of men or else become the dominant sex themselves. These suggestions make fascinating science fiction but are impossible in practice.

Rather than looking for better solutions to the radical feminist problem, it is more fruitful to look critically at the definition of the problem itself. As defined by these radical feminists, the problem of women's subordination is a biological incompatibility between the sexes that makes it impossible for them to live together without one sex dominating the other. Obviously, radical feminists who accept this definition are accepting a form of biological determinism. Such a position is very unusual among advocates of social change because biological determinism is typically used to justify the existence of such social ills as racism, slavery, warfare, laziness, drug addiction, homophobia, rape, poverty, violence, corruption, political hierarchy and, of course, male dominance. Most feminist theorists have taken one of their major tasks to be precisely the revelation of the innumerable flaws in the many arguments that seek to justify male supremacy by arguing that it is determined biologically.

The trouble with attacking specific biological determinist arguments is of course that, no matter how decisive one's refutations may be, they always leave open the possibility that a new and more-valid form of biological determinism may be invented. By using a dialectical approach, however, it is possible to develop an argument that tells against biological determinism in general by showing that it is incoherent. The conceptual framework that can do this is fundamentally Marxist, but it needs to be applied to the question of human sex differences, differences which Marx and Engels, inconsistent with their own methodological commitments, took as biologically fixed.

The Social Determination of Sex Differences

A dialectical conception of human biology sees human nature and the forms of human social organization as determined not by our biology alone but rather by a complex interplay between our biological constitution, our physical environment and our forms of social organization, including our level of technological development. The effect of each of these factors cannot be isolated because each affects and changes the others. In other words, the factors are not only related to each other but dialectically related. For instance, the physical environment does not set rigid limits to the organization of human social life; although the environment may impose certain constraints at any given time, organized human activity also affects the environment—by draining, damming, clearing, terracing, leveling, fertilizing, or polluting. The humanly caused changes in the environment in turn allow for new forms of human social life, which in turn affect the environment in a new way, and so on. As we saw earlier, human biology, like the physical environment, is not just a pre-social given, remaining constant throughout the changes in human social life. Instead, it is a result as well as a cause of our system of social organization. This is as true of sex differences as of other aspects of human biology. Sex differences are in part socially determined both on the level of the individual and on the level of the species.

On the level of the individual, it is easy to see how a sexist society has different effects on the biological constitution of males and females. An obvious example is women's feet which, while no longer mutilated by foot-binding, are often still deformed by what used to be called winkle-picker shoes. In general women have been prevented from developing their capacities for physical speed and strength, and the effects of this prohibition can be seen simply by looking at women's bodies, particularly their upper bodies. The rate at which women's athletic records are being broken and the speed with which women's bodies have changed even over the past decade shows that in the past, social norms have limited the way in which women fulfilled their genetic potential, so that we have no idea of the extent of that potential.

Even the genetic potential that women and men inherit, however, is influenced by the social history of our species. For instance, a relatively advanced form of social organization was a prerequisite for the evolution of human reproductive biology as we know it. In the course of human evolution, the development of bipedalism narrowed the pelvis and reduced the size of the bony birth canal in women. Simultaneously, however, tool use selected for larger brain size and consequently for larger bony skulls in infants. This "obstetrical dilemma" of large-headed infants and small birth canals was solved by the infants' being born at an earlier stage of development. But this solution was possible only because human social organization was developed sufficiently to support a long period of infant dependence.

Just as the process of human reproduction was a social as well as a biological development, so the fairly exaggerated sexual dimorphism that we see in contemporary industrial society may also have resulted, at least in part, from social factors. In some ethnic groups, there is little sexual differentiation between women and men. Women are as tall as men, have equally broad shoulders and breasts so small that it is often difficult to tell an individual's sex even from the front.[20] The relatively smaller size of females in other ethnic groups is often due directly to the social fact that the nutrition of females is inferior because of their lower social status.[21] Differential feeding may also have resulted in selection for genetically shorter females, however, since taller women would have found it harder to survive on minimal food. Andrea Dworkin has suggested that even the sex distinction itself may be in part a social product because "inter-sex" individuals were less likely to be preferred as marriage partners. These are some of the ways in which society produces genetically inherited sex differences as well as sex differences shape society.[22]

The conclusion of this sort of reasoning is not simply that human biology and the forms of social life are more "cultural" and less "natural" than biological determinists suppose. It is rather that,

where human nature is concerned, there is no line between nature
and culture. Dorothy Dinnerstein puts it this way:

> The point is, humans are by nature unnatural. We do not yet walk
> "naturally" on our hind legs, for example: such ills as fallen arches,
> lower back pain, and hernias testify that the body has not adapted
> itself completely to the upright posture. Yet this unnatural posture,
> forced on the unwilling body by the project of tool-using, is precisely
> what has made possible the development of important aspects of our
> "nature": the hand and the brain, and the complex system of skills,
> language, and social arrangements which were both effects and
> causes of hand and brain. Man-made and physiological structures
> have thus come to interpenetrate so thoroughly that to call a human
> project contrary to human biology is naive: we are what we have
> made ourselves, and we must continue to make ourselves as long as
> we exist at all.[23]

When this is understood, biological determinism becomes not so
much false as incoherent. We cannot say that "biology determines
society," because we cannot identify a clear, nonsocial sense of
"biology" nor a clear, nonbiological sense of "society." The thesis
of biological determinism cannot be stated coherently.

Some Implications of This Conception of Human Biology for Feminism

1. A dialectical conception of human biology allows us to avoid
not only biological determinism, but also the "environmentalist"
denial that human biology has any relevance at all. According to
environmentalism, the human mind is more or less a blank slate that
is inscribed by the individual's experiences in society. Various kinds
of environmentalists theories attempt to explain human behavior by
describing the mechanism through which this inscription occurs.
Whether or not environmentalism succeeds in answering this psychological question, however, it can give no insight into larger social
questions, such as why certain messages rather than others are
inscribed on the individual's "slate", why society is organized in
certain ways, or why, indeed, society exists at all. Moreover, it
suggests, falsely, that all alternative ways of organizing future
society are equally possible.

A dialetical materialist approach to human biology allows us to
answer these sorts of questions by recognizing the obvious fact that
our biological constitution does mean that we require food, air,
sleep, and so on. These requirements, together with our approxi-
mate size, strength, speed, etc., have always been important influences on how we have organized our social life. What these requirements do not do, however, is set rigid limits on what is socially

possible. Of course, human beings are a biological species and, of course, as such there is a biological basis for our abilities, limitations, and needs. Human social organization must allow for the satisfaction of these needs by human abilities and in spite of human limitations. But human needs are flexible, and they are modified according to the means available for their satisfaction. And human abilities can be expanded, for example by technology, in order to overcome human limitations. For this reason, we can talk sensibly about human biology or human abilities, limitations, and needs only within a particular social context. For this context determines the specific form taken by our biologically based abilities, limitations, and needs, just as much or as little as our biological constitution in turn determines the specific form of our social organization. Human nature is both historical and biological, and the two aspects are inseparable.

2. A perhaps unexpected consequence of this dialectical conception of human biology is that it challenges the conceptual distinction between sex and gender that earlier feminists painstakingly established. As it is conceived ordinarily, sex is thought of as a fixed set of biological characteristics, whereas gender is construed as a set of variable social norms about the proper behavior of sexed individuals. Yet if we acknowledge human biology, including human sex differences, as created partly by society, and if we acknowledge human society as responsive to human biology, then we lose the clarity of the distinction between sex and gender. As Ann Palmeri puts it, the original clarity of that distinction comes to seem "a false clarity."[24] We see that there is a dialectical relation between sex and gender such that sex neither uniquely determines gender, as the biological determinists hold, nor is irrelevant to gender, as liberals and environmentalists believe. Instead, sex and gender create each other.

3. Given this dialectical conception of sex and gender, we can see that there is no simple answer to the question of whether women's subordination has a biological cause. Instead, we can see that the question itself is misleading, suggesting a linear model of causality that is quite inapplicable to this context. Women's biology is clearly relevant to the sexual division of labor in which their subordination is rooted, but it does not *cause* women's subordination because it is, in part, determined precisely by that subordination.

4. A further implication of the dialectical conception of human biology is that no social activity or form of social organization is any more "natural" than any other. Male dominance is no more nor less natural than female dominance. It is not more or less natural for mothers than for fathers to rear children. Heterosexual intercourse

is not more or less natural than other forms of sexual activity. Giving birth in a field is not more or less natural than giving birth in a hospital or even than providing an ovum for a test-tube baby. Some of these practices have a longer history and more ideological support than others, but none of them is determined by human biology or beyond the reach of conscious social control. Since both sexes are equally human, no sense can be given to the suggestion that women are closer to nature than are men. Going to war is neither more nor less natural than giving birth, and neither of these is more natural nor less than composing music or doing philosophy.

5. If nothing is natural, then the area of human social life that political theory has taken traditionally as its domain can now be seen to be too narrow. Traditional political theory has always made a distinction between the public and the private spheres of human existence. Although the so-called public sphere has been variously defined, it has always excluded the areas of sexuality, childbearing, childrearing, etc., which have been seen invariably as "natural" or biologically determined. If this assumption of naturalness is false, however, then the distinction between the public and the private realm comes to seem philosophically arbitrary, without reason. When so much of women's lives are spent in the private sphere, moreover, it is not just irrational but sexist for political theory to ignore the work of human reproduction and to assume that women will carry on doing this work just as they have always done. Political theory must acknowledge explicitly that humans have a sex, that their sex is defined primarily by differences in reproductive physiology, that women bear children, that infant survival depends on human milk or a close substitute, and that human young require a long period of adult care. Of course, liberal and Marxist theorists know these facts too, but they give them little theoretical attention. Questions of sex, gender, and procreation are virtually ignored by liberal and Marxist political theory. A dialectical materialist conception of sex differences, by contrast, allows us to reflect systematically and constructively on the political significance of human reproductive biology. It provides the conceptual foundations for bringing sexual, childbearing, and childrearing practices within the domain of political theory and of conscious social control.

6. Although these practices have not been questioned by traditional political theory, they have begun to be explored by feminists, especially by the authors of feminist science fiction, such as Dorothy Bryant, Marge Piercy, Ursula Leguin, and Sally Gearhart.[25] In her influential novel *Woman on the Edge of Time,* Piercy outlines her version of the good society. One of the most remarkable features of this society is that neither sex bears children, but both sexes,

through hormone treatments, suckle them. On Piercy's view, the ability to bear and suckle children is not necessarily a disadvantage for women; on the contrary, this ability could become a power and a privilege. It is a privilege, moreover, that women will have to share with men in any society that is truly egalitarian. Thus Piercy envisions a situation where every baby has three social "mothers" who may be male or female, and at least two of whom agree to breastfeed it. The point of this arrangement is not only to guard against sexual inequality. It is also to avoid feelings of reciprocal possessiveness and dependence that Piercy fears may be engendered by having children born to a single mother.

If these sorts of speculations seem bizarre or extravagant, I suggest that this appearance is an indication of the depth of our prejudices regarding the "natural" basis of human social life. The truth is, no significant body of modern political theory reflects systematically on the apparent biological facts that every human being enters the world with a special biological connection to a single human male and, even more evidently, to a single human female. Yet that these apparent facts are of enormous social significance is obvious from the way that they are elaborated in every culture into a gender system that structures and, I believe, restricts not only our physical development but every other aspect of our lives. Feminist theory, perhaps influenced by recent developments in procreative technology, is now asserting that no biological facts are unalterable in principle and hence that there is no "natural" basis for human social life. Monique Wittig writes:

> Our bodies as well as our minds are the product of [ideological] manipulation. We have been . . . distorted to such an extent that our deformed body is what they call "natural", is what is supposed to exist as such before our oppression.[26]

It may be that full equality between the sexes requires the transformation not only of so-called sex roles or of gender norms, but of those biological aspects of human nature that we have thought of hitherto, in Firestone's words, as "the sex distinction itself."

Notes

1. E. V. Spelman, "Bodies and their Persons," unpublished manuscript. On this topic, see also Spelman's "Woman as Body: Ancient and Contemporary Views," *Feminist Studies* 8, no. 1 (Spring 1982): 109–31.
2. Sherry B. Ortner, "Is Female to Male as Nature Is to Culture?" in *Women, Culture and Society,* ed. Michelle Zimbalist Rosaldo and Louise Lamphere (Stanford: Stanford University Press, 1974), p. 174.
3. Hilary Putnam, "Robots: Machines or Artificially Created Life?", *Journal of Philosophy* 61 (November 1964): 668–91.

4. Nancy Hartsock made this point to me in a letter. A similar point is made by Sara Ann Ketchum, "Female Culture, Womanculture and Conceptual Change: Toward a Philosophy of Women's Studies", *Social Theory and Practice* 6, no. 2 (Summer 1980): 159.

5. Ronald Dworkin, "Liberalism," in *Public and Private Morality*, ed. Stuart Hampshire (Cambridge: Cambridge University Press, 1978), p. 127. Naomi Scheman pointed out to me this clear statement of a basic liberal assumption.

6. Mary Gibson, "Rationality," *Philosophy and Public Affairs* 6, no. 3: 193–225.

7. See, for example, Elizabeth H. Wolgast, *Equality and the Rights of Women* (Ithaca and London: Cornell University Press, 1980). Wolgast identifies feminism with the claim that women and men should be treated the same in all possible respects, and she then proceeds to attack this view, often with good arguments. Many ordinary people reject what they think of as feminism for reasons similar to Wolgast's.

8. Iris Young, "Women and Political Philosophy," *Teaching Philosophy* 4 no. 2 (April 1981): 183–89.

9. Frederick Engels, "The Part Played by Labour in the Transition from Ape to Man," in Karl Marx and Frederick Engels, *Selected Works* (New York: International Publishers, 1968), p. 359.

10. Frederick Engels, *The Origin of the Family, Private Property and the State* (New York: International Publishers, 1970), pp. 137–38.

11. Karl Marx. *Capital: A Critique of Political Economy:* Vol. 1; *The Process of Capitalist Production* (New York: International Publishers, 1967), pp. 489–90.

12. Ibid., p. 351. See also p. 78.

13. Lorenne Clark, "A Marxist-Feminist Critique of Marx and Engels: or, The Consequences of Seizing the Reins in the Household," unpublished manuscript.

14. Nancy Chodorow, *The Reproduction of Mothering: Psychoanalysis and the Sociology of Gender* (Berkeley, Los Angeles, London: University of California Press, 1978); Dorothy Dinnerstein, *The Mermaid and the Minotaur* (New York: Harper & Row, 1976).

15. Shulamith Firestone, *The Dialectic of Sex* (New York: William Morrow, 1970), p. 206. Italics in original.

16. Ibid., pp. 9, 10.

17. Jane Alpert, "Mother Right: A New Feminist Theory," *Ms,* August 1973, p. 92.

18. Cf. Adrienne Rich, *Of Woman Born* (New York: W. W. Norton, 1976), pp. 40; Janice Raymond, *The Transsexual Empire* (Boston: Beacon Press, 1979), p. 107; Mary Daly, *Gyn/Ecology: The Metaethics of Radical Feminism* (Boston: Beacon Press, 1978), p. 194.

19. Susan Griffin, *Women and Nature* (New York: Harper Colophon, 1980), p. 226.

20. Ann Oakley, *Sex, Gender and Society* (London: Temple Smith, 1972), p. 30.

21. Ibid., p. 28.

22. Andrea Dworkin, *Woman Hating* (New York: E. P. Dutton, 1974), chap. 9.

23. Dinnerstein, *Mermaid*, pp. 21–22.

24. Ann Palmeri, "Feminist Materialism: On the Possibilities and Power of the Nature/Culture Distinction," unpublished manuscript.

25. Examples of feminist science fiction include the following: Dorothy Bryant, *The Kin of Ata Are Waiting for You* (Berkeley and New York: Moon Books and Random House, 1976); C. P. Gilman, *Herland: A Lost Feminist Utopian Novel* (New York: Pantheon, 1979); Marge Piercy, *Woman on the Edge of Time* (New York: Fawcett, 1976); Sally Miller Gearhart, *The Wanderground: Stories of the Hill Women,* Watertown, Mass.: Persephone Press, 1979); and many of the novels of Ursula LeGuin, especially *The Left Hand of Darkness* (New York: Ace Books, 1969).

26. Monique Wittig, "One is not born a woman," in *Proceedings of The Second Sex Conference* (New York: New York Institute for the Humanities, 1979), p. 70.

3

Is Gender a Variable in Conceptions of Rationality? A Survey of Issues

SANDRA HARDING

Introduction: Shifting the Variables of Interest.

In the history of Western thought, sex has been considered a variable in the *distribution* of rationality. Received wisdom and everyday observation combined to make it appear that Mother Nature had slighted her own kind. From antiquity to the present day, women have been claimed less capable of abstract and systematic thought than men, less capable of developing a mature sense of justice than men, more ruled by the emotions, the passions, and the appetites than men, and more inclined toward subjective assessments and less toward objective ones than men. While the reasons advanced to explain why men are more rational than women are not the same in modern and pre-modern societies, a lesser, immature, or defective rationality consistently has been attributed to women. In the last century, theories in both the social and the natural sciences have continued to explain in considerable and often amusing detail how and why sex is a variable in the distribution of rationality.

During the last decade these theories and observations have been severely challenged. First, scholars in the social and natural sciences are suggesting that not only—and certainly not mainly—sex should be the variable of interest in the scientific examination of such human characteristics as rationality. Our biological inheritances undoubtedly distribute some abilities and talents in some degree or other differently by sex; but when we observe and

This essay is reprinted with revisions from *Dialectica* 36, no. 2–3 (1982). Reprinted by permission of the publisher and author.

theorize about the humans around us, the variation within the species of every characteristic we can observe has been mediated by present-day culture as well as by cultural patterns in the distant past. Instead of just looking at sex, we should also be looking at gender—the impressive and baroque superstructure of social differentiation which culture erects on what it presumes to be the appropriate foundation of our relatively modest and cleanly functional reproductive differences. So gender is perhaps as important as sex in distinguishing the groups to which rationality has supposedly been variably distributed.[1]

Furthermore, gender, as well as sex, also distinguishes the interpreters of nature's regularities from half of those humans whose regularities are interpreted. Once we recognize that the history of Western thought is the history of thought by members of a group with a distinctive social experience—namely, men—we are then led to a new set of questions about the social nature of that thought and about the justifiability and reliability of the interpretations of nature and social life emerging from that thought. We need to understand the distribution by gender of *conceptions* of rationality. What are the "male man" 's and the "female man" 's differing social norms for a rational animal? How do women conceptualize the ideally rational person, rational belief, and rational action differently than do men? What causes these distinctive patterns of conceptualization? Is the historical identification of masculine conceptions of rationality with human rationality justifiable? Should our traditional masculine conceptions of humanly rational belief and action be revised to reflect the contributions to human social life that have been made throughout history by women's differing conceptions of a rational person, of rational belief, of rational action? Should not the social value of women's rationality be recognized and empowered to make greater contributions to women's and men's human progress?

In raising these kinds of questions, this chapter should be understood as attempting to fill in a few of the many missing pieces needed to support a larger hypothesis that is beginning to emerge from—or lies just beneath the surface of—explicit feminist epistemological concerns.[2] This hypothesis maintains that the distinctive masculine perspective that has heretofore defined "human rationality" is not only one-sided but also, in some respects, perverse. Knowledge is based on experience. But in societies with relatively rigid divisions of labor by sex/gender, masculine experience of nature's regularities and their underlying causal determinants is not only necessarily limited, but also necessarily distorting. The master must justify his relationship with the slave as good, and as called for by what the master perceives as the real regularities of his and the slave's "natures." Indeed, because the master dominates the slave, he can force the slave to exhibit for the master's observation precisely the regularities the master takes to justify his theories—hence the dominance relationship. The master fails to understand that his political relationship to the slave provides him with a perverse understanding of the regularities and underlying causal determinants of their "natures" and social relations. Marx argues that the division of labor by class makes perverse understandings seem reasonable to the bourgeoisie. Feminists suggest that because of the division of labor by sex/gender, distinctively masculine interests rule women's daily lives, and that men thus come to have not only one-sided but also perverse understandings of their own and women's "natures" and of the real regularities and underlying causal determinants of social life (see Smith 1979, p. 164-65; Benjamin 1980; and Hartsock 1983). This chapter thus attempts to fill in some gaps in our understanding of the specific ways in which sexual politics shapes legitimated belief.

I shall also note in passing that the models of rationality associated with bourgeois societies, with liberal political theories, and with science are specifically *modern* models of rationality. Why it is that these modern forms of rationality are more distinctively masculinized than models of rationality in pre-modern societies is an important topic for further research.

I first will describe how the philosophic questions about the adequacy of our prevailing conceptions of rationality have emerged from the growing recognition that one cannot simply "add women" as objects of knowledge to the existing corpus of our social and natural knowledge; then review the findings from two areas of empirical research that show the gendered character of the dominant conceptions of rational belief and action; and conclude with some implications this new research has for some of the traditional and current issues about rationality in the philosophic literature.

The Emergence of Philosophic Questions from Empirical Research.

In the last decade, social and natural scientists have realized that descriptions and explanations of the regularities of women's "natures," social activities, and interactions with nature are relatively missing from—or distorted in—the existing corpus of social and natural knowledge. A vast collection of empirical and theoretical studies have attempted to restore women as missing "objects of knowledge" to this body of social and natural knowledge (see *Signs,* 1975). In spite of the vast increase in the "facts" we now have about women and their lives cross-culturally and historically, the assess-

ment is slowly emerging that in a significant respect these attempts
have failed. They have failed because women cannot be added as
objects of knowledge within conceptual schemes and methodologies
which distort our understanding of women in two ways. They
suggest that it is primarily men's natures and activities which should
be of interest to the social and natural sciences, and they report
women's natures and activities disproportionately as they are experienced and observed by men.[3] The prevailing theories of the social
and natural sciences draw on and legitimate a conceptual screen that
systematically distorts our vision of women and their lives. Since
women's lives and men's lives have always been intimately intertwined, the question arises whether this conceptual screen does not
also distort our vision of men's lives. Perhaps we understand even
less than we think about the regularities and causes of all of social
life. And yet, the prevailing theories were constructed by supposedly "value-free" criteria of rationality and objectivity.[4] Are the
"canons of science" themselves socially biased in such a way that
their gender-distortions are invisible?

In literally dozens of research projects in every social science in
the last decade, philosophic questions have emerged from what
were initially thought to be only empirical questions (see *Signs,*
1975). Let us consider just one: what has come to be called the
"periodization issue" in history.

Scholars attempting to do "women's history"—to restore women
as missing objects of our historical knowledge—quickly realized the
inadequacy of the most obvious approaches to understanding wom-
en's role in history. "Compensatory history," as the inadequate
approach is called, could not in principle provide either an undistorted or a complete picture of women's roles in history. One
historian described the problem this way:

> Once we look to history for an understanding of woman's situation,
> we are, of course, already assuming that woman's situation is a social
> matter. But history, as we first came to it, did not seem to confirm this
> awareness. Throughout historical time, women have been largely
> excluded from making war, wealth, laws, governments, art, and
> science. Men, functioning in their capacity as historians, considered
> exactly those activities constitutive of civilization: hence, diplomatic
> history, economic history, constitutional history, and political and
> cultural history. Women figured chiefly as exceptions, those who
> were said to be as ruthless as, or wrote like, or had the brains of men.
> In redressing this neglect, women's history recognized from the start
> that what we call compensatory history is not enough. This was not to
> be a history of exceptional women, although they too need to be
> restored to their rightful places. Nor could it be another subgroup of
> historical thought, a history of women to place alongside the list of

diplomatic history, economic history, and so forth, for all these developments impinged upon the history of women. Hence, feminist scholarship in history . . . came to focus primarily on the issue of status . . . woman's place and power—that is, the roles and positions women hold in society by comparison with those of men.

In historical terms, this means to look at ages or movements of great social change in terms of their liberation or repression of woman's potential, their import for the advancement of her humanity as well as "his." The moment this is done—the moment one assumes that women are a part of humanity in the fullest sense—the period or set of events with which we deal takes on a wholly different character or meaning from the normally accepted one. Indeed, what emerges is a fairly regular pattern of relative loss of status for women precisely in those periods of so-called progressive change . . . if we apply Fourier's famous dictum—that the emancipation of women is an index of the general emancipation of an age—our notions of so-called progressive developments, such as classical Athenian civilization, the Renaissance, and the French Revolution, undergo a startling re-evaluation. For women, "progress" in Athens meant concubinage and confinement of citizen wives in the gynecaeum. In Renaissance Europe it meant domestication of the bourgeois wife and escalation of witchcraft persecution which crossed class lines. And the Revolution expressly excluded women from its liberty, equality, and "fraternity." Suddenly we see these ages with a new, double vision—and each eye sees a different picture [Kelly-Gadol 1976, pp. 810-11].

Let me emphasize that the problem here is not only that women lose status at the historical moments marked as high points of rational progress for "humankind." More problematic is the growing suspicion that the scope and powers of women have been restricted exactly "as a consequence of the very developments for which the age is noted" (ibid, p. 811). According to the prevailing reconstructions of history, what are evaluated as periods of progress in the rational organization of social life appear either to have necessarily resulted in or required reductions in women's personhood—in women's ability to act as rational agents of history, rather than as victims of history others made.[5]

The periodization issue raises at least three kinds of new empirical questions for historians. First, how have changes in women's labor, in the labor of reproduction broadly understood—childbirth, sexuality, family structure, and the like—affected women's lives? Second, how has the history of the making of wars, wealth, laws, governments, art, and science affected the labor of reproduction? Third, and most controversial, how have changes in the labor of reproduction affected the making of wars, wealth, laws, governments, art, and science? Many scholars are already pursuing these new questions, and their research promises to give us a picture of human history very different from the "men's history" to which our official understanding has been restricted.

Beyond the empirical questions are the questions of evaluation. Is it justifiable to mark periods when half the population loses power and status as periods of *human* progress? (see Kelly-Gadol 1976, p. 812.) What kinds of social changes mark increases in the power for *all* men and women to design and control their own destinies and hence would provide a more illuminating index of human progress?

Finally, the periodization issue raises the issues about our conception of rationality mentioned earlier. First, how has the conception of a rational person (upon which the criteria for "human progress" in men's history draws) reflected only men's gender-specific criteria for a rational person? Second, would a broader conception of human rationality lead us to evaluate more critically the contributions to human progress resulting from the making, and the making by men, of war, wealth, laws, governments, art, and science? The third question is raised by the recognition that science itself is one of those social products historically made virtually exclusively by men. Some studies have shown that it appears to practically everyone today (Keller 1978) and at its origins (Merchant 1980) to be even more closely tied to characteristics thought to be disproportionately distributed to men than are the making of war, wealth, laws, governments, and art. How did *the* model for knowledge-seeking in modern societies come to be so closely tied to abilities thought so disproportionately distributed to men? And how does this masculinization of desirable belief distort our understandings of the regularities of nature and social life and of their underlying causal determinants? How does it limit the ability of science to contribute to truly human progress?

These questions are far larger than I—or anyone else at present—can answer. But some clues to the answers are already available in the results of recent social research. Newly detected "regularities of nature" have been identified on which philosophers can and should base their beliefs. Recent studies have critically examined the assumptions, first, whether there have ever been (gender-neutral) *humans,* and second, whether social norms for rational belief and rational action have ever been gender-free.

THE "MALE MAN" AND THE "FEMALE MAN"

The concept of a person is central to each and every problem of philosophy. "Person" is generally treated as an explicitly gender-homogenous concept: both men and women are in the same sense persons. Thus it is thought to be merely a trivial matter of cosmetic revision to substitute "a person" for "man" in such historical claims as "man is a rational animal." It is thought that such a substitution does not change the reference or the meaning of such statements. In the history of philosophy, however, such substitutions of gender-neutral language for suspiciously gender-specific uses of "man" really do violate the integrity of the thought of individual figures in the history of philosophy. In the history of Western thought, "man" is hardly ever used with intended (let alone achieved) generic reference or meaning, except here and there in the natural sciences.[6] Many philosophers, drawing on the received wisdom of their day, explicitly explained why women are by nature less able or less willing to satisfy criteria for full human personhood. Philosophers, like everyone else, have claimed women by nature to be deficient in abilities and talents for abstract thought, objective judgments, and moral reasoning—all of which are believed necessary criteria of rationality. These passages are usually regarded as unfortunate but philosophically irrelevant asides in the writings of Aristotle, Hume, Nietzsche, and so on.

Recent studies show that such attempts to "clean up" the history of philosophy by detaching claims about sex/gender differences from the rest of a philosopher's arguments are both wrongheaded and also doomed to failure (see note 6). They fail because no social characteristic is more basic to individual self-identity than sense of gender. As we shall see, of all social characteristics, gender is the earliest to be solidified in the individual, the hardest to change, and the most inextricably connected with how we conceptualize and relate to ourselves, to others, and to nature. Generally we refuse even to interact with a newborn—to touch it or talk to it—until we know whether it is a boy or a girl. The philosophic conceptions of a citizen, of justice, of a moral person, of "the rational man," of a scientific observer, of what should constitute a "rational reconstruction" of theory acceptance in science, have all been tied to gender-specific masculine conceptions of what the "male man" is and should be. In the history of philosophy, substituting "A person is a rational animal" for "Man is a rational animal" systematically and seriously distorts both the intended and achieved reference and meaning of such claims.

The attempt to separate what now appear to be ignorant and sexist characterizations and evaluations of gender from the history of systematic thought is also wrongheaded. Once we really are willing to admit women into full human personhood, it becomes important to understand how conceptions of the "problems of philosophy" and their proposed solutions do in fact define something less than human problems and human solutions. The (false) universality claimed for distinctively masculine ways of thinking about what a person is, what a mature human should believe, and how a mature human should act distorts our understandings of the regularities of social life and of their underlying determinants. So let us see what help recent research can provide in showing how gender is an inextricable part of personhood for individuals in our society.

Traditional psychological theories have attributed the formation of gendered personalities either to nature—to sex—or to culture—to "social learning" that takes place largely after the age of three. In contrast, the part of gender theory being developed by Dorothy Dinnerstein (1976), Jane Flax (1978, 1983), Nancy Chodorow (1978), and others attributes the formation of gender to the very same social/physical processes within which initially androgynous new-borns are transformed, and transform themselves, into distinctive human persons. This theory proposes that gender is indeed "learned" rather than natural, but that it is initially learned before the age at which most social learning theorists begin their observations. Gender theory draws on post-Freudian psychoanalytic "ob-ject-relations" theory (see Mahler, Pine, and Bergman 1975; Gun-trip 1961; Winnicott, 1965), so-named because it describes how infants come to "objectify" or model themselves, others, and appro-priate relationships between themselves and others. Gender theory shows how male and female infants have different *experiences* of the division of labor by sex/gender with which *they* interact, and these experiences account for the reproduction, generation after genera-tion, of certain general and nearly universal differences that charac-terize masculine and feminine senses of self, others, and the appro-priate relationship between self and others.[7] This virtually universal, but nevertheless socially arranged, male-dominated social division of labor by sex/gender "causes" the inextricably intertwined, simul-taneous production of gender and personhood. The infant's experi-ence of this division of labor creates an "objectifying" sense of self in men and a "relational" sense of self in women.

Object-relations theory distinguishes the biological birth of the infant of our species and the psychosocial birth of the human person. Biological birth is an event of short duration (nine months or a few hours, depending on how one defines it), which is relatively uninfluenced by social variables. In contrast, the psychosocial birth of a human is a process that takes about three years and is greatly influenced by the social environment in which it occurs. Psychoso-cial birth is the first distinctively human labor. The infant is by no means a "passive recipient" of "external stimuli." Instead, it strug-gles to emerge from its initial "oneness" with the psychosocial physical environment of its caretakers—in societies with our divi-sion of labor by sex/gender, the "mother world." The first human labor of the infant is extremely difficult because the infant wants to remain in, or return to, that oneness with the mother-world, but also to become a separate individual. Hence the infant's labor is a struggle to distinguish itself from the mother-world which is not itself, and also to discover/create its own separate identity. As Jane Flax points out (1983), the survival of the species requires that infants separate and individuate themselves. But the male-dominated division of labor by sex/gender causes these separations and individuations to take the particular historical forms they do. The "production" of gender, of "relational" and "objectifying" types of persons, is itself one of the consequences of infants having to separate and individuate in interaction with a male-dominated division of labor by sex/gender.

For children of both sexes, the "world" from which they must differentiate themselves, and in interaction with which they create their own autonomous identity, is in one sense the same "world"—the mother-world. But in another sense it is a very different world for male and female infants: gender-differentiated experiential worlds begin at birth. The masculine "objectifying" personality develops through separation and individuation from a kind of person whom he cannot become biologically and against whom he must exercise will and control not to become socially. A woman and the whole mother-world become for him the first models for the bodies and worlds of "others"—of persons who are perceived as disconnected from him and against whom, at risk of losing his painfully attained self-identity, he must in turn maintain a strong sense of separation and control. The development of this distinctive sense of self and world is assisted by the fact that boys receive different "mothering" than do girls. "Mothers experience their sons as a male opposite," and as a result, "boys are more likely to have been pushed out of the preoedipal relationship and to have had to curtail their primary love and sense of empathetic tie with their mother" (Chodorow, 1978, p. 166). This contributes to boys' development of a "more emphatic individuation and a more defensive firming of ego boundaries (ibid., p. 167).

For girls, in contrast, a "relational" self-identity develops through the female infant's struggle to separate and individuate herself from a person whom she will in fact nevertheless become—a socially devalued woman. Again, differential caretaking contributes to the development of gender. "Mothers tend to experience their daughters as more like and continuous with themselves. Correspondingly, girls tend to remain part of the dyadic primary mother-child relationship itself. This means that a girl continues to experience herself as involved in issues of merging and separation" (ibid., p. 166).

Hence the process by which female infants are transformed and transform themselves into feminine persons is one in which separation and individuation from others are not as critically tied to their own gender identity: self-identity in a girl does not depend as strongly upon the achievement of separation from the mother or on the process of individuation with its goal of social autonomy. The parallel process for male infants leaves separation and individuation critically tied to their own self-identity, since separation from the mother is essential for the development of masculinity and of autonomous personhood.

Carol Gilligan points out how the separate developmental processes of boys and girls become unequally valued developmental processes:

> the quality of embeddedness in social interaction and personal relationships that characterizes women's lives in contrast to men's becomes not only a descriptive difference but also a developmental liability when the milestones of childhood and adolescent development are described by markers of increasing separation. Then women's failure to separate becomes by definition a failure to develop [1979, p. 434].

Gilligan shows how Freud, Piaget, Erikson, and Bettelheim have provided new theories "naturalizing" and legitimating the age-old beliefs that women's developmental stages reflect less-mature or less-complete processes of human development. The feminine "relational" emphasis on developing increasingly complex and intense forms of cooperation and intimacy in human relationships, and on developing the empathy and sensitivity necessary for taking the role of the particular other (the particular person to whom one is relating), is systematically regarded as less mature than the characteristic masculine "objectifying" emphasis on developing increasingly complex forms for achieving separation from others and on learning to take the role of the generalized other (anyone who stands in this kind of relationship) (see Gilligan 1979, 1982).

While "rationality" is used to refer to a variety of human capacities and exhibited traits, in general it is thought of as a capacity of all humans, but one not highly visible or "expressed" in immature humans. The development of expressions of rational belief and rational action is thought to be a part of the general development of mature personhood, however the latter is differently designated in different cultures. Nevertheless, cross-culturally and historically certain constancies are detectable in what men and women take to be expressions of rational belief and rational action. Thus, gender theory offers us clues to an understanding of how gender is a variable in *conceptions* of a rational person. A rational person, for women, values highly her abilities to empathize and "connect" with particular others and wants to learn more complex and satisfying ways to take the role of the particular other in relationships. A rational person naturally has problems when there is too little connection with particular others and when she is expected only to take the role of the generalized other. Furthermore, a rational person's self-identity should be relatively little associated with the firmness of one's gender identity. For men, in contrast, a rational person values highly his ability to separate himself from others and to make decisions independent of what others think—to develop "autonomy." And he wants to learn more complex and satisfying ways to take the role of the generalized other. For a man, a rational person has problems when there is too great intimacy or connectedness with particular others, or when he is expected to take the role of a particular other; a rational person's self-identity should be relatively highly connected with the firmness of one's gender identity. No wonder women's relational rationality appears to men immature, subhuman, and threatening. No wonder men's objectifying rationality appears to women alien, inhuman, and frightening (see especially Dinnerstein 1976; Gilligan 1979, 1982).

Let me emphasize that gender theory is providing a causal account of gender which is both "materialist" and nondeterministic.[8] Socially arranged and male-dominated division of labor by sex/gender causes the production of gender. Both a division of labor by sex/gender and its male-domination appear to be characteristics of every known culture—to be cultural universals. Even anthropologists who are critical of feminist tendencies to overgeneralize from culture-specific observations argue that the male-dominated sex/gender system appears to be a universal organizing feature of recorded social life (see Rosaldo 1980, pp. 394-95). In every known society, men more than women are responsible for ruling the society (in whatever form that takes), and women more than men are responsible for the caretaking of young children and for the day-to-day physical and social maintenance of others. Since the labor of ruling is always socially valued more highly than the labor of infant caretaking and day-to-day maintenance of others, labor is differentially valued by sex/gender.[9] The account is materialist because the form of the actual psychosocial-physical environment with which the infant interacts is the variable determining whether or not gender will be produced. The account suggests that if, societywide, men shared equally in infant caretaking and the day-to-day maintenance of self and others, and if women shared equally in the labor of ruling, gender would not be produced at all. (Notice that *both* of these conditions must be met if gender is to be eliminated.) Although separation and individuation would occur, neither sex infant would have a particular sex/gender from which to separate and against which to individuate itself; hence the characteristic gender divisions of relational and objectifying personhood would not be formed in children.

This indicates one way in which the theory is not deterministic: gender is not biologically determined and hence can be eliminated through political processes. The theory is not deterministic in a second way, as well. A critical stance toward one's own gender outlines can result in eliminating many gender characteristics, albeit probably not completely and certainly not easily. We all know many adults who have at least partially succeeded in achieving less-gendered personality structures. Relational and objectifying aspects of personality can be brought into more-balanced dialectical tension. The theory also raises a number of interesting empirical questions that I have discussed elsewhere (1981a) and will not review here.

GENDERED NORMS FOR RATIONAL BELIEF AND ACTION.

A second and connected area of recent research can help us understand how gender produces distinctive norms for rational belief and action. How should a mature person go about achieving and justifying desirable beliefs and actions? Questions of "practical rationality" lead us to gender-differentiated norms for what it is right and wrong to believe and do—in short, to morality and ethics.[10]

When the differing gender norms for a rational person are used to examine moral theory, it becomes understandable why the moral systems men find desirable typically construe women's moral judgments as inconclusive, diffuse, and incapable of furthering justice, and why women tend to regard men's moral judgments as narrow and incapable of furthering social welfare (see Dinnerstein 1976; and especially Gilligan 1979, 1982). Reevaluation of moral developmental theories, such as Kohlberg's (see Kohlberg and Kramer 1969; Kohlberg 1971), reveals that the descriptions of stages of human moral development provided by such theories correspond, as one would expect, to stages of masculine moral development, but not to stages of feminine moral development. Kohlberg's highest stage of moral development prescribes that justice should be understood as fairness,[11] and that individuals who achieve this stage of development will have maximized the autonomous decision-making characteristic of taking the role of the generalized other. As Gilligan (1979) points out, a number of scholars became suspicious of the value-neutrality of this developmental scheme when they noted that women (as well as members of other "underclasses") characteristically reach only the third of Kohlberg's six stages of "human" moral development.

The fact that not only women but also Afro-Americans and working-class Americans are recorded on scales such as Kohlberg's to have less than a "fully human" sense of ethics, *and* that this kind of conception of the highest "human" morality is so consistent with the conception found in the writings of modern moral thinkers such as Kant and Rawls, should remind us that we are examining here not masculine and feminine rationality per se, but particular modern forms of gendered rationality. Why there is such a "coincidence" between the modern ideal of a citizen and the ideal masculine personality in our society is yet to be fully explained (see note 5).[12]

Gender theory alerted us to the characteristic masculine objectifying emphasis upon developing separations from others, in contrast to the characteristic feminine relational emphasis upon developing attachments with others. Empirical examination of boys' and girls' and of men's and women's moral concerns reveals the characteristic gender outlines in new forms. For men, moral problems arise from competing rights, moral development requires the increased capacity for fairness, and the resolution of moral problems requires absolute judgments arrived at through the formal, abstract thinking necessary for taking the role of the generalized other. Men characteristically worry about people interfering with one another's rights, and objective unfairness appears immoral to men whether or not it subjectively hurts. In contrast, for women moral problems arise from conflicting responsibilities to particular dependent others, moral development requires the increased capacity for understanding and care, and the resolution of moral problems requires awareness of the possible limitations on any particular problem resolution arrived at through the contextual and inductive thinking characteristic of taking the role of the particular other. Women worry about not helping others when they could help them, and a subjectively felt hurt appears immoral to women whether or not it is fair.

Hence, the norms for "practical rationality" that are supposed to guide us in resolving the most-crucial human social conflicts and in everyday social interactions appear, as gender theory predicts, to correspond disproportionately to characteristic modern masculine understandings of what constitutes rational belief and action.

Some Implications for Philosophy.

The array of questions suggested by gender theory unifies and theoretically recasts questions that have arisen here and there in the history of philosophy in isolated contexts. First, I have already indicated respects in which the concepts of a rational person, of rational belief, and of rational action need to be reexamined in light of the hypothesis that they reflect something less than human concepts. This raises a host of questions about the history of philosophy and about the conceptual schemes of contemporary philosophical thought. Are "the problems of philosophy" really human problems, or do they only reflect disproportionately what appears problematic to men? (see, for instance, Flax 1983; O'Brien, 1981.) Are the problems of justifying the "rules" for establishing appropriate relationships between mind and body, reason and the emotions, self and external world, will and desire—relationships painfully sundered for men in their infancy—really fully human problems? Notice that in each dichotomy, the latter is perceived as threatening to overcome and control the former unless the former creates rigid separation from and rational control of the latter. The history of modern philosophy appears disproportionately obsessed with establishing rules by which mind, reason, self, and will can legitimately control body, the emotions, the external world ("nature" and "other persons"), and desire.

Second, moral theory in particular needs to be reexamined from this perspective. For instance, to the observer armed with gender theory, egoism, utilitarianism, and formalism all appear to address characteristically masculine problems of how to elaborate rules for adjudicating competing rights and duties between generalized autonomous individuals.[13] None takes as an equally important problem how to elaborate ways of resolving conflicting responsibilities to dependent particular others. Should moral theory take the development of a concept of justice and political theory and the project of constructing the just state as central when those goals, even if achieved, would not by themselves bring about greater social welfare? Is justice sufficient to maximize social welfare?

Third, the fact that thought is formal and abstract does not seem to protect it from reflecting specific social experiences. Both the partiality and the reification of political relations in this thought distort our understandings. Indeed, formality and abstractness usually hide the social experiences a conceptual scheme reflects. Moreover, the research reviewed above suggests that the insistence on formality and abstractness in the form of "impersonal" rules and procedures may itself be a historically originated, distorting social bias. Hence it behooves philosophers to ask what social biases particular formal systems (as well as the insistence on formality) reflect.

Fourth, these considerations reveal that not all "social biases" are equally detrimental to rational scientific progress. Some social experiences produce "values" that obstruct their possessors' ability to detect regularities of nature and social life. Others increase such abilities. The insistence on epistemological privilege for masculine objectifying ways of understanding nature and social life results in distortions in our understandings, as the recent research on women and gender consistently has shown. Hence, why should criteria for maximally complete and undistorted scientific accounts insist on value-neutrality? Why should they not insist on the neutralization only of epistemologically regressive social values?

Finally, these considerations raise some interesting questions about the conception of the "rational reconstruction" of science that has been so problematic in the philosophy of science literature of the last few decades. I mention just one. Should we not reconsider the discrepancies Hanson (1958), Kuhn (1970) and Feyerabend (1975) find between rationally reconstructed logics of theory acceptance and the actual practices of scientists—especially the practices of scientists during the "revolutions" or paradigm shifts that Kuhn contrasted with "normal science" practices? Logics are norms: they tell us how we *should* reason, what procedures we *should* follow. It may be that actual processes and tacit "rules" of scientific inquiry are far more gender-neutral than one could infer after they have been "rationally reconstructed" by scientists' own accounts or by philosophers and historians who attempt to make these processes conform to abstract logics of theory acceptance. Creating and working with a new theory or paradigm (in contrast to the practices of normal science) requires far more concern with conflicting responsibilities to old vs. new theoretical perspectives, far more relational and contextual decision-making, far more awareness of the possible limitations on any particular problem resolution. Revolutionary scientists—in contrast to normal scientists—are concerned far more with developing theoretically lean and empirically undernourished hypotheses than with the more abstract operations and thinking necessary for elaborating rules for adjudicating competing "evidential rights" in normal science. From this perspective, the problematic logics of the "context of justification" would represent a supermasculinized distortion of the far more gender-neutral or "feminized" processes that actually account for the growth of knowledge. From this perspective, it is not surprising that Kuhn felt forced to label as "irrational" many obviously positive influences on the growth of scientific knowledge.

Let me try to clarify what I can only at this point suggest by these highly controversial remarks. As I noted earlier, a peculiar consistency is evident between what have been identified as distinctively modern and also as distinctively masculine models of rationality. Correlatively, what have been identified as distinctively feminine models of rationality appear to share characteristics with pre-modern models. The historical evidence suggests that modern science could develop only with the emergence also of modern forms of class society and of liberal political theory (see, e.g., Zilsel 1942; Sohn-Rethel 1978). Yet neither the philosophic nor the historical literature notes that this interdependent emergence of modern science, modern class society, and liberal political theory also intensified and "rationalized"—in both the Marxian and Freudian senses—the masculinization of many aspects of social life, including our models of knowledge-seeking (see Keller 1978; Merchant 1980; Harding 1980, 1983; Hartsock 1980, 1983). Once we begin to think of science as a social institution—that is, as a particular, socially legitimated kind of process for coming-to-know, rather than as a set of sentences which correspond to the laws of nature—we can begin to see that the widespread dissatisfaction with the logics of justification should be recast as a dissatisfaction with the legitimation of only stereotypically masculine and modern modes of knowing. Kuhn can then be understood to be arguing that revolutionary processes of coming-to-know are not, in fact, these idealized masculine and modern ones, and that even everyday "normal science" involves far more "feminine" and traditional craft techniques for producing belief than the logics of justification can acknowledge. These kinds of considerations thus lead to the question of whether we should not try to develop a less-masculinized and modern conception of rationality, to provide a more illuminating and reliable account of the history and practice of science?

To conclude, there is a growing body of evidence supporting the claim that gender is a variable in conceptions of rationality. Exactly how it functions as a variable and what implications gendered rationality has for philosophy are issues deserving a great deal more attention.

Notes

A University of Delaware Summer Faculty Research Fellowship in 1980 and a NEH Summer Research Fellowship in 1979 supported the research for this essay. I have benefited from discussions with many people on the issues of this paper over the last four years. In particular I am indebted to Pamela Armstrong, Sarah Begus, Jane Flax, and Nancy Hartsock. This printing of the essay differs from its original version in several places where I have responded to helpful comments from Carol Gould.

1. The best sources to use to begin to grasp the main focuses of the last decade's research on women and on gender are the annual review essays for each discipline published since 1975 in *Signs: Journal of Women in Culture and Society*.

In order to draw attention to genderic social aspects of "human nature" here, I have to produce the mirror-image of biological determinism's distortion of reality. As Alison Jaggar has pointed out, biological determinism is not so much false as incoherent. We should talk about sex/gender, for nature and culture, sex and gender, are mutually "determining." See Chapter 2, this volume.

2. The epistemological issues are most clearly focused in Smith 1974, 1977, 1979;

Keller 1978; Westkott 1979; Hartsock 1980, 1983; Flax 1983; Addelson 1983; Spelman 1983; and the essays in Sherman and Beck 1979.

3. Smith (1974, 1977, 1979) points out some of the implications for sociology of regarding the persons whose actions one wants to understand as potential "objects of knowledge" vs. regarding them as potential "agents of knowledge."

4. I have discussed the problems with associating "value-neutrality" with objectivity in my 1977, 1978, 1980, 1983.

5. Two comments are called for here. First, this claim will seem improbable to those unfamiliar with recent scholarship in history and anthropology. While there yet seems to be no clear and uncontroversial explanation *why* the scope and powers of women so consistently appear to be restricted during periods of so-called "progressive" social change, there is persuasive evidence *that* this occurs: it can be found in records of the new laws limiting women's role in public life and regulating women's sexuality in "progressive" (i.e., more democratic) societies. The forthcoming explanation of this correlation must account for the "necessity" of the following intuitively graspable regularities. After all, from the perspective of democracies, aristocracies and tribal societies appear socially regressive. But in aristocracies and tribal societies, kinship networks structure public life—government, the economy, religion, and the educational system (see Rubin 1975). In these societies, in contrast to democracies, women's status is more determined by their kin status than by state-originating regulations determining who can function as a "citizen" in public life. Several of the papers in Bridenthal and Koonz (1977) present this kind of argument. See, for instance, Eleanor Leacock, "Women in Egalitarian Societies"; Marylin Arthur, " 'Liberated' Women: The Classical Era"; and Joan Kelly-Gadol, "Did Women Have a Renaissance?" In addition to the further references in that volume, see Leacock (1981). In Chapter 5 of O'Brien (1981), the *Oresteia* is interpreted as creating the ideology to justify an earlier "world historic defeat of the female sex" in that part of the world through the creation of the *polis* (see Harding and Bhaya 1982).

Second, the text here obscures the fact that only men of the ruling classes and races have disproportionately received the benefits of these periods of "human" progress. The development of bourgeois society, which made possible both modern science and modern society, required the wage-enslavement of workers and the colonial enslavement of most Africans and other ancestors of today's Third World peoples. In the context of the argument of this essay, this is an important point for epistemologists to consider. The literature on European vs. non-European modes of rationality in particular has flourished anew recently. (See, for instance, Horton and Finnegan 1973 [and especially Horton 1973]; Dixon 1976; and Wiredu 1977 for guides to some of the key issues in this literature.

It was an eerie experience for this writer to discover the similarities and differences in the kinds of epistemological issues raised in discussions of the rationality attributed to both non-European cultures and to women in Western cultures in light of the virtually nonexistent cross-referencing of these literatures. The eeriness is caused here not just by the recognition that women often have been characterized as "primitive" and "savage," and that dominated groups are often thought of in feminized ways. Even more puzzling is the failure of feminist and non-Western writers to build on the different and valuable understandings each group has produced of what the epistemological issues *are*. For instance, Africans have a clearer understanding of the problems with the Negritude perspective than do feminists of the problems with reification of femaleness or "the feminine." On the other hand, "the feminist epistemological standpoint" appears to be more clearly articulated than does an African epistemological standpoint. The shared target of feminist and non-European criticisms appears to be a particular, modern, European conception of rationality that is also distinctively masculine. The explanation for this conjunction of characteristics of Western rationality is perhaps the explanation called for in the first paragraph of this note.

6. My argument here may appear to move too quickly from the bare assertion that the sense of gender is the most important social characteristic, to the conclusion that most important philosophical conceptions have been tied to gender-specific conceptions of the "male man." Much evidence suggests that it is increasingly difficult to find *any* philosophical conception that does not bear the fingerprints of its origination in distinctively masculine experience. For an array of the key arguments supporting this suspicion, see Moulton (1977), O'Brien (1981), and the papers in Clark and Lange (1979), Marks and deCourtivron (1981) and Harding and Hintikka (1983). It is important to note that these arguments are made by thinkers coming from all of the main Western philosophic traditions.

7. For an evaluation of the virtues and limitations of this part of gender theory relative to other psychoanalytic theories that explain the relationship between sexuality and personal identity, see Person (1980). I have critically examined the empirical and explanatory properties of this emerging gender theory in 1981a and 1981b, and some of its implications for the naturalist vs. intentionalist dispute in the philosophy of social science in 1980. The following few pages draw on these first two papers especially.

8. I have discussed this at some length in 1981a and 1981b.

9. Qualificatory and cautionary notes are in order here. Historical, anthropological, and sociological records provide a number of challenges for those interested in understanding women's (and men's) lives. Data is always selectively collected, and the selection handed down to us has been collected by men. Male anthropologists, for example, are often denied access to or are disinterested in observation of women's lives. And their interpretations of what they do observe and of what male informants tell them are based on what is familiar to them from their own sexist and Western cultures. (See the introduction to Millman and Kanter 1975 and Leacock 1981 for discussion of these problems in anthropology and sociology.) Furthermore, through public policy, social theories become part of the "ruling" of social life. Our leading social theories are peculiarly consistent with distinctively masculine and ruling-class understandings of how societies function (see Smith 1974, 1977, 1979; Hartsock 1980, 1983; O'Brien 1983). They often distort our understanding of how more egalitarian societies function. Thus, while Rosaldo's generalization seems to be true, there are very important differences in degree and form between the ways in which the sex/gender system structures social life in pre-state societies and in modern, Western social life. As for the cautionary note, we are led away from asking the important questions about why and how the sex/gender system does function if we fixate on the fact of its universality, as it may be thought I am doing in this essay.

10. Gilligan (1979, 1982) provides the most comprehensive review of the criticisms of moral development theories reported here.

11. This conception is central to Rawls (1971), as well as to the history of liberal ethical and political theory.

12. Carol Gould pointed out to me the importance of noting that the moral preoccupations of Kant and Rawls are not those of Aristotle and Hume. I would stress, however, that the latter are also sexist (see Burns 1979; Marcil-Lacoste 1979; Lange 1983; Spelman 1983).

13. Even the egoism/altruism dichotomy appears to be conceptualized mainly on the basis of the masculine "objectifying" personality construct. This has implications for psychological theories' attributions of the "altruistic personality"—the "other-oriented" personality—to women. Are women's personalities really "other-oriented," or rather oriented to the welfare of relational complexes within which the welfare of "self" and "other" are mutually dependent? This kind of question has already been raised about the personalities of Afro-Americans (see e.g., Jackson 1976).

References

Addelson, Kathryn Pyne. 1983. "The Man of Professional Wisdom." In S. Harding and M. Hintikka, 1983.

Benjamin, Jessica. 1980. "The Bonds of Love: Rational Violence and Erotic Domination." *Feminist Studies* 6:1.

Bridenthal, Renate, and Claudia Koonz. 1977. *Becoming Visible: Women in European History.* Boston: Houghton Mifflin.

Burns, Steven A. Macleod. 1979. "The Humean Female." In *The Sexism of Social and Political Theory: Women and Reproduction from Plato to Nietzsche,* ed. Lorenne M. G. Clark and Lynda Lange. Toronto: University of Toronto Press.

Chodorow, Nancy. 1978. *The Reproduction of Mothering.* Berkeley: University of California Press.

Clark, Lorenne M. G., and Lynda Lange, eds. 1979. *The Sexism of Social and Political Theory: Women and Reproduction from Plato to Nietzsche.* Toronto: University of Toronto Press.

Dinnerstein, Dorothy. 1976. *The Mermaid and the Minotaur: Sexual Arrangements and Human Malaise.* New York: Harper & Row.

Dixon, Vernon J. 1976. "World Views and Research Methodology." In *African Philosophy: Assumption and Paradigms for Research on Black Persons,* ed. L. M. King, V. J. Dixon, and W. W. Nobles. Los Angeles: Fanon Center Publication of Charles R. Drew Post-Graduate Medical School.

Feyeraband, P. K. 1976. *Against Method.* Atlantic Highlands, N.J.: Humanities Press.

Flax, Jane. 1978. "The Conflict Between Nurturance and Autonomy in Mother-Daughter Relationships and Within Feminism." *Feminist Studies* 4.

———. 1983. "Political Philosophy and the Patriarchal Unconscious: A Psychoanalytic Perspective on Epistemology and Metaphysics." In S. Harding and M. Hintikka, 1983.

Gilligan, Carol. 1979. "Woman's Place in Man's Life Cycle." *Harvard Educational Review* 49.

———. 1982. *In a Different Voice: Psychological Theory and Women's Development.* Cambridge: Harvard University Press.

Guntrip, H. 1961. *Personality Structure and Human Interaction.* New York: International Universities Press.

Hanson, N. R. 1958. *Patterns of Discovery.* Cambridge: Cambridge University Press.

Harding, Sandra G. 1977. "Does Objectivity in Social Science Require Value-Neutrality?" *Soundings* 60:4.

———. 1978. "Four Contributions Values Can Make to the Objectivity of Social Science." In *Philosophy of Science Association 1978,* Vol. 1, ed. P. D. Asquith and I. Hacking. East Lansing, Mich.: Philosophy of Science Association.

———. 1980. "The Norms of Social Inquiry and Masculine Experience." *Philosophy of Science Association 1980,* Vol. 2, ed. P. D. Asquith and R. N. Giere. East Lansing, Mich.: Philosophy of Science Association.

———. 1981a. "The Gender Politics of Infancy." *Quest: A Feminist Quarterly* 5:3.

———. 1981b. "What is the Real Material Base of Patriarchy and Capital?" In *Women and Revolution,* ed. L. Sargent. Boston: South End Press.

———. 1983. "Why Has the Sex/Gender System Become Visible Only Now?" In S. Harding and M. Hintikka, 1983.

Harding, Sandra, and Shakuntla Bhaya. 1982. "Review of *The Politics of Reproduction* by Mary O'Brien." *Signs: Journal of Women in Culture and Society* 7:2.

Harding, Sandra, and M. Hintikka, eds. 1983. *Discovering Reality: Feminist Perspectives on Epistemology, Metaphysics, Methodology and Philosophy of Science.* Dordrecht: Reidel.

Hartsock, Nancy. 1980. "Social Life and Social Science: The Significance of the Naturalist/Intentionalist Dispute." In *Philosophy of Science Association 1980*, Vol. 2, ed. P. D. Asquith and R. N. Giere. East Lansing, Mich.: Philosophy of Science Association.

———. 1983. "The Feminist Standpoint: Developing the Ground for a Specifically Feminist Historical Materialism." In S. Harding and M. Hintikka, 1983.

Horton, Robin. 1973. "Levy-Bruhl, Durkheim and the Scientific Revolution." In *Modes of Thought: Essays on Thinking in Western and Non-Western Societies*, ed. Robin Horton and Ruth Finnegan. London: Faber & Faber.

———, and Ruth Finnegan, eds. 1973. *Modes of Thought: Essays on Thinking in Western and Non-Western Societies*. London: Faber & Faber.

Jackson, G. G. 1976. "The African Genesis of the Black Perspective in Helping." *Professional Psychology*, pp. 292–308.

Jaggar, Allison. 1983. "Human Biology and Feminist Theory: Sex Equality Reconsidered." See Chapter 2, this volume.

Keller, Evelyn F. 1978. "Gender and Science." *Psychoanalysis and Contemporary Thought* 1:3. Reprinted in S. Harding and M. Hintikka, 1983.

Kelly-Gadol, Joan. 1976. "The Social Relation of the Sexes: Methodological Implications of Women's History." *Signs* 1.

Kohlberg, L. 1971. "From Is to Ought: How to Commit the Naturalistic Fallacy and Get Away with It in the Study of Moral Development." In *Cognitive Development and Epistemology*, ed. T. Mischel. New York: Academic Press.

Kohlberg, L., and R. Kramer. 1969. "Continuities and discontinuities in childhood and adult moral development." *Human Development* 12, pp. 92–120.

Kuhn, T. S. 1970. *The Structure of Scientific Revolutions*. Chicago: University of Chicago Press.

Lange, Lynda. 1982. "Women Is Not a Rational Animal: On Aristotle's Biology of Reproduction." In S. Harding and M. Hintikka, 1983.

Leacock, Eleanor. 1981. *Myths of Male Dominance*. New York: Monthly Review Press.

Mahler, M. S., F. Pine, and A. Bergman 1975. *The Psychological Birth of the Human Infant*. New York: Basic Books.

Marcil-Lacoste, Louise. 1979. "Hume's Method in Moral Reasoning." In *The Sexism of Social and Political Theory: Women and Reproduction from Plato to Nietzsche*, ed. Lorenne M. G. Clark and Lynda Lange. Toronto: University of Toronto Press.

Marks, Elaine, and Isabelle de Courtivron, eds. 1981. *New French Feminisms*. New York: Schocken Books.

Merchant, Carolyn. 1980. *The Death of Nature: Women, Ecology and the Scientific Revolution*. New York: Harper & Row.

Millman, M., and R. Kanter, eds. 1975. *Another Voice: Feminist Perspectives on Social Life and Social Science*. New York: Doubleday.

Moulton, Janice. 1977. "The Myth of the Neutral 'Man.' " In *Feminism and Philosophy*, ed. Mary Vetterling-Braggin, F. Elliston, and Jane English. Totowa, N.J.: Littlefield, Adams & Co.

O'Brien, Mary. 1981. *The Politics of Reproduction*. Boston: Routledge & Kegan Paul.

Person, E. S. 1980. "Sexuality as the Mainstay of Identity: Psychoanalytic Perspectives." *Signs* 5.

Rawls, John. 1971. *A Theory of Justice*. Cambridge: Harvard University Press.

Rosaldo, M. Z. 1980. "The Use and Abuse of Anthropology: Reflections on Feminism and Cross-Cultural Understanding." *Signs* 5.

Rubin, Gayle. 1975. "The Traffic in Women: Notes on the 'Political Economy of Sex." In *Toward an Anthropology of Women*, ed. Rayna R. Reiter. New York: Monthly Review Press.

Sherman, Julia A., and Evelyn T. Beck, eds. 1979. *The Prism of Sex: Essays in the Sociology of Knowledge*. Madison: University of Wisconsin Press.

Signs: Journal of Women in Culture and Society. 1975 et seq. Chicago: University of Chicago Press.

Smith, Dorothy. 1974. "Women's Perspective as a Radical Critique of Sociology." *Sociological Inquiry* 44.

———. 1977. "Some Implications of a Sociology for Women." In *Woman in a Man-Made World: A Socioeconomic Handbook*, ed. N. Glazer and H. Waehrer. Chicago: Rand-McNally.

———. 1979. "A Sociology for Women." In *The Prism of Sex*, ed. J. Sherman and E. Beck.

Sohn-Rethel, Alfred. 1978. *Intellectual and Manual Labour: A Critique of Epistemology*. Atlantic Highlands, N.J.: Humanities Press.

Spelman, Elizabeth V. 1983. "Aristotle and the Politicization of the Soul." In S. Harding and M. Hintikka, 1983.

Westkott, M. 1979. "Feminist Criticism of the Social Sciences." *Harvard Educational Review* 49.

Winnicott, D. W. 1965. *The Maturational Processes and the Facilitating Environment*. New York: International University Press.

Wiredu, J. E. 1977. "How Not to Compare African Thought with Western Thought." In *African Philosophy: An Introduction*, ed. Richard A. Wright. Washington, D.C.: University Press of America.

Zilsel, E. 1942. "The Sociological Roots of Science." *American Journal of Sociology* 47.

4

A Different Reality: Feminist Ontology

CAROLINE WHITBECK

Introduction

In this chapter I outline a feminist ontology or metaphysics, and argue for its adequacy. This ontology has at its core a conception of the self-other *relation* that is significantly different from the self-other *opposition* that underlies much of so-called "Western thought." Dualistic ontologies based on the opposition of self and other generate two related views of the person and of ethics: the patriarchal view and that of individualism. The proponents of individualism or of patriarchy often argue for their view by attacking the other view, as though the only possibilities were variants of these two masculist viewpoints. The feminist ontology outlined here is based on a conception of the relation of self and other(s) that is neither oppositional nor dyadic, and engenders a view of the person and of ethics that is significantly different from both those of individualism and of patriarchy.

The self-other opposition is at the heart of other dualistic oppositions, such as theory-practice, culture-nature, spirit-matter, mind-body, human-divine, political-personal, public-private (or "productive-reproductive"), knower-known, theory-practice, lover-beloved, that figure prominently in so-called "Western thought."[1] The feminist ontology outlined here yields a distinctive, non-oppositional, and non-dualistic conception of these subjects, as well as a new view of the person and of ethics. Furthermore, because the relation of self to other is not taken to be represented by gender difference, gender is neither taken to be, nor to be symbolic of, an important ontological difference. Because differentiation does not depend on opposition, the differentiation of the proposed ontology from dualistic ontologies does not require that it be interpreted as the "opposite" view, or even the only alternative to dualism.

The ontology presented here must be understood in relation to a certain general type of practice. By "practice" I mean a coherent form of cooperative activity, or "joint action," as Carol Gould calls it, that not only aims at certain ends but creates certain ways of living and develops certain characteristics (virtues) in those who participate and try to achieve the standards of excellence peculiar to that practice.[2] The practice that I consider to be the core practice is that of the (mutual) realization of people. I take this practice to have a variety of particular forms, most, if not all, of which are regarded as women's work and are therefore largely ignored by the dominant culture. Among these are the rearing of children, the education of children and adolescents, care of the dying, nursing of the sick and injured, and a variety of spiritual practices related to daily life.

These practices are sometimes described as "nurturing." Although this language has the advantage of being familiar, it has often been used to evoke a sentimental picture of a woman doing a variety of mindless tasks in response to the demands of others, and for that reason I am reluctant to use it.[3] The creativity and responsibility of all parties in the conduct of the practice in its full, liberated form is inconsistent with the sentimental picture of women's self-sacrifice. These points will be illustrated in the discussion of the practices of family life, below, and will be discussed further in the section on the ontology of the person.

A characterization of the core practice that would be adequate to represent it in its major forms and in a variety of cultural contexts will require discussion of the forms of that practice from a variety of individual and cultural perspectives. It may only be from a few cultural perspectives that it seems plausible to work out the associated ontology, or at least to describe it as "ontology."

The vision of society that fits the ontology outlined in this paper is that of society organized around the practices of mutual realization, practices which by and large have been "women's work." This is close, if not identical, to the vision of society that Barbara Ehrenreich and Deirdre English point to at the end of their book, *For Her Own Good: 150 Years of the Expert's Advice to Women* (p. 292). The views that they characterize as "romantic" and as "rationalist" are the exemplifications in recent Anglo-American culture of the views that I term "patriarchal" and "individualistic," respectively. (Unfortunately they call the feminist view to be developed a "synthesis" of the replaced views. This use of Marxian-Hegelian jargon obscures the point that, as their book documents, *neither* the romantic or rationalist alternative attends to women's experience, as contrasted with men's representations of women. A literal synthesis of two views rooted in dualism would only yield another dualistic view.)

Since the liberation of women's practices is central to this vision, it must be developed by articulating the experience of those engaged in the practices. Although this is a task that can be assisted and midwifed by academics and other theoreticians, I think that little can be contributed by dissociating ourselves from what have been women's practices, and the women engaged in them, since we will then either ignore those practices or inadvertently perpetuate the false account that masculist culture gives of them.

In the second section I summarize some earlier research that uses influential psychological theories to expose the dualistic ontology presupposed by "Western thought." This is followed by an examination of the views of the person and of ethics that derive from the patriarchal and from the individualist variants of dualism. The project of constructing a feminist ontology, and the heuristic function of feminist psychology for that philosophical project, are considered in the fourth section. The main features of the ontology are next presented: reality is understood in terms of the interactions among multiple factors which are often analogous, rather than in terms of dualistic oppositions. The sixth section contains the account of the person that flows from the feminist ontology presented in the preceding section. I argue that the person is a relational and historical being whose creativity and moral integrity are both developed and realized in and through relationships and practices. The correlative ethical viewpoint outlined in the seventh section takes the notion of the moral responsibilities that go with relationships as the fundamental moral notion. Moral rights, including human rights, have their ultimate warrant as the moral claims on others and on social institutions that safeguard a person's ability to fulfill the responsibilities of relationships that person has formed or may form. A summary of the ontology is given in the final section.

The Use of Psychological Theory to Reveal Masculist Ontology

Nine years ago, I documented a remarkable constancy over the 3,000 years in the themes or motifs embodied in the theories proposed by philosophers and scientists to identify and explain sex differences (Whitbeck 1973–74). I shall briefly summarize that research since it reveals some major features of masculist ontology. Three themes repeatedly occur:

1. woman is an incomplete man;
2. there are two opposing or complementary principles, masculine and feminine, that are constitutive of reality; and
3. the strengths or virtues proper to women are defined by male needs.

In some cases a single theory exemplifies two or more of these themes. The recurrence of these themes is all the more notable when one considers that our views about nature, scientific method, and the like have undergone profound changes in that period of time. Each theme shows an androcentric bias; that is, the male, or the male experience, is taken as the norm.

Although the theories of Freud and the Jungians exemplify the first and second themes and are incoherent in their treatment of *female* development, their theories of male development give major clues as to how the three recurrent themes arise in the thoughts and fantasies of little boys. In particular, the view that the masculine and feminine are opposite principles that symbolize other major oppositions, especially an opposition of self and other, is one that the Jungians trace to the (male) infant's differentiation of his masculine self from the feminine primordial nurturer. It is this second theme, which dates at least from Pythagoras, that is central to masculist ontology. (It turns up even in influential theories, such as those of Aristotle and Freud, that for the most part view woman as an incomplete man.) The masculine principle is taken to have whatever attributes the culture sees as appropriate to the conscious and rational self. The characteristics that are viewed as opposite are attributed to the second, the "feminine" principle. Although the two principles are frequently held to be complementary, the association of the masculine principle with rationality leads to a hierarchical interpretation of the relationship between the principles, so that the masculine is viewed as superior and the feminine as inferior.[4]

Norman O. Brown echoes the same ontological dualism based on sexual opposition when he says, "Dual organization is sexual organization. The structural principle is the union of opposites. . . . The *agon,* the contest between winter and summer, night and day is coitus" (Brown 1966, pp. 22–23). (Brown's statement accurately reflects a crucial ambiguity or confusion in the dualistic thought concerning the nature of the relation of the self to the other. On the one hand, the relation is represented as attraction; on the other, it is represented as one of conflict that gives rise to a struggle for dominance. The confusion between attraction and aggression is evident in the view that rape is a normal expression of male sexuality.)[5]

Standing outside the ontology based on dualistic oppositions, one can easily recognize what is odd about the attempt to represent cyclical changes as an alternation between opposing states. If we consider the seasons, for example, we find there is nothing about those cycles that dictates what two points should be taken as the supposed extremes of the cycle. One might select extremes of temperature, or of duration of daylight, or any number of other pairs of points.

It is important to distinguish clearly between dualistic ontology and the ontology proposed in my fifth section. Too often the project of constructing a feminist view is confused with the project of simply affirming the goodness or the primacy of the characteristics associated with what masculist dualistic thought views as "the feminine principle," or appropriate to the feminine gender, or arising from female biology. The latter tendency, which is common in the writing of Jungians and some feminists, was prefigured in the defense of Mother-Right and the Dionysian (as opposed to Father-Right and the Apollonian) in the writings of Nietzsche and Bachofen.[6]

Two Versions of Dualist Ontology: Patriarchy and Individualism

Masculist dualist ontology has been developed along two related lines. The first, and older, line of development generates patriarchy in the strict sense—the rule of the fathers, with its hierarchal organization of political life modeled on the organization of the patriarchal family. This view is followed, and to some extent is replaced by individualism, with what may be called "the rule of the sons." The resulting view of family, political, and psychic life, however, presupposes the preceding patriarchal view.

The sisters are rarely mentioned in the theories of liberation associated with the rebellion of the "sons" against the father. Brothers would be brothers to sisters as well as to one another. The absence of any reference to the sisters symbolizes a key feature of individualism; that is, individualism reflects the concerns of a certain group of men, those whose primary experience of domination was at the hands of a father or a monarch, and provides the basis for an ideological justification for their rebellion against that oppression. It retains the same opposition of self to other. It is therefore hardly surprising that individualism leaves untouched forms of domination other than domination of the sons by the father and of propertied citizens by the monarch. (In Locke's original scheme the right to vote did not extend even to those free men who did not own property. In early America property was widely available, so the distinction between those men who had property and those who did not was not of major significance in creating societal divisions. The denial of the civil and human rights of slaves on the basis that they themselves were property shows the strength of the idea of property rights in early America, however [see Lodge 1977, chapt. 4].) The same dualism underlies Hegel's version of patriarchy and the individualism of Sartre's *Being and Nothingness*. (An illuminating account of the central place of sexual dualism in Sartre's discussion of the dualistic opposition between the for-itself and the in-itself has been given by Margery Collins and Christine Pierce [1973–74].) Indeed, these philosophical frameworks exhibit the features of dualism even more explicitly than do Hobbesian-Lockean individualism and Aristotlean patriarchy, to which I shall give more attention. For example, in Hegel's *Phenomenology of Spirit*, the presupposition of an opposition between self and other is underscored by the statement that "the relation of the two self-conscious individuals is such that they prove themselves and each other through a life and death struggle" (Hegel 1977, pp. 113–14). Indeed, Hegel starts by taking the self-other relation to be a master-slave relation. Some philosophers desire to interpret the notion of dialectic in Hegel in a way that replaces the notion of opposition with something more congenial to the notion of historical development that is also in Hegel; however, the difficulty is in Hegel—opposition is where Hegel starts.[7] If a mother saw the emerging person who is her child in the way that Hegel describes, human beings would not exist. The failure of Hegel's scheme to apply to the mother's experience in the primordial mother-child relation is a significant failure. An understanding of differentiation that does not depend on opposition and "a life and death struggle" is essential to the ontology outlined here.

From the dualistic perspective the other is taken to be opposite to the self. Therefore, if one takes existence itself as a predicate, solipsism becomes a plausible ontological viewpoint; that is, one can ask, "If I am, can anything else even exist?" Indeed, in view of the potential threat to the self of an other assumed to be opposite, solipsism may even be an attractive position. If one is willing to grant the existence of others, their character becomes a question.

Dualism runs through Aristotle's thought, from his early thinking recorded in the *Physics* to his late work in *Generation of Animals*. Aristotle took the dualistic opposition between male and female as his *starting point,* and he used it as the model for the relation of form to matter, which is at the core of his entire ontology (*Physics:* Book Alpha, 192a). Form is rational and active; matter is irrational and passive. Thus far from being a quaint aberration in Aristotle's thought, his construal of the relation between male and female as dualistic opposition is crucial to his ontology.

According to Aristotle, only the free adult male (in fact only the Athenian citizen) qualifies as a full person, because only he has fully functioning and authoritative rational capacity (*Politics* Book 1).

Aristotle says explicitly, and repeatedly, that to be born female is the most common kind of deformity (*Generation of Animals* 728a, 18 and 766b, 20). Because only the free male adult (Athenian citizen) has full and authoritative rational powers, his relation to others, i.e., to female non-slaves), to slaves and to children (presumed free and male), is largely determined by his obligation to reason for them.

In view of Aristotle's analogy between the relation of male to female and the relation of form to matter, it is not surprising that in the *Politics* he needs explicitly to disclaim the view that the relation of a man to a woman is necessarily that of a master to a slave. (This is a view that he attributes to the "barbarians" in a handy bit of projection.) Aristotle argues that wives, for example, are to be managed, whereas slaves and children are to be ruled as a monarch rules his subjects. According to Aristotle, the female is naturally attracted to the male (although not the reverse), and so the wife, unlike the slave or barbarian, willingly accepts management by the husband.

Aristotle's scheme is more egalitarian than those in which only the eldest son eventually matured to take on the full status of a patriarch. This is not surprising since we know the limited democracy in which Aristotle lived. In Aristotle's thought we find some of the seeds of the individualism that was to follow, and his thought gives important clues as to how individualism develops out of patriarchy. (Just as some elements of individualism were prefigured in some patriarchal systems, so elements of the patriarchal view are to be found in the thinking and legal systems of our contemporary individualistic society.)[8]

Let us return to the story of development: if, or to the extent that, children do not identify with their care givers and do not take the skills appropriate to mutual realization as appropriate to the self, then the relation to siblings must be constituted as one of competition for the attentions of the primordial nurturer(s). In what follows, I shall call the adult counterparts of such children "the peers."[9]

The notion of an "equal" or "peer" assumes a hierarchic ranking in which people are identified as superiors, inferiors, and equals. The notion of equality also reflects those peculiar concerns with measurement that seem to enter into men's relations with each other. For example, men "take each others measure" and speak of the need to "measure up." In contrast to the relationship that exists among the sisters (and brothers) who acquire, and aspire to, the skills and virtues necessary for eliciting the strengths of others, the sons' relationships to one another are, at best, enforceable contracts that function to keep competition within bounds, or alliance against some common enemy, like a domineering father or monarch. In view of the centrality of the theme of competition in defining their relationships and the practices in which they are engaged (competitive sports, wars of rebellion, class war, or wars of national interest), alliance against a common enemy, rather than friendship, is the basis for cooperation among the peers. The moral aspects of the relationships among the peers are specified in terms of rights that generate moral requirements that vary only with changes of contract.

According to individualism the self is assumed to be a "peer," that is, only the perspective of the peers is taken into account.[10] Furthermore, only such peers are regarded as full persons, in the sense that the only decisions that are regarded as significant are the decisions of "peers." The person is regarded as an atom, in the sense that individualism ignores both the interdependence of people and their historical character. The denial of interdependence is a consequence of confining attention to the peers or later to "all men."[11] Restriction of the concept of a person so that it extends only to "peers"—and ignores the women, children, and (for a period) enslaved men and laborers—ignores the agency of the latter groups and the dependency of the peers on them. In particular, the practices regarded as women's work are ignored.[12]

The model of people offered in individualism is adequate to model only the transactions among the peers (in a certain type of market society; see Hartsock 1981). What happens, even to the peers, when they are too young or old or sick to compete and contract with other peers is largely ignored and unrepresentable in terms of the atomic model of persons. Just as it ignores all areas of human vulnerability, so the individualistic model ignores human development. In this respect individualism is less adequate than patriarchy, notwithstanding the extension of full personhood to a larger group—the peers rather than just the patriarchs.

The atomistic representation of persons is implicit not merely in the work of those thinkers from Hobbes and Locke through Nozick, who emphasize the individual's right to pursue self-interest, but also in the work of those from Rousseau through Rawls, who assume they can found the notion of a just society on an agreement among ideal individuals who are construed as existing apart from the history of their relationships and, therefore, apart from their own cultural and intellectual history.

The Project of Creating Feminist Ontology

The very idea of a feminist ontology is not likely to sit well in some circles. Those who balk at the idea of a feminist ontology are, nonetheless, usually able to envision the possibility that there is a pattern of psychological development typical for women that is alternative to that typical for men. Furthermore, although construing reality in a certain way is not reducibile to having undergone a certain pattern of psychological development, feminist theories of women's development do serve a heuristic function for the construction of a feminist's ontology.

Freud (and others) tell us that the male infant's differentiation from a Nurturer (who is viewed as opposite) leads to a preoccupation with the possession of the Nurturer, and with the issue of competing with others with similar designs (Rawlinson 1982). These masculist theories of development have an androcentric (not to mention ethnocentric) bias that make them inapplicable to the development of the girl. First, as I have argued, the mother-son relation has itself been read by men in terms of their own (culturally mediated) adult relation to women so that, for example, the attachment of the infant to the mother is interpreted on the model of a man's sexual attraction to a woman (Whitbeck 1983b). It is possible that this has lead to a misreading of the attachment of infants to their mothers. It is certainly an error to interpret the *mother's* attachment to her daughter (and even to her son) as sexual in the narrow sense (although as I have argued it is both sensual and erotic [Whitbeck 1975]), because of the comparative rarity of mother-child incest as compared with father-child, and brother-sister, incest.

The arguments of feminist psychologists may not be read as ontology, however. First, it may be necessary to free the psychological account of any terminology that presupposes the received, masculist ontology. (I would argue that much of the terminology of ego psychology, as well as that of Freudian, Jungian, and Lacanian psychoanalytic thoery, assumes masculist self-other distinction.[13] Therefore, in spite of the importance of the insights to be gained from reading works by feminist psychologists like Juliet Mitchell and Nancy Chodorow, who employ the technical terminology of psychoanalytic theory and ego-psychology, it is important to recognize that concepts such as that of "object relations" presuppose the masculist opposition of self and other. It does so in postulating an either/or "investment" of libidinal energy, that is, in postulating that energy is *either* directed toward the self *or* directed toward an other in a way that makes it impossible to represent caring about the-self-in-relation-to-others.)

Some feminist philosophers in the last five years have discussed feminine development in a way that relies heavily on dualist categories taken from psychoanalytic theory and object relations theory, and in ways that do not provide a heuristic for a feminist ontology.

For example, Sandra Harding says the "feminine personality develops through the struggle to separate and individuate from a kind of person whom she will in fact nevertheless become—a devalued woman" (Harding 1981, p. 315). Such a reading is an account of the perpetuation of women's oppression. If that reading were formative for a women's own self-understanding, it would lead either to despair or to the attempt to dissociate oneself from women and women's practices.

Even where the psychological theory dispenses with masculist categories (or makes as little use as is possible for a contempory speaker of English, Spanish, etc.), it is necessary to distinguish, at least provisionally, those features of women's thinking and practice that are the results of women's oppression. Finally, even where feminist psychologists write without recourse to masculist categories, and explicitly address the issue of distinguishing the results of oppression from other features of women's psychology (as do Jean Baker Miller in *Toward A New Psychology of Women,* and Janet L. Surrey in "The Relational Self in Women"), there still remains the philosophical project of extracting the view of reality and of ethics implicit in women's liberated practice.

I read the girl's development as follows: girls form their self-concepts in large part through identification with their first significant other(s) who share the same socially defined possibilities of a female body. As a result, the self-other distinction is neither symbolized by a distinction between the sexes, nor does it involve the assumption that the self and other possess opposing characteristics. Therefore, I disagree with the view expressed by Chodorow and Harding that mothers internalize the representation of gender difference as a dualistic opposition, and then recreate or pass on this dualistic understanding to their sons (Chodorow 1978, p. 166; Harding 1981, p. 315). I think Chodorow and Harding have missed the crucial distinction between seeing another as an opposite, and seeing the other as distinct and different in a some respect.[14] A girl's (socially reinforced) identification with her nurturers also often leads to an identification with the virtues and skills necessary for the practices of mutual development.[15] Furthermore, since sisters, grandmothers, and aunts commonly care for children in many cultures, the girl is typically involved in a multiagent network of mutual realization.

The heuristic function of the foregoing arguments should not be forgotten: I do not claim that it is *only* by undergoing a particular course of early development that one can come to the ontological position described here. Although a certain history of relationships may incline a person to seek out other relationships and practices that embody a similar ontological outlook, people may become convinced of the superiority of a particular ontology and seek the relationships and practices consistent with that view. (Theory may guide practice!) I agree with Sara Ruddick that "although some men do, and more generally men should, acquire maternal thinking [or, more generally, self-others thinking], their ways of acquisition are necessarily different from ours" (Ruddick 1980, p. 346). I maintain that the extent of that difference is determined by differences in relationships and practices in which a man has participated. (Notable in my experience of mother-reared men who have internalized self-others thinking and practice are men who have internalized the practice of Friends—Quakers.) People who have little familiarity with the practices and relationships that embody self-others thinking seem to need to give and receive arguments to the effect that "no man is an island."

It is not easy to make clear an ontological proposal when basic concepts are involved. The difficulty is that the terminology in which the new ontology is to be articulated is automatically interpreted in terms of the accepted ontology, so that one is always at the risk of having one's statements construed either as nonsense, or as a quaint phrasing of what are familiar truths according to the old ontology. For example, although we can *now* express the changes in our concepts of space and time brought about by the special theory of relativity by saying that "space and time form a single continuum," or by referring to the "relativity of non-accelerated motion," those phrases would have been of little use to Einstein in *introducing* his theory. Such statements would probably have been misconstrued to state what were taken to be truths according to the Newtonian view. If, on the other hand, Einstein had said that simultaneity or, more generally, that the time elapsed between two events, is relative to the observer's state of motion, the statement would have seemed nonsensical. (Einstein actually tried to make his point by describing information gained by the sending of light signals. The predictable result was that his central claim about the nature of space-time was confused with claims about the speed of light and about conventionality of simultaneity for a *given* observer [Whitbeck 1969].)

Today, one of the easiest ways to introduce the concepts of space-time to students who have a background in mathematics is to use the Minkowski graphic representation. It is instructive to recall that not only was this representation no part of Einstein's original thinking, but that when it was presented to him, he did not initially recognize it as expressing what he wanted to say.

This illustrates an important feature of ontological proposals:

further articulation of an ontological position is not separable from the proposal of an ontology, and therefore any significant ontological proposal is unlikely to be the work of a single individual. In particular, the ontology outlined here depends on a deeper understanding of the practices of mutual realization for its development, since to the extent that these relationships and practices have been represented in the dominant culture, they have been misrepresented (Ehrenreich and English 1978). Mother-children relationships and the practice of mothering and/or family living are paradigmatic examples. Nursing and caring for the sick, disabled, and elderly, teaching, psychotherapy and counseling, and various forms of spiritual practice are others. (For some feminist representations of these and related relationships and practices, see McBride 1972; Freire 1973, 1974; Miller 1976; Rich 1976; Boulding 1978; Christ and Plaskow 1979; Ruddick 1980; Gilligan 1982; Lindemann and Oliver 1982; Whitbeck 1975, 1981a and b, 1982, 1983b; Joan Ringelheim's forthcoming research on the women of the Holocaust—1983; Addelson, unpublished; and the references in each.)

Feminist Ontology: After Dualism, or, None of the Above

At the core of the ontology that I am proposing is a self-other relation that is assumed to be a relation between beings who are in some respects analogous, and the scope and limits of that analogy (what Mary Hesse calls points of "negative and positive analogy" [Hesse 1965]) are something to be explored in each case. This starting point is quite different from that which arises from the opposition of self and other, namely, that the burden of proof is on anyone who claims that the other is in any way like the self. A recurrent tendency that results from the opposition of self and other is to deny the existence of the other to a greater or lesser degree or to make any existing other into the self. In the extreme this results in solipsism or in various forms of patriarchy that represent the patriarch or the state as the decision-maker for the family, clan, or nation. (Elsewhere I have argued that this assumption of dualism lies behind the so-called "problem of other minds" in philosophy. In addition to assuming mind-body dualism, this supposed problem assumes that the burden is to show that the other is like the self in "having" a mind [Whitbeck 1983b].)

The question for those who hold the ontology based on a self-other relations is, what are the scope and limits of the analogy between the self and an other? Since an other is not taken to be opposite to the self, the character of the self does not uniquely define the character of the other by opposition to it: others may be similar or dissimilar in an unlimited variety of ways. Even to make the relation a dyadic relation distorts the ontological position I am outlining here. The relation is not fundamentally dyadic at all, and is better expressed as a self-*others* relation, because relationships, past and present, realized and sought, are constitutive of the self, and so the actions of a person reflect the more- or less-successful attempt to respond to the whole configuration of relationships.

Since the relations of the self to others are relations among analogous beings, and the scope and limits of that analogy are to be discovered or, if the other is another person, to be mutually created and transformed, relationships between people are understood as developing through identification and differentiation, through listening and speaking, with *each other,* rather than through struggles to dominate or annihilate the other. That the images associated with transformation are non-violent should not be taken to suggest that the transformations are less profound, or more gradual, or easy, but only that the process of change is more complex than that which can be represented in terms of successive dualistic oppositions. Birth is hardly trivial or gradual, and may be painful or difficult. (Mary Condren argues on the basis of a great deal of textual evidence that whereas women's creativity is expressed in relation to the giving and sustaining of life, men's creativity takes place in relation to death and death-defying activities [Condren 1982].)

In place of an ontology characterized by dualistic oppositions, of self-other, egoism-altruism, theory-practice, culture-nature, mind-body, knower-known, male-female (and therefore, straight-gay), public-private (or "productive-reproductive"), human-divine, political-personal, spiritual-material, etc., the self-others relation generates a multifactorial interactive model of most, if not all, aspects of reality. Because the content of each related term is not defined by opposition to the content of the term with which it is paired, these terms no longer mean what they meant in masculist theory.

Thus, for example, theory aims at the clarification of practice, rather than the discovery or creation of some some sort of Popperian or Platonic World of Ideas, itself immune from decay and death, which might confer an immortality of sorts upon its creators; culture does not aim at the pornographic objectification and domination of nature so brilliantly analyzed by Susan Griffin in her book, *Pornography and Silence.* Culture is a body of developing and decaying interpretations and strategies created by people for understanding and interacting with human and non-human aspects of nature and with other aspects of culture. Not only can the personal be political, for example, but both politics and personal life are bound up with other matters not easily classifiable either as political or as personal.

Not only are our bodies ourselves (rather than being something that we, as minds, possess), but the bodies, intellects, emotions, souls, characters, and configurations of relationships that we are can be adequately understood only in relation to one another.

Ontology of the Person

The model of the person that I propose is a relational and historical model but, unlike the relational and historical models of patriarchy, one that takes seriously everyone's creativity and moral integrity. On this view it is the exercize of human creativity in the realization of aspirations and the maintenance of moral integrity, rather than successful performance of an externally definable role, that are the key elements in a person's well-being.

On this view relationships to other people are fundamental to being a person, and one cannot become a person without relationships to other people. A person is an historical being whose history is fundamentally a history of relationships to other people.[16] This feature of people or "persons" is not adequately captured by saying that people are cultural beings, although the latter statement is also true. By virtue of being the cultural beings we are, we possess the languages we do; but the history of the relationships which, in part, constitute us, is something over and above our cultural heritage.

It is important to emphasize that the relationships I am discussing are *lived* relationships, not legal or biological relationships, although relationships in the latter sense may influence lived relationships. The concept of a relationship also contrasts with the notion of a role as something that a person can take on and later reject and be no more affected by than the clothing one has temporarily worn.

This notion of relationship has some affinities with the notions of practice I discussed in the first section of this essay. Something is lost, however, when the relationships that constitute and are constituted by those practices are not given a primary place in the discussion. Perhaps the tendency to emphasize practices rather than relationships is due to the relative ease with which one can ignore what is taken to be the secondary private world in discussing practices: in discussing practices it is relatively easy to confine attention to practices in the so-called "real" public world, whereas lived relationships are personal and involve much that is regarded as private. If so, the tendency rests on the acceptance of an opposition of public and private. If relationships are necessary to the emergence of a person, then the existence of social practices requires the prior emergence of the people who participate in those practices, and hence the existence of relationships among people.

The ontology based upon a self-others relation is adequate to represent many facts that have been anomalous from the point of view of dualistic ontology, and thus have regularly escaped notice. For example, the customary views of the family, both the sentimental view of it as a haven in a heartless world ministered to by an angel mother-wife, and the disenchanted view of it as a hell-hole in which the neuroses of one generation are visited upon the next, fail to take account of the extent to which all family members, including the youngest, are typically involved in caring for the others. Sociologist Elise Boulding puts the point in the following way:

> We expect parents to nurture children, but forget that children also nurture parents. Even the fact that children often nurse sick and temporarily bedridden parents [or siblings] is by a pathological twist of the social memory simply forgotten. Each act of healing becomes a part of the personality of both the healer and the healed, a part of each person's future [Boulding 1978].

I submit that what Boulding calls "a pathological twist of social memory" is a predictable consequence of an ontology that views matters in terms of dualistic oppositions so that one and only one member of any dyad can be creative in any except competitive relations.

A related finding that is also recalcitrant to representation in dualistic ontologies is the finding that for some clients of psychotherapy, who were themselves children of disturbed parents whom they as children experienced no success in healing, progress in therapy occurred only as the therapist was able to accept healing by the client (Searles 1980).[17]

Other findings that show the inadequacy of the dichotomy between egoism and altruism that arises from the self-other opposition are the facts that led to the World Health Organization's construction of the concept of maternal-child health. One might suppose that if any aspect of a person's well-being could be construed individualistically, it would be health (as contrasted with such things as status or economic security), but the health of the mother and of the child are so intimately connected that neither can be influenced without influencing the other.

The Ethics

It is a measure of how impoverished the view of the person has become in contemporary philosophical discussions that an increasing number of writers now use the term "person" to mean nothing more than a being with certain rights, particularly a right to life.[18]

This restricted view of the moral person arises as the attempt is made to model all moral requirements on the rights that proved so central in arguing for the legitimacy of the "rule of the sons" that replaced patriarchy. The view that the notion of a right is the fundamental notion in ethics is what I call "the rights view of ethics." The overreliance upon and/or loose use of the concept of rights in contemporary ethics has been pointed out by a number of authors, some of whom, like MacIntyre (1981), and Ladd (1979, 1982) specifically link their criticisms to a criticism of modern individualism. It is Ladd's account that I find most helpful in outlining an alternative view of ethics compatible with the ontological viewpoint presented here. That John Ladd has developed this view of ethics, or one very much like it, gives a concrete demonstration that the philosophical viewpoint I am proposing is not unavailable to men.[19]

According to the rights view of ethics, the concept of a moral right is the fundamental moral notion, or at least the one of preeminent significance. People are viewed as social and moral atoms, armed with rights and reason, and actually or potentially in competition and conflict with one another. (It is a testimony to this culture's obsession with competition that so often aspiration is rendered in competitive terms; for example, "I am competing with myself." A key difference between aspiration and competition is that the goals of competition are achieved by making the competitor fail.) If any attention is given to relationships on the rights view, it is assumed they exist on a contractual or quasi-contractual basis and that the moral requirements arising from them are limited to rights and obligations.

In contrast to obligations that generally specify what acts or conduct are morally required, permitted, or forbidden, responsibilities (in the prospective sense of "responsibility for") specify the ends to be achieved rather than the conduct required. Thus, responsibilities require an exercise of discretion on the part of their bearers. People without the knowledge to exercise discretion in some matter can have only moral obligation and not moral responsibilities in that matter. What I call "the responsibilities view" of ethics takes the moral responsibilities arising out of a relationship as the fundamental moral notion, and regards people as beings who can (among other things) act for moral reasons, and who come to this status through relationships with other people. Such relationships are not assumed to be contractual. The relationship of children to their parents is a good example of a relationship that is not contractual. In general, relationships between people place moral responsibilities on both parties, and these responsibilities change over time with changes in the parties and their relationship. (Newborns cannot have any responsibilities, and for that reason may be regarded as immanent people.) Each party in a relationship is responsible for ensuring some aspect of the other's welfare or, at least, for achieving some ends that contribute to the other's welfare or achievement. This holds even in asymmetrical relationships (whether personal or occupational), such as the relationship between parent and child or between client and lawyer.

Rights and obligations do have a place within the responsibilities view. Human rights are claims upon society and upon other people that are necessary if a person is to be able to meet the responsibilities of her or his relationships. Although only moral agents can have moral responsibilities and thus can have moral rights, according to this view, moral agents may, and probably do, have some moral obligations toward, or responsibility for, the welfare of other beings who are not moral agents, that is, beings who do not themselves have the moral status of people. For example, people may have a moral obligation to treat corpses with respect, or not to be cruel to animals.

I maintain that a rights view of ethics yields an inadequate view of the moral status of people or "persons" and disregards the importance of the special responsibilities that go with affectional and occupational relationships. In some cases, notably in situations involving adults who are strangers, the situation may be described adequately in terms of rights and obligations alone. (The question of whether anyone is ever a total stranger is answered differently in different ethical and religious frameworks.) When the relationships between the parties are significant, or even necessary in order for one of the parties to become a moral agent, the moral responsibilities arising out of relationships are of central importance.[20]

It is important that the description of a relationship and the responsibilities that attend the relationship begin with that of the parties to it (although such a description is criticizable by others so that, for example, there may be grounds for saying that a child is being abused even if initially neither the child nor parent sees the relationship that way). This means that the responsibilities approach to ethics has a greater potential for cross-cultural applicability than does the rights approach, which has no means for representing variation in moral requirements with variation in lived relationships. Since the fulfillment of the responsibilities for the welfare of others that attends one's relationships to them is essential to the maintenance of moral integrity, each person's moral integrity is integrally related to the maintenance of the moral integrity of others. Thus, on this view their self-interest is not something that can be neatly separated from the interests of others.

In contrast to the usual dualist accounts, *all* parties to the relationship and participants in the practice emerge and develop and, therefore, the relationships and practices also develop. Furthermore, what counts as *proper* development is itself partially specified in terms of acquisition of the very virtues necessary to engage in the key practices of mutual realization.

The liberation of women's relationships and practices requires that those practices and relationships be so reconstituted that the skills, sensitivities, and virtues, which make it possible for people to contribute to one anothers' development, be the primary traits developed in everyone. This liberation is a social task, and for this reason communities committed to this transformation have often undertaken to separate from those unwilling to take part in it. Faithfulness in relationships and the advancement of liberated practices does require that one sometimes contest another's actions, or cause the other pain or disappointment. As Jean Baker Miller has argued (1976), the liberation of women's practice will mean that developing others will no longer be a matter of self-sacrifice on the part of those engaged in the practice, a self-sacrifice that ultimately contributes to the perpetuation of practices and relationships of domination and competition. It follows that among the virtues that are necessary to engage in and sustain the liberated practices are strengths to resist domination and co-optation of one's development of others.

Summary of the Ontology

In view of the foregoing arguments it may be clear that in spite of the intuitive plausibility and even obviousness of some features of the proposed ontology, a thorough-going replacement of dualistic ontologies with an ontology such as this has major implications for both theory and practice. The ontology is based on an understanding of the relation of self and other as a relation between analogous beings. The nature and extent of the analogy is something to be determined in each case. Therefore, the distinction between the self and an other does not turn on construing the other as opposite; another distinct being may, and usually does, possess some of the same characteristics as the self. Because the distinction between the self and an other does not turn on an opposition, the characteristics of the self do not define a unique other by opposition. There may be many others who differ in character from one another as well as being numerically distinct from one another and from the self. In place of the self-other opposition, therefore, we have the relation of the self and others, and in place of the previously mentioned dualistic oppositions that figure so prominently in so-called "Western thought," we have multifactorial interactive models. Since there is no assumed opposition between the self and other, there is no general motivation to either deny the existence of others, reduce all others to the self—"one soul in two bodies,"—or to interpret the other as mere material for the self's designs.

On this view the person is understood as a relational and historical being. One becomes a person in and through relationships with other people; being a person requires that one have a history of relationships with other people, and the realization of the self can be achieved only in and through relationships and practices. The fundamental moral notion is that of the responsibility for (some aspect of) another's welfare arising from one's relationship to that person. Responsibilities are mutual, although the parties to a relationship may have different responsibilities. Rights (and the correlative obligations) receive their warrant as the claims upon institutions and other people that must be honored if people are to be able to meet the responsibilities of their relationships.

Notes

I thank Margaret Rhodes, Spencer Carroll, Nona Lyons, Carol Gould, and Mary Vetterling-Braggin for helpful criticisms of earlier versions of this essay.

1. For an early and important feminist critique of dualistic thinking, see Ruether (1972). I believe that I heard all or part of the argument of this paper presented at Yale around 1970. A number of the other essays in this volume criticize one or another of these dualistic oppositions. Hilde Hein's critique of the spirit-matter opposition, which is the only one that I have seen at the time of this writing, is very illuminating. Carolyn Merchant's major historical study of the period 1500–1700 both transcends the customary spirit-matter dichotomy and gives an account of some of its historical antecedents (Merchant 1980). Sherry Ortner has discussed the relation between the culture-nature opposition and the male-female opposition in masculist thought (Ortner 1974). A number of other early essays by feminist anthropologists and other feminist scholars outside of philosophy, which deal with dualisms in different cultures, are contained in Rosaldo and Lamphere (1974). Sandra Harding has written on the knower-known dichotomy as it affects investigations in the social sciences (Harding 1981), and numerous feminist and non-feminist philosophers in the last ten years have argued against the mind-body dualism of Descartes and modern philosophy. Not all these treatments are consistent with the view presented in this paper. This is particularly true of those accounts that rely heavily on theories that incorporate dualistic thinking while arguing against some particular polarity or dichotomy. Another recent work on dualism is Glennon (1979). I am indebted to Linda Gardiner for bringing it to my attention.

I regard feminist philosophy as primarily concerned with the construction and development of concepts and models adequate for the articulation of women's experience and women's practices. Many of the most important influences on my work have been the practices and new ways of living that many women have helped to create, and it is difficult to find ways adequately to acknowledge those creations and their creators. In addition to the influence of writers and thinkers mentioned in previous papers, I would like to acknowledge the influence of women's music on the practices in which I have participated and on my theoretical reflections on those practices. I am particularly impressed with the range of women's experience that Holly Near, and Sweet Honey in The Rock have expressed, and with the representation of the self in transformation in Chris Williamson's work. Women's music is all the more impressive in its ability to speak to many people.

In arguing that reality should not be understood dualistically, I am not arguing that oppositional thinking is never helpful in the continuing struggle to liberate our thinking. It may sometimes be important to temporarily reorganize one's experience in terms of an opposition of the self and the oppressive other in order to liberate oneself from fatalistic acceptance of oppression, as Paulo Freire suggests (1973). I am indebted to Kate Lindemann for demonstrating some of the general applicability of Freire's scheme (Lindemann and Oliver 1982).

2. My definition is indebted to MacIntyre's, although Ruddick's use of the term is similar in many ways, and her use is influenced by that of Habermas (Ruddick 1980). Carol Gould's expression "joint action" (Gould 1981) is more likely to highlight the departure from individualism than MacIntyre's "cooperative activity," but for that reason may seem more obscure. MacIntyre defines a practice as follows: "By 'a practice' I am going to mean any coherent and complex form of socially established cooperative human activity through which goods internal to that activity are realized in the course of trying to achieve those standards of excellence which are appropriate to, and partially definitive of, that form of activity, with the result that human powers to achieve excellence, and human conceptions of ends and goods involved, are systematically extended" (MacIntyre 1981, p. 175).

3. Elsewhere I have used the expression "calling forth" for infant care, to emphasize the creativity of the mother in creating the relationships that will make the infant capable of relationship. There is a danger that this way of speaking may obscure the point that "calling forth" involves exquisite sensitivity to the initiatives of the infant. Nona Lyons and Carol Gilligan use the term "response" following H. Richard Neibuhr. The latter avoids the disadvantages of "calling forth," but may be misunderstood to suggest response to the exclusion of initiation. My accounts of mothering and family life are strongly influenced by my own experience of rearing a daughter in community with other women (while working in the male academic world). My accounts of nursing are a result of both academic research and the first-person experiences of nurses and allied health workers who have been my friends and my students, especially Patricia Comer, who created family life with us and with whom I came to understand the influences of the practices in our occupations upon our life together. A brief, readable account of family life that provides an historical and cross-cultural perspective is contained in Boulding 1978. A detailed but less-readable account is contained in Boulding 1977.

4. This same hierarchal organization is also found in many branches of Eastern thought; for example, in the *I Ching,* one of the oldest sources of Taoist thought, the *yang* principal is explicitly viewed as superior and the *yin* as inferior. This hierarchy is less evident in some Taoist practices, such as *T'ai Chi,* that make use of the *yin-yang* symbolism.

5. For a discussion of the prevalence and function of the view that rape is a normal sexual behavior, see Peterson (1977).

6. An interesting discussion of the thought of Nietzsche and Bachofen on this point is contained in a paper by Rebekah S. Perry, "Neitzsche and Bachofen: The Sexual Roots of Morality and Culture," presented at the SWIP session of the 1982 Eastern APA meeting. I disagree with the author's attempt to categorize theirs as a proto-feminist view, however.

7. I am indebted to Mitchell Aboulofia for several discussions on Hegel's thought. Perhaps Aboulofia and other Hegelians can arrive at a non-dualistic ontology beginning where Hegel began, even as those who begin with individualism may work their

way out with arguments that no man is an island, but I see no reason to "enter that fly bottle," to use Wittgenstein's metaphor.

8. What I have described as individualism has developed over centuries. I have not attempted to do justice to the history of that development here. Were I to do so, however, I would trace it from the late Middle Ages, rather than from the 17th century. It shows the strength of the ideas of individualism that anyone would feel obliged to argue that "no man is an island," as John Donne did at the beginning of the 17th century.

9. I choose the term "peer" mindful of the application of the term both to dukes, marquesses, earls, etc., who asserted their rights vis-à-vis the monarch before propertied citizens took on and transformed the role of rebellious "sons," and of the literature on peer relations in developmental psychology.

10. I cannot do justice here to the complex relation and distinction between concepts of selfhood and personhood.

11. *The Declaration of Independence* speaks of the rights of "all men," but civil rights were not extended to male slaves until the passage of the Fourteenth Amendment.

12. Elsewhere I have shown how the patriarchal view that women and women's bodies are a resource to be controlled by men and/or the state is very prevalent in our "individualistic" society as well as in socialist "state patriarchies" (where the availability of contraceptive and abortion services are manipulated to serve state interests), and argued that the individualistic position that is represented as the alternative view to patriarchal control of women's bodies is also inadequate to represent women's concerns about pregnancy and childbirth. The interested reader is refered to Whitbeck 1983a.

13. Arguments for this point are contained in Miller 1976, Gilligan 1982, and Whitbeck 1983b.

14. It may be that some women have internalized a dualistic view of gender, and that may even be common among women exposed to a great deal of masculist theory, but the absence of a nurturer with whom the infant shares characteristics that are socially significant would tend to generate in him a dualistic view of the self-other relation in the cases in which the mother did not see him as opposite, and engages in a great deal of mirroring and teaching by example, as many mothers do with children of both sexes.

15. The extent of such social reinforcement varies and may be minimal in some cases; for example, in the case of upper-class girls reared by women of a lower class.

16. There are some parallels to this notion of a person in the thought of some major thinkers in Western philosophy. For example, I might have taken the notion of an historical object from the middle period of Whitehead's thought, and elaborated the notion of a person using that starting point. It would be an enormous and unrewarding task to discuss the views of each philosopher individually, however, and to draw out the meager parallels and to suggest appropriate epicycles to their formulations. I know no really *close* parallels in Western thought to the ontology that I find in feminist practice and thought. The non-dual ontology of Tibetan Buddhism looks somewhat promising, but I am too dependent on a few translations and interpretations to assert this with confidence.

Of particular interest among contemporary philosophical formulations is the account of the person or "individual" that Carol Gould develops in connection with her view of the ontological foundations of democracy and property (Gould 1979, 1980). Although her characterization of persons as "individuals-in-relation" and her notion of joint action (see note 21 above) are quite compatible with the ontology outlined here, there are some difficulties in reading her views as operating out of a similar framework. Gould criticizes the social ontologies of individualism and "socialist holism" (which I take to be similar to what I have called "state patriarchy") and constructs an alternative designed to avoid the inadequacies of each that she has identified. Many of the terms that Gould uses are borrowed from the positions that she criticizes, and therefore often suggest the same self-other opposition, and individualism in particular. Since these terms may have been chosen to communicate to the audiences she was addressing, I have tried translating her terminology—words such as "individual," "choice," "right," and "self-realization"—in ways that make explicit the interconnectedness of selves. When this is done, however, some of her central theses lose their plausibility. For example, if self-realization is understood to be the realization of aspirations to participate in certain sorts of practices and relationships, then the right to personal possessions or "individual property" (which she distinguishes from social property—including the means of production) does not seem to be required. What is required, instead, is the existence of the relevant practices and relationships, or the people interested in creating those practices and relationships. It is difficult to see how there could be a *right* to the requisite practices, relationships and/or people, since these might not even exist. Although it is easy to see why such things as health care might be important to a person's self-realization, and in this society medical care is a commodity to which people are viewed as having property rights, it is difficult to see why such services would be regarded as personal possessions in a society in which women's practices were central. It would seem, instead, that healing would be an integral part of the life of a community, as Ehrenreich and English suggest (p. 292).

17. I am grateful to Carol Gilligan for this reference.

18. For example, Michael Tooley in "A Defense of Abortion and Infanticide," *Philosophy and Public Affairs* 2, p. 40, stipulates "In my usage the sentence 'X is a person' will be synonymous with the sentence 'X has a (serious) moral right to life' "; and Edward A. Langerak, in his article "Abortion: Listening to the Middle," *Hastings Center Report* 9, p. 25, stipulates that by the term "person" he means a human being that has "as strong a right to life as a normal adult."

19. It is significant, I think, that John Ladd is experienced in the practice of rearing children, in contrast to the bachelors who are seen as the great figures of modern philosophy (and to contemporary philosophers who left to their wives—*not* "spouses"—the rearing of children who were born early in their academic careers) and who found the philosophical framework of individualism so congenial. Ladd has been at a further advantage in participating in the practice of childrearing with his wife, Rosalind Ladd who, being an analytic philosopher herself, could make that practice clear to an analytic philosopher. In keeping with the dichotomization of the public and private, it has been thought impolite or irrelevant to mention a philosopher's experience of relationships, though not the philosopher's intellectual or class background, but the dichotomy between the public and the private is one I reject. (Elsewhere I have discussed some other ways in which the practice of doing philosophy might be transformed in conformity with a feminist vision of reality [Whitbeck 1983b]. Major statements on the subject of doing feminist theory are contained in a paper by Maria C. Lugones and Elizabeth V. Spelman [Lugones and Spelman 1983].)

20. Nona Lyons and Carol Gilligan, in their major empirical studies investigating both women's conception of the self and the ways in which women tend to formulate moral issues, found that consideration of interrelationships among people and responsibility for the welfare of all involved figures prominently in many women's thinking (Lyons, forthcoming, and Gilligan 1982).

References

Addelson, Kathryn. "Respect and Impartiality." Unpublished manuscript.
Aristotle. 1942 ed. *Generation of Animals.* English translation by A. L. Peck. Cambridge: Harvard University Press.
———. 1962 ed. *Physics.* Translated by Richard Hope. Lincoln: University of Nebraska Press.
Boulding, Elise. 1977. *Women in the Twentieth Century World.* Beverly Hills: Sage Publications.
———. 1978. *The Family As a Way Into the Future.* Wallingford, Penn.: Pendle Hill Publications.
Brown, Norman O. 1966. *Love's Body.* New York: Random House.
Caplan, A. C., H. T. Engelhardt, Jr., and J. J. McCartney, eds. 1981. *Concepts of Health and Disease: Interdisciplinary Perspectives.* Reading, Mass: Addison-Wesley Co.
Chodorow, Nancy. 1978. *The Reproduction of Mothering, Psychoanalysis and the Sociology of Gender.* Berkeley: University of California Press.
Christ, Carol, and Judith Plaskow. 1979. *Womanspirit Rising: A Feminist Reader on Religion.* New York: Harper & Row.
Collins, Margery, and Christine Pierce. 1973–74. "Holes and Slime: Sexism in Sartre's Psychoanalysis." *Philosophical Forum* 5, nos. 1–2. Reprinted 1976 in Gould and Wartofsky, eds., *Women and Philosophy.*
Condren, Mary T. 1982. "Patriarchy and Death." Paper presented at the American Academy of Religion Meetings, New York, December.
Ehrenreich, Barbara, and Deirdre English. 1978. *For Her Own Good: 150 Years of the Experts' Advice to Women.* New York: Anchor Press/Doubleday.
Freire, Paulo. 1973. *Pedagogy of the Oppressed.* Translated by Myra Bergman Ramos. New York: Seabury Press.
———. 1974. "Education as the Practice of Freedom." In *Education for Critical Consciousness,* ed. Paulo Freire. New York: Seabury Press.
Gilligan, Carol. 1982. *In a Different Voice: Psychological Theory and Women's Development.* Cambridge: Harvard University Press.
Glennon, Lynda M. 1979. *Women and Dualism.* Longman Press.
Gould, Carol C. 1979. "Ontological Foundations of Democracy." Paper presented to the Metaphysical Society of America, Manhattanville College, March 15.
———. 1980. "Contemporary Legal Conceptions of Property and Their Implications For Democrary." *Journal of Philosophy* 7, no. 11 (November).
Gould, Carol C., and Marx Wartofsky, eds. 1976. *Women and Philosophy: Toward A Theory of Liberation.* New York: G. P. Putnam's Sons.
Griffin, Susan. 1981. *Pornography and Silence: Culture's Revenge Against Nature.* New York: Harper & Row.
Harding, Sandra. 1981. "The Norms of Social Inquiry and Masculine Experience." *PSA 1980,* vol. 2. Edited by P. D. Asquith and R. N. Giere. East Lansing, Mich.: Philosophy of Science Association.
Hartsock, Nancy C. M. 1981. "Social Life and Social Science: The Significance of the Naturalist/Intentionalist Dispute." *PSA 1980,* vol. 2. Edited by P. D. Asquith and R. N. Giere. East Lansing, Mich.: Philosophy of Science Association.
Hegel, G.W.F. 1977 ed. *Phenomenology of Spirit.* Translated by A. V. Miller. Oxford: Clarendon Press.
Hesse, Mary B. 1966. *Models and Analogies in Science.* Notre Dame, Ind.: University of Notre Dame Press.
Holmes, Helen B., Betty Hoskins, and Michael Gross, eds. *The Custom-Made Child?: Women-Centered Perspectives.* Vol. 2 of the Proceedings of the Conference on Ethical Issues in Human Reproduction Technology: Analysis by Women.) Clifton, N.J.: Humana Press.

Ladd, John. 1979. "Legalism and Medical Ethics." In *Contemporary Issues in Biomedical Ethics,* ed. J. W. Davis, Barry Hoffmaster, and Sarah Shorten. Clifton, N.J.: Humana Press.
———. 1982. "The Distinction Between Rights and Responsibilities: A Defense." *Linacre Quarterly.* May.
Lindemann, S. K., and Elizabeth Oliver. 1982. "Consciousness, Liberation, and Health Delivery Systems." *Journal of Medicine and Philosophy* 7, no. 4.
Lodge, George C. 1977. *The New American Ideology.* New York: Alfred A. Knopf.
Lyons, Nona. 1983. "Two Perspectives: On Self, Relationships and Morality." *Harvard Educational Review.* 53, no. 2. May.
Lugones, Maria, and Elizabeth V. Spelman. 1983. "Have We Got A Theory for You!" Feminist Theory, Cultural Imperialism, and the Demand for "The Woman's Voice." *Hypatia* 1, no. 1. Published as the fall 1983 issue of *Women's Studies International.*
MacIntyre, Alasdair. *After Virtue.* Notre Dame, Ind.: University of Notre Dame Press.
Mahowald, Mary Briody. 1978. *Philosophy of Women: Classical to Current Concepts.* Indianapolis: Hackett Publishing Co.
McBride, Angela B. 1972. *The Growth and Development of Mothers.* New York: Harper & Row.
Merchant, Carolyn. 1980. *The Death of Nature.* San Francisco: Harper & Row.
Miller, Jean Baker. 1976. *Toward A New Psychology of Women.* Boston: Beacon Press.
———. 1982. *Women and Power.* "Work in Progress", no. 82-01. Wellesley Mass.: Wellesley College.
O'Faolain, Julia, and Lauro Maritines, eds. 1973. *Not in God's Image: Women in History from the Greeks to the Victorians.* New York: Harper & Row.
Ortner, Sherry B. 1974. "Is Female to Male as Nature Is to Culture?" in Rosaldo and Lamphere, eds., *Woman, Culture, and Society.*
Peterson, Susan. 1977. "Rape and Coercion: The State as a Male Protection Racket." In *Feminism and Philosophy,* edited by Mary Vetterlin Braggin. Totwa, N.J.: Littlefield, Adams & Co.
Rawlinson, Mary. 1982. "Psychiatric Discourse and the Feminine Voice." *Journal of Medicine and Philosophy* 7, no. 2.
Rich, Adrienne. 1976. *Of Woman Born: Motherhood as Experience and Institution.* New York: Bantam Books.
Ringelheim, Joan. 1983. "Communities in Distress: Women and the Holacaust." *Netzach* 1, no. 1.
Rosaldo, Michelle Zimbalist, and Louise Lamphere, eds. 1974. *Woman, Culture, and Society.* Stanford, Calif.: Stanford University Press.
Ruddick, Sara. 1980. "Maternal Thinking." *Feminist Studies* 6, no. 2.
Ruether, Rosemary Radford. 1972. "Motherearth and the Megamachine: A Theology of Liberation in a Feminine, Somatic and Ecological Perspective." *Christianity and Crisis.* April 12. Reprinted 1979 in Christ and Plaskow, *Womanspirit Rising.*
Searles, Harold F. 1979. "Patient as Therapist." In *Counter-Transference and Related Subjects,* ed. Harold F. Searles. International University Press.
Surrey, Janet L. 1983. "The Relation Self in Women: Clinical Implications." "Work in Progress", no. 82-02. Wellesley, Mass.: Wellesley College.
Warren, Mary Ann. 1980. *The Nature of Woman, An Encyclopedia and Guide to the Literature.* Michigan: Edgewood Press.
Whitbeck, Caroline. 1969. "Simultaneity and Distance." *The Journal of Philosophy* 66, no. 11.
———. 1973–74. "Theories of Sex Difference." *The Philosophical Forum* 5, no. 1 & 2. Reprinted in Gould and Wartofsky, eds. *Women and Philosophy.*
———. 1975. "The 'Maternal Instinct'." *Philosophical Forum* 6, no. 1 & 2.

———. 1981a. "Introduction" and "Response" on the Neonate. In Holmes, Hoskins, and Gross, eds., *The Custom-Made Child?*

———. 1981b. "A Theory of Health." In Caplan, Engelhardt, and McCartney, eds., *Concepts of Health and Disease.*

———. 1982. "Women and Medicine: An Introduction." *Journal of Medicine and Philosophy* 7, no. 4.

———. 1983a. "The Moral Implication of Regarding Women as People: New Perspectives on Pregnancy and Personhood." In *Abortion and the Status of the Fetus,* edited by W. B. Bondeson, H. T. Engelhardt, Jr., S. F. Spicker, and D. Winship. Dordrecht: Reidel Publ. Co.

———. 1983b. "Afterword to the 'Maternal Instinct'." In *Mothering: Essays in Feminist Theory,* edited by Joyce Trebilcot. Totowa, N.J.: Rowman & Allanheld.

5

Concepts of Woman in Psychoanalytic Theory: The Nature-Nurture Controversy Revisited

ANNE DONCHIN

For the leading feminists of the 1960s and early '70s Freud's psychoanalytic theory, taken to be the antithesis of feminist theory, was anathema.[1] For them, Freud, in echoing Napoleon's *bon mot* "anatomy is destiny," had placed himself squarely within the ranks of the legion of male supremacists who were responsible for the ubiquitous devaluation and degradation of women. Moreover, not only did Freud *transmit* a tradition of male chauvinism, but in fabricating the venomous doctrine of "penis envy," he actually *furthered* the cause of woman's oppression, providing ideological rationalization for women's inferior status.

As the agenda of the feminist movement advanced, attention began to turn toward the development of a feminist theory that could explain how male dominance had persisted so tenaciously despite revolutionary transformations in other social arrangements. By the mid-70s a few feminist writers had begun to turn back again to Freud in search of fresh insights into the psychology of women and the psychological and ideological workings of patriarchy. To these feminists it had become clear that patriarchal attitudes and institutions were so deeply and pervasively imbedded in the culture that good intention and legal reform alone were powerless to root them out. It would be necessary, first, to understand how patriarchal attitudes *functioned* within social institutions, and how they were acquired and transmitted from generation to generation.

Juliet Mitchell was one of the first feminists to call for reassessment of psychoanalytic theory's relevance for feminist theory. In her 1974 book *Psychoanalysis and Feminism*,[2] she takes her contemporary feminists to task for misunderstanding what Freud had actually said about women. She faults them for misconstruing the implications of his views for feminist theorizing, arguing that Freud was by no means the apologist for the view that anatomy determined destiny that he has been made out to be. On the contrary, it was principally a group of Freud's followers who had pressed the view that recent feminists denounced. The contention that the mental life of the sexes *directly* reflects biological divisions was not advanced by Freud, she claims, but by Karen Horney and, subsequently, Clara Thomson, Freida Fromm-Reichmann, Gregory Zilboorg, and Ruth Moulton—precisely those analysts who have been most closely allied to the feminists. Mitchell believes that this misunderstanding of Freud's position has seriously hampered progress in the feminist understanding of women's psychological development and contributed to a tendency common to many different psychotherapeutic practices (not confined to psychoanalytic circles alone) to readapt discontented women to a conservative feminine status quo, to the presumption that they are inferior beings who should be content to serve men and children. This failure to grasp the central point of Freud's teaching about women has contributed also, she believes, to the propagation of cultural stereotypes about women's "passive nature" and the "aggressive nature" of men that disguise the actual realities of women's social condition and contribute to the perpetuation of oppressive practices.

Since the appearance of Mitchell's book, increasing numbers of feminist writers have taken a second, more-serious look at Freud, though seldom with the rigor and attention to detail that Mitchell brings to her task; at least, not until the publication of Nancy Chodorow's *The Reproduction of Mothering,* which stands as both a corrective to Mitchell's overzealous defense of Freud's views and a valuable extension of the project Mitchell initiated.[3] Chodorow seeks to demonstrate how the psychoanalytic account of the psychological processes through which individuals acquire a culture explains the communication of patriarchal attitudes from parent to offspring. She believes that the institution of mothering provides the crucial link in the perpetuation of patriarchy. Hence, for both Mitchell and Chodorow, to break through the chain transmitting patriarchal attitudes, we must understand the mechanism that holds it together. For both, the unconscious mind mediating between the external culture and the inchoate individual organism forges new beings into masculine and feminine forms. Despite significant differences in their reading of Freud and in their recognition of later developments in Freudian theory,[4] Mitchell and Chodorow share a common orientation: both see psychoanalytic theory as the primary source of insight into women's psychological development, and both interpret Freudian theory as a theory about the comparative weight of anatomy and destiny in the shaping of men and women. They stress the preponderant importance of nurture over nature in the formation of masculine and feminine personality and argue that only the Freudian conception of the unconscious mind can explain how such personalities are forged.

Without calling into question the primary direction of their project—for I, too, am fully persuaded that we are more likely to learn far more about the psychology of women within the psychoanalytic perspective than from any rival viewpoint—I should like to raise some doubts about a presupposition common to Mitchell and Chodorow and shared by many other theorists as well: the doctrine that mental life is shaped exclusively by culture, that bodily differences play no part in determining the outcome of individual development, apart from cultural ways of valuing them. Both Mitchell and Chodorow take this position to be integral to psychoanalytic theory. Both presume that having defended a Freudian conception of the unconscious, they have also established the exclusive primacy of nurture over nature. Each maintains that those who argue for the influence of biology in shaping human personality reject the theory of the unconscious mind. Neither offers an independent argument for the contention that biology plays no significant role in the formation of personality. Both presume that Freud's own views, correctly understood, preclude the possibility that biological factors could play any significant role in the making of men and women as distinctive genders, and that those subsequent psychoanalysts who appeal to biological influences to explain gender-specific development lack Freud's own insight into the unconscious determinants of human behavior.

It is necessary, I believe, to examine the beginnings of psychoanalysis to learn whether this was, indeed, Freud's own view. Despite the fact that Freud explicitly disavowed the need to incorporate biological determinants into his theoretical construction, it does not follow that he succeeded. If he did actually employ appeals to biology, then a new question arises: could a plausible psychoanalytic theory be constructed that is purged of any appeal to biological influences in the shaping of gender? If such an enterprise were not likely to succeed—either by virtue of its own internal inconsistencies or because it lacked explanatory force—then what should be the future relationship between psychoanalytic theory and feminist theory? Unless feminist theorizing could abandon these newly

forged links to the psychoanalytic perspective and return to the
position of the earlier feminists, there would be no choice but to
accommodate some account of biological influences to a feminist
account of gender-specific development.

Feminist antipathy to any suggestion that nature plays a part in
the drama of personal development is surely understandable, given
the employment of nature theories by male supremacist apologists;
but possibly the recognition of nature *per se* is not the villan as much
as those who use this recognition as a weapon to vindicate male
chauvinism. Although empirical research into biological influences
on human sex and gender is still in its primitive stages,[5] much
evidence has already emerged indicating that the work of biological
factors, while it does not determine gender *identity* as such (a mode
of self-awareness that most theorists now believe is fixed by age
three or four), does play a significant part in gender *role behavior.*
Clinical studies, for instance, have shown significant correlations
between hormonally and genetically deviant infants and subsequent
gender-specific modes of behavior. What significance does this data
have for feminist theorizing? Can such data be integrated within a
psychoanalytic model? If Juliet Mitchell is right both about psychoanalysis and about feminism—that central to both is the disavowal of
the conception of an *essential self,* the affirmation that the self is not
born but made—can such empirical research tell us anything interesting about the condition of women? Should it be ignored? Re-
futed? Or is it possible, perhaps, to detach the thesis that patriarchal
attitudes are transmitted unconsciously from the more-inclusive
thesis that all gender-specific modes of behavior are the result of
learning?

As preamble to discussion of such issues it is fitting to reexamine
the nature-nurture controversy that sprang up among the first generation of psychoanalysts to see if we can determine whether it was,
indeed, Freud's view that women's psychosexual development
could be explained without recourse to biological factors and, also,
to place in perspective some problematic issues underlying the
controversy. Among these are, what counted for them as a biological determinant? What features of women's development were they
seeking to explain? What modes of explanation did they take as data
supporting their rival hypotheses? Why did the controversy end
inconclusively—because it was irresolvable, or merely for lack of
sufficient data?

To firmly situate the controversy within the context of feminist
discussion, I will first summarize Mitchell's thesis about the central
significance of Freud for feminist theory. Then I will recapitulate the
principal arguments that engaged Freud and his first generation of

followers. Finally, I will argue that the issue over which Freud and his disciples were joined, though it bore the superficial marks of the perennial nature-nurture dichotomy, ought not to be confused with cruder, more simplistic controversies between biological and cultural determinists. For within the psychoanalytic group the background assumption shared by both parties—that the unconscious mind mediates between bodily drives and their psychological expression—transformed the very nature of the controversy itself. Accordingly, it should be possible for feminist theorists to construct rival accounts of psychosexual development without renouncing the central core of psychoanalytic theory.

Mitchell's Assessment of Freud

Juliet Mitchell's book is an attempt to lay bare the central core of Freudian theory, distorted initially by the revisions and reforms of Freud's followers, then the more "radical" therapists, such as Wilhelm Reich and R. D. Laing and more recently by Freud's feminist critics, principally Simone de Beauvoir, Betty Friedan, Eva Figes, Germaine Greer, Shulamith Firestone, and Kate Millett. All of them, she believes, share a common conviction that beneath layers and layers of acculturation an *essential self* waits, fully formed, ready to be unearthed. She believes that all these critics argue against the fact of an unconscious mind. They attempt to translate mental phenomena into social reality, and confuse the way we *think* our world with the ways it is perceived from without.

Freud, on the contrary, was not principally interested in describing the social realities of his time, but in learning how these realities were reflected in mental life. Even in his nonanalytic works, such as *Totem and Taboo,* it was not the *actual* historical beginnings of social life that interested Freud, but how humankind "thinks" their history, their mythological conceptions of human origins. Through such reconstruction of both social and personal history Freud is able to tell us far more about the sources and conditions of woman's degradation, Mitchell argues, than have any of the more socially conscious revisionists and reformers. For his theory principally explains how the cultural heritage is acquired and internalized in each generation and how the consequences of culturization differ in men and women. Neither the defenders of biological determinism, who presume that the different cultural roles assigned to the sexes are due to innate disposition, nor the cultural determinists, who attribute these roles to the division of labor that assigns childbearing and rearing functions to women, can adequately account for the persistence and the tenacity of sex-role stereotyping. Only a theory that can explain how such roles are imprinted on us from infancy, and how the memories of the cultural process by which we become men and women lies deeply buried within our personal histories, can have sufficient force to explain how we can come to appropriate such roles as our own. Only psychoanalytic theory, Mitchell claims, has the resources to reconstruct such a developmental process. That the theory appears initially implausible is due principally to the enormous difficulty we experience in attempting to make our earliest experiences accessible to conscious understanding and control. But once we have come to view our personal histories from within Freud's theory of psychosexual development, we shall come to understand the process through which patriarchal society shapes us into masculine and feminine roles.

Mitchell argues that it is a common misunderstanding of Freud to presume that he was offering a normative theory of how men and women *ought* to develop. He was not attempting to *prescribe* womanhood, only to *describe* the conditions within which woman was *made* and to show how very trivial later influences were by comparison with the weight of early infantile experiences. Freud shows how misguided it is to presume that the stereotyping of women can be overcome merely by innovative forms of therapeutic intervention or by piecemeal social reform. Until we understand the origin and function of sexual stereotyping, we cannot seek appropriate remedies. We need first to look again to Freud to discover how it all began and what keeps it going.

The Freudian Account of Feminine Development

Central to psychoanalytic theory is the thesis that individual development proceeds through a succession of stages, each marked by the primary bodily source of sensory gratification. From the initial *oral* stage the infant moves on to the *anal* stage of psychosexual organization and into the *phallic* stage before reaching full *genital* development. Freud believed that in the case of boy children, this theory was largely adequate to account for the shift in the boy's primary attachment from the mother to the father. For as the boy entered the phallic period, when he discovered his own sexual organ and fantasized about seducing his first love, fear of the father's enmity acted as a powerful check on the development of these incipient sensual stirrings. Rather than risk loss of his prized organ at the hands of an angry father, the boy-child made a bargain with himself, deferring gratification of such longings until some later time when he could win an adequate substitute for the foregone mother. In exchange he held onto both the organ and his father's love. In renouncing his mother and turning his affectional ties toward his father, the grounds of his own masculine identification were established.

But for the girl-child a very different story would need to be told to reconstruct the turning from the primary infantile relationship with the mother toward the father. For presuming that girl-children started off in the same way as boys and proceeded along the same path through the oral and anal periods and into the phallic period, she would need still to negotiate an additional developmental stage over and beyond the shift from one object to another. If she shared the same desires as the boy, like him she would desire to possess the mother, to penetrate her, and get her with child. The clinical experience of Freud and his followers persuaded them that many of their women patients had actually experienced such fantasies and that they were by no means limited to disturbed women. But if this were a common phenomenon, before girl-children could attain a heterosexual orientation they would need not only to give up the attachment to their mothers, but also the desire to play the active sexual role. Nevertheless, the incentive that propelled the boy out of his primary attachment, the fear of castration at the hands of an angry father, could have no force for the girl. She, who according to the psychoanalytic story imagined herself as having originally been similarly endowed with such an appendage, perceived herself as *already* castrated. Her desire to give her mother a baby could not be merely postponed; it had to be forsaken altogether. Freud surmised that the sense of this irretrievable disappointment led the girl to turn angrily away from her mother and seek solace in her father's affection, imagining that eventually he would give her a baby by way of compensation for the penis her mother had caused her to lose.

Freud recognized that this was a rather patchy solution to his puzzle, and he sought the help of women analysts in attempting to assemble the pieces more coherently. He had first initiated his speculations about women's early psychosexual development in the 1890s, but not until the '20s did Freud's conception of feminine development become a subject of active controversy within psychoanalytic circles. The immediate issue focused about the genesis of the female castration complex. Karl Abraham, one of Freud's most literal-minded disciples, had claimed in a 1921 paper, "Manifestations of the Female Castration Complex,"[6] that it was based upon penis envy, and that a girl turns her attachment from mother to father because she finds that the mother not only cheated her out of a penis, but had been cheated herself. Another member of the psychoanalytic circle, Karen Horney, challenged Abraham's contention. She argued in "The Genesis of the Castration Complex in

Women,"[7] that the complex was not a primary feature of normal development, as the phenomenon of penis envy itself was believed to be, but a regression from a later, more-advanced, developmental stage to an earlier, more-primitive one. In her view, the girl's castration complex was a secondary phenomenon caused by a disappointment that had injured the normal development of the young girl's sense of womanhood, a disappointment that led such girls to pattern their identity after the parent of the opposite sex. Hence, instead of identifying with the role of the mother, these girls would emulate masculine pursuits and interests. Girls who escaped such disappointments would avoid the castration complex too, and grow into more conventional women.

In a later paper, "The Flight from Womanhood,"[8] Horney took issue with Freud directly, extending her attack to the concept of penis envy. She had come to believe that psychoanalytic theory can dispense with the notion of penis envy as well as the female castration complex, that the cultural inferiority of women plays a far more important role than penis envy in explaining the psychology of women. She suggested that Freud's views about the development of little girls bears a remarkable similarity to the fantasies little boys commonly have about anatomical distinctions. Moreover, she claims, the concept of penis envy is superfluous even in explaining a girl's shift in emotional attachment from mother to father, because that shift merely reflects "an elemental principle of nature," the mutual attraction of the sexes.

Freud subsequently referred to this appeal to nature as "biological mystification," and he came increasingly to express serious misgivings about attributing any features of psychosexual development to biological endowment alone. In one of his last works he remarked that appeal to instinct is itself a form of "mythology" and suggested that forms of explanation which appeal to primitive unanalyzable processes and entities have no place within a purportedly scientific theory; they do not answer the question asked, but instead transpose the inquiry to another level of meaning.[9]

Though Freud rejected Horney's proposed solution to the theoretical problem, he was now dissatisfied with his own earlier formulations as well. By his 1933 paper "Femininity,"[10] he had developed grave reservations about the very meaningfulness of the notion of femininity. He had come to believe that prevailing popular conceptions of femininity had little support from either biological or psychological evidence. He noted that available anatomical data seemed to suggest that sexual differentiation probably developed from one, single, innate disposition, so that from a biological perspective an individual is neither wholly man or woman, but is more or less androgynous. In mental life, too, there is evidence of a bisexual disposition. Although masculinity, Freud believed, usually connotes activity and femininity passivity, and although Freud took this distinction to correspond roughly to explicit sexual conduct, he recognized that it is by no means all-pervasive in carrying out other sex-related roles. The mother, for instance, is in every sense active toward her child, and men cannot live in company with other men without a good deal of passive adaptability.

For such reasons Freud recognized that it is theoretically unproductive to use "active" to coincide with men and "passive" with women. He attributed this usage to the explicit sexual practices of his period, which relegated women to a wholly passive role and then modeled her social life upon it, forcing women into passive situations and compelling them to suppress their aggressive impulses. Consequently, Freud concluded, the prevailing conception of femininity is without foundation in either anatomy or psychology. Explanation of the social conception of femininity cannot come, Freud believed, "until we have learned how in general the differentiation of living organism into two sexes came about."[11] Meanwhile, lacking a physical basis for our social discriminations, we cannot describe what a woman *is*. We can only focus our attention on how she comes about—"how a woman develops out of a child with a bisexual disposition."[12] Features of this development which Freud still believed to lie beyond doubt include the little girl's early sexual wish to get the mother with child and bear her a baby. Also, in this same period before the girl comes to perceive the practical significance of anatomical differences between herself and boys, she, too, has seduction fantasies, although she perceives the mother as the seducer.

But there are limitations, Freud acknowledged, to the degree to which it seems possible to reconstruct the early experience of the pre-oedipal girl-child. Although psychoanalysis has established sound theoretical grounds upon which to reconstruct the end of the phallic period, where psychoanalysis believed the developmental paths of boys and girls diverged, and though psychoanalytic observation had established that this turn was accompanied by hostility and jealousy, Freud still believed it very difficult to gauge the strength of such emotional impulses, the tenacity with which they persist, or the magnitude of their influence on later development.[13] What can be inferred, however, is that there must be something specific for girls, and not present in the development of boys, that can account for the termination of the attachments of girls to their mothers.

Freud's later account of femininity is noteworthy, not so much for

its novelty—there is little theoretical advance over his earlier formulation—as its tentativeness. Since the child can tell us directly very
little about her early sexual wishes, all we have available for study
are

> the residues and consequences of this emotional world in retrospect,
> in people in whom these processes of development had attained a
> specially clear and even excessive degree of expansion. Pathology
> has always done us a service by making discernible by isolation and
> exaggeration conditions which would remain concealed in the normal
> state. And since our observations have been carried out on people
> who are by no means seriously abnormal, I think we should regard
> their outcome as deserving belief.[14]

The Nature-Nurture Controversy Transformed

The issue between Freud and Horney is directly subject to neither
empirical confirmation nor refutation. The character of the available
evidence is the same for both. Their theories are not based on
laboratory observations, but on the interpretations of memories,
fantasies, and neuroses. They do not deal with physiological response but with mental phenomena, not with how things are in
physical reality but how they come to be represented to us in our
mental lives. Horney has claimed that in the analysis of a woman
patient when we find residues of the emotions associated with penis
envy and the castration complex, we have not discovered a primary
feature of the normal development of women, but only a secondary
structure that has come about through regression from later developmental conflicts to earlier infantile impulses. A crucial difference
between them is this: how much of the strength of the feelings
associated with the castration complex—envy and jealousy and the
sense of being wounded—is due to early infantile fixations and how
much to later experiences and developments? Freud stressed the
predominant influence of the infantile pattern, Horney emphasized
subsequent experiences.

This strand of the debate between them is still at issue among
analysts, although it is more often waged over other developmental
issues only tangentially related to the psychology of women. But an
increasing proportion of those within the psychoanalytic tradition
have come to view the developmental process as never-ending.
Although the centrality of early infantile experiences remains unquestioned, the influences of both the earlier experiences of the oral
stage and later, post-oedipal experiences have been given more
substantial weight; the presumption, shared by both Freud and
Horney, that no significant distinctions could be made between the

mental life of both sexes until the phallic period, has given way to the speculation that the earliest relational experiences might already bear the mark of gender difference.[15]

But Freud's objection to Horney's position was not based solely on a different interpretation of the clinical evidence, but on more-general methodological considerations as well. Freud and Abraham took the position that until Horney had attempted to take refuge in the biological determinants of psychosexual development, attempts to reconstruct the psychology of women had been defended principally by critical analysis of each proposed alternative path of development. Several different patterns of growth had been noted and characterized by their ultimate outcomes: (a) a "normal" end of development where the girl's castration complex had been successfully overcome (or, in Horney's reformulation, never developed) and she had turned toward the opposite sex and toward *passive* modes of sexual gratification, substituting for the wished-for penis a desire to be given a baby; (b) a "neurotic" resolution of the phallic conflict where all sexual desire—both active and passive—was repressed; and (c) the formation of a "masculinity complex" marked by the predominance of *active* strivings and a preference for traditionally masculine social roles. These "patterns" were taken as observational givens, and the explanatory adequacy of proposed reconstructions of women's early mental life were tested by assessing their capacity to account for the emergence of each of these different patterns of psychosexual development. Horney's move was criticized for invoking a biological principle that was not subject to critical analysis and so could not lead toward the formulation of a more-adequate theoretical construction. By shifting the controversy away from the process by which women are made and suggesting that a woman is not made but born, Horney had, Freud contended, effectively blocked further creative theoretical development.

Yet by the time of Freud's last paper, "Femininity," the fabric of his own earlier speculations had loosened so considerably that the threads of his own biological presuppositions had begun to show through. As the original "bisexual disposition," that he attributed commonly to both men and women began to unfold itself developmentally, the predominance of "activity" in the man and "passivity" in the woman had come to be viewed as "normal" outcomes of the developmental process that required no justification at all. Although Freud noted that the active/passive distinction is not extendable to *all* the sex-related functions of men and women, he never doubted its adequacy as an apt characterization of sexual function per se. No attempt was ever made within the original psychoanalytic circle to expose the active/passive distinction itself, to critical analysis, though the entire account of the psychological development of women rested on the presumption that before women could successfully negotiate the developmental hurdle leading to opposite-sex object choice, she would need to exchange active desires for passive ones. Karl Abraham expressed this picture most graphically in his remark that the woman is only in a position to excite the man's libido or respond to it, and that otherwise she is compelled to adopt a "waiting attitude."[16] The preponderance of passivity in the personality of the "normal" woman was taken to be so conspicuous a mark of femininity that Freud, in his paper by that name, could find no more ultimate answer to what he called the "riddle" of femininity than this appeal to woman's predominant passivity. Although Freud paid lip service to the possibility that passivity might eventually be discovered to have an even more fundamental origin, Abraham had long before given the whole show away. He assimilated to activity the capacity to penetrate, for which a penis is needed. Since women are initially presumed to desire active gratification too, they must also expect to be supplied with a penis. In learning that they are forever deprived of this prized organ, they have no recourse but to turn to passive forms of sensory gratification, a development which Abraham openly attributed to instinctual paths. He wrote:

> I have collected material belonging to the castration complex from a great number of psychoanalyses. And I should like to say expressly that it is solely for reasons of clearness (in writing) that I have only occasionally alluded to the ideas connected with *female passive instincts* which none of my patients failed to express.[17]

Here the appeal to biology to ground sex-specific distinctions is boldly affirmed, removing any doubt that orthodox psychoanalytic theoreticians rested their theory of woman's psychology on any ground other than a biological one. Though Juliet Mitchell is undoubtedly right in emphasizing that within psychoanalytic theory instinctual expression was always mediated by some sort of mental representation, for Abraham, at least, such representations were transparent to their instinctual sources—showing that they were believed to be little transformed by cultural influences.

I shall not dwell here on the consequences for psychoanalytic theorizing of this appeal to biology, but shall only point out that it was as disastrous to fruitful theoretical advance as Freud had believed Horney's appeal to be. For it concealed from exposure the hidden presupposition that as far as mental life is concerned, females are defective males, endowed initially with the mistaken belief that they were originally made of the same stuff as males, only to discover (as was also foreordained) that the most highly valued item of the male body had been denied them. Here, too, contrary to Mitchell's contention, woman's social inferiority is interpreted as the mere shadow of her biological inferiority.

Are we then forced back into the opposite corner? Is our only alternative to adopt the position that culture alone makes us men and women? If Mitchell's rereading of Freud is mistaken in presuming that he placed no reliance on biology in reconstructing feminine development, must we reject her rereading altogether? Is it viable, as was suggested earlier, to separate Freud's teaching about unconscious mental processes from his (covert) appeals to biology? Presuming that both Freud and Mitchell have given an apt characterization of mental life—as a representation of the ways we think our histories rather than as they must actually be—is it not still possible that the shape these histories take is the product of the interpenetration of both sorts of influences, from within and without, that even the attitudes and beliefs we form take shape in their own time in response to pulls and tugs in the shape of both unconscious ideas and biological developments?

Of course, at one point or another in the formation of theory it might be more fruitful methodologically to push the explanatory limits of either mode of explanation exclusively, as Freud himself urged. But acknowledgement of this methodological device need not lead us either to the presumption that there can be no biological determinants of mental life or that, if there are, they cannot be knowable. Of course, it would still be possible to be mistaken in presuming that we had discovered and accurately characterized such determinants. Much as we now understand that Freud and Abraham took their own fantasies about male superiority as biological determinants of sexual choice, we, having learned from Freud something of the labyrinthian workings of the unconscious, can exercise greater caution in moving beyond the scope of cultural explanation. To take Freud's teaching about the unconscious seriously should encourage us to question even Freud's own claim to have moved beyond the reach of cultural influences.

Freud presumed that the need to explain female development demanded an account of how woman is brought to accept the role of propagator of the species, to see herself principally as a passive agency for the transmission of an evolutionary destiny embracing the role of mother and caretaker. Freud's evolutionary functionalism determined at the outset the shape of the psychology of women that emerged from his psychoanalytic speculations. His own teleology—incorporated within the presumptions that women are born to fulfill an evolutionary task, that there is a natural order that shapes the social and moral order around which we govern our lives, and that the primary *aim* of human sexuality is propagation—led him to focus the story of woman's psychological development about the turn toward heterosexual object choice, and to neglect the development of gender identity, a necessary precondition of her attachment to the father.

More recently, psychoanalysts have turned their attention to the conception of gender identity and the conditions that foster it. The object-relations theorists, that group of analysts who have most influenced Nancy Chodorow, have attempted to reconstruct the story of the child's pre-oedipal years before the distinction between self and other is firmly established. They have argued that any account of the oedipal family romance presupposes the prior acquisition by the child of a gendered sense of self-identity. Other nonpsychoanalytic theorists (such as those cited by Susan Baker in note 5) recognize a third distinction as well. They point out that unlike gender identity, which involves the subject's conscious awareness, gender role behavior can be manifested directly without mentalistic representation. They have attempted to correlate such behavior with genetic and hormonal anomalies. Their work is suggestive of Freud's vision of a science of behavior that would ultimately explain "the riddle of femininity." Unlike Freud, however, this new group of theorists does not assimilate gender-specific behavior to sexual-object choice. The results of such research are so recent and so tentative that we cannot know yet how psychoanalytic theory might attempt to integrate them. But considering the tendency within psychoanalysis to view the human organism as an intricate psychophysical structure within which increments in learning are always linked with biological readiness, we would expect the psychoanalytic account to show how the subject's awareness of whatever behavior is viewed as gender-specific comes to be represented in mental life.

This open-textured character of psychoanalytic theory is what renders it so useful an instrument for feminist theorizing. Once this open-texturedness comes to be seen as a feature of the theory of the unconscious itself, the need to buttress the psychoanalytic perspective with claims either for or against the exclusively determinate influence of either biology or culture will have vanished. But first there is need to fill out a theory of female psychology that fulfills the program Juliet Mitchell set before herself. Having shown that Freud himself employed biological explanation and suggested that the specific details of his explanation can be detached from the main body of psychoanalytic theory, the way should be open to pursue feminist theorizing within a psychoanalytic framework. Whether this framework condemns us to forever replicate the controversy between Freud and his followers, we cannot yet know.

Notes

Among those to whom I owe especial thanks for their thoughtful comments on previous drafts of this paper are Eva Feder Kittay and Carol Gould. I also wish to express my thanks to the New York Council on the Humanities, which supported the project that motivated the initial version.

1. See, for instance, Eva Figes, *Patriarchial Attitudes* (New York: Faber & Faber, 1970); Betty Friedan, *The Feminine Mystique* (New York: Penguin Books, 1965); or Germaine Greer, *The Female Eunuch* (London: MacGibbon and Kee, 1970).
2. Juliet Mitchell, *Psychoanalysis and Feminism* (New York: Pantheon Books, 1974).
3. Nancy Chodorow, *The Reproduction of Mothering* (Berkeley: University of California Press, 1978).
4. For a fuller treatment of the distinctive stages in Freud's own thinking about differences in the ways masculinity and femininity are shaped, see Owen J. Flanagan, Jr., "Freud: Masculinity, Femininity, and the Philosophy of Mind," " *"Femininity,"* *"Masculinity,"* and *"Androgyny,"* ed. Mary Vetterling-Braggin (Littlefield, Adams, 1982).
5. Susan W. Baker's review essay on this topic provides an illuminating summary of the current state of research in this area. See her "Biological Influences on Human Sex and Gender," *Signs* 6, no. 1 (1980).
6. Karl Abraham, "Manifestations of the Female Castration Complex," *International Journal of Psychoanalysis* 3 (1921). Reprinted in *Women and Analysis*, ed. Jean Strause (New York: Dell, 1974).
7. Karen Horney, "The Genesis of the Castration Complex in Women," *International Journal of Psychoanalysis* 5 (1924): 50.
8. Karen Horney, "The Flight from Womanhood," *International Journal of Psychoanalysis* 7 (1926): 324.
9. Freud, *New Introductory Lectures in Psychoanalysis. Collected Works*, vol. 22. Lecture 32: "Anxiety and the Instinctual Life" (p. 95 of the Norton ed.).
10. Ibid., Lecture 23: "Femininity."
11. Ibid., p. 116 (Norton ed.).
12. Ibid.
13. Ibid., p. 123 (Norton ed.).
14. Ibid., p. 121 (Norton ed.).
15. Freud based this claim on the belief that the libido was sexually undifferentiated. Nancy Chodorow argues the point on other grounds (see note 3, above). Several recent empirical studies suggest that the capacity to distinguish gender is manifested much earlier in life than had previously been presumed. A study of "Infants' Recognition of Invariant Features of Faces," *Child Development* 47 (1976): 627–38, reports that babies, by seven months of life, are able to distinguish between male and female faces.
16. Abraham, "Female Castration Complex."
17. Ibid., p. 159 (Dell ed.).

PART III

Women and Spirituality

6

Sexism, Religion, and the Social and Spiritual Liberation of Women Today

ROSEMARY RADFORD RUETHER

The participation of women in the received historical religions of dominant cultures is in crisis today, particularly in the West. This is a startling new phenomenon. It is true that this is not the first time women have realized that religion was one of the primary tools of their oppression. Nineteenth-century feminists such as Sarah and Angelina Grimké realized early that the Bible was a basic authority for women's subordination in their society not only in religious matters, but in secular matters as well. The Grimké sisters believed that the true message of the Scriptures was liberating for women, and that exegesis had to be wrested from the male clergy and their use of Scripture to justify subordination. At the turn of the century Elizabeth Cady Stanton gathered a group of women exegetes and ministers for a thorough critique of the sexism of the Bible. Unlike the Grimké sisters, Stanton was not sure that the Bible as a whole was liberating for women and needed only better interpretation. Stanton believed that the Bible reflected sexist patriarchal societies and that at many points its authority needed to be contested and discredited for modern times.

Few women wanted to take on Stanton's direct challenge to biblical religion. Most women in the National-American Women's Suffrage Association preferred to bypass the issue, believing that it would only make women's struggle for social rights more difficult. Thus, the present decade is the first time in known history in which large numbers of women have been able to gain both the educational means and the collective strength to challenge the redemptive meaning of biblical religion for women, and either demand significant transformation of its traditional understanding or else call for a rejection of biblical religion altogether in favor of an alternative women's religion.

The question of whether biblical religion is irredeemably sexist has emerged as critical not just for a few groups in counter-cultural movements, but for many women who are involved in churches and synagogues. It also is proving to be an increasingly divisive issue within the women's movement itself. In addition, the women who take the need for a new culture or spirituality as primary, and therefore start with the need for a new women's religion, differ from those who are mainly concerned with a new social order and who assess the negative or positive role of religion in relation to this social agenda. I would place my own position more in this second camp. In my view, biblical religions have both sexist and liberating traditions, and the question is how to establish the hermeneutics for distinguishing between the two.

How does one establish alternative traditions that are helpful to women in the Christian tradition? How does one find principles in the tradition itself to criticize its dominant sexism? For women's studies in religion, the first task was simply to document the history of sexist bias toward women in the dominant tradition. This involved locating this sexist bias in the worldview of the male authorities, but also discovering the economic and legal reality of the actual status of women, which is quite different from what the official tradition suggests! Feminists quickly realize that what men have wanted women to be and what they have actually been are two quite different things. In fact, we can almost take it as a principle that violent diatribes against women in religion or culture occurred at those times when women were escaping somewhat from patriarchal limitations. Vehement dicta forbidding women to teach, speak, lead, or learn in public places is hardly necessary unless there is some movement of women to do these things!

This principle forces us to look at church and synagogue traditions in new ways. The rabbinic dicta of early Talmudic tradition, such as "Cursed be the man who teaches his daughter Torah" or "He who teaches his daughter Torah teaches her corruption," certainly point to the long tradition in Judaism of excluding women from the religious learning that led to the rabbinate and which was regarded as the crown of Jewish (male) existence. The similar statement in the New Testament, "I do not permit a woman to teach or to have authority over men; she is to keep silence" (*I Tim.* 2:12), shows the exclusion of women from the Christian teaching tradition. These statements became the norms for 2,000 years of a tradition that has sought to keep the definition of the public cultural tradition, including the definition of women's "nature" and role, in the hands of males. The effect of this exclusion of women from participation in theological education is massive. It means that women are eliminated as shapers of public culture and are confined to passive and secondary roles. Those who do manage to develop as religious thinkers are forgotten or have their stories told through male-defined standards of what women can be. In addition, the public theological culture is defined by men not only in the absence of, but against, women. Theology not only has assumed male standards of normative humanity, but is filled with an ideological bias that defines women as secondary and inferior members of the human species.

Many examples can be cited of this overt bias against women in the theological tradition. Thomas Aquinas's famous definition of woman as a "misbegotten male" was based on Aristotle's biology, which identified the male sperm with the genetic form of the embryo.

Aquinas regarded women as contributing only the matter or "blood" that fleshes out the form of the embryo. Hence, the very existence of women must be explained as a biological accident that comes about through a deformation of the male seed by the female "matter," producing a defective human or woman who is defined as lacking normative human standing.

Women are regarded as deficient physically, lacking full moral self-control and capacity for rational activity. Because of this defective nature, women cannot represent normative humanity; only the male can exercise leadership in society. Aquinas also deduces from this that the maleness of Christ is not merely a historical accident, but a necessity. In order to represent humanity, Christ must be incarnated into normative humanity, the male. Only the male, in turn, can represent Christ in the priesthood.

This Thomistic view of women is still reflected in Roman Catholic canon law, where it is decreed that women are "unfit matter" for ordination. If one were to ordain a woman it, quite literally, would not "take," any more than if one were to ordain a monkey or an ox. The Episcopalian conservatives who declared that to ordain a woman was like ordaining a donkey were fully within this medieval scholastic tradition. Whether women were defined as inferior or simply as "different," theological and anthropological justifications of women's exclusion from religious learning and leadership can be found in every period of Jewish and Christian thought. Sometimes this exclusion of women is regarded as a matter of divine law, as in Old Testament legislation. Christian theologians tend to regard it as a reflection of "natural law" or the "order of nature," which, ultimately, also is a reflection of divine intent. Women's exclusion is also regarded as an expression of woman's greater proneness to sin or corruption. Thus, as in the teaching of I Timothy, women are seen as "second in creation but first in sin" (I *Tim.* 2:13–14).

The male bias of Jewish and Christian theology not only affects the teaching about woman's person, nature, and role, but also generates a symbolic universe based on the patriarchal hierarchy of male over female. The subordination of woman to man is replicated in the symbolic universe in the imagery of divine-human relations. God is imaged as a great patriarch over or against the earth or creation, imaged in female terms. Likewise, Christ is related to the Church as bridegroom to bride. Divine-human relations in the macrocosm are also reflected in the microcosm of the human being. Mind over body, and reason over the passions are also seen as images of the hierarchy of the "masculine" over the "feminine." Thus, everywhere the Christian and Jew are surrounded by religious symbols that ratify male domination and female subordination as the normative way of understanding the world and God. This ratification of male domination runs through every period of the tradition, from Old to New Testament, through the Talmud, Church Fathers and Canon Law, Reformation Enlightenment, and modern theology. It is not a marginal, but an integral part of what has been received as mainstream, normative traditions.

Nevertheless, as one digs deeper into the history of the traditions one discovers that this exclusion of women from leadership and education is not the whole story. There is much ambiguity and plurality concerning the views of women in religious traditions and the roles women have actually managed to play at different periods. For example, evidence is growing that women in first-century Judaism were not uniformly excluded from study in the synagogues. Some synagogues included them, particularly in the Hellenistic world. One thinks, for example, of Philo's strange description of the Therapeutae, an idealized account of a contemplative Jewish sect that spent its life in study of Torah. This community consisted of a double monastery of men and women. Philo assumed that the female community equally spent its life in contemplative study of the Scriptures. Where were Philo's precedents for such an assumption? In the light of this material, the rabbinic dicta against women studying Torah become not the statement of a consensus, but rather the assertion of one side of an argument against an alternative practice and viewpoint among other Jews.

Similarly, the teachings of I Timothy about women keeping silence now appear to us not as the uniform practice of the New Testament Church, but as a reaction against the widespread participation of women in leadership, teaching, and ministry in first-generation Christianity. This participation of women in the early Church was not an irregular accident, but rather the expression of an alternative worldview. Women were seen as equal in the image of God. The equality of women and men in the original creation was understood as restored through Christ. The gifts of the Spirit of the messianic advent were understood (in fulfillment of the prophet Joel) as poured out on the "menservants" and "maidservants" alike of the Lord (*Acts* 2:17–21). Baptism overcomes the sinful divisions that divide men from women, Jews from Greek, slave from free, and makes us one in Christ (*Gal.* 3:28). The inclusion of women in early Christianity expressed an alternative theology in direct contradiction to the theology of patriarchal subordination of women. The New Testament must be read not as a consensus about women's place, but rather as a conflict over alternative understandings of male-female relations in the Church.

This alternative theology of equality, of women as equal in the image of God, as restored to equality in Christ, and as commissioned to preach and minister by the Spirit, did not just disappear with the reassertion of patriarchal norms in I Timothy. It can be traced as surfacing again and again in different periods of Christian history. The strong role played by women in ascetic and monastic life in late antiquity and the early Middle Ages reflects a definite appropriation by women of a theology of equality in Christ that was understood as being particularly applicable to the monastic life. Celibacy was seen as abolishing sex role differences and restoring men and women to their original equivalence in the image of God. As the male Church deserted this theology, female monastics continued to cling to it and understood their own vocation in terms of this theology. The history of female monasticism in the late Middle Ages and the Counter-Reformation is one of the gradual success of the male Church in suppressing this latent feminism of women's communities. It is perhaps not accidental that women in renewed female religious orders in Roman Catholicism today have become militant feminists, to the consternation of the male hierarchy.

Left-wing Puritanism in the English Civil War also became a period when the latent egalitarianism of Christian theology surfaced to vindicate women's right to personal inspiration, community power, and public teaching. The reclericalization of the Puritan congregation was a defeat for this renewed feminism of the Reformation. The Quakers were the one Civil War sect that retained the vision of women's equality and carried it down into the beginnings of 19th-century feminism.

Finally, the 19th century became a veritable hotbed of new types of female participation in religion, ranging from the evangelical holiness preacher, Phoebe Palmer, to Mother Ann Lee, understood by her followers as the female Messiah. New theologies that attempted to vindicate androgyny in humanity and God expressed a sense of the inadequacy of the masculinist tradition of symbolization.

Feminists who are engaged in recovering alternative histories for women in religion recognize that they are not just supplementing the present male tradition. They are, implicitly, attempting to construct a new norm for the interpretation of the tradition. The male justification of women's subordination in Scripture and tradition is no longer regarded as normative for the Gospel. Rather, it should be judged as a failure to apply the authentic norms of equality in creation and redemption. This is to be judged as a failure, in much the same way as the political corruption of the Church, the persecution of Jews, heretics, or witches, or the acceptance of slavery has been judged as a failure. This does not mean that this "bad" history is suppressed or forgotten. This also would be an ideological history that tries to "save" the moral and doctrinal reputation of the Church by forgetting what we no longer like. We need to remember this history, but as examples of our fallibility, not as norms of truth.

The equality of women, as one of the touchstones for understanding our faithfulness to the vision, is now set forth as one of the norms for criticizing the tradition and discovering its best expressions. This will create a radical reappraisal of Jewish or Christian traditions, since much that has been regarded as marginal, and even heretical, must now be seen as efforts to hold onto an authentic tradition of women's equality. Much of the tradition heretofore regarded as "mainstream" must be seen as deficient in this regard. We underestimate the radical intent of women's studies in religion if we do not recognize that it aims at nothing less than this kind of radical reconstruction of the normative tradition. These considerations lead feminist criticism to two questions: (a) what is the vision of social reconstruction adequate to the liberation of women, and (b) what new theology or worldview would express liberation from sexism? The limits of this format allow for us more than a cursory treatment of these complex issues.

The Vision of Social Reconstruction Beyond Patriarchy

Once some part of the story of women's subjugation under patriarchy and its various ideological justifications has surfaced, women are often outraged, while men often resist the notion that they should feel "guilty" for this history. Two opposite viewpoints tend to emerge among those who desire change. At one extreme is the view that this whole history was an inevitable expression of a certain stage of social evolution, due to the female rule in childbearing and the consequent division of labor between the sexes, possibly also because of the lack of medical technology for birth control. In the modern world, this situation of women's marginalization can be overcome; things can be changed, but men cannot be held responsible for the past. Obviously, males prefer this viewpoint, but so also do some women who are afraid of confrontation with the males in their lives.

The opposite view sees the suppression of women as a great historical crime. It is said that men have deliberately and continually conspired, and continue to conspire, to perpetuate this crime. This reflects the socialization of males into roles of dominance, which they identify with the very essence of their masculinity. Debate then arises whether this socialization of males is "nature" or "nurture." However deep this socialization, is it the psychological reflection of patriarchal social structures which could be changed once this social base is changed? Or is it a reflection of something essential in male "nature"? Feminists who take the latter view come close to suggesting that males, by nature, are intrinsically oppressive. Even if it is socialization, it is now so deeply structured into male psychology that women who wish to affirm their full personhood should shun bonding with males. Feminist separatism is the logical expression of this viewpoint. In theological circles, Mary Daly has come closest to this viewpoint of males as demonic by nature.

My viewpoint lies somewhere between these two extremes. First, I believe we must absolutely consider sexism to be a massive historical crime against the personhood of women. This crime was neither biologically inevitable nor the expression of "unconscious" forces. A social division of labor along lines of biological roles in reproduction undoubtedly took place on the tribal level and corresponded to certain necessities of survival. But it varies considerably in different ecologies. Depending on the relationship of hunting to food-gathering, women often have had a preponderant role in food production and have initiated many of the productive technologies. The translation of these roles into social power also differs.

The social incorporation of biological roles is a cultural artifact, not a necessity of nature. Particularly once social power is freed from direct prowess in hunting and war and becomes incorporated into legal and cultural superstructures, all biological reasons for eliminating women from leadership roles disappear. The fact that patriarchal societies have arisen that legislated such marginalization of women is the expression of the will-to-power of a male ruling class, not of a biological necessity. This marginalization, moreover, is not maintained by mere unconscious forces, but by the constant reiteration of laws and pronouncements by the guardians of the prerogatives of this male ruling class against women who seek to emerge from their limits. This is a culpable history, in the same way as slavery or racism is a culpable history. Even lack of birth control cannot be used as an excuse because, in fact, most of the basic principles of contraception have been known for thousands of years, but have been withheld from women by patriarchal law and religion.

One must differentiate between individual and corporate responsibility. Our ethical traditions have developed very little reflection to help us analyze the distinction between individual and social sin. (This itself is a reflection of the ideology of the dominant class. The individualization of sin keeps the dominant culture from having to confront its own particular responsibility for evil.) The social incorporation of unjust roles means that these roles, and the ideologies that enforce them, are passed on from generation to generation— neither men nor women can remember having chosen these roles. This is why it is so difficult for the oppressors to feel personal responsibility for such crimes. The burden of justifying these roles is shifted from the individual to the corporate instruments of the culture. Its justification is lodged with "nature" or "God," which serve as ultimate sanctions of the culture.

It is almost impossible for a lone individual to dissent from this culture. Alternative cultures and communities must be built up to support an alternative consciousness. Those who began such dissent in the past can be shown to have had the beginnings of such an alternative community and culture. But even then, if the alternative is not stable and authoritative enough, the individual dissenter is likely to become a mentally unhinged crank, rather than a viable role model of mature personhood. All this means that consciousness is more a product of social relations than we like to admit. Individual consciousness is not merely passive; it is critical as well. But it can leap only a little way ahead of the available social options. It has to be fed by some community that responds to it and moves along with it.

The social base for the birth of feminist consciousness in modern society began with industrialization and the dramatic shift of many of the productive roles, formerly exercised by women, away from the home. This created a class of women who enjoyed some affluence and culture but an increasingly narrow sphere of activity. Feminism began as a protest against this effete existence by this class of women. Its expression was liberal feminism, a wide-ranging effort over the last 200 years to break down the legal boundaries that barred women from professional education and leadership roles.

Many of these civil rights appear now to have been won in Western industrialized societies. Yet the resistance to passing the ERA reflects the refusal to ratify this fact systematically in American society. Simultaneous with industrialization, however, an opposite tendency appeared that subjugated women in a new way. The location of productive or salaried labor exclusively in the public sphere means that women who remain home become increasingly unskilled and economically dependent. Their dependency no longer needs to be ratified by laws excluding them from education and jobs. It now becomes structural to their marginalization from the workplace. Women are forced to choose between "family" or "work." Housework appears as a new category of unpaid labor, outside the sphere of wage labor. Women in the home are structured into a new level of intensive nurturant activity toward men and children, housework, and consumer management that becomes increasingly complex and culturally demanding as the society more and more points to this activity as the compensation for the alienations of the workplace. Women are blamed for all the failures of men and children to make it in the "world."

Women who work are tied to a "double shift" of domestic and wage labor. They are responsible both for the full span of the male work-day, plus all the activities associated with the female sphere. Since it is virtually impossible to do both equally well, most women are defeated from the start and accept their economic marginalization and dependency (and become committed to defending the ideologies that justify it). The large number of women who must work become structured into a menial level of low-paid and low-security jobs, or irregular and part-time patterns of employment. The few women who aspire to the full professional careers of the male ruling class necessarily remain exceptional "tokens" and often sacrifice marriage or children to do so. They are also "punished" as "unnatural" and "unfeminine" thereby. Thus, the system of patriarchy keeps itself intact despite the appearance of full acceptance of women's cultural equality and legal rights.

With the modern industrial split of home and work, new cultural and religious ideologies also appear that justify women's "different" nature. Woman's nature becomes correlated with the nurturant and escapist functions of the home, over against the capitalist work world. Woman is said to be more religious, spiritual, loving, and altruistic than man. Men are seen as more strongly sexed than women (a reversal of the medieval Christian view!), more rational and aggressive, but less capable of "delicate" feelings. Men need women to "uplift" them, but women retain this elevating role only by remaining in strict segregation in the home. To venture outside the home to play public roles is to coarsen and destroy her "femi-

nine" nature. It is obvious that "femininity," while presumed to be
an expression of woman's biological nature, is a socially precarious
possession! The old patriarchal ideology saw woman as defective and inferior.
The new bourgeois ideology replaces inferiority with complementarity. Complementarity is often designed to make woman appear not
only different, but even superior to males. Yet this ideology masks
the reality of dependency. This whole concept of femininity is, as
Engels recognized, a middle-class ideology. It was applicable only
to those women whose husbands could afford a "non-working"
wife. Poor and working-class women fell below the ideology of the
"lady" and were not accorded its respect or protection.

Today this ideology has been somewhat modified to accommodate
the reality of working women in the middle classes, but the same
contradictions between the female domestic role and the work world
remain largely unalleviated. Religious authorities are often the most
vehement defender of the ideology of complementarity and are
constantly trying to restore it to normative status in new forms.
Both the Vatican and Protestant fundamentalists today have assumed an all-out assault on the woman's movement and its threatened redefinition of male-female relations, as well as the relations of
family and work.

Feminists are divided about what kind of vision best points
toward full liberation. Liberal feminists continue to pursue the
agendas of equal rights, equal pay, full access to the work world and
to professional status. Countercultural feminists move in the direction of separate community building, often informed by new principles of ecological lifestyle. Socialist feminists, on the other hand,
see the conflict between women and men as embedded in a hierarchical economic system that relates housework to paid labor, and
structures women as an unpaid and low-paid labor class at the
bottom of both of these systems.

Any feminist solution, whether liberal or utopian, will remain
token if this total system is not reconstructed. This demands not
only the equality of women with men in the work world, but the
overcoming of the conflict between woman's domestic and paid
labor roles. The temporal and spatial shape of work itself has to be
restructured to allow men and women to participate equally in both
worlds. Paternity leaves, shorter full-time work shifts, more-flexible
work hours, child care on the job, and decentralized workplaces
more integrated with living communities are all part of what would
be necessary. Shared home and work roles can't simply be carried
out as a private struggle between men and women. This possibility
must be incorporated into the normative ideologies and social

systems. As long as the home-work dichotomy burdens primarily women with a double work load, all hopes for full equality between men and women will be an illusion even under socialism.

Religious Reconstruction Beyond Patriarchy

Several trends appear in feminist religion today. These correspond roughly with the liberal reformist, utopian counter-cultural, and socialist feminist options mentioned above. Liberal and evangelical feminists believe that equality of the sexes is the real meaning of Scripture. This can be made evident by better translations and exegesis. Reformers seek greater access for women to education, ordination, and employment in the churches and synagogues. They assume that Judaism and Christianity are reformable in the direction of equality between the sexes.

Liberation feminists believe that a critical and transformatory tradition within biblical faith can be the basis of the liberation of women and men from sexism, but they see this tradition existing in the biblical and theological past in a more conflictual way. Just as society is divided by class, race, and sexual hierarchies, so churches and their theologies are divided between an ideological use of religion to sanctify these ruling classes and a prophetic tradition that denounces this use of religion. The salvation message of the prophet points toward a "new age" when these unjust relations are overcome in a new society.

Counter-cultural feminist spirituality, on the other hand, rejects the idea that there is any critical or messianic tradition in the Bible or Church history that has any relevance to women. What liberation feminists call patriarchal ideology within the biblical tradition, they declare to be the *only* biblical tradition. They take the most reactionary spokesmen for patriarchal religion at their word when they say that God and Christ are males and only males can represent them. They believe that Judaism and Christianity exist for one purpose and one purpose only, to sanctify patriarchy. Consequently, any woman who is concerned to find a feminist spirituality must get out of these religious institutions, purge any attachment to their authoritative symbols she may have inherited, and seek an alternative female-centered religion.

Since there are no established female-centered religions around, counter-cultural feminists have been engaged in trying to rediscover or create them. Following 19th-century anthropologists, such as Jakob Bachofen, counter-cultural feminist spirituality accepts the idea that human society was originally matriarchal. They believe that the original human religion, during the long millenia of Stone

Age culture, was the cult of the mother Goddess and her son, the hunter, which reflected matriarchal society. This religion was subdued by the patriarchal nomadic warriors who conquered the Indian subcontinent and the Mediterranean world in the second millenium B.C. These nomadic warriors replaced the dominant symbol of the mother Goddess with that of the sky God, and subsumed the Goddess into the cult of Zeus Pater, or Jupiter, as his subordinate wives, mistresses, or daughters. From the eighth century B.C. to the seventh century A.D., the patriarchal reform religions of Judaism, Christianity, and Islam suppressed the Goddess altogether and substituted the exclusive reign of the sky Father.

According to this view, however, the cult of the mother Goddess did not die out altogether. It survived underground as a persecuted religion, named witchcraft or devil worship by its patriarchal enemies. According to the writings of Dame Margaret Murray, medieval witchcraft was believed to be the continuation of the cult of the mother Goddess and the horned God. Either in exclusively female or in mixed groups, her followers gathered in secret societies, called covens, limited to the mystic number 13. Nine million women were sacrificed to the fires or persecution. Nevertheless, a remnant of the true believers survives into the present world. Today this "old-time religion" of humanity is being revived in the movement known as Wicca (supposedly the Anglo-Saxon word for witches). Followers of the Wicca movement identify with the above story as their religious history and believe that the dominant patriarchal history suppresses the truth about these matters.

Feminist Wicca, as delineated by its theoreticians, such as Starhawk (Miriam Simos) in her book *The Spiral Dance,* is believed to be a feminist and ecological religion. It operates on the natural rhythms that connect our bodies with the cosmic body around us. It is not without its ethical code, since to bring the human community truly into harmony with nature is not merely a personal, but a social discipline. We must not only rectify our personal lifestyle, but struggle against the polluting systems of corporate capitalism that proliferate warfare and waste. In her book, Starhawk teaches spells and incantations and describes how to found one's own coven. But she rejects the notion that such spells are manipulative of others or can be used to do harm to others. Rather, she sees such spells as ways of transforming one's own consciousness, purging oneself individually or in groups of depression, anger, and hatred, and putting oneself in right relation to the self, others, and the universe.

Starhawk also rejects female-dominant and separatist forms of Wicca. Such tendencies may be understandable compensation for millenia of patriarchal repression of women. But she believes they lack the full redemptive vision of the "craft" and could be as wounding to men as patriarchal religion has been to women. Rather, her version of Wicca includes males and females as equals. Through relating to the dual symbols of the Goddess and the horned God, females and males find the full androgyny of the human potential. Women find the authority and power, and men the gifts of poetry and intuition that have been repressed in them. Both men and women are able to integrate the intuitive capacities of the right half of the brain, which has been repressed into unconsciousness by the one-sidedly cerebral patriarchal religions.

The Mother Goddess is fundamentally an immanent deity, the maternal ground of being of the coming-to-be and passing-away of all things, the womb of creation. Goddess feminists believe that, in basing ourself on her, we base ourselves on the true divine foundations of reality that do not force us to deny our bodies and our material existence, as does patriarchal transcendence. Matriarchal religion allows us to accept the naturalness and goodness of things as they are. It teaches us to "go with the flow," rather than existing as the destructive "rogue elephant" of the world; to see not only all human beings, but the animals and plants, stars and rocks as our sisters and brothers. American Indian religion and other religions of tribal people also preserve much of this immanentist ecological religion of pre-patriarchal humanity.

I have a great deal of sympathy with this option for Goddess religion, as well as the communitarian and ecological values that are being expressed through it. In many ways it takes me back to my concerns with the relation of pagan and biblical religious worldviews with which I dealt as an undergraduate more than twenty years ago. I have been acquainted for many years with the Great Mother of Syria, the many goddesses of the Mediterranean world—Ishtar, Anath, and Isis—as well as the Greek poetic rendition of these figures as Athena, Hera, Aphrodite, and Artemis. When I visited Greece in 1978 I made a special pilgrimage to Eleusis to see the spot where Persephone was "raped" into the underworld, and her mother, Demeter, began her sorrowful quest for her return. My classical professors taught me long ago about "matriarchal origins" and the conflict of maternal chthonic and paternal sky deities, so these themes are not surprising to me.

Moreover, I retain a fondness for the ancient mother. I would even say that my model of divine being has, for a long time, been more that of cosmic "matrix" than of transcendent phallic "act." I reject religious exclusivism. So I have no objection at all to people finding religious nurturance through theophanies of the divine outside the biblical or Christian traditions.

When such options are translated into a sectarian faith that declares that feminists must reject all biblical traditions and instead identify with a counter-myth of the Goddess, I do have some objections. Much of this counter-myth is drawn from a very simplistic take-over of what is now an outdated anthropology and history of religions that originated in the 19th century. Many basic assumptions about the Goddess taken for granted in contemporary feminism are quite dubious. These are not just superficial matters (such as the great exaggeration of the number of witches burned in the Middle Ages, or the description of the victims only as women). It is a matter of fundamental assumptions, such as whether any such religion of witchcraft as a Goddess-and-nature religion actually existed; and whether the ancient goddesses represented counter-cultural feminist values, were a woman's religion, and mandated leading social roles for women.

In the ancient Babylonian psalms to Ishtar, the devotees who address the Goddess are ruling-class, propertied figures who are concerned with the restoration of their economic prowess and victory over enemies in war and politics, exactly as they are in the Old Testament psalms (which were modeled after Near Eastern psalms). While this might refer to an aristocratic woman as well as a man, the concerns are neither feminist, equalitarian, or counter-cultural.

This concern with historical accuracy is not a matter of academic quibbling, but rather of truthful self-knowledge. We do not construct our own identities truthfully if we base them on tendentious falsifications of the past. But, and most important, the particular scholarship of ancient religion on which feminist spirituality relies reveals all to clearly its own cultural biases. Historically, this scholarship was a product of 19th-century romanticism. Its account of paganism over against biblical religion was woven into that same system of complementarity. It is not surprising that pagan versus biblical religion is described in terms of a dualism between femininity and masculinity, nature and civilization, the instinctual and the rational, the immanent and the transcendent.

Feminist spirituality seems to me to have bought into this radical version of romantic complementarity in a separatist and utopian form. There is a lack of critical awareness of the 19th-century romantic origins of these patterns of thought and their inappropriateness to ancient religion. Not only are alternative, perhaps more helpful, elements of the ancient Goddess missed by this mistake; more important, feminist spirituality identifies itself with a doctrine of woman's nature as intrinsically linked to motherhood, earth, and instinct over against civilization and rationality. This formula marginalizes woman in separatist, utopian sects incapable of addressing realistically the dominant world. It also imbues counter-cultural feminism with a problematic anthropology about women, as well as men. Women, like nature, become the unfallen innocents of history, victimized but naturally good. One has only to withdraw from the evil world and "get in tune" with one's bodily and cosmic "lunar" rhythms to recapture paradise.

This kind of romanticism is very congenial to Americans, but it must be questioned. It sets women apart from men, as possessing a different nature, and projects alienation and evil onto males. This not only falsifies the capacity of women themselves for self-alienation and oppression, but it deprives us of an appropriate way for deciphering the reality of human history.

Feminists have tended to reject biblical ideas of sin, the Fall, and inherited evil because they have been used to scapegoat women. It seems to me, however, that this biblical religious pattern should be understood in quite a different way. Sexism means self-alienation and the transformation of the primal relation of men and women into an oppressive dualism. This is the root sin upon which the crimes of history have been constructed. Underneath this history lies an alternative reality of harmony, with each other, with God, with nature, as our true nature. But it cannot be recovered by retreat of women from men or from civilization, but rather by historical repentence. We need a realistic recognition of the capacity for evil as a human (not a male) capacity, and the restructuring of society to maximize the incentives for mutuality, rather than oppressiveness. This biblical pattern of thought gives a critical and transforming tool for dealing with the reality of our own ambiguity in a way that is not possible with romantic ideologies of complementarity. This is why I see in biblical religion an important key for any genuine theology of liberation, including liberation from sexism, which we cannot afford to discard.

This does not mean that all the values which counter-cultural feminism seeks to affirm do not have to be reclaimed. The understanding of divinity as Goddess, as well as God, the reclaiming of the repressed parts of our psyche, new harmony with nature; all this is a part of that "redeemed" existence which we should seek. But it needs to be sought through a liberating, rather than a romantic, escapist project, if we are to be truthful about ourselves and effective in the world.

I do not expect the tension between biblical and "pagan" feminists to be soon overcome. Indeed, it corresponds to a classical tension within Western culture. This is *not* a dualism between biblical religion and actual ancient paganism (which was not a

counter-cultural, feminist, ecological religion), but a dualism between the dominant and suppressed parts of the Western consciousness, which is mythically translated into a conflict between the
biblical and the pagan, the rational and the instinctual, the "masculine" and the "feminine." The problem with counter-cultural feminism (and the romantic scholarship on which it relies) is that this
projection is taken to be an actual historical description, which thus
casts people into false options between the dominant and the
suppressed consciousness. I expect this tension between these two
expressions of feminism to continue for some time, until some new
synthesis appears that can incorporate them both. I hope only to
keep critical and creative lines of communication open to allow for
an eventual transforming synthesis, rather than just a noncommuni-
cating impasse.

7

Liberating Philosophy: An End to the Dichotomy of Spirit and Matter

HILDE HEIN

The concept of spirituality is amply interpretable. It has been identified with the transcendent and supernatural, but also with the immanent and natural. It has been associated with the mental and intellectual, but also with bodily feeling and passion. It has been considered the "besouling" or animating principle, but also to be other-worldly or beyond life. It is often regarded as of positive moral value, but it can be perverted to evil ends. It is most commonly opposed to the material. But even this claim is problematic, for some theories regard matter and spirit as continuous or even as merely aspectival. Matter becomes spirit as it flows from the indefinite infinite into the "utterly subtle." The notion that matter complexified or rarefied becomes spirit has been one of the classic alternatives to philosophical dualism.

The ascription of spirituality to women has also been problematic. Women are sometimes understood as fundamentally incompatible with the spiritual, but at other times as its primary human representation. If one looks for patterns of intelligibility in these attributions, they are hard to discern. One thing seems clear: women have had little to do with making the assignments and associations. Furthermore, the associations have not been coordinated with any particular changes in the lives of women. Throughout Western civilization, women's lives have been predominantly devoted to and defined in terms of procreation, including preparation for reproduction and its aftermath of nurturance, homemaking, and child care. Yet despite this historic sameness of women's experience, their alleged relation to spirituality has fluctuated wildly.

The affirmations and denials of spirituality to women have generally been made by men, and so we must look to men's philosophical preconceptions to make sense of the apparently random vacillations. I have argued elsewhere that male-generated philosophy, and specifically the Western mainstream that descends from Greek philosophy, tends to regard the universe in terms of dichotomies— light and dark, permanence and change, finite and infinite, dry and moist, even and odd, male and female, day and night, intelligence and emotion.[1] The extremes are then opposed to one another upon a hierarchical value scale and so grouped that, with few exceptions, the positive ends of each pair are assimilated and so are the negative poles. Thus the female is associated with the cluster including the moist, the dark, the odd, night, and other negative qualities, while the male lines up with the positive attributes at the opposite pole. I have discussed some of the philosophical and practical implications of this polarizing and hierarchicalizing tendency, pointing out its irrelevance to women's experience as it systematically devalues it.

Spirit and matter, however, do not appear on this scale as primary oppositions. Sometimes they are held to be compatible and sometimes not. I suggest that they should nevertheless be understood as secondary oppositions, at least insofar as differentially applicable to men and women. Where male and female are opposed, spirituality is derivatively affirmed of the one and denied of the other. Whatever state of spirituality (or its absence) men claim for themselves within the Western tradition, they automatically declare the opposite for women. However men see themselves with regard to spirituality at any given moment, and whatever the logic or rational justification for that representation, women are automatically relegated to its antipode. Thus, their identification of women as spiritual or not has relatively little to do with men's actual perception of women, much less with that which women might have of themselves, but only with an historic male self-perception.

I suggest that this mechanical designation of spirituality or its opposite to women, depending upon the primary and orthogonal status of men, accounts for its apparent arbitrariness and lack of conformity to either reason or experience. I will here consider four distinct analyses of the association between women and spirituality. The first three, all argued by men, are radically incompatible with one another. Yet they reveal no significant differences in the actual traits and functions they ascribe to women, apart from the specific involvement with or incompatibility with spirituality. These analyses may best be understood as reflecting shifts in the sociohistoric self-representation of men. The fourth view of women's spirituality, currently held by some women, is largely reactive and therefore follows the pattern of understanding women as defined by men, i.e., as their opposite. Hence the attribution of spirituality to women continues to be consequent upon their gender, and that, in turn, is represented by negation, although it is positively evaluated.

I. The Aristotelian/Christian View:
Spirit Is to Matter as Man Is to Woman

Aristotle is clear, especially with respect to procreative functions, that woman plays an essentially material role, while the male parent is the source of "besoulment."[2] Women, he says, do have vegetative and locomotive souls and even some degree of rationality, but it is "without authority."[3] Women lack the combustible soul-making element, the entelechy, which is the male contribution to reproduction—transmitted by means of the notably material semen. While women are obviously not altogether devoid of the animating principle or spirit, Aristotle depicts them as primarily receptive to it. Women are passive receptacles who nurture life. Spirit is active agency; only spirit, the male principle, generates life.[4]

On this account, the female parent has little influence on the positive character of her offspring. The mother's intrinsic defectiveness limits the child's possible perfection, but its actual identity is fixed and imparted by paternal agency. It is merely temporarily domiciled in her nurturant womb.*

Woman's preeminent materiality also renders her morally deficient. Aristotle does not follow Plato's belief that the possession of virtue is ultimately a consequence of knowledge of the Good. But he does regard virtue as a kind of knowledge, following from an intellectual, hence spiritual, capacity. The practice of virtue is the result of a state of character acquired by habitual action and good judgment.[5] The recognition of the appropriate action to perform is a cognitive act of syllogistic reasoning. One who lacks intellect is incapable of such judgments, and the virtue appropriate to persons who are constitutionally so deprived is therefore obedience. Whereas men are fit to rule, thanks to their rational souls, Aristotle affirms that obedience is the virtue appropriate to woman. Thus woman's lack of spirituality, her lack of a full-fledged active intelligence, justifies her social subordination as it rationalizes her moral inferiority. Biologically and metaphysically deficient, she lives at the level of matter, where her moral and social aspirations are accordingly fixed.

Aristotle, who never believed that all human beings are created equal, did not perceive women's consignment to inferior status as

---

*No wonder the notion of "renting" a womb for purposes of artificial insemination seems plausible and so attractive to so many.

either a punishment or an injustice. It was simply a matter of observable fact which, happily, supported the existing social order. His doctrine was carried over with some modifications into Christian doctrine. The notion of the woman's body as nurturant host to the paternally provided embryo persists to this day, despite the 16th-century discovery of the reproductive role of the ovum and the modern understanding of genetic dimorphism.[6] But rhetoric and "common" sense agree that men have children "by" (i.e., through the instrumentality of) women, just as race horses are "sired by" male stallions "out of" mares.

Women's material nature (carnality) was much discussed by the Fathers of the early Church, who held it in horror as much for its inherent depravity as for its capacity to evoke the uncontrollable lust of men.[6] St. Augustine, for example, clearly indicates that the Fall of Man brought in its wake not sexual intercourse, which must have existed prior to that event, but its accompaniment with concupiscence.[7] Women's lack of spirituality is thus no mere deprivation, nor is materiality a neutral, if deficient, state relative to a high mode of being. Matter, insofar as it is a privation of Spirit (God), is a positive evil. Hence woman as matter is evil and, furthermore, threatens to unleash the potential for evil in man.

Thomas Aquinas actually expresses a view closer to that of Aristotle in describing female materiality as essentially passive. But it is ironic that, in his view, in consequence Eve as mere passive vehicle is responsible neither for the commission nor for the transmission of original sin.[8]

> it has been stated that original sin is transmitted by the first parent in so far as he is the mover in the begetting of his children. And so it has been said that if anyone were begotten only materially of human flesh, they would not contract original sin. Now it is evident that, in the opinion of philosophers, the active principle of generation is from the father, while the mother provides the matter. Therefore original sin is contracted, not from the mother, but from the Father; so that if Eve and not Adam had sinned, their children would not contract original sin, Whereas if Adam, and not Eve, had sinned, they would contract it [*Summa Theologica*, Q 81, Art V].

It does not follow, of course, that Eve is *good*, but only that she lacks responsibility for evil. The commission of sin presupposes active agency, i.e., a soul; if Eve is sheer material potency, then she is no more capable of sin than she is of doing good. She is the occasion of sin; but not the performer of it. Neither does she transmit it to the next generation.

Strictly speaking, Eve's materiality ought to render her morally neutral, or amoral—a being to whom ethical attributes are inapplicable. In fact, we do speak in morally neutral terms of inanimate objects which, however offensive they may be to us, are not taken to act deliberately.* In the case of such nonresponsible beings, we assign their supervision to a higher authority, and that is exactly what Aristotle had in mind. But the Christian Fathers did not equate Eve's lack of spirituality simply with lack of intellect, although they undoubtedly regarded her as benighted in that dimension, as well. They considered the defect of Eve's nature to be more sinister. As nature abhors a vacuum, so does spiritual deficiency invite the seduction of the Evil one. Pure spirit is not properly opposed to the absence of spirit, pure indeterminate matter, but to its diametric opposite, the depraved and corrupted spirit—Satan. Eve is subject to the beguilement of the fallen spirit, the serpent, and she, in turn, passes its seduction on to her imperfect companion, Adam.

Woman's capacity to elicit reprehensible thoughts (and deeds) in men can hardly be a post-lapsarian fault, since Adam succumbed unprotestingly to her blandishments when Eve offered him the apple. Yet this ability to tempt and seduce, preeminently associated with her materiality, has caused woman to be most despised.† Evidently the contagion of her spiritual weakness is to be feared, for if men were spiritually perfect beings, they would be unmoved and unaffected by women's attraction.

Ultimately, then, men detest the dark forces within themselves on consideration of women's lack of spirituality. Yet in all cultures the reasoning is the same, regardless of what women are or do. They must be covered, shaved, disfigured, maimed and locked away—not as a corrective for their own spiritual lack, for which they are in a sense blameless, but as a protection against men's spiritual fallibility. The point is not that women must be protected against men. Rather, the denunciation of women's materiality is a means devised by men for deflecting attention from their own spiritual fallibility (as they understand it.) It is odd that little effort has been made to correct that fallibility. Instead, moral and spiritual weakness is projected upon woman as "the weaker vessel," and she is incarcerated and mummified to forestall the greater temptations of men.

On this view, matter and spirit are opposed to one another and are attributed, respectively, to the female and male principles. Spirit is

---

*The National Rifle Association has capitalized on that distinction, declaring that "Guns do not kill: People do." Guns, however, are designed by people exclusively for the purpose of killing.

†This horror of woman's charm is certainly not unique to Christianity. It is the heart of Hesiod's fable of Pandora's box, and of countless fairy tales and popular stories in which woman, the enchantress, is also reviled as "troublemaker." It is the familiar notion "cherchez la femme" whenever things go wrong.

furthermore associated with the rational, the principled, and the ethically sound, as well as with the generative and divine. Spirit is in all respects superior to matter and is rightfully destined to dominate it. Yet matter, the passive female potency, has its dark powers that must be curbed and suppressed. Thus it is that wherever it appears in women, in the physical world of nature, and not least in man himself, material nature must be ruthlessly surveyed and controlled. The presumption is, of course, that the universe is well served by such hierarchic domination.

II. Woman as Nature: Spirit as Immanent

Woman's materiality may be affirmed without denying her spirituality. An alternative conception of spirituality assimilates it to the natural forces that animate the physical universe, rather than to the intellect or to a word-reifying deity.

Some archaeological evidence supports the argument that regions of the Mediterranean and Middle East were once inhabited by matriarchal societies that worshipped a Mother-Goddess.[9] Perhaps, as feminist scholars have claimed, the scant evidence of these societies has been further invalidated and discredited by patriarchal scholarship,[10] not to mention the ruthless extermination of the societies in the first place. There are some indications even in patriarchal history and literature that alternative cultures might have existed with different social structures, different values, and different patterns of thought and feeling. I am concerned here only to explore the concept of spirituality that might have been derived from such prehistoric societies and which surely has been a persistent mythological strand of patriarchal culture. I am not arguing in defense of the actual existence of prehistoric matriarchal societies.

It is plausible that there once was a time when men were ignorant of their own role in procreation and were aware only that women had a miraculous, life-giving capacity. It is not unlikely that this ability would be regarded with reverential awe, and that women might be esteemed as goddesses and exercise considerable power. One may imagine that matrilineal descent would be the norm in such a society and that kin groups would be matrilocal. It does not follow that there would be matriarchy, a pattern of domination which seems dictated only by analogy to later patriarchal power structure. One can speculate, however, that once men discovered their part in the drama of birth, they might wish to aggrandize that role.

The agricultural model would surely be available to them, and could reasonably be extended to human generation. It allows men to claim preeminence as planters of seeds and producers of crops, harvesting women as women harvest nature. The assimilation of the fecundity of women to the fecundity of nature then seems justified and warrants similar rituals and practices. Thus woman as nature becomes the object of religious ceremony—not as transcendent being, but as the incarnation of natural processes whose rhythms must be respected and whose rites observed.

Natural processes, however, as Simone de Beauvoir has pointed out,[11] are not highly valued in our patriarchal culture. Only such activities as are deliberate, intentional, and represent the project of a self transcendent over nature qualify as truly human acts. Sheer process is perceived as unreflective and passive. The woman in childbirth is taken to be an acquiescent medium. She is impregnated: the child comes to fruition within her body and is expelled. She participates as in a dream, but she is not responsible for the event. Few women who have undergone the experience of pregnancy could subscribe to this description of their uninvolvement, but that is how it appears from the vantage point of patriarchy. By contrast, the deliberate taking of life is a transcendent act. To impose death (as distinct from suffering it) is to declare oneself a Self. Thus men have glorified death, awarded themselves authority over it, and mystified it where their power to control it was lacking. Meanwhile, they have devalued the capacity to engender life, treating it as a force to be reckoned with and even feared, but above all to be husbanded and controlled like any natural resource, such as water power or electricity. Women thus become a repository within which that force resides, a garrison of nature that must be held hostage for the sake of life.

On this account spirituality is not denied of woman and is indeed equated with her materiality. But it is not an individuating, intellectualizing, or morally elevating property. It is rather an elemental and undifferentiated force which "passes through" and occupies a woman as heat may be conducted through a metal or an electrical impulse through a wire. Woman's spirituality is in no way incompatible with her passivity or with her lack of moral authority.

This very neutrality or omnipotence of spirituality renders it suspect from a male perspective. Since women have no preordained commitment to patriarchy nor investment in it save the habit of subservience, their fidelity to it is not to be counted upon. That is why women are easily enlisted in conspiracy. (Witness again the guile of the serpent. Why did he not approach Adam directly?) That is why women's "gift" is precariously placed and may as readily be "perversely" applied as used to the benefit of patriarchy. Viewed from the standpoint of patriarchy, spirituality as so conceived is clearly a mixed blessing.

Nowhere is this ambivalence more clearly reflected than in the rich literature of Lilith, Eve's predecessor as Adam's consort.[12]

Banished from Adam's side because she refused to submit to his importunings, Lilith is said to have wandered throughout Asia Minor, consorting and coupling with a variety of quasi-human creatures. A menace to men, she was an aide to women, presiding over child-birth and bringing them mid-wifely comfort. The legend of her autonomy, her bad reputation, her ostracism from civilized society, and the particular arts that she is alleged to have practiced certainly suggests the uneasy grafting of a patriarchal mythology and value system upon some more-ancient and more female-oriented trunk.

No claims of superiority may be drawn either from the priority of the older system or the victory of patriarchalism. Neither antiquity nor power are measures of value, nor are they indices of greater or lesser spirituality. But patriarchy has continued to pay a grudging and ambivalent respect to the subterranean forces of life and passion that are viewed as woman's spirituality. Benevolently represented, these forces empower women as healers and comforters. Women are herbalists, alchemists, nurturers, and bringers of solace and repose. Malevolently feared, the same forces reflect women's trafficking with diabolical agents as witches and enchantresses, with dangerous hands as murderous as they are seductive.

Spirituality as thus depicted is a natural force attendant upon woman's materiality and closeness to nature. Intrinsically, it is neither good nor evil, but instrumentally it may be a means to the production of either. The control and domination of women who harbor this spirituality are therefore essential to the survival of patriarchy. Whether through witch burnings or the apotheosis of maternity and the "eternal feminine," women are culturally and politically collectivized, used as a resource, and "contained" as a potential hazard.

III. Spirituality Domesticated

Still another representation of spirituality distinguishes it from both matter and the realm of intellect and places it in a pseudo-morally refined dimension of sentiment. This view arose with the advent of modern science, which treats nature as an abstraction and matter as inanimate and inert. Neither invested with spirit nor viewed as a menacing evil, no longer the repository of secret forces and powers, nature is neutrally objectified. Its conquest and control are rationally achieved and methodically maintained. Reason is the instrument of control, and its function is largely utilitarian.

Far removed from the Nous or Logos of the Hellenic-Christian tradition, modern reason adjudicates means to ends which it neither originates nor justifies. It will take us to outer space and to the moon, but it is essentially pedestrian. It is not the crowning glory of humanity, but is perhaps better exhibited in such machines as are unimpaired by human flaws and fallibilities. Little spirituality is left in this conception of reason, which has been denounced by mystics and romantics as the preserve of small-minded shopkeepers. Yet the power of this reason is not to be underestimated, for it is capable of building empires and destroying nations. Indeed, it may destroy the world altogether if it is not opposed by something other than reason. Scientific reason adjusts human destinies and may, with genetic engineering, redesign human potentialities. Thus it is a powerful manipulator of values, but it does not ground or preserve value. It has ceased to be the link between mankind and the divine.

Matter too has been demoted to an inert status. It is transformable into energy and is fluid and volatile, but it is not besouled. Unreceptive to spirit, it is a dead mechanism. Whatever spirit inspirits the world is not immanent in matter or its nature, but alights upon it as from another sphere and is held captive or enshrined.

Women, or rather "the Feminine," are the hostage to this transcendent spirit. Intuitive and feeling, they are nonrational; nurturant, and caring, and not purely material. Identified by default with spirituality, they are required to satisfy the dimension of affect and sensitivity that both reason and matter ignore. This spirituality gives meaning to life and makes it worthwhile. It imbues action with value and suffuses character with worth. But it is not to be confused with moral righteousness, which is lawful and derives from reason. Love, not morality, is the realm of the spirit, and love is the domain of women.

The home is also the domain of women, and there spirituality is enshrined. According to the doctrine of "separate spheres," which came to particular prominence in the 19th century and is still deeply embedded in patriarchal mythology, the home is the sanctuary of the spirit, and there the woman presides. From her pedestal she relieves the harsh reality of the lives of men (a reality from which she herself is supposedly protected), and indirectly she dispenses an inspiriting influence upon the public sphere by softening the hearts of the men to whom she ministers.[13]

Men are governed by reason and occupied with material concerns from which women have been largely excluded, but men are also the chief beneficiaries of women's spirituality. The solace and comfort which women purvey, not to mention their unpaid labor, are no doubt renewing both to men who are themselves oppressed and to those who oppress them. The spiritualizing role of women is thus a socially stabilizing force, and it has been harnessed to politically and economically conservative causes. We see again in this instance how the attribution (by men) of spirituality to women works to subjugate and to imprison women while it uses that spiritual capacity as a device for the maintenance of social order.

While from a woman's perspective the comparative social esteem of being regarded as a font of spirituality may be preferable to (and certainly safer than) being burned at the stake as a witch, the caliber of spirituality involved is somewhat truncated and ultimately degrading. Far from the romanticized "at-oneness" with a transcendent spirit from which it is alleged to stem, this hearth-bound spirituality is miniaturized and manicured. The little mother is all sweetness and tenderness, as depicted in countless sentimental works of literature and art, and the same slightly eroticized affection is displayed toward her errant man. No sign is apparent of the ferocity and bitter calculation which often mark genuine maternal concern. Nor are violent tremors of sensual passion allowed to mar the serene face of spirituality that romantic patriarchy ascribes to women. Above the crass materialism and rationalism of the world of men, the sentimentally spiritualized woman is removed from the rough traffic of life. But woe unto her if she descend, for she is instantly transformed into her mirror image—cold, hard, unnatural, and desexed. The compromise of her spirituality denatures her femininity, though not necessarily her sexuality. Hence the distinction, ridiculed by both feminists and their abusers, between the lady and the woman. The spiritualized lady is "pure" in her wifely dedication and motherhood; the de-spirited woman is depraved, either as sexually wanton (the whore) or as sexually neutralized and frigid.

As a heuristic paradigm for living, such tender spirituality must be deeply dis-spiriting. The survival of such a fragile artifact as the "spiritual" woman, or even the perpetuation of her illusion, is possible only through the beneficence and organized protection of men. The very special femininity that makes the hot-house flower vulnerable and dependent evokes in men a sense of power and sometimes responsibility. Male protectiveness is the obverse of male aggression, and both are linked to the ideal of manhood and virile self-esteem. That is why rape is the inevitable and salacious underside of male protection, the ultimate degradation and the greatest tribute to male power.

Though woman's spirituality is alleged to arise from her communion with a transcendent being, she is in fact cut off by the social arrangements that protect her from actual communication with those resources that would empower her. These constraints, experienced from infancy, prohibit the female child from acquiring those kinesthetic and calculative aptitudes later denied of her as a "natural" deficiency.

Women continue to be discouraged from following the pursuits or entering the professions that have been denominated as belonging in the male domain. But long before these choices are articulated, the gender roles are cast, dictating conventional fears and expectations, rewarding patience and docility in girls and aggressive probing of limits in boys. The wonder is not that so many are turned away from the "male" activities, but that so many girls apply themselves to their achievement. It is clear that the societal rewards, including the esteem awarded to occupants of the male sphere, are higher than those of the female sphere. Yet women are rewarded as women, if not necessarily as people, for remaining in their "proper" sphere.

Lest this account of woman's spirituality and the "proper" sphere of womanhood appear quaintly archaic and absurdly out of date, I suggest that with only small modifications of language, it is still very much with us in the form of such contemporary doctrines as sociobiology. As its preeminent promulgators, E. O. Wilson and his associates, have maintained, the nurturant, maternal inclinations of the female are inherent expressions of the genetic drive for replication.[14] Male dominance and aggressiveness are similar genetic manifestations. Given the difference of their biological roles, the male is motivated to impregnate as many females as possible, a hit-and-run tactic calculated to preserve a widely distributed genetic progeny. The female, on the other hand, since her destiny includes the care and nurturance of her young, is motivated to associate sexual affiliation with long-term protection. She seeks a provider as well as a mate and so distributes her favors less casually. She evaluates a potential partner qualitatively as well as quantitatively and thus preserves a higher, less-promiscuous standard of behavior. These patterns of conduct are described as "naturally" fixed in gender identity, and therefore the efforts of individuals to extricate themselves from their tyranny are ill-fated and ultimately deleterious to one's own genetic heritage, not to mention the established social order.

It might be observed that there is no glorification of the female sphere in this account, no rhapsodizing over woman's spirituality. Indeed, the very notion of any kind of spirituality or even moral worth has become debased. Altruism is reduced in significance to the status of a device for the perpetuation of a kindred gene pool. Where egoistic self-preservation is precluded, it is a shrewd alternative.

Strictly speaking, even the dubious merits of egoism are superceded by sociobiology. This is no philosophy of a transcendent spirit any more than it is of an immanent one. The apparently conscious and deliberate intentions of individuals, now represented as gene bearers, are all but immaterial in view of the exigencies of biological destiny. It is the genes which exhibit a rather demented if not demonic "purposiveness without a purpose." This presumed triumph of evolutionary selection assures the personal characteristics and social arrangements by means of which the relentless perpetuation of homologous genes is achieved. Not even the survival of the individual is at stake; nor that of the species which some varieties of ethical humanism have promoted as a naturalistic version of spiritualism. According to sociobiology, the end and order of all things, that to which all human and biological endeavor is ordained, is the indefinite replication of ordered sequences of DNA. Sic transit gloria mundi!

In characterizing sociobiology as a reformulation of the 19th-century sentimentalized view of women, I do not mean to suggest that it is a theory of spiritualism. On the contrary, it renders the very notion of spirituality insignificant and even makes nonsense of the concept of significance. But it is a very effective and highly persuasive modern "scientific" defense of traditional beliefs regarding the ultimacy of gender dichotomy. And insofar as these beliefs embody previously established dogma linking sex identity with spirituality, that dogma is automatically and uncritically reinforced. It is in fact subtly incorporated into the rhetoric of the scientific theory itself. The popularized language of the "selfish" and "sneaky" gene capitalizes on prior prejudice and conveys a classic image of the war between the sexes in which the wily, intelligent, and adventurous male impregnates the dumb and passively receptive female.

Perhaps any defense of radical gender differentiation would, in the wake of the history I have described, carry the associative burden of making polarized attributions of spirituality. Clearly, differences between male and female do exist. The most obvious difference is physical, but it is not evident what further differences of a moral, intellectual, or spiritual nature might follow from these. Assuming that the material and functional differences lead to gender-specific experience, one might expect some social accommodations that would enlarge the original difference. The converse is also possible. One might make social arrangements that would minimize the effect of the natural disparity. Thus, nothing follows with necessity, even granted the fact of an initial material difference between the sexes. There is certainly no self-evident basis for drawing conclusions about comparative spirituality. I have tried to show that the dissociation between matter and spirit is not constant. But the polarization of male and female is constant, and therefore whatever qualities are taken to be essential to the one are promptly denied of the other. This gender opposition has pervaded the mainstream of Western philosophy as it has been transmitted under male domination, but there are indications of its presence even in some forms of feminist philosophy. And where the polarization persists there is a similar tendency to preserve the unnecessary and irrelevant orthogonal assignment of spirituality to the sexes. I will consider one example of such a theory.

IV. Woman's Spiritual Supremacy: The Feminist Claim

Among the most-ardent opponents of patriarchy are some feminists who insist not only upon the existence of gender differences, but upon the spiritual superiority of the female. Some of these advocate the repudiation of patriarchal religion and the return to a reconstructed form of the Goddess religion described in Section II. It must be emphasized that this is not a recommendation of matriarchy as a replacement for patriarchy. The notion of matriarchy is in fact a male invention conceived as a parallel counterpart to existing forms of governance, including their mode of hierarchy and domination. But there is no particular reason to believe in the historicity of such forms.

The Goddess religion as represented by its contemporary proponents stresses female symbolism and immanence. The Goddess animates all of nature and is especially evident as female power. Power in this context does not refer to control or mastery over others, but to creative self-engenderment. Z. Budapest calls it "self-blessing" and invites the worshippers of the Goddess to personal rituals and communal celebrations.[15] To honor the Goddess is to honor and elevate, rather than denigrate, the "traditional" female attributes—closeness to nature, nurturance, sensuality, and receptiveness. Adherents of the Goddess religion do not deny the role ascribed to women by patriarchy, but they reverse the patriarchal estimation of its value. Where patriarchy sees weakness, incompetence, and dependency, they see strength, wisdom, and freedom. Proponents of this religion, while they do not invariably exclude or reject men, tend to regard the established, male-contrived religions as immature in their rigidity, excessively formalistic, and defective in their inhumanity and lack of universality. The Goddess religion denies transcendence and stresses community. It emphasizes the continuity of natural phenomena, including human life, and their interdependence. It encourages mutual aid, while not excluding the

affirmation of individual will and purpose. It rejects formal subordination and servility and a mechanical system of reward and punishment. It is clearly based upon a compassionate analysis of women's
cultural experience and thus offers an historic alternative to "the
religion of the fathers." In this respect it is an attractive rectifica-
tion.

But while the exaltation of the Womanspirit is producing a
groundswell of women's communities and some collaborative political and social action, I believe that its ultimate effect is both
politically and theoretically regressive.[16] However vitalizing to
women's self-esteem, and however truly meritorious are the spiritual values which it extols, the Goddess religion, like sociobiology,
tends to reaffirm existing prejudices. Here again, the polarities are
overstated and are presumed to entail unrelated distinctions whose
gender-specificity has not been established. Even where men are
invited to take part in the rituals of the Goddess religion and to learn
from women's experience, the old pathways of the male-suprema-
cist tradition are not abandoned. They are a constant beckoning
presence, inasmuch as they are allowed to define the terrain of
human experience. Given the profound maldistribution and mis-
definition of power that has emerged so far, its mere realignment is
not a sufficient corrective. It will not do to glorify as virtue what men
have labeled vice, or to denounce what they have celebrated. Such
transvaluations are hardly new. But the very notions of virtue and
vice must be called into question and the polarities themselves
discredited.

Women theologians (or thealogians, as they sometimes call themselves)[17] have rightly noted that the so-called primal sins of pride,
lust, greed, and avarice, and the corresponding virtues of humility,
modesty, and generosity are male-identified.[18] They are not unheard
of in women, but not notably common. Women are more prone to
such offenses as triviality and self-wastefulness. But this is not to
indicate that a standard of female merits and demerits should be set
alongside of, separate but equal to, those of males. Instead, it
implies that we must reappraise the entire system of cataloguing so
fundamental to male reflection. Perhaps the whole contextless abstraction of virtue and vice, good and evil, along with their attendant
praise and blame, punishment and reward, damnation and redemption are mere instances of simplistic patriarchal dichotimization.
Little would be gained by a duplication of the list of simplifications.

The affirmation of a female ascendant thealogy, although its
symbols be pleasing, its rituals satisfying, and its doctrines benevo-
lent, nevertheless seems to perpetuate just those metaphysical and
epistemological errors of traditional male philosophy which ought to

be corrected. Furthermore, the political and psychological edge which male-generated polarizations already possess admonish us to cautiousness in the construction (or reconstruction) of yet another bipolar religion. At the same time, we must avoid insensitivity to the psychological and political fortification which the enunciation of such a religion might provide to women. The role of symbol and ritual in the establishment of beliefs and attitudes cannot be underestimated, especially in this instance where the entire counter-weight of masculine culture must be offset.

But counter-weapons will not serve where disarmament must be our end and wars of opposition rendered meaningless. My point is not simply that the Goddess is likely to be out-gunned and defeated, but that even her triumph would be a form of defeat where victory is to become an outmoded concept. In my view, the very notion of religion, though not devoid of features which may be gratifying to women as well as to men, must be so contaminated with patriarchal structures and residual associations of polarized values, hierarchy, and transcendence that even the most scrupulous feminist expurgation could not disinfect it. Something more radical than the resurrected Goddess is required.

I will end by sketching the beginnings of a possible reconceptualization of spirituality. I have indicated several historic analyses of spirituality and suggested that neither the opposition of spirit and matter nor the positive value of spirituality has been invariant. The more-fundamental dichotomy between male and female has been determinative. However patriarchy has defined the nature of man, it has accorded the opposite qualities to women. But suppose we take an altogether different approach, and examine spirituality not as an adherent to this or that type of being, but rather as an end in and of itself. One feature that is commonly ascribed to spirituality and that may be an essential condition of its possibility is freedom, which concept we will next explore.

V. Beginnings of a Proposed New Analysis of Spirituality

The spirit can be bound by ignorance or dogmatism, by false consciousness, or by tyrannical oppression. Nonetheless, it is of the spirit that freedom is quintessentially predicated. A free-falling body acts according to law, but the spirit unencumbered is truly free. Philosophers have for centuries exhorted us to be mindful that even where the body is enchained, the spirit can be free, and some have urged the cultivation of spiritual freedom. Indeed, where that freedom is lacking, the uncoerced body is hardly significant. What would a spiritless freedom mean?

Assuming this inherent integration of freedom and spirit, an analysis of spirituality in its relationship to freedom and especially as pertinent to a philosophy of women's liberation seems appropriate. In patriarchal philosophy, freedom is classically defined in relation to constraint. It does not usually mean the absence of constraint. Most philosophers reject the absence of constraint as formlessness, lawlessness, anomie, anarchy, disorder, and chaos. Hence it is not only morally and politically undesirable, but ultimately conceptually absurd. We could not describe a condition of lawlessness, we could only react to it, for without definition as given by law and hence constraint, things have no identity. They cannot be objectively experienced. A world without law is a nullity, and so cannot be said to be free.

It is noteworthy that women are frequently taken to be just such nullities. Lacking ego boundaries, they are not defined as selves. They do not extricate themselves from their environment as transcendent beings, but remain contextually integrated. Consequently, the attribute of freedom is mis-applied, though not falsely applied to women. In other words, women are neither free nor unfree, just as success and failure have not been appropriate female characterizations until recently.

If freedom is not the absolute lack of constraint, it may be more fruitfully and is more commonly understood as self-imposed limitation or autonomy. The subject is not independent of all law, but only of that imposed by sources other than itself.[19] It is acknowledged that constraint is not only inevitable but essential to the very possibility of freedom, indeterminacy being the opposite of freedom. By this definition the meaning of freedom does not exclude lawful constraint, but the reality of freedom excludes heteronomy. One who is subject to the law of another is unfree and, *a fortiori*, one whose very being is defined by the perception of another is unfree. According to this representation of freedom, women are thus irretrievably unfree. They live in a world whose laws are contingently dictated by men, and they exist as creatures categorically designed by and for men. If spirituality has to do with self-legislation, then women are clearly without spirit—but so also are most men.

Yet another view of freedom defines it as the recognition and acquiescence in necessity.[20] Here there is no question of self-determination, much less the absence of determination. Instead, the harmonious subordination of self to the necessary order of things is taken to be the intellectual and moral equivalent of freedom. This is not meant as a passive surrender, but as an act of comprehension in which the understanding self is in voluntary attunement with the ultimate (and usually rational) order of things. Because of the emphasis on the active, the voluntary, and the intellectual, the capacity for such attunement is usually denied to women. Though they too are bound by necessity, it is as object which is unfree, not as freely willing subject.

It seems then that by all the classic definitions of freedom, women are unfree and the very notion of women's liberation is a contradiction in terms. Yet I have argued that spirituality which is quintessentially associated with freedom is not incompatible with women and has sometimes been regarded as their specific domain. A redefinition of some key concepts is clearly called for.

I suggest that spirit be defined as an active, generative, and generous source—its materiality is irrelevant—whose fulfillment is the exercise of freedom. While the presence or absence of constraint is pertinent to the full realization of freedom, it is not included in its definition. Bondage is a restriction of freedom, as may be bodily conditions, such as illness or physical impairment. But inasmuch as human beings are corporeal, their spirituality as well as their freedom is expressed in and through bodies present in a physical world. This is as true of men as it is of women and does not represent a difference between them.

Furthermore, the freedom of such beings is not manifested in their coping with constraints, but in their enablement and accomplishment. Freedom is an impetus from within, not a reaction to what is without the agent. It expresses the nature of a being rather than defining its limits. Just as one's lived space moves as one moves, so does one's spiritual freedom expand as one expands. To the extent that spirituality entails freedom, it is because the spirit is the theater of freedom, not its legislator. And the spirit is neither self-contained by self-made law nor uncontained by license.

The freedom of spirit is expressed and evidenced in the capacity to formulate purposes and act in accordance with them. It does not follow that these purposes are always successfully accomplished. Their achievement may be concretely obstructed or variously frustrated, but freedom is not thereby, or not necessarily, denied. One is not unfree because one has failed in an attempt, but the inability to try is a failure of freedom. It is also a failure of spirit, for spirit is the purposing agent.

There is no reason to deny spirituality of beings other than women and men. Perhaps it is appropriately ascribed even to collective bodies and communities whose purposes are emergent from and irreducible to the aims of constituent members.

While spirituality may be characterized by intelligence, it is not reducible to it, nor is it a tributary of some irrational cosmic force.

Spirituality is surely not antithetical to matter but, as we have seen, may well be found there. And since the only certain distinction between men and women is a physical one, it is most improbable that spirituality is a gender-linked capacity. In all likelihood it is found throughout nature. We know it best through those objects that human beings make as a consequence of its presence, such objects as works of art and science, but also through other human beings and human relationships.

I suggest that children, the offspring of joint parenthood and like their parents a complex of physical, mental, and moral being, are a paradigm spiritual product. Controversy over the disposition of credit seems absurd. Whether we look at the child from the patriarchal perspective as "ensouled seed" implanted in a passive vessel, or alternatively as a "dead seed" quickened and animated by the maternal environment, both contributors seem to carry considerable responsibility. Furthermore, both parents as parents are products of one another's history and one another's interactions. Neither conceives or is conceivable without the other. Their offspring is a commingling of both, not drawn from mutually exclusive segments of each.

I cite children as obviously of bisexual origin, but cultural artifacts more generally are the spiritual products of communal enterprise, though not necessarily of gendered pairs. Here, too, the description of formed matter or embodied spirit as applied, say, to a code of laws, a work of art, or an institutionalized ritual practice seems hopelessly inadequate. Such descriptions invariably mystify both matter and spirit while failing to grasp the rich integrity of the objects they purport to describe.

I conclude, then, that the best way to understand spirituality is to consider those objects that are its acknowledged products. Such reflection reveals that matter and spirit are not exclusive, that intellect and spirit are not identical, that neither men nor women have a monopoly on spirituality, but that an analysis of the relationship of woman to spirituality is warranted in order to rectify the philosophical biases of the past.

Notes

1. Hilde Hein, from "Half a Mind: Philosophy from a Woman's Perspective" (unpublished manuscript, 1979).
2. Aristotle, *On Generation and Corruption* (1930) Vol. II in *The Works of Aristotle*, ed. W. D. Ross (London: Oxford Univ. Press, 1962).
3. Ibid., Vol. X.
4. Ibid., Vol. III.
5. Ibid., Vol. IX.

6. Tertullian, "De cultu feminarum" (The Apparel of Women) in *Disciplinary, Moral and Ascetical Works,* tr. R. Arbesmann et al., (New York: Fathers of the Church, Inc., 1959); Clement of Alexandria, *Paedogogus* (Christ the Educator), tr. Simon P. Wood, C. P. (New York; Fathers of the Church, Inc., 1954).

7. St. Augustine, *Treatises on Marriage and Other Subjects,* ed. Roy J. Deferrari (New York, Fathers of the Church, Inc., 1959).

8. St. Thomas Aquinas, *Summa Theologica,* tr. Fathers of the English Dominican Province (New York: Benziger Brothers, 1947).

9. Merlin Stone, *When God Was a Woman* (New York: Harcourt Brace Jovanovich, 1976); Carol Ochs, *Behind the Sex of God* (Boston: Beacon Press, 1977).

10. Mary Daly, *Gyn/Ecology: The Metaethics of Radical Feminism* (Boston: Beacon Press, 1978).

11. Simone de Beauvoir, *The Second Sex* (1940) (New York: Bantam, 1970).

12. Robert Graves and Raphael Patai, "Adam's Helpmeets," *Hebrew Myths: The Book of Genesis* (New York: McGraw-Hill, 1966); Lilian Rivlin, "Lilith," *Ms,* December 1972.

13. Barbara Walter, "The Cult of True Womanhood: 1820–1860," *American Quarterly* 12 (Summer 1966).

14. E. O. Wilson, *Sociobiology* (Cambridge: Harvard Univ. Press); Richard Dawkins, *The Selfish Gene* (New York: Oxford Univ. Press, 1976); David Barash, *Sociobiology and Behavior* (New York: Elsevier, 1977).

15. Szuzsanna E. Budapest, "Self-Blessing Ritual," in *Womanspirit Rising,* ed. Carol P. Christ and J. Plaskow (San Francisco: Harper & Row, 1980); Starhawk, "Witchcraft and Women's Culture," in Christ and Plaskow, eds., *Womanspirit Rising.*

16. Judith Christ, "Why Women Need the Goddess: Phenomenological, Psychological, and Political Reflections," in Christ and Plaskow, eds., *Womanspirit Rising.*

17. Naomi R. Goldenberg, *Changing of the Gods* (Boston: Beacon Press, 1979).

18. Valerie Saiving, "The Human Situation: A Feminine View," *The Journal of Religion,* April 1960.

19. Immanuel Kant, *Foundations of the Metaphysics of Morals,* trans. L. W. Beck (Indianapolis: Bobbs-Merrill Co., 1969).

20. Benedict De Spinoza, *Ethics,* ed. James Gutman (New York: Hafner Publishing Co., 1949).

PART IV

The Analysis of Domination

8

Pornography and the Erotics of Domination

EVA FEDER KITTAY

Pornography is a feminist issue. This means that it is also a moral and political issue. Like other moral issues, it requires reflection and inquiry to understand the proper grounds for its condemnation; like other political issues, its analysis does not stand apart from a political position. Some feminists have claimed that pornography has a causal efficacy in maintaining patriarchy; others have argued that pornography is merely the symptom of deeper underlying social ills. But feminist issues, perhaps because of the historically long-standing and culturally pervasive nature of the subordinate position of women, do not fit easily into a "disease model" of social issues. In particular, I believe, there is no one underlying cause of women's oppression such that by removing it, all the symptomatic manifestations of oppression will be relieved. If this is so, feminist issues such as pornography must be regarded as being simultaneously symptom and cause.

As symptom, pornography is reflective of certain social and political relations between men and women; although as a mirror, it reflects through hyperbolic distortions. As a cause, pornography is a contributing factor, perpetuating a social order in which men dominate. In its causal aspect, pornography is hate literature (where "literature" is meant to cover not merely the written word but spoken, graphic, and cinemagraphic materials as well) and is morally wrong, for it contributes to a political and moral injustice. As such, it deserves the same moral and legal sanctions as other defamatory materials. In its aspect as symptom, we can see the disturbing reflections of a mode of social interaction so prevalent that the pornographic hyperbolic image is not only tolerated, but is experienced as an occasion for sexual, that is pleasurable, arousal for many.

The aim of this essay is twofold: first, to explore the moral-political questions concerning the objectionable nature of pornography in its causal aspect as hate literature, and as hate literature with a sexual charge; and second, to consider the conceptual-political questions concerning pornography in its symptomatic aspect, asking what we can learn about sexual relations in a sexist society by looking at the limiting case of pornography.

A word about the use of the term "political" is in order. When I speak of the political nature of pornography, I use the term in a manner that feminists have been accustomed to, referring to the power relations that exist between men and women, power relations which often remain invariant across different patriarchal political systems.

The use of the term "power" also requires an explanatory note. The power one has may be regarded as one's causal efficacy in the world and includes the ability to exert control over one's own destiny. Too often, however, power is understood only in terms of the control one can exert over the lives of others. When I speak of power relations, I speak of the latter sense of power—a sense coincident with relations of dominance and subordination.

Identifying the Pornographic

Before pursuing the question of pornography, it will be useful to cite some instances of what I and other feminists call pornographic:

An article in *Oui* magazine (published by *Playboy*) entitled "Jane Birkin in Bondage," in which Jane "explains the solution to all disciplinary problems." It is illustrated with several photos of Jane Birkin handcuffed, gagged, whipped, and beaten.

A magazine entitled *Brutal Trio,* in which three men successively kidnap a woman, a 12-year old girl, and a grandmother, and beat them senseless, kicking them in the face and body. After they have passed out, they are raped and beaten again.

A *Hustler* magazine item called "About Face" in which a man sticks a gun into a woman's mouth and forces her to suck it. A variation of this theme is seen in a magazine called *Dynamite,* available for fifty cents. One month this magazine featured a cover story called "Women Under the Gun," in which a gun is shown pointed at a woman's head on the cover of the magazine and at her breasts, vagina, and buttocks in three separate pictures in the centerfold.[1]

A photograph of a woman with hands bound as if in crucifixion, her body naked and bruised, her face turned to the side in agony, and her nipple squeezed and pulled by a wrench. The caption below is "Snuff lib—The incredible and mysterious saga of a film none of us will ever see. By Cheri's resident master of gore."

An article entitled "Good Sex with Retarded Girls," categorized as "non-fiction" in a *Slam* magazine that was being sold at a supermarket counter. The article begins "retarded girls say 'gumf' a lot, but they also like to fuck a lot. They take off their clothes and diddle with themselves all the time. If they can get someone to do their diddling for them, they laugh and jump merrily around." The text continues to talk about how easy it is to rape a retarded girl because "who would people believe—a squash-faced girl or you." And it continues to talk about how, if you play your cards right, you can not only get the girl to be your sexual slave, but to perform all sorts of duties for you.

The cover of *Hustler* magazine, June 1978, which carries a quotation from the magazine's owner, Larry Flynt: "We will no longer hang women up like pieces of meat," and features a glossy cover photo of the naked torso of a woman being fed into a meat grinder. Her upper half has already been transformed into chopped meat, while her legs and buttocks (no genitalia) await processing. An imitation of a U.S. meat grade stamp on her body says, "Last all-meat issue / Prime / Grade 'A' pink."

A young blond woman in a magazine called *The Bondage Parade* is portrayed in an innocent pink floral dress, with her legs, arms, and body bound with large, thick, and multiple white ropes; her feet, hand, and eyes are taped with shiny blue tape; her face is in a face harness and she has a red ball gag in her mouth. She is seated and bound to the stool in an extraordinary awkward position with the top of her head forced upward by another rope. The text inside reads:

> Leslie answered the ad: WANTED: attractive 18–21 year old with exotic tastes for high paying job as model. She was offered $1500.00 for three day's work—more money than she had ever seen. The conditions of her job? To first be fitted with a new experimental sexual stimulator front and back, then to be dressed in a comfortable stylish dress and pantyhose and then to be expertly bound, gagged and blindfolded in an excruciatingly uncomfortable posture and photographed for posterity in all her excited splendor. Of course, Leslie never had a more gratifying working experience.

These examples suffice to illustrate that pornography, while often involving the depiction or display of exposed genitalia and explicit sexual behavior, has neither as a necessary condition. Nor does sexual explicitness in exposure or behavior constitute a sufficient condition for material to be pornographic. The infamous *Hustler* cover, the photographs of clothed women bound and gagged, an album cover with a woman's buttocks stamped "prime meat" on a record album entitled "Choice Cuts," all show neither explicit genitalia nor explicit sexual acts yet are more clearly pornographic than the photographs of nude prostitutes taken by the photographer Belloque. And this, notably, in spite of the etymology of the word "pornography," which is a "depiction of prostitutes."

EROTIC VERSUS PORNOGRAPHIC

Do the artistic merits of Belloque's photographs make them immune from the charge of pornography? I do not believe so. The proper distinction is not between erotic *art* and pornography, but between what is erotic and what is pornographic. Jean's Genet's *Thief's Journal* is pornographic, at least in part, although it is nonetheless a work of art. Susan Sontag, in a provocative article, "The Pornographic Imagination,"[2] argues for the recognition of the artistic merits of such clearly pornographic works as *The Story of O*. In a work by photographer Helmut Newton, a very attractive blond woman, garbed in shiny black pants and vest with a leather-studded bracelet, is attempting to close a partially opened though still chain-latched door, behind which a sinister-looking man is attempting to force his way in. The photograph subtly, but very insistently, suggests the intrusion of a rapist and depicts the scene as a thrilling moment of high fashion. Artistically, the work is far from crude. Its content and intent, though not *explicitly* sexual, are pornographic.

Abstracting from these examples, we may provide a *provisional characterization* of pornography:

> *Pornography deals in the representation of violence, degradation, or humiliation of some persons (most frequently female) for the sexual gratification of other persons (almost exclusively male).*

This is not a *definition* of pornography, for a definition will, of necessity, be not specific as to the descriptive content of pornography. To see why, we need to consider Joel Feinberg's analysis of the term "obscene."

Under the Moral Penal Code, obscenity is defined as the "shameful or morbid interest in nudity, sex, or excretion."[3] But Feinberg argues that the Penal Code is ultimately useless in determining what is obscene, because the term "obscene" is not purely descriptive. We cannot simply pick out or somehow find the elements of what constitutes obscenity in the work or behavior which we so designate. Borrowing a notion from P. H. Nowell-Smith, Feinberg calls "obscene" an "aptness" word, that is, a word that "indicates that an object has certain properties which are apt to arouse a certain emotion or range of emotions."[4] In using an aptness word, we generally mean to say that when the given word is applied to some particular entity, it predicts of others, expresses of ourselves (unless we explicitly disavow it), and endorses as correct and appropriate certain reactions to our seeing or experiencing that to which the word is applied. In the case of obscenity, we find the obscene thing to be "disgusting," "shocking," "revolting."

I would like to claim that "pornographic" is also an aptness term, as is the term "erotic," which I want to contrast with pornographic. When we claim a work to be "erotic," we mean to express, predict, and endorse as appropriate a response of what I will call "sexual interest", that is, sexual arousal or satisfaction. To call a work erotic is to focus, specifically, on the following condition:

That we regard it as being apt to evoke what we think to be the appropriate response of sexual interest which is more sensuous and voluptuous than lewd or prurient.

When we say that something is pornographic, we are also saying that it is apt to arouse certain feelings in us. Here, however, it is less clear what those feelings might be and what we might endorse as an appropriate response. In the case of pornography, I think that we have in mind something like the following:

That we regard the work as having certain characteristics which are apt to arouse an intended (the intention being on the part of those responsible for the work) response of sexual interest which we now qualify not as sensuous but as lewd and licentious.

That which is licentious is that which is lawless—is taken to be illegitimate. Every society, from the most austere to the most free, makes some distinction between a legitimate and an illegitimate sexuality. What we call erotic as opposed to pornographic, sensuous as opposed to lewd, is expressive of this distinction (though it may not be coincident with what the prevailing ideology holds to be legitimate), a distinction one may regard as part of the "sex/gender system" inherent in a given society at a given historical moment.[5]

LEGITIMATE VERSUS ILLEGITIMATE SEXUALITY

Where the lines between the erotic and the pornographic are legally or morally or aesthetically drawn varies from culture to culture. This is perhaps because almost anything can trigger sexual desire, providing only that it has been *eroticized* at some time in a person's history (and each person's individual history is both reflective of and a part of a culture). The breaking of taboos, of constraints, can in itself be eroticized, but the constraints serve to restrain the voraciousness of our impulse to eroticize.

In the breaking of taboos, sexual taboos which are sometimes in the service of other forms of political or economic oppression, pornography has at times been hailed as progressive. Indeed, what is sanctioned as legitimate sexual behavior, and by extension legitimate sexual interest, is often more a matter of cultural mores (sometimes politically motivated), and as such the illegitimacy is merely contingent. But in other cases, I will argue, the sexuality is illegitimate in an intrinsic sense and is a moral matter, and as such it is necessarily illegitimate. What follows, then, is not that in order to be progressive and value human liberation, we must endorse pornography. Rather, when a work is judged pornographic, we must ask why and to whom the represented sexuality is considered illegitimate, that is, whether to regard it as contingently or necessarily pornographic.

We may agree to call some things pornographic only in a contingent, i.e., a qualified sense, meaning that we recognize that the work in question may depict sexuality that many, but not we ourselves, consider illegitimate—thus predicting a certain response on the part of the many. For example, completely explicit sexual intercourse, in which neither person is degraded, but which is not particularly artfully veiled, may be an image one could argue is only contingently "pornographic."

Indeed, on some views of what constitutes a legitimate sexuality no distinction can be drawn between the erotic and the pornographic. In all depictions of sexuality there is a voyeuristic element, so that what is regarded as "legitimate" when hidden may be viewed as illegitimate when made public, since privacy in the sexual experience is often part of what lends legitimacy to the act. Those who regard any public display of sexuality as illicit can hardly make the sort of distinction I am trying to make between what is erotic and what is pornographic.[6]

Regardless of how we draw the line between a legitimate and illegitimate sexuality, it appears that there are nonsexual grounds, purely moral considerations which apply to human actions and intentions, that render some sexual acts illegitimate—illegitimate by virtue of the moral impermissability of harming another person and particularly for the purpose of obtaining pleasure or other benefit from the harm another incurs. Such a moral injunction is but a particular statement of the Kantian imperative not to treat persons as means only. Therefore, I maintain that sexual activity involving the violation of such moral imperatives is *necessarily* illegitimate. And because what I have termed "sexual interest" is itself sexual activity, sexual interest in necessarily illegitimate sexual activity is also necessarily illegitimate sexuality. I leave aside the issue of whether it ought to be the only form of sexuality we consider illegitimate. I am concerned here only to indicate that a *prima facie* case can be made for the view that, regardless of the general relativity of the distinction between legitimate and illegitimate sexuality, at least some sexual activity has a claim to be considered universally and necessarily illegitimate—an illegitimacy that derives not from any particular sex/gender system, but from a universal moral imperative.[7]

For the remainder of this essay, I will leave aside questions of contingent illegitimacy. When I use the phrase "illegitimate sexuality" I will mean sexuality that is illegitimate in the necessary sense, and when I speak of the pornography that relies (in the manner I specify below) on the necessarily illegitimate sexuality, I will be referring to pornography that is necessarily and not contingently (i.e., only relatively) pornographic.

In the case of pornography, illegitimate sexuality is generally represented rather than actually carried out, as in a literary rendering or drawing of an imagined scene, a faked photograph, or acting on film or in theatre. We can imagine depictions of illegitimate sexuality that are not apt to evoke sexual interest, or at least, are not intended for this purpose—for example, news coverage, particularly by a feminist press, of sexual abuse, or films (including scenes of sexual violence) that attempt to explore and understand the feelings and attitudes underlying such violence. The same material might be exploited in the name of news coverage, let us say, for its titillating effects on the same callous sensibility that is sexually aroused by the pornographic depictions described earlier. One might further argue that there is a significant difference between the depiction of actually occurring illegitimate sexuality and fictionalized accounts; that in most pornography the audience is presumed to believe that what is portrayed is fictional: that there is no actual injury to the portrayed "victim"—that this is not "for real." I will later argue that there is something morally repugnant in the desire to derive sexual gratification from the actual injury done to another, from the representation of such behavior, and even from imagined injury and fictionalized accounts of harm done to another.

A pornographic depiction might then be a depiction of illegitimate sexual behavior, such as a rape, where characteristics of the depiction endorse the illegitimacy and the viewers' sexual interest in the scene as an appropriate response. A pornographic depiction may also be one where the subject of the depiction is not itself illegitimate sexuality, but where the characteristics of the depiction endorse a certain response on the part of the audience, that is, the sort of sexual interest we would say is itself illegitimate. For example, when a photographic model is posed for an audience of strangers who would be apt to view her posture as humiliating or degrading, and is so presented that an aroused sexual interest by virtue of the degrading posture of the subject is endorsed, then the depiction is pornographic. We are now ready to provide a definition of pornography:

> *Pornography is a depiction or enactment which has characteristics apt to arouse sexual interest because of the actual or intimated sexual illegitimacy of what is portrayed, and endorsing as an appropriate response the arousal of sexual interest by virtue of the illegitimacy of its sexuality. It may, either instead of or in addition to such intended effects, also arouse feelings of disgust and revulsion, i.e., feelings appropriate to obscenity as defined above.*

The above definition is meant to incorporate much of what is often called "hard-core" pornography, but also some of what is generally labeled "soft-core," and it is meant to capture the relation between what is obscene and what is pornographic. I believe that the definition is consonant with what Rosemary Tong has called "thanatic" as opposed to "erotic" pornography, in an attempt to tie the former to the idea of death as opposed to love. Thanatica, writes Tong,

> represent sexual exchanges devoid or nearly devoid of mutal or self-respect; they display sexual exchanges which are degrading in the sense and to the degree that the desires and experiences of at least one participant are not regarded by the other participant(s) as having a validity and a subjective importance equal to his/her/their own[8]

My formulation may be still stronger in that I explicitly tie the depictions to a sexual activity that is to be censured as morally impermissible, on nonsexual grounds, although it casts the net wider in that it encompasses depictions that are not necessarily depictions of sexual exchanges as such. I will, however, adopt the term "thanatic" pornography for the phenomena with which I am here concerned.

The recent attack on pornography by feminists is, I assume, a response to whatever may be included under the term as I have specified it above, when what is illegitimate is necessarily and not contingently so. This may mean that neither everything nor only those things normally (contingently) called pornographic are under scrutiny. Although I am concerned only with pornography as so characterized, when the possibility of ambiguity might arise, I will speak of thanatica or thanatic pornography to clarify the issue. In what follows I will be concerned with all thanatic pornography, but I will speak particularly of violent pornography. This is not because I believe that the less-violent images are not harmful, but because I find the violent images the most frighteningly problematic. These images speak most clearly and loudly to the misogyny of patriarchal cultures, and illuminate the extent to which sexuality, which ought to be a self-affirming power, is distorted into a destructive force within misogynist cultures. They force us to raise questions about our conceptions and experience of sexuality within a context of sexual domination. For how can we understand that even the more extremely thanatic pornography can arouse a pleasurable response in sufficient numbers of persons (men) to make such materials profitable? How is it that within our society, men can derive a sexual charge out of seeing a woman brutalized, a sight which ought to evoke a response of pity or revulsion, not sexual titillation?

A NOTE ON SADO-MASOCHISTIC SEXUALITY

My claim that sexual activity in which one person is harmed for the sake of another's pleasure or benefit is illegitimate sexuality would appear inevitably to make sado-masochist sex, even between mutually consenting parties, appear to be illegitimate. Nevertheless, the question of the legitimacy or illegitimacy of sado-masochistic sex centers around the question of what constitutes *harm,* where "harm" is to be distinguished from "hurt." It is conceivable that partners in mutually desired sado-masochistic sex (not just mutually consented to—one partner may consent to sado-masochistic sex only because one fears the consequences of not pleasing one's partner) may hurt one another by engaging in physically painful or psychologically humiliating behavior, without causing harm to one another. The "masochist" might claim that physical pain can, at times, heighten the intensity of sexual pleasure. Similarly, the sadistic role may conceivably be undertaken out of a genuine concern and even love for a partner who desires the masochistic behavior. The "sadist" may receive pleasure not from the other's pain per se, but from the satisfaction the other receives through one's own actions. Moreover, one can claim that, given the inhibiting socializing factors in our society, certain role-playing can release inhibitions to sexual pleasure, allowing us to explore psychic and physiological potential for increased sexual satisfaction in relatively safe circumstances.

Nevertheless, persons might desire to be humiliated or physically pained in a sexual role-playing or fantasizing because they really believe themselves unworthy of love and can attain sexual release only when they can fantasize that they are being punished. For some persons, at least, this masochistic role may serve to reinforce their lack of self-respect and self-esteem through their sexually demeaning behavior. In these cases we can claim that the person who willingly engages in masochistic sex is nonetheless harmed by it. Similarly, at least some persons may undertake the sadistic role because they receive pleasure from the thought that they are really harming another, psychologically or physically. For these persons the partner's humiliation and suffering whets the sexual appetite. The apparent willingness of the partner to suffer the abuse is not regarded as an indication of the anticipated pleasure of the partner, but rather as an indication to the sadist of that domination over the masochistic partner which heightens his satisfaction. If we take genuine sadism to include the intent to harm as well as the intent to hurt, then the latter is a genuine sadism which is harmful, at least in intent, to the masochistic partner, even when the partner is a willing one. As such it is morally objectionable and should be considered illegitimate sexuality.

Beyond this, we should note that mutually desired "sado-masochistic" acts are generally highly "represented actions," that is to say, they are actions that are given meaning by having them, in fact, be representations of some sort—e.g., punishment for some imagined evil. However one may judge the moral fiber of the individual who receives sexual gratification from being degraded in such theatrical role-playing, one may not immediately conclude that the person's moral character is the same as that of the person who accepts the degradation in their life generally, when it is "for real" and not a role-playing. The character of our sexual life, the sorts of ways in which things become eroticized for us, and the ways in which we carry such feelings into the rest of our life are sufficiently complex and obscure to force us to be cautious in our moral judgments.

Much pornography presumably depicts sado-masochistic scenes; but such depictions are representations of representations, so the meaning of the act in the pornographic representation does not necessarily have the same meaning as the act might have for two mutually consenting and desiring adults. That is, the viewers of the pornographic depiction see only a scene in which one person is gaining mastery over another through the latter's physical or psychological mortification. Unless the representation is quite subtle, we will fail to see the meaning each participant attaches to the actions. If our previous discussion is at all accurate, it may be the case that the mastery actually lies with the one who is the "maso-chist" rather than with the "sadist." Given the crudity of most pornography, sado-masochist scenes generally show pain and cru-elty mixed with sexual acts and give little evidence of the concern and caring that might mitigate the harm one normally associates with the hurt. Thus, it seems most always to depict an illegitimate sexuality.

Pornography as Hate Literature

PORNOGRAPHY AND MISOGYNY

It may be argued that the pornography I have identified reflects only the bizarre tastes of the perverse few. Pornography, as more gener-ally defined, is a big business, grossing 4 billion dollars a year, according to the California Department of Justice.[9] But how much of this is thanatica? Increasingly, pornographic images depict the torture, mutilation, and even murder of women. A longitudinal study between 1973 and 1977 of *Playboy* and *Penthouse,* the two best sellers among best-selling "erotica magazines," involved a "content analysis of sexual violence," meant to determine whether there was any significant increase in violent and exploitative sexual content.[10] Content was considered sexually violent if the stimulus portrayed sado-masochism, rape, or hostile or exploitative sexual relations. The analysts were instructed to consider the material not sexually violent if the stimulus was ambiguous. An increase in the violent content of the pictorial material was clearly evident, al-though the trends in cartoon material were less clear. By 1977 about 10 percent of cartoons and 5 percent of the pictorial content was sexually violent, by a relatively conservative estimate. When we consider that the combined circulation of the two magazines is approximately 9.6 million[11] and that these are, by industry stan-dards, "soft-core," we can presume that there is a considerable proliferation and consumption of sexually violent material already available. Countries such as Denmark, where pornography has been legalized for some time, indicate a trend of increasingly violent pornography.[12]

Of course, we know from the content of television and film, that portrayals of violence and abusive behavior can be very profitable. The violence in pornography is distinctive in two ways: first, the victims are almost always women and, second, the abuse is seen as a means to sexual gratification. Unlike cowboy westerns, "fair fights" rarely occur in pornography—the violence is directed almost exclu-sively at hapless, though often presumably deserving, victims. Violence is rarely pandered as raw violence, as the portrayal of violence for the entertainment value of seeing other sentient beings brutalized. The brutality is usually given some acceptable frame: a moral tale, an apocalyptic vision, a competition in sports, occasionally "art."

In all fairness to the run-of-the-mill misogynist, raw violence against women is most likely less marketable than violence made sexual. When the aggression is sexualized, the anger, hostility, and fear that motivate the brutality is masked as a pleasure for the woman-victim as well as for the man-perpetrator or consumer of the images. Let us recall the text accompanying the bondage pictures of "Leslie" bound in "an excruciatingly uncomfortable posture . . . in all her excited splendor [who] never had a more gratifying working experience." Whatever the violence and degradation, it is perpetrated with the rationale of giving the victim sexual pleasure. This serves as a rationale to excuse the normally inexcusable and to allow the man to hide from others and perhaps from himself the destructive feelings to which he is giving vent. In addition, we can speculate, on the basis of studies suggesting men's fear of intimacy,[13] that the very situation that is sexual and hence intimate gives rise to a violence that is a defensive reaction to the fear of the intimacy of sexuality. Rather than the violence being made more palatable, as it is in the service of sexual pleasure (that of the male consumer and, presumably and libelously, of the female victim), curiously the intimacy of the sexual situation is made more palatable *by virtue* of the violent lacing.

It may be remarked that, except where violence is indiscriminately meted out to persons of both sexes, most portrayals of violence against women, whether or not the intent is overtly pornographic, are tinged with sexuality. For in our cultural setting, women are defined primarily in terms of their sexuality. Jean-Jacques Rousseau voiced this attitude when he said that a man is a male only some of the time, while a woman is a female always.[14]

But the images from pornography not only depict violence against women that has sexual overtones; they also involve an advocacy of the acts they portray. The advocacy takes the form of a suggestion or an explicit statement or portrayal of sexual pleasure, which results from the activity described, pictured, or enacted. It is this advocacy, implicit or explicit, that makes pornography a form of hate literature.

PORNOGRAPHY AS HATE LITERATURE

In defamatory material we see the oppressed group portrayed in humiliating or demeaning ways. Violence directed against the victims is seen as justified by their own presumed weakness, evil, or vileness. The humiliating portrayals are sometimes masked as scientific or sociological fact and sometimes as the exercise of good fun on the part of the propagators of the hate literature. The violence, shown as justifiable and satisfying, is thereby implicitly advocated—sometimes the advocacy is forthright. In racist hate literature, the hate and the consequent abuse are justified on the basis of racial characteristics. Pornography justifies the abuse of women on the basis of their sexual characteristics.

But in pornography the pernicious message comes in sheep's clothing. Hedonistic celebration of sexual pleasure should not blind us to what is more than a mere analogy between hate literature and pornography. In pornography one's gender, usually female, is a sufficient condition for one's use and abuse, just as in hate literature a person's race or national identity is a sufficient condition for his/her use and abuse.

The assumption in both cases is that those in the victimized group are simultaneously "inferior" and menacing. The perserve "logic" of the oppressor—the "logic" of the bully—is that because someone is "inferior" power can be exerted with impunity, and if it gives the oppressor pleasure to exert that power, there is no reason not to. Furthermore, since she who is inferior is also seen as menacing, that power not only can, but must be exerted. In pornography, the woman is portrayed alternately or simultaneously as inferior—a mere hunk of meat—and as menacing—the castrating bitch. Women and the victims of hate literature, generally, are groups which are both oppressed and yet viewed as needing to be continually conquered and subdued. Violence and psychological abuse are the means to further conquer and mark that conquest: again in perverse "logic," "Because I have conquered you, I can mark my conquest in your flesh."

To see pornography as defaming women, when thanatic pornography is widespread and growing still, lends considerable justification to the claim that misogyny pervades our patriachical culture. As Simone de Beauvoir writes, "Few myths have been more advantageous to the ruling caste than the myth of women; it justifies all privileges and even authorizes their abuse."[15] In connection with this remark, she quotes the following from Balzac's *Physiology of Marriage:*

> Pay no attention to her murmurs, her cries, her pains; nature has made her for our use and for bearing everything: children, sorrows, blows and pains inflicted by man. Do not accuse yourself of hardness. In all the codes of so-called civilized nations, man has written the laws that ranged woman's destiny under this bloody epigraph: Vae Victus! Woe to the weak![16]

If we add to abusive pornography the high incidence of rape and the persistence of wife-battering, we see the pious and chivalrous banter about the delicate care owed to the "weaker sex" revealed as the hypocritical masking of male hostility and violence. Whether or not we acknowledge it, the fear of that hostility is something that women learn to harbor in our innermost consciousness, a fear from which few of us are ever free. Violence against women is part and parcel of a power hierarchy created by and for men, in spite of noble sentiments that serve to disguise the force of male domination.

Rousseau writes in *The Social Contract* (never suspecting that he might be speaking of the domination of woman by man, which he took to be only natural and right), "The strong are still never sufficiently strong to ensure them continual mastership, unless they find the means of transforming force into right and obedience into duty." In degrading and reducing the dignity of those dominated, the right of the dominant group is fortified by the seeming inferiority of those dominated. But in thus fortifying their "right," the dominant group also reveals the force and threat of force that underlie that "right."

THE HARM OF PORNOGRAPHY CONSIDERED AS HATE LITERATURE

Only the morally blind would not recognize the moral evil of hate literature. To the extent that hate literature has as its aim the advocacy of abusive behavior toward certain groups of people, its moral evil lies in its intent to cause injury to innocent persons. Not only are the ends of hate literature objectionable, but also its means, for the expression of the hatred normally results in false and misleading portrayals of the objects of the hate. Thus, hate literature is usually libelous. To the extent that our concept of some entity influences our behavior toward such an entity, these false and misleading portrayals, if believed, can be supposed eventually to influence behavior directed to the entity in question. In this causal relation between our beliefs and our actions, the intent to harm is seen in defamatory materials.

Unfortunately, the libelous nature of pornography is only too often obscured by the false characterization of female sexuality that is rampant in our culture. For example, a study by Malamuth, Haber, and Feshbach reported that although each female subject recognized that she personally would not enjoy being raped under any circumstances, many female as well as male subjects believed that as much as 25 percent of the female population would derive some pleasure from being the victim of a rape.[17] It is no mystery why the false claims and assumptions made by the hate literature are not recognized as libelous within a society that tolerates such literature, since these falsehoods are often implicit in the ideology of the larger oppressive society, e.g., that female sexuality *naturally* thrives on abuse.

Hate literature may be immoral in still another way. For it is not only characterized by the advocacy of injury to others and the intentional propagation of libelous claims; it also often panders to those who derive pleasure in witnessing the real or fictive abuse of the despised group. Insofar as pornography by definition aims at arousal and pleasure from its depictions, it clearly shares this feature with other hate literature.

While it is immoral to harm and cause another to suffer, it is less clear, but still intuitively correct, that we ought to consider the immorality of such actions aggravated if the perpetrator receives pleasure from the harm he causes and from the suffering he brings about. Moreover, these actions are particularly repugnant if their sole motivation is the enhancement of the pleasure of one party. Indeed, if the one who is harmed is aware that another is deriving pleasure from her/his actual or imagined suffering, she feels additional humiliation and pain. Yet, according to many accounts, pleasure as such is always a good, albeit sometimes a non-moral good, hence pleasure per se cannot be morally reprehensible. While pleasure per se may be morally indifferent, the fact of deriving pleasure in such circumstances may indeed be morally significant. This is, at least in part, because the pleasure derived from the experience of seeing or contemplating or imagining another's victimization involves the exploitative use of the victimized person and her/his pain for one's own interests.

What is morally reprehensible in deriving pleasure from causing another pain or injury over and above the actual injury incurred is, I believe, related to the immorality of *using* another person. And if this is so, then the harm comes about even if we have not been the cause of another's suffering, but only derive enjoyment from that suffering. Moreover, when the pleasure is derived only from a real or fictive portrayal, the moral objection of using another, which includes using their image, is still present.

In other words, the moral objectionability of "using" another applies not only to using an individual and the image of the individual, but also to using an image of an individual, real or fictive, as representative of a class of individuals.

Let us pursue this point further. Consider, as an example, the case of John who befriends Mary, a woman in a politically powerful position who can help him advance in his career. John pretends great friendship toward Mary in the hope that she will take an interest in him and help him attain promotions. Once John has achieved his goals he becomes indifferent to Mary and shows relatively little concern for her fate. John has merely "used" Mary for her potential to help him secure his own ends. A case of "using" another need not be so overt, or may be more overt still. When using occurs not in interpersonal relations but in more public contexts, we often speak of the "exploitation" of persons.

When we say that A "uses" B, where the phrase has moral repercussions, we mean to say, at the very least, that (a) A takes B's interests to be so significantly less important than A's interests that A acts as if the moral worth of B is of less consequence than the moral worth of A; (b) there exists a relation between persons A and B so that for A to pursue A's interests involves B's actual, likely, or eventual forfeiture of interests; and (c) A will pursue these interests regardless of B's interests and desires; and while B might well be willing to forfeit these interests either because of a recompense (money, love, or other benefit) or out of sheer altruistic feeling, B would be unwilling to forfeit these interests were B to believe that, in so doing, A would construe B's behavior to indicate that B was inherently of lesser moral worth than A. (That is to say, in acting altruistically we do not want our benefactors to believe that we act to benefit them rather than ourselves merely because we do not morally value ourselves. Rather, we want our benefactors to see that we have concern for their well-being and that their well-being is of great importance to us.)

While we may allow our own interests to be subservient to another's if the interests of the other are of a more pressing kind than ours (e.g., if A's survival depends on B's diminished comfort), we are less likely to consent to this when we believe that the interests we forfeit are more important than the benefits another gains. In our example, had John been seeking a promotion to take care of pressing financial needs (and had he not sought Mary's friendship on false pretenses), Mary might have been willing to take some risks to secure the position for John, which she would have been unwilling to do if John's promotion simply increased an already comfortable income or was only a matter of ego-building.

Even when a good case can be made for B forfeiting her interests to allow A to benefit, A, prima facie, ought not to disregard the interests of B. A's total disregard for B's interests might be thought to involve A's exploitative use of B, while B's unwillingness to put the more-pressing interests of A before her own less-pressing ones could be thought of as B's egotism. When an exploitative use of another cannot be justified even on the basis of a supervening interest on the part of A, then there is no moral justification whatsoever for the use of B. The more gratuitous is A's benefit and the more costly is B's loss, the more morally reprehensible is the use of B. A's gratuitous pleasures, his *mere enjoyment,* cannot justify his causing B pain, it being a far more pressing interest not to endure pain than to obtain an incidental pleasure. A's gratuitous pleasure also cannot justify someone else causing B pain. That is, C would not be justified in causing B pain because it would give A pleasure to witness B's pain.

To return to defamatory depictions, it is often the case that no one, in fact, causes B pain or any actual injury, but that C portrays a situation where a person *like* B is made to suffer, and C intends thereby to elicit pleasure from A. When A derives pleasure from even the contemplated suffering of B or a B-like person (i.e., a person who is like B in certain salient regards), it is implied that, as far as A (and all those who, like A, derive pleasure from the portrayal) is concerned, the interests and well-being of B and B-like persons are of lesser importance than the gratuitous enjoyment of A. To fail to assign an equal moral worth to all persons is already to fail to recognize the central principle of moral and just interactions between persons.

But if this were to remain a mere thought in A's mind, possibly no greater harm could result than the moral degeneration of A, since A's fantasies are accessible to no one else. If the contemplated suffering of B were made accessible to B, while B might not suffer hurt he could be harmed from the humiliation of seeing that another viewed his moral status as significantly beneath that of the other. Even if B does not learn that his contemplated suffering gives pleasure to others, but others than A do, while B may not be hurt, he will still be harmed inasmuch as others share the pleasure and thereby implicitly concur with his diminished moral standing. Not only is B harmed in this way, but society as a whole is harmed in its moral fiber when the moral status of all its members is not considered of equal worth by all the members of society.

Deriving such pleasure or seeking benefits from the suffering of another may have more direct consequences in that such pleasure may become the basis for a vested interest in perpetuating the unjust state of affairs responsible for the suffering. In addition, it may serve to brutalize those who so profit. It is a brutalization which causes a breakdown in our moral imagination, the source of that imaginative possibility by which we can identify with others and hence form maxims having a universal validity.

Recent studies on the effects of viewing violence and violent pornography offer suggestive confirming evidence that the very pleasure gained from watching the abusive behavior facilitates, under the right combination of circumstances, a change in attitude toward the behavior and affects self-predictions of engagement in such behavior. In other studies conducted by Malamuth, Haber, and Feschback pertaining to rape,[18] those who were aroused by viewing violent pornography reported that they would not rule out the possibility that they would engage in sexual assault if they could not be caught, and they also exhibited the attitudes often held by convicted rapists toward rape and rape victims. This is not to imply that all or even any of those who made such self-reports will ever become rapists, but only that the pleasure derived from viewing sexual violence *may* modify attitudes and *possibly* alter inhibitions regarding the actual carrying out of violent behavior. If hate literature is indeed successful in its advocacy, then it is not only morally reprehensible in and of itself, but it is also the source of further harm and injury and so is morally reprehensible for the harm to which it is casually related.

PORNOGRAPHY AND THE LAW

I have argued that thanatic pornography is hate literature and have given some arguments concerning the moral sanctions appropriate to hate literature. As hate literature reflects, promulgates, and endorses the morally repugnant attitudes of those who produce, believe, and enjoy it, it is harmful and inimicable to a just society. As such, one might well argue that such materials ought to be legally sanctioned, and look for the appropriate legal grounds on which to censure them. Because of the stringent requirements for censorship established by the First Amendment, such legal grounds are difficult to establish without at once jeopardizing the protections enjoined by the First Amendment. Whether we are dealing with hate literature of the usual sort or with pornography, the central question is whether the material under consideration is "protected speech." Speech is not protected under the Constitution if it is obscene or if it constitutes "a clear and present danger" to others. Nor are libel and slander protected speech.

Arguments for the censorship of pornography have traditionally been based on the alleged obscenity of such materials. In the past, questions of obscenity have been closely tied to traditional Judeo-Christian conceptions of sexual morality, in which illegitimacy in sexuality is based on grounds quite different from the grounds for illegitimacy I have sketched above. In my definition of pornography I indicate that while the pornographic and the obscene do, at times, have the same referents, not everything that is pornographic is obscene. Therefore, the fact that obscenity is not protected speech will not help in determining possible legal sanctions against pornography. Nor should it. We can recognize in the dual consideration of pornography as an aptness term, and in the relativity of the distinction between a legitimate and an illegitimate sexuality, the danger that what is merely contingently pornographic will be censored by those empowered to do so, while at least some material that we have called necessarily pornographic, or thanatic, will escape censure. The intent in delineating thanatic pornography has been to show that it is indeed possible, as Tong contends, to provide a definition of pornography that delimits only the material that is harmful in the sense that it impedes the creation of a just society, and to ensure that any efforts to banish this material do not at the same time endanger sexual material not thanatic but proscribed by our traditional sexual mores, such as literature favorable to homosexuality. Nonetheless, the distinctions are, at times, sufficiently subtle that one must exercise great caution before advocating censorship based on the premise that the individual judges, the legislative bodies, and the enforcement personnnel are able and willing to make the necessary distinctions.

One could also argue that while obscenity has traditionally been tied to a Judeo-Christian sexual morality, one could similarly distinguish a contingent from a necessary sense in which material was obscene. In the case of obscenity one might argue that when an object is apt to evoke a response of "disgusting, revolting, etc.," it is only contingently obscene when that response is based on cultural mores, prejudices, etc., but it is necessarily obscene when it is based on a universal conception of what is morally impermissable. Such an argument would have to be spelled out, but if it had validity then one could say that what is necessarily pornographic is necessarily obscene and vice versa. Therefore, one ought to apply obscenity laws to pornography, given that one argues for the proper construal of obscenity. Such an argument seems very hypothetical, given the tenor of legal debates and the current definition of obscenity in the Moral Penal Code.

In recent years feminists have been more likely to argue that pornography ought not to be protected under the First Amendment because it constitutes a "clear and present danger." Rosemary Tong has distinguished three stances feminists have taken in arguing the harmfulness of thanatic pornography:

> (1) Although such thanatic material may not be harmful per se, it causes people to engage in harmful behavior; (2) Thanatic material does not have to be harmful in order to be constitutionally censorable; and (3) Thanatic material is harmful.[19]

She claims, correctly I believe, that the third is the strongest argument, that the first is the weakest, and that the second might be useful in making pornographic material less visible. Let us briefly review some of these arguments.

While some suggestive data links violent pornography to a disposition to behave with hostility and aggression toward women, the legal requirements for censoring such material are far too stringent to make such generalized data useful in meeting the criteria for the "clear and present danger" test. Wendy Kaminer, an attorney and a member of Women against Pornography, writes that were one to adopt a clear-and-present-danger standard to prohibit pornography, one would need to "demonstrate in every case, with direct factual evidence" that a particular case of pornography presented such a " 'clear and present danger,' and it is unlikely that a link can be proven in individual cases, that is, between a given viewing of such material and a particular act." She writes:

> This does not mean that the speech at issue might be or could be dangerous, and it does not refer to the cumulative effect of a certain kind of speech. It means a tangible, immediate and individualized danger that can only be avoided by suppressing publication.
> Sociological studies and expert testimony pointing to a connection between pornography generally and violence against women would not establish a clear and present danger in an individual case, as a matter of law. . . . Use of this sort of generalized evidence to demonstrate that a given instance of speech is dangerous would be like trying a defendant in a criminal case with evidence of "similar" crimes committed by "similar" people.[20]

James Q. Wilson, professor of government at Harvard, after reviewing psychological and sociological experiments meant to establish a link between the viewing of violence and violent pornography and violent behavior, expresses his doubts that such evidence would ever be successful in establishing a clear-cut causal relation, at least one strong enough to satisfy the "clear and present danger" criterion.[21] While he would like to see legal sanctions against pornography, he writes; "The irony is that social science may be weakest in detecting the broadest and most fundamental changes in social values, precisely because they are broad and fundamental."

In the following passage, Wilson articulates the view of the second argument, that even if thanatic material is not harmful, there ought to be a public commitment, presumably in the form of some sort of legal sanction, to eliminate it. Wilson continues:

> Perhaps I should be worried that I cannot prove my belief that human character is, in the long run, affected not by occasional furtive

experiences but by whether society does or does not state that there is an important difference between the loathsome and the decent. I would, for example, want my government to say that race is not to be used as a basis for granting or denying access to public facilities even if social science could not show that such racial restrictions harm individual Negroes—indeed, even if social science could show that such restrictions benefit (what one might wonder, is the measure of benefit in this case) Negroes. A public commitment to equal opportunity and public opposition to disgusting racial distinctions should be made as a matter of right and propriety, whatever the immediate effects: I would also imagine that, over the long term, such public commitments would play a part in shaping individual attitudes in what I take to be a desirable direction.

Another direction this argument takes follows that argued by Feinberg regarding the legitimacy of prohibiting "harmless" offences. That is to say, even if thanatic pornography is not harmful per se, it is offensive to most women and, one hopes, to most men; and to the extent that it is publically flaunted and thus difficult to avoid by reasonable means, it should be actionable. The view here is that I should not be subjected to material that I find extremely offensive, presuming that most others find it so as well, and that it should not be necessary for me to greatly inconvenience myself in order to avoid such offensive material.

Legal action, in such cases, would essentially involve getting thanatic pornography "back in the closet." This may be valuable in that it would be less accessible to minors, it would not subject women to the barrage of offence the public proliferation of this material entails, and it would indicate some public commitment to the undesirability of the behaviors endorsed by the pornography. Yet banning the public display of these materials would still have to be weighed against the dangers of the public expression of political views. The more one argues that pornography is a political issue, the more one weakens the argument against the public display of pornographic materials, for if one argues that one set of political views is a public offense and therefore ought to be curtailed, then the same argument may be used against political views espoused by feminists. It is a road feminists must tread with great caution.

In arguing that pornography is a form of defamation and arguing the immorality of such materials, I am also arguing for the view that hate material and thanatic pornography are harmful per se. Do these arguments provide a ground for a legal sanction against pornography? In arguing that pornography is hate literature, can we use whatever sanctions exist against defamation to apply to pornography? Legal sanctions against defamatory materials do not, unfortunately, provide us with clear models we can adopt for the case of pornography. The difficulty centers on the issue of "group libel" as a viable legal concept. As Tong points out, quoting Zechariah Chafee, the concept of "group libel" has proved embarassing for legal theorists because of its close association with the sedition laws of English common law, laws which made it illegal to make statements construed as hostile or injurious to the state or as intending to "promote feelings of ill will and hostility between different classes."[22] Recall that the First Amendment was framed against the background of the English common law. Tong writes (on pages 10-11), "legal theorists are not likely to turn to the criminal law to forge a group-libel doctrine. . . . Consequently, the only salvation for the notion of group libel would seem to be the civil law."

As long as the libel is distributive over all the members of the class who are libeled, that is, as long as the defamatory remarks claim that a certain fact or characteristic holds for all members of the libeled class, any particular woman can engage in a civil suit claiming a defamation of her character due to libelous claims.

This may indeed sound promising, but I fear that this course of action may promise more than it can deliver. For a statement to be libelous it must be a statement of fact that can be proven to be false. The libelous content of much pornography does not easily lend itself to such proof, particularly when much of it (a) is so widely assumed to be true and (b) is also believed to be the sort of thing that a woman will not easily admit to it. Take, for example, the implicit or explicit claim that women want to be raped as a characteristic but libelous claim found in much pornography. Within our culture, men and women alike think that a woman saying "no" does not justify a belief that she means "no," and girls are still taught that they ought not to be open and honest about their sexual feelings. Under such social conditions, a defendant can argue that regardless of what any individual woman claims, any presumably seductive behavior warrants the conclusion that she "secretly" desires to be forced to engage in sexual intercourse. Precisely these sorts of presuppositions make it difficult to prosecute actual rape cases. Efforts to establish legal resolutions to pornography suffer by virtue of the fact that the legal system itself is embedded within a patriarchical society; even if the abstract system of rules can be made free of patriarchical bias, the implementation of those laws still depends on persons who are largely male and largely insensitive to the oppressive nature of our sexual relations. The woman taking the witness stand in such a suit against libelous pornographic claims would be subject to the sort of mental rape endured by the woman who testifies against her rapist, and the fate of the suit would most likely be as unsuccessful as that of attempts to prosecute rapists.

Nonetheless, certain instances of pornography might be suitable candidates for libel claims. Consider the article entitled "Good Sex with Retarded Girls," which I cited at the beginning of this essay. The article makes statements about retarded girls that would not be difficult to disprove; for example, the putative claims that "retarded girls say 'gumf' a lot, but they also like to fuck a lot. They take off their clothes and diddle with themselves all the time." Furthermore, a retarded girl would not have to take the witness stand and be subjected to the same legal indignities to which another woman, who would take the stand in her own behalf, might be subjected. The guardian of the retarded woman would be the one to speak for claimant.

To what extent could one isolate actionable libelous claims that might feasibly be won in court cases? What would such suits accomplish? Would they make a serious dent in the growing mass of thanatic pornography? The answers to these questions are unclear. What does seem clear is, as Tong concludes, "there is nothing inherently unconstitutional about group-libel doctrine or civil suits aimed at impeding the flow of publically disseminated thanatica." But it is also clear that legal remedies alone cannot *stop* the flow of all and only that pornography we deem thanatic, and that other means, such as education and consciousness-raising, not only are advisable and preferable, they also are necessary.

The Limits of the Erotization of Domination

I spoke earlier of the pleasure that certain persons may derive from hate literature. But the pleasure derived from pornography is particularly sexual. In considering the specificity of its sexual nature, we move from viewing pornography in its causal aspect as hate literature—that is, from a consideration of the ways in which pornography contributes to a male-dominated order—to a consideration of pornography's symptomatic aspect—that is, to the ways in which pornography reflects that order. At the outset of this essay, I stated that pornography reflects through hyperpolic distortion. From this exaggerated image of male-female sexual relations within cultures where men dominate, we can see "writ large" the ways in which our conceptions of sexuality are permeated with conceptions of domination, conceptions that we must alter radically if we hope to realize the goal of sexual equality. Feminists, in attempting to draw our attention to rape as an act of power and aggression against women and to dispel the idea of rape as lust not sufficiently contained, proclaimed that rape is not sex, it is assault. But we know that we cannot assimilate rape to assault—the horror of rape is not exhausted by the fear of physical assault. A residue remains that renders such a reduction a falsification. Similarly, while the characterization of pornography as hate literature directs us to its humiliating and violent nature, here too a residue remains. That residue is the erotic intermingling with the abusive and the violent. To this unholy alliance I now turn our attention.

It seems clear that violence expressed sexually reveals to us the frighteningly destructive possibilities of the same sexuality that is often the source of our most intense pleasure and the binding of loves and friendships. The legitimatization of sexuality in marriage may be seen as the societal harnessing of the binding force of sexual attachments. To see how sexuality is linked with violence, and why this linkage can be exploited in a $4 billion a year industry, we need to examine the relation between eroticism and power.

Most pertinent is the extent to which we have eroticized the relations of power. We have done so in a manner consonant with the dominant power relations between men and women, so that women generally seek male sexual partners who are their superiors, while men regard as erotic women who are their inferiors. The parameters may be height, age, social status, wealth, education, intellect, physical strength, or whatever other qualities are regarded as salient hierarchical differentiations. Women eroticize being possessed, conquered, overwhelmed, etc. Men have eroticized the conquering, possessing, subduing. Simone de Beauvoir writes: "It is not only a subjective and fleeting pleasure that man seeks in the sexual act. He wishes to conquer, to take, to possess; he penetrates into her as a plowshare penetrates into the furrow; . . . and these images are as old as writing."[23] And we have all, male and female, learned the lesson that to heighten eroticism, we often need only to increase the resistence of the prey to the conqueror. Indeed, we can reason that if the relation of power is erotic, then the increase of power, either through an increase in polarity between the relata or through a heightened resistence on the part of the one to be conquered, will increase the erotic potential of the relationship.

To be in a position of dependency is to be in a position in which another can exert power over you. That power may involve the potential exercise of physical force or psychological coercion. The exercise of that power in its extreme forms involves the capacity to inflict pain and injury on another. Physical violence (and in some cases psychological violence) is the exercise of the ultimate power over life and limb. If the direct proportionality of power and eroticism was not in any way bounded, then we should expect to find a great deal of violence in our sexual relations. And perhaps there *is* more than we care to admit. There are, however, good reasons to suppose that, in real life experiences, the increase in the polarity of power has limits to its erotic potential.

C. A. Tripp argues that men must engage in delicately balanced interactions with women. On the one hand, a woman's oversubmissiveness is a turn-off "lest it bleed him dry." On the other hand, if a woman is too resistant, she offends his status and his ego.[24] From the woman's point of view, the woman "is not supposed to look for the inert qualities of an object in him, but for strength and virile power . . . she longs for a strong embrace that will make of her a quivering thing, but roughness and force are also disagreeable deterents that offend her."[25] An excess in polarity of either sort, it seems, can kill eroticism.

Furthermore, when we consider power in its physically or psychologically violent expressions, i.e., physical force or crude humiliation, additional factors dampen the eroticism of extreme power. We must recognize that power has many subtler and more attractive forms. The more-violent extremes of power are generally exercised when other forms of control are ineffectual or unavailable. Paradoxically, brutality is an extreme of power often exercised by those who feel themselves or who actually are otherwise powerless. And the force of the brutality is fed as well by the anger and the frustration of that sense of powerlessness. It seems reasonable to expect that to the extent that he who relishes his superior position has access to other forms of domination and is secure in his dominance, his exercise of power will assume less-violent forms.

A preference for the subtler forms of domination is buttressed by what are, we can speculate, certain internalized censors that limit the extent to which both women and men can experience as erotic the extreme power *cum* violence. For men, there is a moral censor that it is wrong to inflict pain and injury on another person; for women, there is the actual pain and fear of injury of the abusive behavior.[26] Thus, while relatively few men and women might engage in physically violent or extremely degrading behavior in their sexual interactions, many more can enjoy it vicariously through its representation in pornography where the censors can be stilled.

In fantasy and in fictional representations we engage in a sort of suspension of moral belief so that we can sympathize where in a comparable real life situation we might be outraged. This is particularly the case when the offending acts are convincingly depicted as not having the expected harmful consequences. In the case of pornography, the victim of the sexual brutality is portrayed as experiencing pleasure, or as afterwards thanking her tormentor. Feschbach and Malamuth report:

Reading about a rape generally inhibited the sexual reponses of both men and women. But the responses depended quite a bit on whether the victim was described as being in pain or whether she finally succumbed to—and enjoyed—the act. . . . For men, however, the fantasy of a woman becoming sexually excited as a result of a sexual assault reversed inhibitions that might have been mobilized by the pain cues and by the coercive nature of the act.[27]

To portray the victim as enjoying her plight, in some sense, is not to portray her as victimized. The censors can then be stilled.

These experiments indicated, however, that for women "high pain cues resulted in low sexual arousal" and were not altered by suggestions that the victim ultimately submitted. This agrees with the fact that not only are men by far the major consumers of pornography, but also with the fact that women seem to enjoy pornography less. This is most often true of women who consider themselves in other regards to be in revolt against prudery. But if the increase in power lends itself to a direct proportional increase in eroticism for men and women alike, why should women not similarly enjoy pornography as the fantastic, uncensored playing out of this relation? I believe that women are generally less responsive to pornography because the facility with which women identify with the victim makes it harder for them to silence their censors.

Moreover, I think that women find it easier to enjoy written than visual pornography. In the case of visual material, I suspect that women can best relate to drawings, less to photographs, and still less to film. Here I venture to surmise that there is an intrusive quality to visual pornography: in photographs the figures, either through their posture or their glance, draw the viewer in, as someone who is more than a voyeur; or they seem to make an appeal to the audience in a way that is similar to intrusive advertising. Film is a medium with a special potential for immediacy: the darkened room, the larger-than-life figures, and the eye of the camera through which we easily become the spectator-participant. The difference in media is (generally, not necessarily) a difference in the amount of distancing required of the viewer. The less-mediated and distanced the material is, the more the woman experiences the threat of pain and humiliation and the stronger are the censors which inhibit erotic response.

Women, however, notoriously fantasize scenes of rape, humiliation, and submission to pain and brutality. That women have such fantasies is a sign of how deeply the "internal colonization" of women has taken hold. Women have, to some measure, adopted the negative self-conceptions that serve the advantage of their oppressors. But conceptions that allow for rape fantasies are still at variance with an acknowledged public morality that condemns rape and sexual violence. In the shadowy world of our fantasizing, the censors, not faced with the fleshy images of the screen, are not aroused, and the proportional relation of domination and sexuality can be played out. It is a freedom with a significant restraint: we are in control of our fantasizing; if the images become more disturbing than erotic, we can stop the internal projector and the internal reel.

Conclusion

As a symptom, as a reflection of the society in which it thrives, pornography displays an extreme in the erotization of domination. It portrays a fantasy world in which the ordinary limitations we bring to such eroticizing are suspended. Can these remarks, then, be seen as justification of pornography as, after all, merely a harmless outlet for repressed sexual desires, with no actual consequences other than some possible self-injury to the pornography consumer as he wallows in his morally unwholesome pleasures? I do not believe so. Here the dialectic between symptom and cause propels us back to a consideration of the consequences of pornography's presence.

There is, I have argued, nothing harmless in the vicarious enjoyment of the representations of this eroticized domination. On the contrary, pornography escalates the dimensions of the problem by making it appear that violence is intrinsically erotic, rather than something that is eroticized. And as I and others have argued, it is libelous, since it portrays women as essentially masochistic, enjoying rape, and as being sexually fulfilled only when sufficiently humiliated and dominated. Beyond this, we must pay attention to the empirical data suggesting that pornography may weaken the censors that inhibit the sexualization of domination from pervading our sexual life in its most extreme forms. Men (particularly those with a low level of aggression anxiety) watching pornography are, at least momentarily, convinced that the brutality they see is not really brutality if it is a means to a felt sexual gratification.

Contrary to the claims of some of its apologists, pornography is not cathartic. Catharsis is a purging of unpleasant, undesirable emotions, particularly the emotions of pity and fear, by first exciting and then allaying them. Both the excitement and allaying of the emotions are accomplished by images accompanied by pain. In pornography the images that would excite and allay the sexual discharge are made to appear pleasurable. When murderous rage is portrayed in an appropriately cathartic work of tragedy, it is seen as leading to the most awful consequences. But sexual desire that must be satisfied by brutalizing a woman is portrayed in pornography as leading to the most ecstatic pleasures. To claim that the overflow of unhealthy sexual desires is "purged" in pornographic consumption is completely unsupported by psychological research into the effects of violence and pornography. Pornography, rather than purging sexual desires of a dangerous sort, exhibits horrid violence, sexually—that is pleasurably—charged, as permissable, as well as possible.

The problem, in the end, is more than pornography. It is the eroticizing of the relation of power. Without this, pornography would simply revolt us all; it would not be stimulating to many. If the erotization of domination is so prevalent, is there perhaps something in the nature of eroticism that calls for the differentia of power relations? Plato spoke of Eros, as of necessity seeking what it lacked. Simone de Beauvoir (p. 498) says, "Eroticism is a movement toward the Other." The creation and maintenance of hierarchical relations between men and women is itself a guarantor of alterity. Yet, any reasonable reflection allows us to see what the defenders of patriarchy obscure by the motto "Vive la difference," namely, that among human beings, equality is not identity. Alterity and its consequent eroticism can be preserved in relations of equality. Indeed, the mutual and reciprocal giving and receiving of sexual pleasure, such that the other's desire and pleasure are constitutive of our own, would seem the very model for the interrelationship between equal persons.[28]

The eroticism of domination, rather than being demanded by the nature of eros, is an instrument for the maintenance of male perogatives. Deirdre English writes, it is "a fantasy that is intended to make male supremacy more palatable to both sexes."[29] And given that what we have eroticized is so deeply embedded in our collective and individual psyches, be we sexist or feminist, pornography serves only to feed and rouse the lion within. It not only reflects, but also contributes to the difficulties women face in their struggle for autonomy: difficulties in their own sexual identity, in establishing equality in intimate relations, and in their safety and freedom of movement as they try to Take Back the Night.

Notes

Various versions of this work have been read at the Stonybrook Colloquium for Women in Philosophy, the Eastern Division of Society for Women in Philosophy, the Society for Philosophy and Public Affairs—New York Chapter, and the Trenton State College Philosophy Colloquium, as well as at the Conference on the Philosophy of Women at Milwaukee. It has greatly benefited from the comments of these audiences. I particularly want to thank Professor S. Baumrin for helpful suggestions on the legal issues as well as for his help in other sections of the essay. I also want to thank E. Casey, P. Grimm, C. Gould, D. Hausman, J. Kittay, L. Miller, and J. Rajchman for their helpful comments.

1. Quoted in the introductory essay, Laura Lederer, ed., *Take Back the Night* (New York: William Morrow & Co., 1980).
2. In Douglas A. Hughes, ed. *Perspectives on Pornography* (New York: St. Martin's Press, 1970). Also in Susan Sontag, *Styles of Radical Will* (New York: Farrar, Strauss and Giroux, 1966).
3. American Law Institute, *Moral Penal Code* §251.4 (1), 1962.
4. Joel Feinberg, "The Idea of the Obscene," The Lindley Lecture given at the University of Kansas, 1979. Feinberg discusses the notion of an aptness word only in regard to "obscene," not in regard to "pornographic" or "erotic."
5. See Gayle Rubin, "The Traffic in Women: Notes on the Political Economy of Sex," pp. 157–210 in Reyna Reiter, ed. *Toward an Anthropology of Women* (New York, Monthly Review Press, 1975), for an explication of the sex/gender system. Rubin does not discuss questions of legitimate versus illegitimate sexuality as such, but I believe that the notion is clearly part of the same complex of ideas that informs her formulation.
6. Nevertheless, there are depictions of nudity or sexual behavior in which the voyeurism is somehow masked, so that the sense that someone is present and viewing the scene depicted is minimal. Just as in the case of narration, the narrator's presence may be more or less felt, so in a depiction of a sexual act the presence of the depictor may be more or less felt. The less presence, the more the privacy of the sexual act is preserved, even in its public presentation.
7. It may be more difficult to justify such a claim on utilitarian grounds or even on the basis of rights. Clearly, if one is abused or injured, there is some sense in which one has had some rights violated, even if the right be as general as the right to personal security and the right to the pursuit of happiness. In cases involving pornography, however, it may be very unclear precisely whose rights have been violated and what those rights are that have been violated. In many cases, a claim that rights have been violated would be less than obvious, and I am not certain that a strong claim could be made out in this manner. A justification on utilitarian grounds is still more problematic. It raises the dilemma faced by utilitarians when a situation is presented in which a number of persons may obtain a great deal of pleasure cumulatively, whereas the harm to a single person is great but not as great as the cumulative pleasure of the benefactors of the victim's injury. To the extent that utility theory can handle the more-general case, it can handle the more-specific case.
8. Rosemarie Tong, "Feminism, Pornography and Censorship," *Social Theory and Practice* 8, no. 1 (Spring 1982): 4.
9. James Cook, "The X-rated Economy," *Forbes,* September 18, 1978.
10. Neil Malamuth and Barry Spinner, "A Longitudinal Content Analysis of Violence in Best-Selling Erotica Magazines," *Journal of Sex Research,* August 1980.
11. Cook, "The X-rated Economy."
12. J. H. Court, "Pornography and Sex-crimes: A Re-evaluation in The Light of Recent Trends Around the World." *International Journal of Criminology and Penology* 5 (1976): 129–57. The sexual violence of which I speak here is found in materials geared to a heterosexual audience. Apparently only 10 percent of all pornography is directed at homosexuals, and that is almost exclusively directed at male homosexuals. There is no significant body of female homosexual pornography. My remarks are confined to heterosexual materials for two reasons. First, some women familiar with male homosexual pornography have thought much of it to be derivative of the male-female patterns, but where a male plays the role of the female. If this is true,

then male homosexual literature does not require a separate analysis. Second, if this is not true, then I, not being a member of the male homosexual community, do not see myself in a position to make pronouncements as to what is erotic and what is pornographic within that community, at least up to a certain point. A homosexual "snuff" film, in which a male is treated as is the women in a heterosexual snuff film, warrants the same moral, if not political, judgement.

13. Susan Pollack and Carol Gilligan, "Images of Violence in Thematic Apperception Test Stories," *Journal of Personality and Social Psychology* 42, no. 1 (1982): 159–67.

14. William Boyd, ed. and trans., *The Emile of Jean-Jacques Rousseau* (New York: Teacher's College Press, 1962), chap. 5.

15. Simone de Beauvoir, *The Second Sex*, trans. by H. M. Parsley (New York: Vintage Books, 1974), pp. 288–89.

16. Quoted in ibid., p. 289, footnote.

17. Neil Malamuth, Scott Haber, and Seymour Feshbach, "Testing Hypotheses Regarding Rape: Exposure to Sexual Violence, Sex Differences and the 'Normality' of Rapists," *Journal of Research in Personality and Social Psychology* 30 (1974), write:

> Subjects (female) believed that over 25% of the female population would derive some pleasure from being victimized. For the female subjects this finding is particularly interesting in light of their very clear assertion that they personally would not under any circumstances derive pleasure from such victimization.

18. Ibid.

19. Tong, "Feminism, Pornography, and Censorship," p. 5.

20. Wendy Kaminer, "Pornography and the First Amendment, Prior Restraint and Prior Action," in Lededer, ed., *Take Back the Night*, p. 246.

21. James Q. Wilson, "Pornography and Social Science," in *Where Do You Draw the Line*, ed. Victor Clive (Brigham Young University Press, 1974), p. 305.

22. In Zechariah Chafee, *Free Speech in the United States* (Cambridge: Harvard University Press), p. 506. Quoted in Tong, p. 11.

23. S. de Beauvoir, *The Second Sex*, p. 171.

24. C. A. Tripp, *The Homosexual Matrix* (New York: Signet Books, 1976), p. 43.

25. S. de Beauvoir, *The Second Sex*, p. 421.

26. Both the censor and the fear exist for both men and women. I am here describing those factors operative in curbing the erotization of the relation of power in the situation where men dominate.

27. Seymour Feschbach and Neil Malamuth, "Sex and Aggression: Proving the Link," *Psychology Today*, November 1978, pp. 16–17.

28. See Virginia Held, "Marx, Sex and the Transformation of Society," *The Philosophical Forum* 5 (1973–74): 168–84.

29. Deirdre English, "The Politics of Porn," *Mother Jones*, April 1980, p. 50.

9

From Domination to Recognition

MITCHELL ABOULAFIA

Freud's notorious question, "What does a woman want?", succinctly crystallizes the perspective that has nurtured the oppression of woman. It is the view of woman as other analyzed by Simone de Beauvoir in *The Second Sex,* which, ever since its publication, has served as a source of dialogue for those seeking to understand and overcome the subordination of woman to man. This chapter takes as its point of departure a suggestion found in *The Second Sex:* "Certain passages in the argument employed by Hegel in defining the relation of master to slave apply much better to the relation of man to woman."[1]

Hegel's dialectic of master and slave is justly famous, for it exhibits the manner in which the oppressed are related to their oppressors, and how they can overcome their otherness to achieve independence. When this dialectic is applied to the relation of man to woman the following points are disclosed: both men and women are oppressed by woman's subordination; the liberation of women entails the liberation of men from roles that deny true independence; the importance of mutual recognition in this liberation; and how unalienated work enables women to overcome otherness and subservience. By exploring Hegel's dialectic in the following pages I will articulate the manner in which the above points are entailed in the roles of man as master and woman as servant.

The essay is divided into two sections: the first provides a brief prefatory *social-psychological* reading of key elements in the chapter on "Self-Consciousness" from Hegel's *Phenomenology of Spirit,* which contains the dialectic of master and slave; I then convert the dialectic of master and slave to a dialectic of man and woman, to demonstrate how the confinement of women to certain roles necessitates the confinement of men to other roles, and how this, in turn, precludes mutual recognition and liberation.

An Account of Hegel's Master and Slave Dialectic

In his chapter on "Self-consciousness," Hegel wishes to exhibit the quest of the human subject to gain a sense of itself as a unified independent being after it has begun to achieve self-consciousness. Hegel calls the subject as self-consciousness a desiring consciousness, because it experiences a lack of self-unity, of wholeness, which it desires to overcome.[2] In its quest for self-unity, self-consciousness seeks to prove that it is whole through asserting that it stands apart from all else. If this subject were to speak it would declare: "I am above the things of nature, for they have not the power to resist me. I deny them any independent status; as a subject, a self, I am the only self-conscious, independent being." To demonstrate its mastery and independence, self-consciousness proceeds to consume the vegetation and animals of the natural world, and by digesting them affirms that natural things cannot stand apart from itself. Yet, consumption of this sort can never fully satisfy self-consciousness' desire for independence, because self-consciousness *depends* on the things which it consumes in order to have something to consume.

What self-consciousness really wants is to demonstrate its self-unity by ridding its world of anything that challenges its claim to total independence. Consumption cannot gain this for self-consciousness, for the very act of consumption implies the existence of independent objects, which it wishes to deny. One answer to its need might be to have whatever is "out there" deny that it has an independent existence, while affirming that only self-consciousness is the true, independent, whole being. Only another human being has the power to speak, however, to publicly declare that it is not independent, so self-consciousness needs another human being to deny its own independence for the sake of affirming self-consciousness' independence. In this manner self-consciousness can do away with the other's claim to independence, while this other asserts that self-consciousness is the only independent being to be found (the perennial having your cake and eating it too although, in this case, it is more like the cake eating itself so that one does not have to deal with its existence, i.e., its independence). Self-consciousness requires *recognition* of its status by another human being who, it turns out, is also a self-consciousness.

It has already been noted how self-consciousness wishes to deny the independence of objects it finds outside itself; self-consciousness seeks to show that it is not attached to the things of the world, and "hopes" that another human being will recognize its independence while denying itself independence. But self-consciousness discovers that the greatest threat to its claim of independence comes not from mere objects, but from just this other who is also a subject, a self-consciousness. If self-consciousness asserts its independence by consuming—negating—that which it finds in the world, then a second self-consciousness would do the same and wish to deny the independent existence of the first self-consciousness. It also wishes to declare itself an independent self, because it is the character of every self-consciousness to desire to be affirmed as an independent, unique being. If two such self-consciousnesses meet they will find themselves mutually threatening each other; they will both desire to negate the existence of the other as an independent being. In order to continue to define itself as the only independent being, each must seek the destruction of the other.

The result of self-consciousness' intolerance regarding the existence of another self-consciousness is a life-and-death struggle between them. Each is bent on gaining the certainty and the truth of its own being, and the other cannot be allowed to manifest independence; there is no reconciliation yet possible. The willingness of the foes to risk their lives, literally or figuratively, in a struggle to the death proves to be crucial for the development of the master and slave dialectic; each cannot tolerate the existence of the other, and must be willing to go to any extreme to prove it is worthy of being called independent.[3]

Yet, death would bring the most futile of all victories over the other; self-consciousness realizes that biological life is necessary if it is to be an independent self-consciousness: "self-consciousness learns that life is as essential to it as pure self-consciousness."[4] A simple point, but one that marks a crucial turning-point in the dialectic. The result of the struggle unto death must not be the death of both participants, nor even the death of one of the participants. Self-consciousness not only wishes to rid its world of otherness, but also desires to be recognized as the independent self, and only another human being can recognize a self-consciousness; both must survive if there is to be this recognition.

As a result of this life-and-death struggle, the self-consciousnesses involved are transformed. One, as we now find out, was prepared to die for its conviction regarding independence, and becomes the master; the other was not so prepared, and becomes the slave. The slave is looked upon as being locked into thinghood for not being prepared to die for an ideal; it remains part of the merely natural world, and as a living "thing" it is "the dependent consciousness whose essential nature is simply to live or to be for another."[5] As the master's servant, the slave manipulates the things of the world in working upon the world for the master. The desire of self-consciousness, now embodied in the master, is satisfied through the work of the slave, for the slave brings the master things to consume so that the master does not have to directly deal with the objects of the world, which would threaten its independence. We find, however, that the actual situation is somewhat different from the way in which it first appears to the master and the slave. The master actually *depends* on the slave to recognize him as the master, while the slave, on the other hand, comes to embody independence by working on and transforming the world. The master lives under the illusion of independence, for he thinks that by being recognized as an independent consciousness by the slave he has achieved the status of independence. But, of course, he *depends* on the slave in order to be recognized. The slave, who is actually becoming independent, thinks of himself or herself as dependent on the master, and views the master as the ideal of independence that is beyond reach. The slave is alienated from himself or herself because his/her actual reality, independence in work, is denied; and as long as (s)he views him/herself as a dependent being, incapable of independence, the alienation will remain. Neither the master nor the slave can truly be recognized by the other for what each actually is.

Mutual recognition entails a basic respect for the other, which is impossible in a master-slave, independence-dependence, relationship. Take the case of the master. He views the slave as a dependent consciousness unworthy of respect, yet he expects to be recognized by the slave. The slave, however, as a dependent thinglike consciousness can only appreciate independence in an abstract manner, as something which "belongs" to the other. The master cannot be satisfied with the "recognition" he receives from the slave because the slave, as a dependent consciousness, is not in a position to recognize his independence. This dilemma is quite familiar: the old scholar wishes to be recognized, not by novices, but by those worthy of his own recognition, his peers. To be satisfied with "recognition" from those who are not worthy of giving it is to prove oneself unworthy of recognition; we can only be authentically recognized by those who share the quality or characteristic for which we wish to be recognized.

The barriers to authentic recognition are numerous and entail obstacles more insidious than the mere lack of peers; one of these is that we must be in a position to be cognizant of our own character in order to recognize or to be recognized. In this regard, both master and slave reveal a lack of self-awareness. For example, the slave, Hegel claims, "sets aside its own being-for-self, and in so doing itself does what the first [the master] does to it."[6] In other words, the slave's image of him/herself is the image the master has of him/her, the image of a dependent thinglike consciousness. The reality of the situation is that the slave is far from a merely thinglike consciousness which (s)he believes him/herself to be. But how can the slave be recognized for what (s)he is if his or her own self-image belies reality? On the other hand, if the slave's image of him/herself so distorts reality, can an other, the master, expect authentic recognition from him or her? To be authentically recognized one must be recognized by those who know something about what they are recognizing. Clearly, one whose perception of the social world inverts or completely distorts and confuses one's own place in it is in no position to confirm another's social role, especially when that role is being played opposite his or her own role. The slave is neither prepared to give nor to receive authentic recognition, and neither is the master.

Dependence, Independence and the Pursuit of Recognition

If we set aside—as a speculative account of prehistoric events— Hegel's claims regarding the origins of the master and slave through the struggle unto death,[7] we can apply his dialectic to the roles women and men often take in the contemporary Western world to show how these roles militate against mutual recognition and, therefore, liberation. The man has been and is taken to be the figure of independence, the master of the household. The woman is viewed as the dependent one, the household servant who looks to the man as the ideal of independence. Woman takes herself to be the dependent individual who must work in the home at the beck and call of her master, even if she is also working part- or full-time outside of the home. The woman is supposed to recognize the man as the independent one; she does this by telling him what a *man* he really is, often by acknowledging his achievements in the world, while he derides and trivializes her work in the home as "woman's work," slave's work, thus making it clear that it is inferior to his own labors.

The home is enjoyed by the male through the work of the woman, while the woman works directly upon the household, ordering it, keeping it. In her role as servant she must not let the things of the household disturb his enjoyment of them; her function is to manage the household in such a manner that he does not have to be soiled by involvement with things that require woman's work. It is the woman who is required to directly deal with things in their natural state in order to remove their naturalness, e.g., in *cooking and cleaning*. Man must never directly engage the natural in this fashion lest he relinquish his manhood, his independence. (Perhaps the fact that men often must take the role of the servant during the "working day" heightens their need to demarcate in some manner women's work from their own.)

The master believes he has achieved the recognition he had desired because he has the slave to recognize him as the independent self-consciousness. In doing so the woman sets aside her own claims to independence in order to recognize the man; she sees herself attached to and identified with the needs of her man: his needs are her own needs, she must work to satisfy him, and this she sees to be her duty, her life. This, in turn, tends to perpetuate the roles as they stand, in that the master is viewed by both himself and the servant as that which is essential and deserving of honor, while the slave is the unessential. In this relationship the "unessential" looks to the master for a model of independence and essentiality and appears to depend on him, while the master exists for himself, to be served. The servant is invested in her lord, she *must* take care of her man; though he may support her financially, she directly serves him. Woman is often required to shed or bury her own feelings for the sake of serving the feelings of man; she must recognize his feelings, and her own feelings and needs cannot be acknowledged because she is living for his. She is alienated from herself in serving him, for she is other to herself in only being-for-him.

The problem with this arrangement becomes apparent when one tries to understand how recognition can come out of such a situation. The master, the man, is calling for recognition of himself and his role in the world, though the nature of her work and her role prevents the fulfillment of this desire for recognition; and of course the converse is also true—he cannot possibly recognize her. We find the man in the same precarious position as Hegel's master: he needs to be recognized in order to be the independent one, but how can a dependent "womanly consciousness" recognize a *man?* How can a servile consciousness appreciate an independent consciousness? What she can do is acknowledge his maleness, as that which is different and other, and he can do the same in turn with her femaleness, so that they only acknowledge the other as other and know the other as an abstraction.

Given the nature of independence-dependence relationships, neither man nor woman can gain satisfaction in being recognized, because each cannot authentically recognize the other. Take the situation of the man: he is living a lie, living under the pretence of being independent when his very self-definition *depends* on woman. He asks to be recognized by one he has himself labeled inadequate, who is not the independent consciousness he takes himself to be. The man, not willing to acknowledge his dependence, is in bad faith.

This situation can also lead the woman into bad faith; that is, if she comes to realize the degree to which he depends on her, if she has a sense of her own independence and yet continues to act totally dependent. I should note in passing that by suggesting that both men and women can be in bad faith I do not mean to imply that this is all that keeps mutual recognition from taking place. The socializing forces that produce these relationships are great, and they are supported by the social system as a whole. We are not quite the free agents the early Sartre would have us be—in order to be truly free we must in some sense be recognized as being capable of freedom— but this is another essay altogether.

"Recognition" by an other for qualities which distort my character should be labeled *pseudo-recognition,* for the other, through false or limited images, does not recognize me as I am. The woman, for example, "recognizes" the man for his independence and self-sufficiency, when the reality of the man's existence belies this recognition. The man, on the other hand, "recognizes" woman as dependent, though she reveals independence through managing the household. This state of pseudo-recognition, which may have begun in complete ignorance on the part of each regarding his or her situation, is often perpetuated in the partial ignorance of self-deception. Deception can easily become a way of life, because the alternative, full awareness of the masquerade, entails a confrontation with the contradictions each has been living in the roles of independence-dependence, roles each has assumed to be the inevitable foundation of his/her experience.

If one cannot be recognized as one actually is and is consigned to living a role that does not accurately reflect who one is, the result is alienation. The situation we have been discussing leads to alienation from oneself, and therefore from others who might be able to recognize one. (It would also be correct to say that the situation leads to alienation from others, and therefore prevents one from being able to recognize oneself.) Being alienated here means having to live a lie, because it is through this lie that one can continue to function in a role that allows one to be a social being. The woman has come to see herself as a servant, a dependent consciousness, and the man as a master. To give up these roles appears to them as having to yield their sociality, because they define their sociality in terms of these roles. Tragically, the quest for recognition can lead in precisely the wrong direction. Instead of coming to recognize each other outside these limited roles, the alienated individuals are led to believe that the way to become whole is to fit more deeply into the roles. We then have men trying to be ever more independent, and women believing servility to be their path to nonalienated existence.

What then is the remedy for this lack of recognition that alienates men and women from each other? Perhaps they should strive to be as little different from each other as possible. This solution would make sense if we assume that we can only be recognized by those who totally share our qualities or capacities. Yet, if I end up looking to others who are as much like myself as possible for recognition, the logical extension of this might be to look only to myself. After all, who is in a better position to recognize me than myself? Has our discussion of recognition led to the rather bizarre conclusion that recognition is really a form of narcissism? Is the only solution to the alienation arising from a lack of recognition to surround oneself with those just like oneself? From this perspective, are those who argue for the importance of recognition to be seen as attempting to collapse distinctions, which alienate individuals from themselves and others, by making individuals as much like each other as possible?

Difference and differentiation, however, are not in themselves the source of the lack of mutual recognition. As a social being, my differentiation from the other is as crucial to me as my unity with the other. If I were totally other, I could not be recognized, nor could I recognize the other; if I were completely similar to or unified with the other, recognition would clearly be a meaningless concept since recognition assumes that there be an other whose otherness can be at least partially overcome through recognition. It can be safely said that we have the capacity to identify the qualities we share with the other, so as to be able to recognize the other, without having to be just like the other. For example, when someone recognizes me as a moral agent, he or she does not have to make the same decisions that I have made in order to recognize me, but he or she must be able to appreciate the qualities of a moral agent. To expect that everyone should be able to recognize us in all things is to do away with otherness, and would mean an end to authentic recognition. A complete denial of differentiation, a longing for others to be just like oneself, is to step, narcissistically, in the direction of the false totality of totalitarianism.

It is not differentiation in itself that is primarily responsible for the lack of mutual recognition between men and women, it is the independence-dependence relationships which lead to self- and other deception. This is not to say that there may not be other types of relationships that prevent recognition; it is to say that the structure of these relationships tends to create and foster deception. They are, in essence, relationships of domination, for one individual, the apparently independent one, is seen by both individuals as endowed with the right to rule. Relationships of domination fail to promote mutual recognition precisely because they prevent individuals from seeing others as anything but totally other; and they accomplish this false othering by promoting differences meant to keep individuals on one level of a hierarchy from being able to recognize individuals on different levels, especially by making those at the top feel somewhat more human than those at the bottom.

Those who claim they are endowed with the right to be at the top dupe themselves; the master is not the independent power he believes himself to be, for his self-consciousness is *dependent* upon the slave's consciousness, "his truth is in reality the [so-called] unessential consciousness and its unessential action."[8] Without the slave he could not be the master; the slave's consciousness *recognizes* his self-consciousness, so that ground for the master's self-consciousness actually lies in the consciousness of the slave. Man discovers at the moment of glory that he needs woman to be the independent self-consciousness that he takes himself to be. He is not independent after all: he depends on woman, he needs to be recognized by her, though he has called her the unessential. What man fears has come to pass—his masculinity is dependent upon (a specific) woman recognizing him. Is it any wonder that men have ambivalent feelings toward women! The question "What does a woman want?" is fathomable only in light of the question "How can I, as man, control what woman wants?" (i.e., recognizes).

There is a path from bondage. At first the slave trembled before the alien things of the world; only the master seemed to have a power over them. But the slave has come to see that she can remove the alien-ness of things by working upon them. That which was external—alien—comes to be viewed as her own through the power to change things, to shape things, which Hegel calls the power of negativity. Through work the servant learns that its own power manipulates and shapes the world.

> Through work . . . the bondsman becomes conscious of what he [she] truly is . . . consciousness, qua worker, comes to see in the independent being (of the object) its *own* independence.[9]

> Since the slave works for the master and therefore not in the exclusive interest of his [her] own individuality, his [her] desire is expanded into being not only the desire of this particular individual but also the desire of another. Accordingly, the slave rises above the selfish individuality of his natural will.[10]

It is crucial that the slave work upon the world *in a context* that permits her to see the independence of that which she shapes. Through the independence of what she "makes" her own independence comes to be reflected, for the independence of the thing made reflects her own independence. The independence which she originally thought she saw in the master, the ideal (or idol) which she could only long to be, becomes a reality for her in the forms that she shapes. The lord, on the other hand, remains hindered by his dependence on others to work upon the world for him. Independence truly occurs only when we are able to recognize ourselves in the creations of our own labor, and this happens only in unalienated labor.

By locking men and women into relationships where one member of the relationship dominates the other, and by fostering alienated working conditions, we prevent the possibility of mutual recognition. We deny the full humanity of each, the full potential of each and, in so doing, deny it of the other. While differentiation is in itself necessary, there are differences that debilitate relationships, and the difference of master and slave, or variants thereof, I hope I have shown to be just such a damaging configuration. Relationships of this sort foster pseudo-recognition, thereby preventing us from knowing the other and ourselves and achieving liberation. Hegel tells us:

> I am only truly free when the other is also free and is recognized by me as free. This freedom of one in the other unites . . . in an inward manner, whereas needs and necessity bring them together only externally.[11]

Notes

1. Simone de Beauvoir, *The Second Sex,* trans. H. M. Parshley (New York: Vintage Books, 1974), p. 73.
2. G. W. F. Hegel, *Phenomenology of Spirit,* trans. A. V. Miller (New York: Oxford University Press, 1977), p. 109.
3. "To prevent any possible misunderstandings with regard to the standpoint just outlined, we must here remark that the fight for recognition pushed to the extreme here indicated can only occur in the natural state, where men exist only as single, separate individuals; but it is absent in civil society and the State because here the recognition for which the combatants fought already exists." G. W. F. Hegel, *Philosophy of Mind,* trans. W. Wallace (London: Oxford University Press, 1971), p. 172, para. 432, Zusatz.
4. Hegel, *Phenomenology of Spirit,* p. 115.
5. Ibid.
6. Ibid., p. 116.
7. Hegel comments that, "The individual who has not risked his life may well be recognized as a *person,* but . . . not . . . as an independent self-consciousness" (*Phenomenology of Spirit,* p. 114), the implication being that merely natural creatures do not risk their lives for an ideal, and cannot develop culture. In order to account for women's original servitude, de Beauvoir suggests, along these lines, that men risked their lives on the hunt or in combat and, in doing so, overcame mere naturalness, while women, not being allowed or able to risk their lives on the hunt, did not overcome being linked to the "merely" natural. She states, "the hunter was no

butcher, for in the struggle against wild animals he ran grave risks. The warrior put his life in jeopardy to elevate the prestige of the horde, the clan to which he belonged. And in this he proved dramatically that life is not the supreme value for man, but on the contrary that it should be made to serve ends more important than itself. The worst curse that was laid upon woman was that she should be excluded from these war-like forays. For it is not in giving life but in risking life that man is raised above the animal" (*The Second Sex,* p. 72). This position is clearly a variant of the man/culture vs. woman/nature school of explaining woman's servitude. Regarding this position, see Sherry Ortner, "Is Female to Male as Nature Is to Culture?" in *Woman, Culture and Society,* ed. Michelle Rosaldo and Louise Lamphere (Stanford: Stanford University Press, 1974), pp. 67–87.

8. Hegel, *Phenomenology of Spirit,* p. 117.

9. Ibid., p. 118.

10. Hegel, *Philosophy of Mind,* p. 175, para. #435, Zusatz.

11. Ibid., p. 171, para. #431, Zusatz.

PART V

Work, Personal Relations, and Political Life

10

Women's Work and Sex Roles

JANICE MOULTON AND
FRANCINE RAINONE

Most contemporary feminist critics maintain that sex roles ought to be abolished. Their argument is that sex roles restrict freedom and opportunity, and if they were abolished individual freedom would be enhanced and opportunities made more equal. On this view the interests of males as well as females would be served by such a change. We agree that much of what are called sex roles should be changed. But we consider this argument for their abolition to be inadequate because it neither tells us why women in particular are disadvantaged by sex roles, nor does it give a correct account of what is wrong with sex roles. In this essay we will argue that the problem is not that sex roles restrict freedom; rather the problem is that sex roles reinforce the sexual division of labor (SDL) that functions in most existing societies to subordinate women.

The concept of "role" is used quite widely—and very loosely—in contemporary social science. The more specific concept of a "sex role" is equally widespread: every college student who has taken an introductory sociology or psychology class can discuss roles and sex roles. Some have argued that these concepts are hopelessly inexact and foster confused thinking about the way society actually functions. We do not wish to enter into that debate here. Instead, we hope to show that theorists who criticize current sex roles base their criticisms on the wrong grounds. They do not understand what is really wrong with sex roles.

By focusing on sex roles one can easily lose sight of the main problem: subordination. Even if women freely choose their sex roles, these roles are still wrong whenever they subordinate women to men. We believe that sex roles and subordination are in principle independent; only under certain social conditions are sex roles pernicious.[1] Whether or not sex roles are pernicious depends on how they affect the total structure of society. When sex roles are used to effect the subordination of women, to prevent women from having an equal share in the distribution of social resources, they should be changed. On the restricts-freedom view of sex roles, sex roles are intrinsically wrong: because sex roles restrict the freedom of individuals to do certain things they are wrong. In the next section we challenge this claim, arguing that many roles that do restrict freedom are not wrong.

All Roles Restrict Freedom

Dictionaries define a role as a part, an office, a duty, or a function. In addition to roles that people assume are roles that people just have, sometimes by choice and sometimes not. There are actors' roles and advisory roles, personal and professional roles, child, parent, and adult roles. The term "role" is used so broadly that nearly any pattern of behavior or function in a group or system can be called a role.

It is not sufficient for a behavior pattern or function to exist in a society for it to be a role; there must be expectations or standards about the behavior for it to be a role. It might even be said that social roles are characterized more by expectations and standards than by what people actually do. The expectations might be so unrealistic or impossible that no one, or hardly anyone, could ever meet them, but the role would still be characterized by the expectations and not by its fulfillment. For example, very few ballerinas in the world achieve the perfection of Makarova, yet her flawless performances help set the standards for that role. To give a different kind of example, it is almost impossible to be an ideal father, as that role is currently defined. Ideal fathers work long hours to provide the maximum in material benefits for their children, yet they are also supposed to spend long hours playing with and caring for their children. These two demands are incompatible, but they may still form the basis of our expectations of fathers.

On the other hand, people might follow a pattern of behavior or perform a function with no concomitant expectations or standards, which consequently would not be a role. For example, we all, in exhaling carbon dioxide, perform a function, but there are no expectations or standards about such behavior. We are not enjoined to exhale deeply near plants nor expected to produce certain amounts of carbon dioxide. Exhaling carbon dioxide is a pattern of behavior and a function, but it is not a social role.

Where there are expectations and standards in a society, rewards and penalties will be given according to how well people conform to the behavior patterns set by those expectations and standards. Some penalties may be merely the withholding of desired rewards, while in other cases social and legal sanctions may exist for ensuring conformity. The restrictions on freedom and opportunity that these penalties produce have been the subject of debate in previous discussions of sex roles.

It is certainly true that sex roles limit individual freedom and opportunity, but so do roles other than sex roles. One must be qualified to fill certain roles. The law restricts who may fill some roles and determines penalties for playing disallowed roles. Immigrants cannot be President; convicted felons cannot legally be gun owners. Freedom and opportunity are restricted because having one role can prevent a person from having another. Just as society tells us that men are not supposed to act like women, it also tells us that adults are not supposed to act like children and that lawyers are not supposed to dress like rock stars. One cannot simultaneously take a vow of silence and be on a debating team, have two nine-to-five jobs, be a boxer and a concert pianist, nor be a member of a city council and live in another city.

So sex roles are not alone in imposing limitations. The arguments used against sex roles will apply to any roles whatever: roles in general impose limitations on the people in them, and roles come with expectations about conduct, style, behavior, and so on, incurring sanctions when the expectations are not met.

Yet someone might argue that the sanctions imposed on sex role violators are particularly unfair; that while the severe sanctions imposed on felons and other disrupters of the social order are appropriate, those imposed on people who do not or cannot live up to sex role expectations are unjust. The argument might be that sanctions and restrictions arising from roles freely chosen are justified, but since sex roles are certainly not freely chosen, sex role restrictions are not fair.

This argument does not recognize that a great many occupations and social roles are not freely chosen, but rather are determined by economic necessity, social pressures, or ignorance about alternatives. And many of the roles that are chosen are done so with little information about the actual requirements of the roles. For example, all the roles involved in public entertainment attract many people, but most aspiring performers usually overlook the actual working conditions—low pay, job insecurity, long periods on the road. Influences such as early childhood experience (e.g., exposure, or lack of exposure, to team sports, musical training, or role models) often determine one's roles in later life. It is not clear, for example, that Wanda Landowska's being a harpsichordist was any more freely chosen than was her being a woman. Distinguishing acceptable roles from sex roles cannot be done on the assumption that the first are all freely chosen.

Let us emphasize this conclusion. The claim is that sex roles are unjust because they are not freely chosen. Nevertheless, many roles that most of us would allow to be unobjectionable, fair, and perhaps even beneficial to their holders are not freely chosen. Many factors interfere with free choice: ignorance, economic and social pressures, lack of ability. Yet the roles themselves might be rewarding, enriching, even desirable, and not at all unjust. Therefore it cannot be lack of free choice that makes sex roles unjust. It must be something else.

Many feminist critics argue that sex roles are wrong because they are assigned from birth rather than chosen. But we also do not choose whether we will be tall or short, attractive or ugly; and many roles depend on such attributes. Some might object that this analogy is faulty. It is true that one's height cannot be chosen any more than one's sex. But height materially disqualifies a person from fulfilling certain social roles, while sex does not, because it is not a relevant characteristic for fulfilling any social role. The answer to this objection is that *no* characteristic is relevant to the performance of a role if one is willing to change society and/or develop new technology. Short people could be basketball players with other short basketball players, or if gym shoes were designed to propel their wearers several feet into the air. Wealth would not be a relevant characteristic of potential political officeholders if campaigns were funded solely by public money. So the question is not what *is* relevant, but what *ought* to count as relevant. We do not believe that sex ought to be a relevant characteristic for the performance of social roles. But we are arguing against the claim that it ought not to be relevant *because* making it relevant limits women's freedom of choice. Let us examine the concept of freedom of choice and how it applies to this issue.

In the ordinary sense of free choice, someone chooses freely if s/he has alternatives, knows what the alternatives are, and chooses among them on the basis of preference rather than as a result of coercion. Unfortunately, it is very difficult to know what counts as coercion. Moreover, after enough coercion, people tend to have certain preferences. The feminist concern about sex role stereotyping in early education stems from this realization. But is it sensible to say, for example, that a 35-year-old woman is coerced into wearing make-up because of influences on her during her childhood and adolescence? And if not, can we say she freely chooses to wear make-up? Even if we could resolve these issues, the argument would still be unconvincing, for two reasons.

First, not all coercion is bad. In fact, education could hardly proceed without it. Children are coerced into learning many rules and types of behavior that curtail their freedom of choice about what sort of adults they become, in ways that we approve of. So proponents of this argument need to distinguish between acceptable and unacceptable coercion. Second, this argument cannot tell us why women are more severely disadvantaged by sex roles, because it ignores the issue of power and domination.

Boys are as coerced as girls to learn their socially determined role. A strong case can be made that men have *less* freedom to choose their sex roles and less latitude of behavior within them. Yet the sex roles of women attract more concern about injustice. This indicates that the real issue about sex roles is not freedom of choice, but the other effects of sex roles on their bearers. The real issue concerns the respective positions of women and men in the distribution of social resources, which result from sex roles. The central effect of sex roles is the perpetuation of a worldwide SDL in which:

> women are one-third of the world's formal labor force, and do four-fifths of all "informal" work, but receive only 10 percent of the world's income and own less than 1 percent of the world's property.[2]

The fact that sex roles reinforce the SDL, and thereby perpetuate the subordination of women to men, is what makes sex roles wrong. Even if it were true that many housewives had more freedom of choice in their daily lives than their husbands, this would not change the feminist problems with the position of housewives. The issue of whether men or women have more freedom to choose their social roles, or even whether they have any freedom at all, does not address the problem with sex roles. In sum, the free-choice argument is inadequate because it is based on a vague concept of free choice, and because it fails to confront the issues of power and domination.

One could try to distinguish sex roles from acceptable roles by claiming that the acceptable roles are restrictions on occupational roles, while sex roles are restrictions on persons. Restrictions on occupational roles include training and licensing requirements and rules in games and sports, and they are justified by the purpose they serve. But restrictions on persons as persons are not justified. This argument ignores the extent to which sex roles *are* job roles and how important that is for this issue. Let us consider it nonetheless. It claims that sex roles serve no purpose. But don't they? One can claim they tell people how to "play the game," if nothing else, and serve at least as much purpose as any other game. Or one can argue that they tell people what to expect of others. Perhaps they add stability to a culture. In a world where economic and political roles may fluctuate greatly, sex roles can provide a focus for one's self-identity because they are stable. So sex roles may serve a purpose just as some other roles do. This does not mean that their purpose cannot be served some other way, just as the purposes served by many other roles can be served in other ways. But it does mean that lack of purpose is not a reason for eliminating sex roles.

In addition, restrictions on occupations are, like sex-role restrictions, also restrictions on persons, namely the persons who have those jobs and who must do certain things, and the persons who do not have those jobs and therefore are not allowed to do certain things. A person not accepted to medical or dental school can never legally prescribe certain drugs; that is a restriction on that person whether or not she or he wanted to prescribe drugs. So sex roles do not appear to be significantly different from occupational roles after all.

Suppose one argues that the degree of severity of the sanctions and restrictions makes sex roles wrong. The trouble with sex roles, one might say, is that there are only two, and the social cost of nonconformity is very great. To show that this is true, one would have to show that the social cost of disobeying sex role expectations was greater than that of not living up to other standards and stereotypes. And it is not clear that this is true. It would seem, for example, that the social cost of breaking the law, of being poor or illiterate in an industrialized society, of being handicapped, old, or naive is greater than the social cost of being unmasculine or unfeminine (however they are characterized). One might contradict this by pointing out the threats of violence, the ostracism, or the fear of being locked up or left unprotected that come with sex role nonconformity. Yet felons, the mentally handicapped, and others have the same problems. The sanctions for sex role violations are not essentially different from the sanctions for other role violations. We may think sex role sanctions are worse than other sanctions because we think that they are wrong *and* can be corrected.

Roles Aren't Wrong

Freedom cannot be used to distinguish sex roles from other, acceptable roles. But instead of looking elsewhere to find out what is wrong with sex roles, we might conclude that all roles are wrong— that to guarantee individual freedom there should be no roles at all. We are going to argue that this second alternative is mistaken as well. We shall claim that roles are essential to our freedom because they provide information about what to expect when we make decisions, and that only with roles are informed choices possible. On our view, a society without roles would be impossible; roles could neither be abolished nor ignored when we act.

Suppose there were no roles. How then could we decide what specific activities to undertake, what is worth training for, or whether some activities will be rewarded well in the future? If there were no roles, there would be no expectations about patterns of behavior and functions and therefore no reason to believe that a person's current actions or situation are part of, or prerequisites for, particular future actions or situations. We could not require an education, apprenticeship, or practice to prepare an individual to become an X (driver, teacher, scuba diver) because that would amount to a role restriction. And if we went to school, served an apprenticeship, or practiced with the aim of becoming an X in this society-without-roles, we would be deluded. If there were no roles, no one would be able to gain an advantage by special training to fulfill some X, for that would restrict the people who had not trained to be Xs. We could not say that something was done well or ill because that would impose sanctions, restrictions on the way something was done; it would show that we had standards and expectations about doing X well. Work done toward a goal produces expectations that can, and very often will, be exhibited by rewards for some and punishments for others. If there were no roles, we could never decide between occupations or hobbies on the grounds that one appeared to involve more interesting activities, or more material rewards, or attracted more praise or respect than another, for all these attributes are part of the rewards and punishments that are supposed to be eliminated. If we chose occupations based on knowledge or beliefs of what we would do in those jobs, we would be using role expectations to make our decisions. Surely such a society without roles is both undesirable and impossible. Different sorts of things to do will always require training for some and produce expectations about performance, with praise for success and penalties for failure.

Consider the following analogy. Our theories and beliefs about the world affect our perceptions by restricting what we perceive, so that we see things one way and not another. But this restriction is what allows us to understand and make sense of the world, by organizing our experience and relating it to other knowledge. Similarly, roles constitute restrictions. They limit our freedom so that some choices are possible and others are not. But in so doing, roles provide information about the future—what behavior is possible, how behaviors are related, what treatment to expect from others. And this information is essential for making choices. If we had no theories and beliefs we would have no coherent perceptions at all, and if we had no roles in our society we would have no reason for making choices. The limitations that roles produce do restrict freedom, but without roles there would be no reason for freedom.

If our arguments so far are correct, we have established that all roles limit freedom and opportunity, but that this does not prove them unjustified. In fact, a world without roles would be impossible. This does not mean that every particular role is justified; far from it. But it does mean that to show what is wrong with sex roles we must show something other than that they limit freedom.

What Is Really Wrong with Sex Roles?

We have argued against the contention that the wrongness of sex roles is simply that they restrict individual freedom and opportunity. On this view there could be sex roles and sexual divisions of labor that are not at all morally objectionable. If we want to find out what is wrong with sex roles, we should look at their particular effects. For example, roles that can be characterized as women's roles are given fewer rewards, less respect, more menial chores, and less recognition than those that can be characterized as male roles. In this section we are going to claim that what *is* wrong with sex roles is that they provide the rationale, and even the ideology, for a sexual division of labor that subordinates women to men.

We have to show that sex roles do function to give women their subordinate status in society, and that alternative explanations for the subordinate status of females are inadequate. And to do that we have to discuss more specifically what sex roles are.

To say that there are sex roles is to say that females perform and/ or are expected to perform functions different from those of males. In some societies (ancient Greece and 20th-century Arab countries, for example) sex roles dictate that one sex does the shopping and that the other sex does the cooking. In other societies one sex is expected to do both the shopping and the cooking, and the other sex, neither. In our society, women are expected to raise children, and men are expected to repair cars, but not the other way around. Another part of our sex roles is that women are expected to earn less money than, and be shorter and younger than, their sexual partners.

There is no universal agreement about what each sex ought to do, and no single view about what sex roles are. We will consider two main versions of sex roles and show how they work together to promote women's subordination. There are "modern" versions that tell us what each sex's primary roles ought to be, but do not rule out the possibility that they can do other things as well, and "traditional" versions that specifically rule out certain roles for either sex. Someone might have a modern version of women's roles and a traditional version of men's roles, or vice versa. In fact, most people probably hold some combination of the two.

The modern version of female sex roles can be divided again into two, somewhat inconsistent, but nevertheless often held, requirements. The primary responsibility for a woman on this view is either to be a successful wife and mother, or to be attractive to men in general. Within this view may be a wide range of views about what counts as successful or attractive. The modern version of women's roles does not directly subordinate women to men, although it does assume that women's nature and value are given mainly in terms of their relationships with and acceptability to men. It is the one that is promoted in current advertising and suggests that women can be nuclear physicists, professional athletes, or workers on the Alaskan pipeline, as long as their jobs do not interfere with their roles as wives and mothers or with their attractiveness.

According to the modern version of sex roles, nothing in principle prevents women from doing other things, as long as they do not violate their primary roles. Success as a traditional wife and mother, however, requires considerable work in caring for a husband and teaching and caring for children. The work that wives and mothers do is unpaid and has low prestige, and this work leaves less time for other work. Since being a wife and mother is supposed to come first no matter what one's other work, problems with marriage or children are often blamed on the other roles, and a woman will be expected to curtail those other roles, making them subordinate to her job as a wife and mother, which is subordinate to the interests of her husband and/or children.

One might argue that the primary fault of this version of sex roles is that it is deceptive, a bit of false advertising. Being a wife and mother is touted as a desirable role, when in fact the working conditions are likely to be pretty poor. But this is not the whole problem. Even if the unpaid, low-prestige duties were made clear, the assignment or requirement of unpaid low-prestige duties to women is wrong. Would work-saving appliances and paid homemaking be a solution? (Of course, such suggestions would not help poor families, who could not afford the homemaker's salary and the appliances.) Suppose that housework were paid for from outside the family and independent of the earnings and evaluation of the others in the family who are employed outside. Poorly paid males might, if they married wisely, have excellent housekeepers with high salaries. But if such an institution were a reality, it is hard to believe that only wives or women would be housekeepers. Competition would arise, and skilled, professional housekeepers would want employment in the best home environments, not necessarily their own. Even for affluent families, the problem would remain that the woman's role is supposed to be that of a subordinate.

Let us consider the other requirement for the modern version of female roles. Sexual attractiveness is determined by the approval or disapproval of men. This may not seem different from many other roles where success is dependent on others—those of a colleague, employer, or supervisor, for example. The important difference, however, is that this particular role relegates women *as a group* to a position subject to the approval of men, and hence to a lower status.

Couldn't one argue that this version of female roles has a parallel version for males and therefore does not subordinate one to the other? After all, many boys and unattached men feel that their success depends on female approval. Teenage boys and girls may both be particularly unhappy because they feel dependent on approval by the other sex. It seems to them that they will be failures if they are not appreciated by the other sex, despite their other accomplishments. Yet if male and female dependence on sexual approval were exactly parallel, there would be no difference in their status. But males *can* become respected and appreciated for their other accomplishments and be attractive to females as a *result of* their other accomplishments. In contrast, the primary way for females to be attractive to males is to be pretty. Simone de Beauvoir has pointed out that women are expected to wear a variety of clothing, keep up with fashion changes, and wear cosmetics and elaborate hair styles, and that all this leaves women with much less time (as well as less money) to pursue their other roles.[3] The expectation that they accomplish this in addition to other roles handicaps women in competition with men and contributes to their lesser status. In addition, being attractive to males is often considered a disqualification for some professional roles and/or an invitation to sexual harrassment, which can make functioning in the other roles very difficult.[4] Another significant problem is that much physical labor, although well paid, is not thought appropriate for women. Physical strength is usually cited as the problem, but women can operate forklifts and many other power tools as well as men. The real problem seems to be that the work clothes, hard hats, sweat, and dirt involved in these jobs are not considered "feminine."

These modern versions of sex roles indirectly create and support a dominance hierarchy that places women on lower levels because they are women. Being successful as a wife and mother requires one to be subordinate to men and spend a great part of one's life doing unpaid, low-prestige work with less time available for well-paid, high-prestige work. Being attractive to men also requires considerable time taken away from other work, as well as being subordinate to the opinions and preferences of men in one's primary role. Still, the modern versions allow some latitude, and even though they place serious restrictions on women's ability to achieve other goals, it is possible on these views to play some other roles and still be a sex role success.

Since women do much more than fill the roles of wives and mothers or be sexually attractive, one could not say that men were dominant over women in general, or that sex roles supported this dominance, if women were not subordinate to men in their other roles. After all, they might be peers, colleagues, and even supervisors in their other roles. The subordination of someone in one role might only be one side of the story. Women might be subordinate to men in some roles and dominant over men in others. This is where the traditional version of sex roles complements the modern version, designating certain jobs as suitable for males and other jobs as suitable for females. Far fewer jobs are considered traditionally suitable for females, and they are concentrated at the lower ends of scales of pay, power, and prestige. So the more than 40 percent of the workforce that is female is crowded into a very small number of occupations. These occupations—nursing, clerical, secretarial, teaching (at the lower levels), domestic service, textile and electronic industries, food service jobs—pay little and/or require work largely under the supervision of men (nursing and secretarial work are clear examples of the latter).

The usual argument for a sexual division of labor is that women are more suited for certain jobs and men for others. On this view, the function of the division of labor is economic efficiency, and the lower status is a side effect. It may be unfortunate, so the argument goes, that what women are suited for is not worth much, just as it is unfortunate that what mentally handicapped people are suited for is not worth much, but that's the way it is.

But let us look at some of the *activities* of the low-prestige, female-assigned occupations and compare them with those of some of the high-prestige, male-assigned occupations. If this division of labor *were* based on economic efficiency we would expect the actual work done to be of very different sorts. The skills and abilities required for female work ought to be different in kind from the skills and abilities required for male work. But are they really so different? It is expected that a woman can follow an intricate pattern for a dress or jacket, while reading a blueprint for a building or a road is thought inappropriate for her. Yet both activities require much the same skills: following a graphic representation, keeping note of dimensions and materials, and translating a two-dimensional outline into a three-dimensional object. The concepts dealt with by computer scientists might be thought more easily understood by males than females, yet at least two well-known books on computer programming explain the basic principles in terms of an analogy with knitting patterns.[5] We expect women to clean up the various excretions of babies and care for the diseased and dying, but morticians who do the same washing and dressing of the dead are almost always men. Women office workers are expected to manage switchboards, typewriters hooked to computers, photo-duplicating machinery, and dictaphones. Women homemakers may operate food processors, floor waxers, microwave ovens, sewing machines, and other machinery. But women are not supposed to be good at operating lathes, radial arm saws, or engine-tuning equipment (except during wartime). Women assemble most of the electronic equipment produced in this country, but electronic technicians are expected to be men. This list could go on, giving more evidence that there is no clear division between the activities that women are expected to perform at low or no pay and those that men are expected to perform.

Perhaps one might think that the assignment of women to subordinate positions is just a side-effect of the beliefs in different abilities of men and women. Women are assigned to the jobs that are less important for the society or to the jobs that do not require much training, because they are thought to be less important themselves or less able. However, it is easy to find examples to show that the importance of a job and the training required for it do not determine the status of the job when women's work is at issue. For example, women are responsible for creating the future citizens of the society and for the socialization and early cognitive training of these children, and for a society not much could be more important. Nurses, social workers, and school teachers receive more education and training than plumbers and garage mechanics, but are usually paid less. And female office workers usually come to their jobs with more of the relevant skills than do male office workers. So it does not look as if women are relegated to occupations that in fact deserve less prestige, but rather that those occupations have less prestige and pay because they are filled by women.

Furthermore, even if it were true that the subjugation of women were a secondary effect of other factors that determined job status, or a secondary effect of an interaction of haphazard factors, objecting to the sexual division of labor because it subordinates women would be no less appropriate. One does not have to attribute a motive or purpose to a social structure to condemn its ill effects. Since sex roles are not based on the activities themselves, since women's jobs are not distinguished from men's jobs by amount of training or other incidental properties, and since the difference in salaries, status, and other benefits between women's and men's jobs cannot be explained in terms of training or importance to society, we can conclude that the main function of the sexual division of labor supported by sex roles is to keep women subordinate to men.

Changing Women's Work

It looks like the next approach ought to be to reduce the sexual division of labor. With this problem in mind, it has been argued that sex roles ought to be abolished.

In this chapter we have argued that sex roles are not wrong because they restrict freeedom; all roles restrict freedom by directing our choices and providing frameworks for future action. If there were no such restrictions, making decisions would be like operating in a world without other physical objects: there would be no obstructions to movement, but also no reason to move in one direction rather than another, no reference points to guide our movements, and so no reason to move at all.

But sex roles *are* wrong because they foster the subordination of women to men. And we've considered the various ways different views of sex roles do this. Note that we have not claimed that sex roles or a sexual division of labor are necessarily wrong. They do subordinate women, but there could be sex roles or a sexual division of labor in which neither sex were subordinate. And this difference allows us to consider alternative strategies for changing this wrongness. No matter how well-trained or how necessary to society the work is, if it is characteristically done by women it is rewarded far less than work traditionally done by men. In the United States, for every dollar a man earns, a woman earns 59 cents. The average American woman with some college education will earn less in a full-time job than a man with less than seven years of schooling. In attempts to alter these inequities, many have argued for equal pay. This is an important and necessary step, but it is not enough because most women and men work at different sorts of jobs. Sixty percent of all working women are crowded into a few, predominantly female, professions—clerks, salespeople, waitresses, and hairdressers. Only 1 percent of all registered apprentices are female; 97.6 percent of all secretaries are female. And of course most of the work traditionally done by women is unpaid. So although equal pay for people with the same job classification is important, it will not end the subordination of women.

Another approach is the attempt to obtain for women equal pay for work of comparable value. On this approach, evaluation criteria are developed that attempt to measure the value of work in terms that are neutral with respect to the specific jobs. For example, truck drivers and secretaries would be assessed differently, and wages for "women's work" would rise dramatically. This is an innovative and important strategy for improving women's position in society. If it worked, it could equalize men's and women's salaries, and that would be a great step toward equality. But questions can be raised about its overall efficacy.

But would the actual outcome be the expected one? First, the strategy could backfire. Because of the higher status of men, identical accomplishments by men and women tend to be perceived differently.[6] So the criteria developed might result in *lowering* women's wages.

Second, it will be difficult to compare solidly female jobs with other jobs. For example, wages for child care might not rise at all. As more women move into a primarily male occupation, hierarchies and status differences could be created where there were none before, so that women would continue to have lower status than men in that profession.

Third, this strategy would leave women in the same subordinate positions in the job hierarchy they now occupy—female secretaries would still work for male management trainees—and therefore would leave them exposed to much of the same exploitation they now confront. Despite increased numbers of women entering the paid work force, women continue to have only token representation, if at all, in the highest ranks of highest status positions.

Fourth, nothing can be done to equalize the division of reproductive work, short of ceasing it altogether. We might acknowledge that making babies is a form of work that should be valued and rewarded like other forms of production. But this might not change the actual value accorded such work.

Last, this strategy would tend to reinforce the SDL, making it more difficult to challenge the notion that women and men are different "by nature." And this could make it even harder for women in this society to rise to the real positions of power, which are at the top of the hierarchy.

A dilemma confronts feminist organizers. To create sexual equality, women need to gain control of social resources. They cannot do this without doing "men's work." Men's work in the institutions by means of which social resources are controlled (for example, banks and governmental agencies) is based on a hierarchical power structure of domination and exploitation. Working in these institutions requires acting in accordance with these values, at least to some extent. But acting in accordance with these values strengthens the bases of oppression rather than weakening them.

To try to reduce the subordination of women by placing them in positions formerly reserved for men is to accept the value and status already accorded such positions. But perhaps we could do as much or more by questioning these values and trying to change the working conditions that support them. For example, what in the structure of office organization and job conceptions makes secretaries more subordinate to the people they type for than grocers and car salespeople are to the people they sell to? What kind of fringe benefits, tax deductions, promotion opportunities, etc., that add to the status of men's work are not available for women's work? Does unionization or some other factor determine the larger salaries for construction workers than for nurses? Professional child-care centers and home appliances can relieve the work required for women's family roles, but do they improve the status and dignity of these roles—and if not, what else would?

This essay is just a preliminary to raising these questions, but we hope it leads to the consideration of other alternatives to remedy the subordination of women beyond trying to minimize the distinctions between women's work and men's work.

Notes

1. See Eleanor Leacock, *Myths of Male Dominance: Collected Articles* (New York: Monthly Review Press, 1982); and Peggy Sanday, *Female Power and Male Dominance: On the Origins of Sexual Inequality* (Cambridge: Cambridge University Press, 1981), for discussions of societies that have sex roles based on a SDL, but in which women are not oppressed.
2. Lisa Leghorn and Katherine Parker, *Woman's Worth: Sexual Economics and the World of Women* (Routledge and Kegan Paul: Boston, 1981), p. 14.
3. Simone de Beauvoir, *The Second Sex* (New York: Alfred A. Knopf, 1953).
4. We do not mean to imply that only "attractive" women are subject to sexual harassment. In *Sexual Shakedown* (New York: Warner, 1980), Lin Farley argues convincingly that the sexual division of labor is sustained largely by male sexual harassment.
5. Margaret Boden, *Artificial Intelligence and Natural Man* (New York: Basic Books, 1977), pp. 9–12; Douglas Hofstadter, *Gödel, Escher, Bach,* (New York: Vintage Books, 1979): pp. 149–50.
6. For documentation of this phenomenon, see Phillip Goldberg, *Transactions* (April 1968): 28–30. Other works on this subject both criticize and support the original claim.

11

The Political Nature of Relations Between the Sexes

PAULA ROTHENBERG

The contemporary movement for women's liberation has contributed many insights to our theory and our practice, not the least of which is the claim that the personal is political. Kate Millett's catalytic book *Sexual Politics* armed us with a new and liberating perspective, and other feminists and social critics on the left besieged us with a variety of works, which ranged from an examination of the politics of the family, to the politics of guilt, to the politics of housework. A women's movement classic, *Sexual Politics* typifies the kind of analysis generated by the view that even so-called "trivial" aspects of our personal existence reflect the fundamental relations of power that extend throughout our lives. Even more to the point, it challenges the whole attempt to portray areas of greatest concern to women as "trivial" as in itself reflecting the politics of our society.

For all its seeming novelty, the recognition that the personal is political is not entirely new. It can be found as far back as Aristotle, who spends a portion of Book One of the *Politics* discussing household management. He begins the topic by quoting Hesiod approvingly: "First house and wife and an ox for the plough" and then goes on to assure us that "the male is by nature superior, and the female inferior; and the one rules, and the other is ruled," adding later, "the courage of a man is shown in commanding, of a woman in obeying." While the usefulness of Aristotle's insights into household management is questionable, at least he correctly understood the nature of his subject and saw clearly that the issue of power between the sexes was political. As time passed, this view became hidden from us, and it remained for the Marxist feminist movement of the '60s and '70s to remind us once again that the split between the personal and the political, between private life and public life, between home and work, is itself a reflection of the political needs of capitalism and patriarchy, not some eternal, historical truth of human relations and social organization.

The question that concerns us here—"Are relations between the sexes necessarily political?"—emerges from this recent history. It would not have been asked, certainly not in this form, during other periods of the twentieth century.

The Politics of Interpersonal Relations

We begin by asking what makes relations between human beings political. Aristotle has already given us a preliminary answer: relations are political when one rules and the other is ruled, when relations are predicated on inequalities of power, when dominance and submission are built into the relationship. Thus, a relation is political insofar as it involves a struggle for control between individuals of unequal power and status, who confront each other with essentially opposed interests. This description applies to most if not all of the situations in which we find ourselves in contemporary society. For within capitalist society, we tend to meet as buyer and seller, doctor and patient, teacher and student, owner and worker, landlord and tenant, corporate executive and secretary, clerk and customer, supervisor and laborer, and so on. That is, we are under pressure to assume a series of roles and to interact with each other according to the logic of the relations that the roles carry with them. While the personality of the individuals involved may modify the equality of the encounter slightly, the power dynamics of the relation itself really determine the nature of the interaction. And though it is true that each of us occupies a variety of such roles each day, sometimes performing more than one at a time, unlike Marx's ideal for human growth—hunter in the morning, fisherman (sic) in the afternoon—our roles do not so much express the infinite variety of human capacities as they reflect the alienating and dehumanizing categories of an economy organized around private property and profit.

The terms for survival, let alone success, dictated by the capitalist system pervade all aspects of our lives. This point is often made in simple terms by contrasting capitalism, an economic system organized around production for profit, with socialism, an economic system organized around production for use. Without belaboring the point, it should be obvious that, for example, where use is really the operative criterion for production, such considerations as durability become merits, while in production for profit, durability will more than likely be regarded as a deficiency. Similarly, there will be a significant difference between the kinds of personality traits that are rewarded and thus promoted in an economic system that stresses competition and those in an economic system that stresses cooperation. The logic of an economy organized around expanding profit will tend to place people in antagonistic relations quite apart from the particular wishes of the individuals involved.

Perhaps a few examples will help clarify this point. Let us begin with the relationship between customer and clerk. Most of us, I think, feel somewhat uneasy when dealing with a salesperson we know to be dependent upon commissions to earn his or her living. We always suspect that their answers to our questions may be motivated by the prospect of their own immediate gain, rather than by an unbiased appraisal of our needs. The logic of capitalism reduces most encounters between people to such a relation. In an economy organized around private property and profit, each of us is forced, in some significant sense, to operate on a commission basis all the time. No wonder, then, that we try to avoid explicitly commercial transactions with friends—or worse yet—family. No wonder that we feel surprise when a merchant stands behind a guarantee, or when a salesperson warns us against buying a particular item because it is known to be defective, or when a professional person seems motivated by some kind of human rather than financial concern. Such things happen within capitalist society, but when they do it is in spite of, and not because of, the logic of the system.

Another example is the relation between a professional and his or her client. While some who enter the professions are genuinely motivated by a desire to help others, many are more concerned with the financial rewards reaped by doctors, dentists, lawyers, and other professionals in this society. And it has long been true that the economic realities of life under capitalism, the explicitly racist and sexist admission policies of the professional schools, and an educational system designed to reproduce hierarchy have tended to tilt the balance in favor of the latter sort of professional person. The high cost of obtaining professional credentials, the elite nature of that training, the enforced scarcity of professionals in medicine and dentistry—all create the context in which relations between individual patient-clients and practitioners occur. The pressures on the professional are to maintain control over their knowledge and skill rather than share it, since it has been acquired at great expense. The patient in such a relation is clearly dealing with someone who operates on a commission basis and must feel all the concern and vulnerability such a relation generally entails exacerbated by the fact that what is being dealt with are not automobiles or toasters, but gall bladders and Caesarean sections. In the professional/patient-client relation, we have a clear-cut case of a relation between individuals of unequal power and status who more than likely confront each other with opposed interests. This relation, like that between buyer and seller, teacher and student, and so on, is a political relationship. While, in some cases, the pleasing personality of some of the individuals who occupy these roles may tend to obscure the political nature of the exchange (just as the paternalistic or humanist temperament of certain slave owners tended to mitigate that inhuman relation somewhat), the relation in essence remains the same. It is the logic of capitalism that requires such interaction and reduces most relations within our society to politicized role oppositions.

But what of relations not explicitly commercial? Don't they manage to escape the dictates of this logic and provide us with an area of personal life that gives us a respite from the values and transaction of the marketplace? Marxist-feminism has already pointed us toward the answer to this question. All attempts to isolate the so-called personal from the political are more reflective of the impact of bourgeois ideology than of the reality of our lives. The dynamics of the relation between buyer and seller begin to pervade all aspects of life under capitalism and provide a sometimes conscious, sometimes unconscious paradigm for all human relationships, even those which on the surface do not appear to be concerned with some kind of commercial transaction. Our language reflects the metaphors of commodity exchange, and we are encouraged to regard ourselves as potentially valuable commodities whose marketability can be improved in a variety of ways. These include improving external packaging through clothing, hair care, cosmetics, deodorants, etc.; improving skill level through learning to disco dance, play racquetball, skin dive, increase our vocabulary, etc.; improving basic personality via sensitivity training, art appreciation courses, image building, etc.; and the ultimate weapon, improving our relative status by acquiring cars, stereos, saunas, furs, and a wine cellar. The values and lifestyle portrayed in television commercials creep into our daily life, and no interaction is entirely free from the logic of commodity exchange.

To say that relationships between human beings are political at this moment in history is to recognize the contradictions that define the roles available to us under capitalism and to recognize that, as a consequence, most significant encounters between people occur within relationships marked by inequalities of wealth, power, and skill, which are only exacerbated further by the fundamentally opposed interests attached to those roles.[1] Who's in control becomes a key issue in human relations. This can be expressed in a variety of ways, ranging from the firing of an extremely competent subordinate whose power threatens to undermine his superior's, to the struggle between two friends over who will pick up the check, to the tension during a phone conversation over who will end it. The pervasive nature of such struggles was recognized by the new left movement of the '60s and early '70s insofar as it emphasized minimizing the inequalities of power that politicize relationships. Teachers tried to equalize relations with students by giving up, or at least sharing, the power to grade and determine curricula; some people rejected styles of dress that had built into them the expression (assertion) of different social status (and power); a handful of radicals in the medical and legal professions challenged the exclusive control over access to information and skill exercised by doctors and lawyers, and so on. In some areas, these efforts met with moderate success, but substantial long-term success was rare. This, of course, should not surprise us. For in recognizing that relations between human beings are political, we thereby recognize that personal struggle carried out on an individual basis can have only limited success. These relationships, no matter how seemingly "personal," are part of the broader fabric of capitalism. Capitalism creates and maintains inequalities of power and status. It establishes antagonistic relations and limits our participation in the world to a set of roles based upon and defined by competing interests. Most attempts to transcend those roles are doomed to failure by the internal logic of the capitalist system.

Sexual Politics

What are the implications of this preliminary analysis for our central questions about relations between women and men? Are such relations political? It should be clear at the outset that our answer must be, "Yes, only more so." Insofar as all relations are political, relations between the sexes are clearly political as well. But the imposition of the additional roles of man and woman on individuals already engaged in the kinds of interactions considered earlier introduces additional inequalities of power and privilege, which further politicize these exchanges. For example, when we know that two individuals confront each other as employer and worker, we already have some basic idea of the form their interaction will take and of the needs and interests that guide each of them. But consider how much our knowledge of the gender of those individuals adds to our knowledge of the probable nature of that interaction. The same can be said about the additional factor of race. This is true because differences in race and gender carry with them differences in power and privilege that further complicate the inequalities and antagonisms defining the basic relations of contemporary society. The relation between teacher and student has built into it certain inequalities of power and status. Yet the nature of the interaction, if the student is female and the teacher male, will be markedly different than if the two are of the same gender or if the gender of those occupying the roles is reversed. A similar claim can be made for all other such relations: doctor-patient, lawyer-client, gas station attendant-car driver, etc.

In addition to politicizing further all the relations of our daily life, the roles of man and woman entail their own set of highly unique and politicized forms of interaction. An examination of two such relations can further expose the politics of relations between the sexes. For the purposes of this discussion, I have chosen to limit myself to relations between women and men in marriage, although much of what emerges from an examination of these relations holds true for similar interactions outside marriage.[2]

The paradigm I have chosen to elaborate assumes that the husband is the primary breadwinner and the wife, the primary homemaker. Although it is a fact of modern life that a large number of women who are married and/or have children also work, and that a large number of black families are single-parent households headed by females, it continues to be true that women are defined and taught to define themselves in terms of the dependent (and subordinate) role of "homemaker" and/or "mother" regardless of their participation in the paid labor force. These women are encouraged to regard themselves as either "working wives" or "working mothers," in contrast to male workers who are *never* referred to as "working husbands" or "working fathers."

Economic realities may well force many families to replace the single-wage with one-and-a-half wages (derived from two workers), but capitalism and patriarchy have an interest in seeing to it that the female's identity continues to be shaped by her role in the home and her position in the patriarchal family, rather than by her activity in the workforce. In consequence wages remain low, demands for health and retirement benefits fail to emerge, and a more-flexible pool of self-defined "marginal workers" is available to employers—all in the interest of capital. At the same time, men can maintain their privileged position in the family by denying the significance of women's paid-labor contribution to it. The force of (largely unconscious) sexist ideology has been remarkably successful in encouraging "working wives" to regard their paid labor as "just helping out," "working for pin money," etc., so it threatens neither their husbands' image and position nor their own definition of femininity.[3]

Marxist Feminism has exposed the family as a political institution that reinforces capitalism and maintains patriarchy. It functions in the interests of male privilege by teaching our children to regard a particular set of roles and, most important, an accompanying unequal distribution of power and responsibilities as natural and inevitable. It teaches them and us to translate the already political categories of man and woman into the infinitely more-complex roles of husband and wife. The issue of control and the struggle to gain and maintain it lies at the heart of the family as an institution. Aristotle recognized this two thousand years ago and Engels, in comparing the husband to the bourgeois and the wife to the proletariat, reminded us of this truth a hundred years ago, recasting it in a form that remains appropriate for understanding the family today.[4]

Like the factory worker, who each day adds to the power of the capitalist while increasing his or her own relative impoverishment, the housewife's productive activity strengthens her husband's power while reinforcing her own sense of powerlessness. The nature of her labor leaves her without a feeling of satisfaction or accomplishment, and the status of her labor outside the system of wages assures her that her work is valueless. At those times when she contemplates selling her labor to the capitalist, she finds that her skills have little or no market value and thus concludes that she has no skills. Her husband's superior position in the family is heavily dependent upon his status as wage earner. By caring for his material and emotional needs, the wife makes it possible for her husband to continue his wage labor and obtain the paycheck that keeps her dependent. Thus, the labor of the housewife ensures her husband of the material basis for his dominance within the family. Like the worker, the more she labors, the more she strengthens the powers over her.[5]

We can take the parallel further. With the help of the science of scientific management, the capitalist reduced skilled craft work to tasks and thereby guaranteed himself control over the productive process. Just as the extraction of maximum surplus value from the worker requires this complete control, the ends of patriarchal society are furthered by robbing women of their knowledge and skills and exercising control over their labor. Women are taught to regard housework as unproductive labor, and the relation of the work they perform to the wealth of the family is masked, hidden from them, mystified, in the same way the worker is kept ignorant or confused about the way in which the capitalist's wealth is generated. Thus both the woman and the worker are kept dependent on the very forces their labor imbues with its power.

Further, men have taken control of the skills and expertise once the exclusive domain of women. While childbearing, childrearing, and household management were formerly presided over by women, men have assumed responsibility for these areas by assuming legal and professional control over them, and women are forced to seek the expertise that was once theirs from doctors, psychologists, and others. The woman who wishes to breastfeed her child reads books by male doctors and seeks counsel from male practitioners. The way in which the almost exclusively male medical profession has attempted to deprive mid-wives of their status has been well documented, as have the laws of patriarchal society that deny women control over their bodies by prohibiting abortions, and so on. (We need not provide a comprehensive list here because the women's movement has already produced a vast body of literature documenting this case.)

But capitalism and patriarchy are not content to achieve and maintain control by legal or formal means alone. The role of ideology in maintaining the exploitation of both the worker and the housewife can never be overemphasized. And here too we find an interesting parallel.

Insofar as we have seen that the interests of the worker and the capitalist are diametrically opposed, the capitalist is faced with a difficult task. He must use every means possible to obscure the true nature of the worker's interest and convince the worker that his/her well-being is tied to the prosperity of the capitalist. This, of course, is the agenda of the capitalist state. Sometimes it goes about its task openly, as during the Reagan presidency; at other times, it adopts a more-subtle approach. In either case, workers are assured that decreasing corporate taxes, decontrolling oil prices, and in general subsidizing corporate pursuit of profits are the best ways, indeed the only ways, to create and maintain jobs and increase wages. The success of this approach is evident everywhere. It reaches deadly heights when union leaders side with management to oppose health guidelines at the workplace for fear that meeting the minimal requirements laid down by the Occupational Safety and Health Act (OSHA) will severely cut into profit margins and cause firms to leave the country. Thus, workers and their labor leaders often end up insisting that it is not in the interests of workers to reduce exposure to carcinogenic agents, even when the cancer rate of employees at a particular worksite is astronomical. This example and others like it indicate how well the capitalists have succeeded in getting working people to define their own interests as the interests of the capitalist class.

We find a similar tactic employed and similar success achieved in the realm of male-female relations. Just as men are taught to define their interests not as human beings but as wageworkers,[6] women are

taught to define their interests not as human beings but as wives or
helpmates of men. Several years ago a book appeared on the market
that proposed to tell us how to become *The Total Woman*. Advertising copy for this popular book read as follows: "Any wife who
wants to can become the total woman and give her husband the
immense satisfaction of living with one!" Evidently the possibility
of becoming total women was beyond those of us without husbands!
This equation of woman with wife is crucial to the perpetuation of
patriarchy as well as capitalism. Women are taught to see their
husband's interests as their own. Insofar as my real identity as a
woman is to be found in my role as some man's wife, it follows that
my satisfaction will come from satisfying my husband's needs. His
comfort, success, happiness become of utmost concern to me. It is
not merely more important than my happiness, it *is* my happiness—
for my reality is defined in terms of this relationship. By washing his
socks and dishes and cooking his dinner, I will find satisfaction.
How extraordinarily convenient for men that their interests and ours
coincide so completely. And how convenient for the capitalist that
my interests as a worker are best served by maximizing his profits.
We recognize the extraordinary pervasiveness of such coincidence
in designating our society as capitalist and patriarchal and in acknowledging the political nature of relations between women and
men.

But many will protest this way of describing the marriage relation.
They are likely to argue that a genuine community of interest is at
issue here; that, for example, both the woman and the man have a
stake in his success on the job because, in fact, *his* income will
largely determine how and where they both live; that when the wife
performs those housekeeping duties that make it possible for him to
perform paid labor outside the home, she is in fact furthering her
own interests as well. Marriage, we are told, is a partnership. True,
each partner has different responsibilities, but the net result will
accrue benefits to both.

In fact, the community of interest that locates the woman's
satisfaction in her wifely role of homemaker or helpmate is about as
legitimate as the community of interest that gives the worker a stake
in maintaining lethal levels of carcinogenics at the workplace. Marx
exposes the fallacy of such reasoning in *Wage Labour and Capital:*

> To say that the interests of capital and those of the workers are one
> and the same is only to say that capital and wage labour are two sides
> of one and the same relation. The one conditions the other, just as
> usurer and squanderer condition each other.
>
> As long as the wage worker is a wage worker, his lot depends upon
> capital. That is the much vaunted community of interests between
> worker and capitalist.[7]

In other words, the drug addict and the pusher, the prostitute and the pimp, the worker and the capitalist, the wife and the husband, may each be said to have their respective community of interest. What is at issue, of course, is the relationship itself. Presuppose any one of them and a kind of mutuality of interests, a kind of symbiotic relationship, may follow. But what must ultimately concern us is the community of interests we can be said to share as human beings, and this is not merely different from the interests engendered by these other relations; it is, in fact, in complete opposition to them.

An additional but not unrelated objection to our description of the marriage relationship focuses on the unpleasant aspects of the husband's responsibilities. After all, he is forced to go off to work at a job that is very likely to be alienating and exploitative. He is expected to assume extensive responsibilities for the economic well-being of his family, etc. Of course there is some truth to this objection. That is why Marxist feminism rejects equal treatment and status as its goal and talks about transcending existing roles. The former implicitly accepts the male role as the standard, while the latter rejects all existing roles and looks to a revolution to produce new forms of human relations along with new forms of relations of production. Attempts to portray the husband as *equally* oppressed within the family are fundamentally unsound, however we may say that the alienating aspects of the husband's role are adequately acknowledged when we consider him as worker and as consumer. When we analyze his role in the family and focus on the parallel with the role of the bourgeoisie in relation to the proletariat, we find his role is essentially privileged. He benefits directly from the exploitation and oppression of the wife within marriage.[8] True, his responsibilities subject him to a certain amount of stress, tension, and pressure, but the same may be said for the capitalist whose endless attempts to extract more surplus value from the labor of his workforce no doubt often leads to ulcers, alcoholism, and hypertension.

If Marxist feminism helped us to appraise the family in a new light and recognize it as political, it was radical feminism that urged us to see the political nature of sexual relations. Early in the history of the women's movement of the '60s, T. Grace Atkinson offered us an analysis of sexual intercourse as a political institution. Jill Johnston wrote in *Lesbian Nation,* "Lesbian—the meaning of the word is not primarily sexual, but political."[9] And in similar vein, Charlotte Bunch argued, "Women-identified Lesbianism is, then, more than a sexual preference, it is a political choice. It is political because relationships between men and women are essentially political. They involve power and dominance. Since the Lesbian actively rejects that relationship and chooses women, she defies the established political system.''[10] While some women eagerly embraced this way of understanding a portion of their lives that had previously seemed beyond political analysis, many more women and men were frightened and angered by the claims of radical feminism. Their fear and anger was understandable, for if these claims were correct, we would be forced to subject the most-personal and intimate relations of our lives to a potentially devastating critical perspective.

In fact, the fundamental insight of radical feminism *is* essentially correct. Sexual relations in the narrowest sense of that term are political. When women and men engage in sex they do not leave inequalities of power at the bedroom door. The privacy in which those relations are usually carried out should not be mistaken for lack of political context, for the real inequalities of power and privilege that separate women and men in their daily lives cannot be banished from the bedroom by fiat.

The extent of the power struggle entailed in what we might call ordinary sexual relations within marriage can be inferred from the comments of some working-class women who were interviewed in a study by Lillian Breslow Rubin.'' In response to a question about oral genital sex, some of the women answered as follows:

> Even though I hate it, if he needs it, then I feel I ought to do it. After all, I'm his wife.
>
> I tell him I don't want to do it, but it doesn't do any good. If that's what he wants, that's what we do.
>
> I don't use excuses like headaches and things like that. If my husband wants me, I'm his wife, and I do what he wants. It's my responsibility to give it to him when he needs it.

These comments reflect a contractual attitude toward the marriage bed. These women regard sex as an activity required of them in their role of wife. They perform various sexual chores in addition to housekeeping and childrearing in return for economic security and social status. Two of the women refer explicitly to the unequal nature of that contractual relation. It is the husband who determines their sexual responsibilities, and it is the wife, like the discontented factory or office worker, who grudgingly performs the responsibilities assigned but not without some struggle. The third woman, while recognizing the unequal nature of the relations, seems to accept it. What interests us most about these comments is their recognition of the power struggle within their sexual relationship, and their recognition of the unequal nature of the relationship in general, which predetermines the outcome of that struggle. Among other things, the partners in the relation have opposed interests. Rubin's study indicates that many of these women, as a consequence of their socialization, do not postulate sexual gratification as a desirable or appropriate goal for themselves, and so they engage in sexual activity as a means to another end. The husbands in each case see the activity as an end in itself. The struggle that ensues results from their opposed interests and unequal power. These in turn are reflections of inequalities in other aspects of their lives as dictated by capitalism and patriarchy.

Of course, the political nature of the sexual relationship means that the struggle in the bedroom is often more complicated and more intense than the comments of these three women would indicate. While they seem to acquiesce to the power differential in their marriages, other women do not. Some women are quick to perceive that the opposed needs and interests of the partners provide some room for negotiation and some possibility of compensating for lack of power in other areas. For example, another wife interviewed in this study responded to the question as follows: "He gets different treats at different times, depending on what he deserves. Sometimes when he's *very* good, I do it to him."

And how do the husbands of these women experience this kind of sexual contact? The politics of the relationship do not escape them. One man interviewed put it this way.

> Either I'm forcing my way on her or she's forcing her way on me. Either way, you can't win. If she gives in, it isn't because she's enjoying it, but because I pushed her. I suppose you could say I get what I want but it doesn't feel that way.

While the plight of the husband here might initially call forth our sympathy, he is very similar to the ruler who commands loyalty and love from his subjects and then complains that he can't be sure anyone's love is genuine, or to the rich man who marries the woman of his dreams, only to spend his life wondering whether she married him for himself or his money. Assuming his doubt and the accompanying pain to be real, we can surely sympathize with his emotional suffering when we view his problem from a narrow perspective; but in the broadest sense, his pain is a consequence of the power his position and wealth bring him, power over other human beings, power to get them to do his bidding (to impose his will on them). Rather than deserving our sympathy, such a relation to other human beings requires our anger and our opposition.

An even more blatant example of the politics of sex is included in Rubin's study in the case of a woman who never had an orgasm during the ten years of her marriage, although the couple routinely had sex four or five times a week. When questioned about his wife's passivity, the husband responded, "If she couldn't, she couldn't. I didn't like it, but I took what I needed." After a moment's hesitation he continued, "She's always been hard to handle." Their relationship began to change when the woman experienced her first orgasm. According to her own account, it happened because she began to read about female sexuality and even to explore pornography. Her ability to attain orgasm altered their sexual relationship radically. Suddenly her husband lost all interest in sex and, she told the researcher, "Now I can hardly ever get him to do it anymore, no matter how much I try or beg him." The only comment Rubin was able to elicit from the husband was: "She's always asking for something or hollering about something. I don't have any control around this house anymore. Nobody listens to me." There was no longer even a pretense of talking about sex, for clearly they were talking about power. As Rubin observed the husband's change from active to passive role was his attempt to remain in control. Initially, he exercised his control by being assertive and aggressive, but once his wife became an active participant in their sexual relationship, he was forced to become essentially impotent in order to remain in control. The reality that emerges from the comments we have read is that what goes on in the marriage bed has very little to do with making love. Both the women and men involved correctly experience these relations as an extension of the politics of their lives.

The problems that characterize sexual relations within marriage (or outside it, for that matter) for the upper-middle-class couple may be different in substance but continue to expose the struggle for power that politicizes even the most-intimate relations between women for men. For example, Robert E. Gould, a psychiatrist dealing with a sampling from a much higher income bracket, has written about the way many men equate masculinity with their ability to make money.[12] In a number of the cases, he believes, the ability of the husband to perform sexually within the marriage was severely affected by their own self-appraisal of success in economic life. Thus, Gould cites cases of couples whose previously satisfactory sexual relationship deteriorated markedly when the income of the wife increased. Unless we acknowledge the political nature of sexual relations, we are at a loss to understand how a change in the wife's salary could possibly have any relevance to the husband's potency. But once we acknowledge that sexual relations reflect the power struggles that occur throughout our lives, it makes perfect sense. Gould's findings and others like them make it increasingly difficult to maintain the view that our sex lives are somehow separate from the rest of our interactions and that they remain unaffected by them.

But the claim that our sexual relations are themselves political is even more profound than this preliminary survey might indicate. To this point, we have simply been considering the dynamics of particular sexual encounters, and although they have indeed reflected a power struggle between unequals, we could surely cite other cases of sexual interactions where the husband did not become impotent when his wife got a raise, or where her orgasm was a matter of mutual interest and pleasure. To understand the political nature of sexual relations, we must look beyond the particular dynamics of particular interactions to the very definition of sexuality within our society.

Society's emphasis on heterosexuality and vaginal orgasm is itself political and reflects the interests of both the work ethic and male privilege. It reflects the work ethic of capitalism insofar as it posits production rather than pleasure as the appropriate end of sexual contact; and it reflects male privilege insofar as it virtually guarantees male orgasm, while leaving female gratification as an accompanying possibility but not an inevitability. A now-classic article from the early days of the women's movement, entitled "The Politics of Orgasm," provides an excellent political analysis of the way in which men have defined feminine sexuality according to their own interests. If, after all, woman's pleasure is obtained through the vagina, then she is totally dependent upon man's erect penis to achieve orgasm. On the other hand, clitoral orgasm defines her pleasure as independent of the male's; thus, "the definition of normal feminine sexuality as vaginal was part of keeping women down, of making them sexually, as well as economically, socially and politically subservient."[13]

When subjected to analysis from this Marxist feminist perspective, other commonly accepted beliefs about sexuality prove to be equally political. For example, it is often maintained that a significant difference between male and female sexuality is that the woman is always ready while the man is not. Ready for what, we might ask, penetration? But surely it is a male, not a female or neutral, perspective that equates being ready for sex with being capable of being penetrated by a penis. On this criterion both a woman and a sugar doughnut may be described as being ready. But ask any woman who has been penetrated when she was not aroused and in the absence of foreplay and she will assure you that women are *not* always ready. Not only does this belief emanate from a masculine perspective, but it clearly serves the interests of the male to assure him of the constant availability of a sex partner and to absolve him of all responsibility for his partner's pleasure, let alone her comfort. In short, it is a myth especially reassuring to lazy lovers and would-be rapists.

We could cite other examples of such distorted descriptions of human sexuality, but even a long list of such politically motivated descriptions offered as science would not fully expose the ultimate basis for our claim that relations between women and men are political. In fact, when properly understood the claim stands as an analytic, not a synthetic, truth. The very categories of woman and man reflect a political decision rather than a biological reality, and must be abolished.

This way of understanding the division of the sexes has been defended by Gayle Rubin in her important essay, "The Traffic in Woman." There she argues that every society transforms biological males and females into socially defined men and women. This is accomplished by a sex/gender system, "the set of arrangements by which society transforms biological sexuality into products of human activity and then satisfies these transformed sexual needs."[14] According to this view, "sex is sex, but what counts as sex is culturally determined and obtained."[15] When understood in this way, our society's division of males and females into heterosexual women and men with an attendant set of complimentary dispositions and desires that be seen as a political rather than a biological given. If, in fact, we believe that the fundamental building blocks of human society are women and men as defined by our culture (and by definition each is incomplete without the other), then we preclude a whole range of social organization as incompatible with the nature of human beings.[16] There is, of course, a remarkable similarity here with the view that portrays people as naturally antisocial, greedy, competitive, and selfish, and then argues that the only economic system compatible with human nature is capitalism. A significant source of support for both capitalism and male privilege has been this ideology, which defines the biological givens of the human race in such a way as to reinforce existing social-political-economic divisions of power and privilege. At the same time, this ideology masquerading as science makes it difficult, if not impossible, to even conceptualize alternative forms of social organization and interaction. Thus Gayle Rubin writes, "But we are not only oppressed *as* women, we are oppressed by having to *be* women or men, as the case may be."[17]

At this moment in history the needs and interests of class privilege and male privilege have become inextricably intertwined (and perhaps they always were.) For the most part the institutions the reinforce the one, reinforce the other. It is not accident that men who work on the assembly line, performing the same repetitive functions day in and day out, often tape pictures of scantily clad women to their machines to alleviate their boredom. Capitalist patriarchy robs them of their dignity as workers while it subordinates men to machines, and human needs in production to the requirements of maximizing profit, but it buys them off with fantasies of male domination and the promise that they can regain their power (if not their dignity) in the continued subordination (sexual and otherwise) of women by men.

Insofar as relations among human beings under capitalism reflect fundamentally antagonistic sets of needs and interests and reinforce the inequalities of power that provide their context, all relations are in some significant sense political. Add to these already politicized relations the further inequalities of power and privilege that accompany differences in race and gender, and the political nature of all human relations becomes intensified. Thus the role of revolutionaries is to set about the task of creating conditions that produce neither buyers and sellers, nor owners and workers, nor women and men, but human beings.

Notes

An early version of this chapter was presented at a meeting of the Society for Philosophy and Public Affairs, New York Group, February 13, 1979. I am grateful to the participants in that discussion for lively remarks. I am particularly grateful to Marlene Gerber Fried and Linda Nicholson, who served as commentators on the paper and whose constructive criticism and support were extremely important to me. Finally, I would like to thank Gregory Mantsios for reading several versions of this manuscript and commenting in detail in each one.

1. I do not wish to claim that domination *begins* with capitalism, rather that the logic of capitalism is a major determinant of the forms of domination that prevail in contemporary social relations.

2. In this connection, the reader is urged to read the chapters on Love and Romance in Shulamith Firestone's *The Dialectic of Sex*. NY: Bantam Books, 1970.

3. The reality is that women's increased participation in the paid labor force does not in itself alter male/female roles within the family. For an important discussion of this and related points, see Heidi I. Hartman, "The Family as Locus of Gender, Class and Political Struggle: The Example of Housework," *Signs* 6, no. 3 (Spring 1981): 366–94.

4. By extrapolation, the analysis that follows can be said to apply to single-parent, female-headed households, black as well as white, if we recognize that women's contribution to the family in such cases is subordinated and devalued in relation to "the welfare" or "the system" that in these cases replaces the individual husband. The result is the direct intervention of patriarchal institutions that perform analogous roles and subordinate the woman in the family in similar ways—both literally and metaphorically.

5. If we wish to translate this analysis so that it applies to single-parent, female-headed households, we can talk about their labor in the family as reinforcing the patriarchal relations (in part by reproducing those values and attitudes) of capitalism and thereby strengthening those forces responsible for their subordination and marginality in the first place. In line with this approach, we would rewrite the four

concluding sentences in this paragraph as follows: "The state's controlling position in the family is heavily dependent on its role as primary provider. By reproducing the material needs, values, and attitudes of capitalist patriarchy in herself and her children, the female head of household makes it possible for the patriarchal state to continue her subordination and dependency. Like the worker, the more she labors (in the family), the more she strengthens the powers over her."

6. This is, of course, very different than defining oneself as a member of the working class and should not be confused with the existence of class consciousness.

7. Karl Marx, "Wage Labour and Capital," in *The Marx-Engels Reader,* ed. Robert C. Tucker (New York: W. W. Norton, 1972), p. 180.

8. In *Sexual Politics* Kate Millett observes, "the service of an unpaid domestic still provides working-class males with a 'cushion' against the buffets of the class system which incidentally provides them with some of the psychic luxuries of the leisure class."

9. Jill Johnston, *Lesbian Nation* (New York: Simon & Schuster, 1973).

10. Charlotte Bunch, "Lesbians in Revolt," in *Feminist Frameworks,* ed. Mison M. Jaggar and Paula Rothenberg Struhl (New York: McGraw-Hill, 1978), p. 136.

11. Lillian Breslow Rubin, *Worlds of Pain,* New York: Basic Books 1976).

12. Robert E. Gould, "Measuring Masculinity by the Size of a Paycheck," in *Feminist Frameworks,* pp. 29-33.

13. Susan Lydon, "The Politics of Orgasm," in *Sisterhood Is Powerful,* Robin Morgan ed. (New York: Random House, 1970), pp. 197-205.

14. Gayle Rubin, "The Traffic in Women: Notes on the 'Political Economy' of Sex," in *Toward an Anthropology of Women,* ed., Rayna Reiter (New York: Monthly Review Press, 1975), p. 159.

15. Ibid., p. 165.

16. This as in the popular song of the '50s, men and women go together like "love and marriage" and "a horse and carriage" so that "you can't have one without the other."

17. Rubin, "The Traffic in Women," p. 204.

12

Feminist Theory: The Private and the Public

LINDA J. NICHOLSON

The primary purpose of this chapter is methodological: to clarify certain confusions in feminist theory connected with the use of the categories "private" and "public." These categories have played an important role within feminist theory, and I believe rightly so. Many feminist theorists have correctly intuited that these categories point to societal divisions that have been central to the structuring of gender in modern Western society, at least. Some theorists have even argued that a more-general separation, expressed in the opposition between "domestic" and "public," has been universally important in organizing gender.

Even so, I sense among feminist theorists a suspicion of such categories conjoined with a suspicion toward employing dualistic frameworks altogether. The following remarks by Rosalind Petchesky illustrate this tendency:

> This, in turn, led to a further analytical insight: that "production" and "reproduction," work and the family, far from being separate territories like the moon and the sun or the kitchen and the shop, are really intimately related modes that reverberate upon one another and frequently occur in the same social, physical and even psychic spaces. This point bears emphasizing, since many of us are still stuck in the model of "separate spheres" (dividing off "woman's place," "reproduction," "private life," the home, etc. from the world of men, production, "public life," the office, etc.). We are now learning that this model of separate spheres distorts reality, that it is every bit as much an ideological construct as are the notions of "male" and "female" themselves. Not only do reproduction and kinship, or the family have their own historically determined products, material techniques, modes of organization, and power relationships, but reproduction and kinship are themselves integrally related to the

social relations of production and the state; they reshape those
relations all the time.[1]

Iris Young's article on dual systems theory elaborates this position.[1] She notes that Marxist feminists, in their attempt to make
Marxism more explanatory of gender, have often merely added onto
the Marxist categories an additional set, creating models composed
of two systems. Thus, many have tended to think in terms of
"production" *and* "reproduction," "capitalism" *and* "patriarchy."
The specific oppression of women is then accounted for by appealing to the interaction of these basically separated spheres of social
relationships. Young persuasively points out the many problems
with this type of approach. She notes that the "production/repro-
duction" model, or those similar to it, tends to universalize the
division of labor peculiar to capitalist society. Only in capitalism has
"production" become separated from "reproduction," or have
some of those activities associated with the making of food and
objects been separated from such domestic activities as childbearing
and childrearing. To make this separation the basis for one's theoretical model is thus to project onto much of history a separation
unique to modern society. Moreover, Young argues that dual systems theory suffers from other major problems: it obscures the
integration that exists between the separated spheres; it fails to
account adequately for the nature of women's oppression outside
the home; and at the most fundamental level, it leaves unchallenged
the assumption that women's oppression is a separable and thus
peripheral element in social life.[2]

Michelle Zimbalist Rosaldo has also criticized early work by
herself and others that stressed a "domestic/public" opposition as
helpful in explaining the social organization of gender.[3] Rosaldo has
argued that this opposition, as earlier formulated by herself and
others, tended to explain gender in psychological, functional terms.
She now claims that such formulations obscure cross-cultural diversity in the structuring and evaluation of gender.

All these arguments are extremely helpful and need to be taken
seriously. I do, however, see a possible confusion in the conclusions
that might be drawn. From such arguments we might be led to
abandon oppositions, such as "private" and "public" that, properly
interpreted, do provide an important clue for understanding gender.
What is wrong with some of the dualisms Petchesky and Young
pointed to, in particular the opposition of "production" and "reproduction," follows not from their duality, but from the fact that the
categories chosen obscure history. As Young correctly notes, the
use of the opposition "production/reproduction" inaccurately pro-

jects backward onto all human history a division of labor specific to capitalism. Similarly, many of the ways in which the opposition "domestic/public" has been formulated tend also to universalize falsely a late capitalist division of labor. In the same way, I would suggest, certain understandings of the opposition "private" and "public," as this is used to describe modern Western society, tend to treat it as a homogeneous separation and not one to be interpreted differently from century to century and from country to country.

In short, I would stress that what was wrong with the models Petchesky, Young, and Rosaldo were attacking was their ahistoricity. If we interpret such oppositions as that between "domestic" and "public" or "private" and "public" historically, that is, as separations rooted in history and not in some biological or otherwise stipulated cross-cultural division of labor, we might then retain tools to help us understand important components of our own past history of gender. Moreover, by so historicizing these separations we may be able to see what is wrong with much existing social theory, which tends falsely to universalize aspects of these separations.

Marxism, for example, tends to universalize the modern separation between family and economy. Thus Marx, and many Marxists following him, have tended on occasion to assert that changes in the family can be understood as effects of changes in the economy.[4] The difficulty with such a position is that it assumes one can cross-culturally separate claims about the "family" from claims about the "economy." Yet not until the establishment of a market economy in the modern period, did activities emerge on any significant scale, concerned with the production and distribution of food and objects that are organized separately from activities considered the province of the family. Indeed, part of what we mean by the term "market economy" is that such activities become freed from governance by such institutions as family, church, and state, and become organized only by the laws of the market. Of course, this separation, even in our own times, has never been complete. For example, even within contemporary society, where fast-food chains absorb ever more of the final stages of food production, this activity is still largely carried out within the home. The point, however, is that we adequately understand neither the existing divisions nor their limitations if we do not view them in historical terms.

By ontologizing the separation of family and economy, we also lose sight of the kinds of connections that have existed between the separated spheres, connections that have occurred in the very process of their separation. Thus, as many feminists have pointed out, even while many women have left the home for wage-earning activities in the course of the 20th century, the social relations of their paid jobs often replicate the social relations of the homes they have left. This transference of gender roles from the home to the work world has been described by some feminists as the rise of "public patriarchy" and may indicate certain weaknesses in the traditional Marxist cure for ending women's oppression: "Get thee to the workplace!" In any case, this phenomenon illustrates one weakness of a theoretical framework that fails to understand the separation of family and economy as an historical process rather than as an ontological given.

If Marxism has been guilty of obscuring our understanding of gender by universalizing the separation of the family and the economy, liberalism has been equally guilty of providing a comparable obstacle, that of universalizing the separation between the family and the state. Again it appears that the task for feminist theory is to disprove the universalization of this separation while also elaborating the grounds for its development.

What is meant by the claim that liberalism universalizes the separation of family and state? A basic explanation is that theorists associated with the liberal tradition assume that there are two different kinds of human needs best satisfied by two different kinds of institutions. On the one hand are the needs for intimacy, affection, sexuality, and the various kinds of aid and support that other human beings can provide. The family is the institution best designed for satisfying such needs. Within liberalism's history, the exact specification of these needs has varied, corresponding to real changes in the institution of the family. For example, the need for intimacy and affection on the part of all family members begins to become stressed only during the 18th century. Also historically valuable is the extent to which sexual needs are attributed to women. But no matter what the specification and allocation of needs is, what is consistent is the claim that there exist some needs, naturally present in whomever they are allocated to, that can best be met through the family.

In conjunction with the claim that the family exists to satisfy certain natural human needs is a further claim that the family alone is insufficient to regulate social life adequately. Early liberal "state of nature" theorists, such as Locke, while admitting families within the state of nature, did not believe them capable of preventing or solving the problems endemic to that condition. Locke and others have argued that some type of political institution, such as the state, is also necessary. The most fundamental purpose of the state is to prevent or resolve conflict arising among individuals who are not members of the same family. According to this theory, if the human population were small enough and constituted by only one family or by a few families widely scattered (a situation Locke attributes to the beginning days of human history), states would not be necessary. Given, however, a human population composed of more than one family, and given the problems Locke and others attribute to a stateless society, the need for a state arises.

It is important to stress that for liberal theory, while the state "organizes" relations between members of different families in a manner somewhat analogous to the way families "organize" their individual members, states are *not* families writ large. Not only is there a difference in size between the two institutions, they also differ widely in purpose and in terms of the nature of the relationships that constitute both. Of course, within liberal theory, there has been much diversity in the description of the extent and nature of the differences between families and states. Such diversity is evident, for example, in the 17th-century parliamentary responses to the royalists' identification of monarchal and paternal authority. At times the 17th-century parliamentarians sought to discredit the identification; at other times they used the identification to justify parliamentarianism.[5] In Locke's writings, one finds arguments supporting both the similarities and differences of familial and political relations. For example, Locke argues against Sir Robert Filmer, for the contractarian nature of political relationships, in part through a claim about the contractarian nature of the marriage relationship. He also points to certain differences between the two, such as the rights over life and death, which states, but not families, have over their members. In general, however, all liberal theorists assume certain dissimilarities in the governance of families and political institutions based upon a belief in certain qualitative differences in the nature of the two institutions. While these differences are not always made explicit, a not untypical list would include reference to such features as their respective sizes and purposes, the composition of their members, the respective relation of their members to property, etc.

The point I believe feminist theory needs to make against this position is not that families and states are similar. While the slogan radical feminism introduced, "the personal is political," may aid us in seeing certain similarities between personal and political relationships and between families and states, we cannot ignore the real differences between both personal and political and family and state. In opposition to liberal theory, however, feminist theory needs to show the historical nature of these differences. Liberal theory has been correct in describing the social divisions that have existed, and sometimes its arguments on the normative implications of these divisions are sound. What has remained untested, however, is the thesis of the inevitability of such divisions.

There are reasons why it is particularly appropriate for feminist

theory to begin making such a challenge. Earlier I argued that
Marxism creates obstacles to understanding the history of gender by
universalizing our contemporary separation of the familial and the
economic. I would also accuse liberalism of creating similar obstacles by tending to naturalize the family and universalize its separation from the state. As a consequence, it has little to tell us about
why the social relations of the family are as they are, or why the
political sphere has excluded women to the extent that it has.
Answers to such questions can be obtained only by viewing the
family, the state, and their interconnections in historical terms.

The above point can be demonstrated by examining certain work
by feminist scholars and others in the history of the family. One
example is an analysis of the relationship between the family and the
state by Marilyn Arthur. While Arthur's focus is primarily on the
evolution of the Greek city-state, she perceives certain parallels
between that evolution and the development of the early modern
state in western Europe. In both cases, a basically aristocratic or
feudal society organized around kinship gave way to a society
dominated by a more-egalitarian state. She describes the changes
occurring in pre-classical Greece as follows:

> Aristocratic or feudal society is usually dominated by a landholding
> nobility defined by birth whose social relationships preserve many of
> the features of tribal society. . . . In the midst of this society a class
> of commercial entrepreneurs arises. They derive from all social and
> economic groups: wealthy landowners interested in trade, younger or
> illegitimate sons of the nobility involved in maritime ventures, crafts-
> men and other specialists and wealthy, independent peasants. In
> archaic Greece the rise of this class was associated with the discovery
> of iron, whose ready availability made possible small-scale cultiva-
> tion of land and thus transformed the method of production. The
> artisans worked the new materials, the merchants traded in it, and
> agriculture was intensified through its use. This new middle class was
> thus still strongly tied to the land (the economic base of society was
> agriculture throughout all of antiquity), but it was a larger and more
> diverse group than the landowning aristocracy. At this point in
> history the small household emerged as the productive unit of society,
> and any head of a household (who was simultaneously a landowner)
> automatically became a citizen or member of the state. Conversely,
> the state itself, the *polis,* was defined as the sum of all individual
> households.[6]

One can carry a parallel between pre-classical Greece and early
modern Europe only so far; too many obvious factors differentiate
the two periods. On a very general level, however, there is one
important similarity: in both periods a connection appears between
the development of a democratic state and the emergence of a

relatively nuclearized household/familial unit. This connection makes sense conceptually if we consider the extension of political power in the early modern period and in the pre-classical period. Political power, in both cases, rather than resting in a tribal chief or head of kin, becomes more widely shared among the diverse constituents of a new middle class, whose justification for political representation lay in a position as head-of-household. Thus the growth of a more-widespread political representation and the development of a more-nuclearized household/familial unit appear as correlate phenomena. This thesis on the interconnection of a more-democratic state and a more-nuclearized family unit finds support in the work of others. Hannah Arendt, for example, long ago pointed out that the foundation of the *polis* was preceded by the destruction of all organized units resting on kinship, such as the *phratria* and the *phyle*.[7] In reference to the early modern period, Lawrence Stone has argued that kinship, lordship, and clientage, the forms of social organization that structured medieval aristocratic life, were antithetical to the functioning of the modern state:

> The modern state is a natural enemy to the values of the clan, of kinship, and of good lordship and clientage links among the upper classes, for at this social and political level they are a direct threat to the state's own claim to prior loyalty. Aristocratic kinship and clientage lead to faction and rebellion, such as the Wars of the Roses or the Fronde, to the use of kin loyalty and client empires by entrenched local potentates to create independent centres of power and to make the working of the jury system of justice impossible by the subordination of objective judgment to ties of blood or local loyalty.[8]

Stone claims that one of the tools used by the emerging state in its battle for power with existing feudal lords was to transfer the idea of "good lordship" from these lords to the individual male head-of-household. The subordination of the household members to their head was in turn described as analogous to and supportive of the subordination of subjects to the sovereign. Thus, Stone notes that the principle of patriarchy was transformed by the state from a threat to its existence into a formidable buttress for it.[9]

Both Arthur and Stone derive implications from their analyses for changes in gender roles. Arthur, for example, after noting the status of woman as object of exchange in the period prior to the one with which she is concerned, argues that the transformations that resulted in the rise of the household's importance as a political unit in ancient Greece in turn added a new dimension to this status. As the integrity of each individual household came to possess political significance, so also did the biological activities of women, who could potentially violate that integrity. Adultery, for example, when practiced by women, became seen as a crime against society and not merely as a personal transgression.[10] The corollary to the legal sanctions against adultery by women was the idealization given to the citizen wife who produced legitimate heirs. This idealization has caused some to argue that the overall status of women in classical Athens was not all that bad.[11] Arthur's position is that the idealization given to the citizen wife does not mitigate the fundamental misogynistic attitude of classical Athens. The proper Athenian housewife may have been praised when she acted as she ought, but beyond the praise stood the fear that she might not:

> This praise of women in the marriage relationship does not invalidate the idea that the fundamental attitude of the Greeks toward women remained misogynistic. As social beings, women in the polis entered into a partnership with men that fostered civilization, and only in this relationship did women gain favor. As we have seen, the misogyny of the Greeks originally sprang from the association of women with the world of instincts and passions, which was hostile to civilized life. Unlike man, the woman of the polis was regarded as a hybrid creature, a domesticated animal who could be adapted to the needs of society but whose fundamental instincts were antagonistic to it.[12]

Insofar as the polis depended upon the autonomy and inviolability of the individual household and thus the legitimacy of each man's heirs, it is understandable that women's sexuality would be highly feared. Women, whose sexuality had the power to disrupt the political order, were idealized for acting rightly while being hated and feared for their power to do wrong. In such a context it follows that women's activities generally would be closely watched. This deduction is supported by other accounts on the situation of women in classical Athens, such as that of Sarah Pomeroy, whose work documents the degree to which the lives of women in classical Athens were dominated by restriction and seclusion to the interior of the household.[13]

Stone similarly argues that the nuclearization of the family unit in the early modern period had certain distinct implications for gender roles. Women's declining ties to an extended kinship system meant a loss of their countervailing power to their husbands' authority. An increased power of the male head-of-household was also brought about during this period as a consequence of other related phenomena. The Lutheran Reformation increased the spiritual authority of the father and husband while reducing the countervailing authority of the priest and the Church.

While Arthur's and Stone's analyses seem to suggest that the rise of a democratic state is on the whole bad for women, I do not want to be taken as committed to that claim. The status of women is always an extremely complicated phenomenon, and while the kinds of broad generalizations I have been delineating may be helpful for providing a first step in understanding gender relations, they provide only a first step. To go on we must pay more attention to the specificities of the particular period in question. In the case of early modern Europe such specificities must include reference to the fact that if, as in classical Greece, the production unit was a household, it was a very different kind of household. The idealization of marriage as a type of partnership, for example, which began to emerge in the early modern period, importantly differentiates the status of women in early modern Europe from the classical era, as does also the emergence of the concept of the individual with natural rights. Thus the purpose of the above use of Arthur's and Stone's analyses was not to derive specific conclusions on the status of women in the early modern period, but rather to suggest the type of procedures we need to employ even to begin the process of reaching such conclusions. The point is that unless we view the family and the state in historical relation to one another, the status of women must remain for us, as it does in much of liberal theory, an unsolvable mystery. In other words, within liberal theory the social relations of the family are assumed as universal and a function of such facts, to quote Locke, that men are "stronger" and "abler." In the 17th century, while liberalism was breaking new ground in extending political representation to male heads-of-households, it had little to say on why women were not also to be included in the political sphere. Even by the 20th century, when women's rights to political participation were becoming recognized, liberalism has provided little insight into its previous position. The failure of understanding in all cases can be attributed to an inability to see the family in conjunction with the state as a social institution, with the two sharing interrelated histories.

Thus the conclusion I wish to draw from the above is primarily methodological: that an important task for feminist theory is to show the historical origins and evolution of those divisions others have assumed to be inevitable. Phrasing the project in this way enables us to clarify certain confusions. Rosalind Petchesky, in her remarks I earlier quoted, stated that the separation between the public and the private, between the family and work, is ideological. This claim is similar to what was intended by the radical feminist slogan "the personal is political." In both cases it was recognized that such divisions as between the private and the public or the personal and the political do obscure our understanding of the dynamics of gender. The ironic point I have been emphasizing is that to prove such claims, we need to show how the private did become separated from the public or the personal from the political. In other words, to break the ideological hold that such divisions maintain over our lives, we need to show their historical origins and their changing dynamics. A breaking of this ideological hold need not necessarily entail a rejection of such divisions. While feminist analyses have brought us to recognize much of women's oppression within existing personal and familial relationships, and have enabled us to recognize the entanglement of at least part of this oppression with the very separation of these relationships from political and economic relationships, the continued analysis of such divisions need not entail their complete rejection. Unless we can begin to see these divisions in historical terms and not as universal givens outside analysis and change, we will be unable to influence intelligently the future of such divisions.

Notes

1. Rosalind Petchesky, "Dissolving the Hyphen: A Report on Marxist-Feminist Groups 1–5," in *Capitalist Patriarchy and the Case for Socialist Feminism*, ed. Zillah R. Eisenstein (New York: Monthly Review Press, 1979), pp.376-77.

2. Iris Young, "Socialist Feminism and the Limits of Dual Systems Theory," *Socialist Review* 10, no. 2–3 (March–June 1980): 169-88. See esp. pp. 179-81.

3. Michelle Zimbalist Rosaldo, "The Use and Abuse of Anthropology: Reflections on Feminism and Cross-Cultural Understanding," *Signs* 5, no. 3 (1980): 389-417.

4. See, for example, Karl Marx, *The Poverty of Philosophy* (New York: International Publishers, 1963), p. 180. Mary O'Brien cites other examples in "Reproducing Marxist Man" in *The Sexism of Social and Political Theory*, eds. Lorenne M. G. Clark and Lynda Lange (Toronto: University of Toronto Press), p. 107.

5. For a discussion of some of these differences, see Mary Lyndon Shanley, "Marriage Contract and Social Contract in Seventeenth Century English Political Thought," in *The Western Political Quarterly* 32, no. 1 (March 1979): 79-91; and Gordon Schochet, *Patriarchalism in Political Thought* (Oxford: Basil Blackwell, 1975).

6. Marilyn Arthur, " 'Liberated' Women in The Classical Era," in *Becoming Visible*, eds. Renate Bridenthal and Claudia Koonz (Boston: Houghton Mifflin Co., 1977), p. 67.

7. Hannah Arendt, *The Human Condition* (Chicago: The University of Chicago Press, 1958), p. 24.

8. Lawrence Stone, *The Family, Sex and Marriage in England 1500–1800*, abridged ed. (New York: Harper & Row, 1979), pp. 99-100.

9. Ibid., p. 111.

10. Arthur, " 'Liberated' Women," p. 69.

11. This controversy, with its respective adherents, is noted by Sarah Pomeroy in *Goddesses, Whores, Wives, and Slaves: Women in Classical Antiquity* (New York, Schocken Books, 1975), pp. 58-60.

12. Arthur, " 'Liberated' Women," p.43.

13. Pomeroy, *Goddesses, Whores, Wives*, pp. 57-92.

PART VI

Law, Ethics, and Public Policy

13

Women and Their Privacy: What Is at Stake?

ANITA L. ALLEN

Introduction

Privacy is an obscure object of desire. Widely regarded as commanding legal protection in a just liberal state, privacy and its value are nevertheless poorly understood. There is considerable disagreement about the theoretical basis and extent of the privacy rights recognized by our laws, social practices, and moral theories.

To a great extent the sphere we call "private" overlaps the traditional sphere of women's concerns: marriage, home, and family. Under the yoke of their traditional roles, however, women have been less able than men to secure privacy for themselves, and have been less able to enjoy and benefit from any privacy they *have* been able to secure.

In response to ongoing philosophical and jurisprudential efforts to understand the right to privacy and the interests it protects, I want to identify the special privacy interests of women. I also want to consider whether some of the more recent formulations of the right to privacy take into account the full range of women's special privacy interests. By "special" privacy interests I mean those interests women have in virtue of traits, roles, and experiences mainly or exclusively belonging to women in our society. These are apt to be overlooked or understressed in theoretical arguments for the protection of privacy rights.

For present purposes it is unnecessary to argue what Ruth Gavison and many others have argued extensively: that the law should recognize a personal right to privacy, and that the state as well as individuals have an interest in the protection of privacy. Today it is usually assumed that women, no less than men, have a fundamental right to privacy. This would not have been assumed a century ago. I start with the assumption that men and women have equal moral claims to privacy, but I focus on the special privacy interests of women.

As will be shown, the privacy interests of women are multi-dimensional. I maintain that a conceptually adequate theory of privacy and the right to it should account for these dimensions. I also maintain that protecting the privacy interests of women requires more than the recognition of equal rights for men and women under the law. It requires promoting respect for women in those areas of social and family life outside the reach of the law. It also requires the recognition of extensive freedom of choice for women with respect to sexual, marital, and reproductive concerns.

What Privacy Protects and Promotes

We can begin to identify the privacy interests of women by examining accounts of the privacy interests of persons in general. Existing analyses of the right to privacy have sought to characterize those interests. Judith Thomson's "The Right to Privacy" was among the first careful attempts by philosophers to clarify a right to privacy and the interests it protects.[1] Thomson suggested that the right to privacy is not one distinct right, but a group or "cluster" of rights, all of which are derivative of other familiar rights. So, the analysis went, to understand the rights of privacy we need only understand these other rights. What are they?

The privacy rights that no one look at my property unless I want them to, Thomson proposed, are derivative of property rights; privacy rights that no one look at or listen to me unless I want them to are derivative of rights over the person; privacy rights not to be coerced or threatened into giving away personal information are derivative of rights against threat and coercion; privacy rights against being harmed or tortured to get information are derivative of rights not to be harmed or tortured; and finally, privacy rights against giving away personal information are derived from the right of confidentiality. Accordingly, the interests protected by the right to privacy are those very interests protected by the putatively more-basic rights designated: the interests of undisturbed possession, bodily integrity, freedom from mental distress and coercion, and confidentiality.

Thomson's often-cited analysis has been largely rejected in subsequent discussions of privacy. The gist of the criticism has been that privacy has meaning and value not captured or elucidated by

Thomson's "cluster" theory. What her critics have rightly demanded is an account of privacy that maps out its peculiar conceptual territory—what it denotes and how it differs connotatively and denotatively from related concepts, such as intimacy and solitude—and an account of its instrumental or intrinsic values. In this vain, Thomas Scanlon objected that even if it were true that all the rights in the privacy cluster were derivative of other more-basic or familiar rights, some account of what distinguishes it conceptually as the *privacy* cluster would be required.[2] This objection was well taken. Having focused on invasions of a sort for which legal protection should be available and their putative derivativeness, Thomson has indeed left the concept of privacy itself in obscurity.

A number of Thomson's critics, including Scanlon, have correctly observed that complete analysis of privacy would give an account of the extent to which social rules, norms, conventions, and practices define and protect what is considered private. Jeffrey Reiman characterized privacy as a complex social practice serving the important function of communicating and recognizing personhood.[3] But for these privacy practices, Reiman argued, human young would not learn that their bodies and minds are *theirs* in the moral sense; they would not learn that they have "moral title" to their existence. On Reiman's view, the right to privacy is the right to "the existence of a social practice which makes it possible for me to think of this existence as mine."[4] The right to privacy in this sense is more basic than rights of property, or rights over the physical person, since there would be no person to whom any rights could be meaningfully ascribed were it not for the person-creating and person-sustaining social practices that we call privacy.

Reiman's account departed sharply from Thomson's in two ways. Both philosophers characterized privacy and the right to privacy as in some sense complex. Thomson, however, emphasized what she viewed as conceptual disunity among the elements of the privacy "cluster"; Reiman emphasized what he perceived to be a coherent set of social practices with a morally valid function, viz., creating persons. Reiman also departed from Thomson by rejecting her pivotal thesis that privacy rights are derivative of rights to property, person, or confidentiality. He accurately pointed out that her claims concerning derivativeness are arbitrary. Why not suppose that these other rights derive from the right to privacy, rather than that the right to privacy derives from them?

Assessing Reiman's highly suggestive account in detail is barred by its lack of specificity. He does not isolate the specific acts, conventions, norms, or rules that constitute the "social practice" of privacy. Of course, we have a good idea of what many such practices are. Privacy is not a complete mystery. Yet it remains unclear just *how* and *which* aspects of what Reiman terms our "social rituals" bring about a situation in which there are individuals who believe they have and ought to be respected as having "moral title" to their existence. In addition, his notion that persons have a right to a way of life that confers "moral title" to their existence is ambiguous. His appeal to the property concept of "title" suggests that protecting privacy entails promoting practices that communicate a familiar Lockean tenet: individuals have proprietary interests in their bodies, talents, and work products. Alternatively, self-identity rather than self-ownership could be the notion Reiman is getting at; that is, the understanding that individuals have of their existence as their own might consist in their having a certain conception of themselves as more or less continuous, distinct persons.

If the ambiguity and generality of Reiman's account did not lead to its rejection, its inclusiveness might. The right to privacy, he said, is a right to a complex social practice that creates, sustains, and promotes personhood. But many practices not typically regarded as having anything to do with privacy appear to confer "moral title" in at least one of the senses delineated above. It would seem, for example, that practices that restrain non-consensual physical contact are practices that create and promote personhood. But are all such practices part of the social practice of privacy? The usual way of viewing the matter is that while a person who, for example, grabs a stranger's breasts without permission violates her privacy, one who non-consensually knocks another down harms her but does not violate her privacy. The usual way of looking at the matter may well be wrong. Perhaps both contacts are violations of privacy, or perhaps neither is. But taking the view Reiman takes, that both amount to violations of privacy, requires an argument. If we are to accept the theoretically paramount and novel notion that the moral imperative to respect privacy is virtually as broad as the Kantian imperative to respect persons, a precise rationale is needed for abandoning what has been referred to here as the "usual way" of looking at privacy.

Reiman's account strikingly contrasts with theoretically less-inclusive accounts of privacy offered by most other theorists. It is more typical of privacy theories that the value of privacy is found in its capacities to make possible important human relationships, rather than to create and sustain persons, as Reiman contended. According to Charles Fried, privacy is a necessary context for relations of love, friendship, and trust.[5] Robert Gernstein argued that privacy is essential for the existence of intimate relationships.[6]

James Rachels maintained that privacy performs a number of important functions, including the prevention of embarassment and the disclosure of incriminating or damaging information.[7] Rachels argued that privacy's most important function is that it enables us to secure a variety of relationships with others. Privacy allows us to control information about ourselves, and thereby to shape relationships—allowing some to become intimate, keeping others at a distance. A frequent criticism of analyses like Fried's and Gernstein's is that although it is no doubt true that privacy can foster and promote intimate, loving, trusting interpersonal relationships, it is not a strict prerequisite for such relations.

Whereas Reiman's theory emphasized the importance of privacy relative to the individual's own personhood interests, these theorists assert that privacy's ultimate value lies in the individual's interests in interacting (or not) with others. Is it necessary to choose between these conceptions of the value of privacy? Note that both treat privacy as a means to another valued end. Is the conception of privacy as a means to personhood true, while the one that treats it as a means to desired personal relationships false?

Both conceptions appear to be true. Privacy promotes *both* individuals' personhood interests, as Reiman emphasized *and* their interests in interpersonal relationships, as others emphasized. To illustrate: *P* lives alone in a secluded dwelling. For *P* this is an ideal setting for reflection and self-analysis, which promote her development as a person. But the seclusion is also ideal for getting to know her prospective spouse. Privacy is important for *P*'s love relationship, freeing her from unwanted observation and distraction. *And* it is important for *P* as an individual, providing quiet and solitude for relaxation and self-expression, and for developing perspectives on herself and her experiences. Thus, privacy's importance stems from (at least) two interrelated sources. For the privacy that contributes to her development as a person thereby contributes to the development of her personal relationships; and the privacy that contributes to the development of her personal relationships thereby contributes to her development as a person.

To say that privacy, in general, protects interests individuals have in personal development and interpersonal relationships still leaves the nature of those interests—and privacy itself—in the dark more than necessary. For it is still possible to ask about the particular respects in which persons and interpersonal relationships are enabled to flourish where privacy is enjoyed. Toward this end Ruth Gavison has demonstrated, in her analysis of privacy and the right to it, that it is possible to characterize privacy less abstractly by reference to the multiplicity of specific interests it promotes.[8]

Privacy's Many Protective Functions

Ruth Gavison's analysis of privacy is a useful, straightforward catalogue of interests protected and promoted by privacy. Her analysis seeks to demystify the concept of privacy in a way that is theoretically cogent and consistent with common theoretical understandings of cognate concepts. Gavison defined privacy straightforwardly as "limited accessibility." Privacy and accessibility, on her characterization, are inversely proportional. The more privacy an individual has, the less accessibility; the more accessibility, the less privacy. Secrecy, anonymity, and solitude are the three chief dimensions of privacy. Secrecy (or confidentiality) is limited accessibility in the sense of *limited information about a person;* anonymity is limited accessibility in the sense of *limited attention paid to a person;* and solitude is limited accessibility in the sense of *limited contact with or sensing of a person.* The distinction between anonymity and solitude is important. The anonymity interest is an interest in not having attention drawn to us, not being singled out or identified when we wish otherwise. Anonymity may be desired when solitude is not. Anonymity is a kind of privacy we may desire, and reasonably desire, even in a public place. On the other hand, as film stars know very well, anonymity is sometimes impossible without retreat to a solitude that seals one off from others. A breach of secrecy may have as its consequence a loss of the possibility of either anonymity or solitude.

Rather than seek to justify a right to privacy on the basis of a single, ultimate value, as many previous theorists had sought to do, Gavison advanced what she termed a "functional" analysis of privacy. Rachels had to some extent stressed the multi-purposive character of privacy. But he selected a particular function and ranked it the "most important," something Gavison sought to avoid. On Gavison's account, privacy furthers a number of valued interests individuals have respecting their own persons and their lives as social and sexual beings. Individual autonomy, mental health, creativity, and the capacity to form and maintain meaningful relationships with others are some of the specific interests of the sort to which privacy contributes. Privacy, understood as secrecy, solitude, and anonymity, promotes relaxation and intimacy by removing persons from view; it relieves pressure to conform; it promotes freedom of thought and (hence) of action; it promotes inventiveness and creativity. Privacy also limits unfavorable social responses to a person's actions, history, or plans, including public ridicule, moral censure, unfavorable decisions, and the formation of unfavorable opinion.[9]

I will use Gavison's analysis of privacy, limited accessibility, to structure my examination of the ways in which privacy functions to protect the interests of women. By pointing out the special privacy interests of women through the windows of Gavison's tripartite analysis, two things will be made clear. First, Gavison's analysis contains an important theoretical inadequacy that relates directly to the privacy interests of women. Second, other existing privacy theories are similarly inadequate.

WOMEN AND INFORMATIONAL PRIVACY

The general value of informational privacy has been much discussed by lawyers and philosophers in the privacy literature. I want only to identify the interests of women that their right to limited information access (i.e., secrecy or confidentiality) could be expected to protect. Legal informational privacy rights protect by providing judicial remedies and deterring invasions. Moral informational privacy rights protect insofar as they become the basis of legal rights, and through their power as individually and socially effective action guides.

An important class of informational privacy interests relate to employment.[10] Female job applicants and employees are commonly asked to supply information about their marital or family status, which has no direct bearing on job qualifications or performance. Invasions of privacy of this type can occur during personal interviews or because of sex biases built into standard application forms. The invasions occur where women are presumed less independent or less dependable in light of their sex or of the roles they are presumed to have in their families. They also occur where being female or unmarried is improperly treated as a qualification for employment by a male employer or personnel officer who may anticipate sexual favors. Premised on female inferiority and subservience, these invasions are demeaning. But female victims of these invasions also suffer material consequences, such as loss of self-esteem and emotional distress. Substantial career and economic losses may accrue, as well, where a woman's employment is contingent upon her marital status or sexual availability.

Women commonly suffer unwarranted losses of informational privacy in the hands of the state.[11] In some states female rape victims still have inadequate statutory protection of their informational privacy rights, with the result that prosecutors are permitted to grill them about irrelevant aspects of their sexual histories. Women seeking welfare aid from the state are also asked irrelevant questions about their sexual lives and have an informational privacy interest in not answering them. Some disclosure of information is indeed necessary to the determination of qualifications and the prevention of fraud. But the state's interest in effective programs does not absolutely and automatically override the privacy interests of needy women and their families. Even if it were conceded that humiliation in the hands of the state's judicial and administrative officials has some justification, given the important goals of the criminal justice and welfare systems, women's interests in not suffering humiliation would not lose their relevance in the determination of what are acceptable practices.

Female students in colleges and universities have their privacy interests compromised by male instructors who press them under the guise of authority for information they would not seek to elicit from male students. Female students who are unwilling to disclose personal information to their professors risk retaliation in the form of low grades and lost educational opportunities. Physical forms of sexual harassment in the university and in the workplace are typically accompanied by prying questions.[12] This verbal harassment is another form of informational privacy invasion.

Discrimination against women by banks and lending institutions has been a much-discussed phenomenon to which the legal system has begun to address itself. Even so, widespread use of computerized information sources facilitate unfair expropriations and the exchange of financial histories by bad-faith lenders and creditors. Historic economic deprivations have resulted in institutions and prejudices that make women more likely than men to be disadvantaged by these practices.[13]

Injury to a woman's career, financial losses, losses of self-esteem, and emotional distress can follow invasions of her informational privacy. Emotional distress can include "fright, horror, grief, shame, humiliation, embarassment, anger, chagrin, [and] worry."[14] Explicit legal provisions and the existence of legal remedies cannot eliminate all the informational privacy invasions to which women are routinely subjected. Some of these are bad-faith invasions out of reach of the legal system. Suppose, for example, that in a one-on-one employment interview a woman is asked irrelevant personal questions in violation of law and company policy. Whether blatant or clothed in ambiguity, the invasion is one the interviewee will be unable to prove; she is unlikely to have the time or financial resources to seek redress; she may wrongly blame herself for the invasion. To bring about an end to this kind of informational privacy invasion it is necessary to strike a blow to the source of attitudinal sexism. Both small-scale "consciousness-raising" efforts and fundamental changes in social and legal institutions will be required to eliminate discriminatory attitudes. Personnel officer-training programs could teach men—and women—with hiring responsibilities ways to avoid informational privacy invasions. Public discussion and media exposure of these practices and their effects on women could work attitudinal changes.

The philosophical rationale for promoting change to protect these privacy interests of women can be couched in the terms of either a deontological or an instrumental ethic. From a Kantian deontological perspective, protecting these interests is in keeping with respecting them as full and equal moral persons. By protecting these interests, what some feminists term the ideology of sexual hierarchy and male domination is supplanted by respect for individuals. A society which so dignifies women is to that extent on the road to becoming a just society. Instrumentally, the special privacy interests of women promote their emotional and economic well-being, which in turn can be expected to promote the aggregate well-being of society.

ANONYMITY FOR WOMEN

Anonymity privacy invasions are commonly experienced by women in public places. Women of all ages are approached by men seeking their names, phone numbers, or other personal information. Women are followed, taunted, and mocked. Fearful, resentful, and distressed, women come to accept not being left alone. They come to accept deprivations of informational privacy (being questioned about personal matters by strangers) and anonymity (being singled out by strangers) as a way of life. But acceptance has a cost. Its cost is to be measured by its cumulative effects on the victimized women, and on the quality of the social life of their communities. One evident effect of continual invasions of anonymity is that women come to believe they are "fair game" if they venture into public places into which men may go to find repose. This can only lead to a perpetuation of the hostility and mistrust many women have for men.

I have stated that invasions of anonymity have a cost. But are these typically minor invasions of any moral consequence? Thomson's account of privacy dealt only a little with minor privacy offenses; she focused instead on privacy offenses of a sort persons would ideally have a *legal duty* to avoid. Minor offenses were characterized as "bad behavior" offenses of no legal *or* moral consequence.

But suppose one passenger on a public bus reads a personal letter over another's shoulder when he might as easily have gazed out the window. It will be readily agreed that nothing the legal system should strain to address directly has occurred. Thomson, I believe, would say that nothing of *moral* consequence has occurred. We have no right against having our letters read by strangers if we chose to read them on a public bus. Yet the letter's owner is likely to experience a distressing loss of privacy due to a perfectly avoidable act of someone who, let us presume, knows the privacy conventions respecting letters. The offense against privacy is not the greatest conceivable offense—imagine a more aggressive passenger who would dare to snatch the letter for a better look. But it is not obvious (as Thomson seemed to think it is) that such offenses should not be described as violations of moral rights or as some other recognizable moral offense.

Willingness to say that a moral privacy offense has been perpetrated against the letter owner depends upon questions of theory Thomson did not discuss. I cannot venture into the complexities of moral theory here. But the letter reader's behavior is surely behavior that should be discouraged. Neither should minor invasions of anonymity and informational privacy to which women are frequently subject in public places be encouraged. That they should not be encouraged does not turn "bad behavior" into moral offense or harm. The argument could be made, however, that where they are frequently perpetrated against the same class of persons, and their actual effect is emotional distress fed by the cumulative impact of similar offenses, minor privacy offenses *are* of moral consequence. *P*'s sitting uninvited next to a woman on a park bench, asking for her name, or leering at her would be mere annoyance but for the fact that this is an extremely frequent kind of unwanted experience suffered by women. At least to the same extent as men (in the communities in which this is a problem), women should be able to enjoy the experience of not being singled out *because they are women* when they appear in public. A degree of repose in public is a reasonable expectation of privacy.

It is the anonymity interest of women, as a *class,* that argues against the public display of sexually explicit publications.[15] The so-called "men's entertainment" magazines call attention to women by graphic display of what in our society are still regarded as private— the sex organs. The configuration of the female body is no secret to adults of either sex. Nevertheless, public uses of pornography contribute to the syndrome of male "leering" whereby women in public places are subject to pointed comments about individual parts of their bodies by strangers.

WOMEN AND SOLITUDE

Enjoying privacy in public has been a problem for women; but so has enjoying privacy at home. Limited accessibility within their homes is perhaps the most important—and most complex—privacy interest of women. Women have not always had the freedom, nor the independence of mind, needed to secure solitude and enjoy it once secured. To begin, the traditional caretaker functions of women have allowed them little time for themselves. The enjoyment of privacy becomes possible for women only as they yield certain traditional family roles. The roles to be yielded are not their roles as mothers and wives per se. As psychologist Jean Baker Miller has pointed out, most women do not want an autonomy which

> carries the implication—and for women therefore the threat—that one should be able to pay the price of giving up affiliations in order to become a separate and self-directed individual. . . . Women are quite validly seeking something more complete than autonomy as it is defined for men, a fuller not a lesser ability to encompass relationships to others, simultaneous with the fullest development of oneself.[16]

If this is correct, it is clear why the quest for solitude has been particularly difficult for women unwilling to eschew the family. With modern standards of nurture and education, motherhood can be the antithesis of solitude. Moreover, women's often-unreciprocated, often-subservient caretaking functions with respect to their husbands have denied them both the *opportunity* for solitude and the *ability* to enjoy and exploit the modicum of privacy their lives as wives and mothers afforded.

Jeffrey Reiman and others who have written about the relationship of privacy to personal development have suggested that privacy functions to maintain boundaries that can and should be drawn between ourselves and others. Solitude as a privacy convention contributes to the process of self-definition and personality development. To be a subservient caretaker is to be denied the possibility of both. Again, quoting Dr. Miller:

> To concentrate on and take seriously one's own development is hard enough for all human beings. But, as has been recently demonstrated in many areas, it has been even harder for women. Women are not encouraged to develop as far as they possibly can and to experience the stimulation and the anguish, anxiety, and pain the process entails. Instead, they are encouraged to avoid self-analysis and to concentrate on forming and maintaining a relationship to one person.[17]

Thus, the problem of privacy for women has been in part the problem of achieving a degree of solitude notwithstanding their roles and responsibilities; and upon achieving it through shared parenting, egalitarian marriages, or total abrogation of traditional lifestyles, using it to formulate and further their ends.

Women have a special privacy interest in a solitude that affords them the possibility of the full development of their unique personalities. And this implies yet a further special privacy interest, namely, the freedom to choose when and to what extent the privacy-limiting experiences of motherhood and marriage are undertaken. Thus, although there can be no legal right to domestic solitude enforceable against a woman's children and spouse, her interests in domestic solitude can be legally protected indirectly, through the protection of her freedom to choose when and to what extent the privacy-limiting experiences of motherhood and traditional marriage are undertaken.

Sexual politics and politics proper reveal that men and the state are co-choosers and regulators of the choices women make. Questions concerning the precise extent to which men and women, husbands and wives, ought to have equal voice in decisions relating to childbearing and child nurturance remain some of the most difficult. Social and political morality also pose unanswered questions about the just limit of state regulation of sexual relations and parenting.

Privacy and Choice

It was just suggested that women must have a freedom to choose if they are to secure much-needed privacy; an important dimension of privacy, domestic solitude, is protected only if women have the freedom of choice respecting sex, childbearing, and marriage. Does this mean that a right to certain choices is included in the right to privacy the state ought to recognize? Let us recall that Gavison did not include a "right to choice" among the rights she designated as the rights of limited accessibility constituting privacy. Nor did Judith Thomson's cluster of privacy rights include a "right to choice" component. Indeed, none of the theorists whose privacy right analyses have been mentioned here expressly included freedom of choice respecting sex, childbearing, and marriage as a privacy interest to be protected by the right to privacy they defended. What *is* the conceptual relationship between privacy and choice, the right to privacy and the right to free choice?

Free choice is an important means by which privacy interests may be promoted in a liberal society. If women cannot choose among motherhood, marriage, and their alternatives, they will continue to find it difficult to secure privacy and conditions requisite to the meaningful enjoyment of privacy. Sexual inequality is perpetuated if women are choiceless and thereby confined to roles that have historically denied them the opportunity for and ability to enjoy privacy. Free to choose, women enjoy privacy in the sense of *limited control by others of matters affecting their sexual and familial life*.

Thus women's privacy interests can be seen as falling into two classes: (a) liberty interests, or interests in limiting their accessibility to others through non-regulation and non-control by others of their sexual and familial lives; and (b) privacy per se interests, or, interests in limiting their accessibility to others through secrecy, anonymity, and solitude. Ideally, a right to privacy would protect both classes of women's privacy interests. For women have *both* kinds of privacy interests at stake.

That privacy interests are both (a) liberty interests and (b) privacy per se interests has led to considerable confusion about what the right to privacy is and what it ought to protect. So, for instance, while Gavison cast only privacy interests of class (b) under the privacy rubric, another theorist, June A. Eichbaum, limited a recent privacy study to privacy interests of class (a).[18] And although both acknowledged the existence of other privacy concerns, neither adequately considered the implications of her respective exclusions.

It is clear that Eichbaum restricted her discussion to class (a) privacy interests as a matter of expedience to narrow its scope. Her quite specific aim was to argue that the right to privacy could not with justice be interpreted as a right of individuals in traditional family roles to have interests protected relating to the promotion of male-headed nuclear families. She adduced evidence from *Griswold v. Connecticut*, 381 U.S. 479 (1965), and its progeny strongly suggesting that privacy in the United States still threatens to be about, as Kate Millett put it, "keeping taboos in their place."[19] Appealing to the equal protection clause and to Ronald Dworkin's notion of a right to equal respect and concern, Eichbaum argued that persons generally—homosexuals, the unmarried, pregnant teens— have a liberty interest in matters directly affecting their personal lives. This interest in free choice, not the sanctity of the traditional family, is the genuine basis of the right to privacy.

Eichbaum did not explain how class (a) privacy interests, which she defended as basic to the right to privacy, relate to informational and other class (b) privacy interests commonly thought to be protected by the right to privacy. No unified conception of the right to privacy was provided.

Whereas Eichbaum limited her discussion of the right to privacy for reasons of convenience, Gavison limited hers to privacy per se interests under the felt force of theoretical necessity. She excluded from the right to privacy umbrella "prohibitions of such conduct as abortions, the use of contraceptives, and 'un-natural' sexual inter-

course; insulting, harassing, or persecuting behaviors [and] regulation of the way familial obligations should be discharged."[20] Remaining under the umbrella were:

> such "typical" invasions of privacy as the collection, storage, and
> computerization of information; the dissemination of information
> about individuals; peeping, following, watching, and photographing
> individuals; intruding or entering "private" places; eavesdropping,
> wire-tapping, reading of letters, drawing attention to individuals,
> required testing of individuals; and forced disclosure of information.[21]

Gavison maintained that the exluded offenses involve losses of
liberty rather than *privacy*. The class of excluded offenses was
removed from the privacy umbrella for the sake of conceptual
clarity. Only privacy interests per se were to be protected by the
right to privacy she defended.

In some respects Gavison's exclusions and inclusions are arbitrary. Why, for example, is harassing a loss of liberty, but calling
attention to someone a loss of privacy per se? How would she
classify harassment-by-drawing-attention-to? Is it a loss of liberty or
of privacy?

Gavison argued that unless a line is drawn between privacy *per se*
and liberty, the concept of privacy loses its theoretical distinctness.
A broader conception of privacy as "being let alone," she argued,
would encompass all of the intuitively includable privacy interests,
whether interests of liberty or privacy per se. But it would also
encompass virtually any other harm or offense perpetrated against
persons. For what insult or injury could not be construed as the
failure to let someone alone?

Gavison is not convincing on this point. It is not self-evident that a
definition of privacy broad enough to include the items she excluded
from the privacy umbrella would have to be as broad as the "being
let alone" formulation of privacy. Jeffrey Reiman, for one, heartily
embraced a broad account on the theory that our privacy is a broad
complex of social practices and our privacy interests a broad
complex of person-creating and person-sustaining interests. From
the vantage point of Reiman's theory it could be argued that liberty
interests do not have to be excluded for the sake of clarity. It was
earlier contended that Reiman's account suffers from ambiguity and
lack of specificity on the matter of which practices are privacy
practices and just what it means to say a person has "moral title" to
her existence. I also pointed out that it might be rejected for its
inclusiveness. But inclusiveness per se is not an objection to
Reiman's theory. Nor is exclusiveness per se a virtue of Gavison's.
For this reason Gavison should have offered a reason in principle for

supposing that all possible inclusive theories will be inadequate if she was to convince us of the reasonableness of her exclusive account.

The plain recognition that certain class (a) and (b) privacy interests are often experientially inextricable also renders unconvincing Gavison's attempt to justify simplifying privacy and the right to it. A woman who is told she is not free to have an abortion is likely to experience both a loss of liberty and a loss of privacy. Indeed, the feeling that privacy has been invaded may be stronger than the feeling that her liberty has been diminished. The state has entered the most intimate domain of her life and has determined how she is to order the most personal aspect of her life, and in that sense invaded her privacy. Some such invasions by the state are no doubt justified by appeal to legitimate governmental functions or political duties of individuals. But because privacy interests are implicated in certain diminunitions of liberty, a right to privacy that adequately protected the full range of women's privacy interests would also have to protect an array of personal liberties. It was therefore proper and natural that the Supreme Court in the landmark *Griswold* decision would frame the *liberty* to purchase contraceptives as a right to *privacy* question.

Theoretical difficulties are posed by a right to privacy inclusive enough to protect both class (a) and class (b) interests. But other difficulties are posed by the fiat of declaring class (a) interests to be "really" liberty interests, rather than genuine privacy interests. For the fact of the matter is that they are *both* privacy interests. Liberty in the area of sexual and familial concerns and privacy per se are interrelated privacy interests. This interrelatedness is one of the things those who seek to explain our privacy interests must explain.

The foregoing discussion has made some progress in that direction. The interrelatedness of privacy and a certain kind of liberty has been explained by showing that privacy as solitude in one's home, so important for the continued development of women as persons, often depends upon freedom or liberty to choose one's lifestyle. Thus, while solitude outside the home depends upon a privacy right to anonymity, confidentiality, and solitude in Gavison's sense, a woman's solitude in her home will depend much more on a privacy right to choice.

We are left with the difficult problem of articulating the standards, legal and moral, of justifying limitations on a woman's free choice in matters affecting her sexual and familiar life. Whatever else is true, the standards would be expected to reflect an egalitarian conception of men and women. Yet, *many* lifestyles and family forms are consistent with the social ideal of sexual egalitarianism. Meaningful moral standards would have to be formulated in relation to particular lifestyles and family forms, and the particular vows and commitments of the parties involved.

That the development of legal standards of free choice for women is complex is well-illustrated by the dilemmas posed by prostitution.[22] Some women claim a privacy interest for themselves against criminalization of prostitution. They argue that laws which make prostitution a punishable offense violate their *privacy* right to have sexual relations with consenting adults of their own choice. That prostitution is a commercial enterprise distinguishes it from marital and other noncommercial forms of sexual activity. But the commercial aspect of the "oldest profession" may simply make the case for complete legalization stronger: private enterprise rights join with sexual privacy rights to give distinct plausibility to the legalization argument. Opposition to the legalization of prostitution comes from those who argue that women lose more in dignity and opportunity than they gain through prostitution, that prostitution is a product and symptom of male domination, or that prostitution encourages vice and crime, including physical injury to prostitutes themselves.

While considerations of free choice argue for allowing prostitution, dignitarian considerations and related social ideals argue for prohibition. That certain dignitarian objections are temptingly construed as "merely" moral and of no interest to liberal states whose aim is to be morally neutral and to avoid paternalism is a further complication. Articulating a legal standard that is something other than the ubiquitous mandate to "balance interests" is barred where it is clear neither where affected parties' interests lie nor which of their interests are relevant to the determination of laws. It remains unclear whether freedom to prostitute is among the genuine sexual privacy interests of women.

Conclusion

As attempts to articulate moral and constitutional rights to privacy continue, the privacy interests of women must not be overlooked or underemphasized. Women have special privacy interests in what Gavison called secrecy, anonymity, and solitude. But they also have a special privacy interest in freedom of choice in marital, sexual, and reproductive concerns. Women need this freedom of choice to structure their lives in ways that afford the domestic solitude requisite for their continued development as persons. A legal right to privacy must protect all of privacy's dimensions—secrecy, anonymity, solitude, *and* choice—if women's privacy interests are to be adequately protected. A society which protects these interests shields women from low self-esteem, emotional distress, and loss of opportunities and income. Liberal ideals such as liberty, equality, equal opportunity, and personal productivity are more surely advanced where women are treated with respect and they are free from discriminatory legal institutions, social policy, and customs.

Notes

1. Judith Jarvis Thomson, "The Right to Privacy," *Philosophy and Public Affairs* 4, no. 4 (1975): 295-314.
2. Thomas Scanlon, "Thomson on Privacy," *Philosophy and Public Affairs* 4, no. 4 (1975): 314-22.
3. Jeffrey Reiman, "Privacy, Intimacy, and Personhood," *Philosophy and Public Affairs* 6, no. 1 (1976): 26-44.
4. Ibid., p. 39.
5. Charles Fried, "Privacy," *Yale Law Journal* 77 (1968): 475-93.
6. Robert S. Gernstein, "Intimacy and Privacy," *Ethics* 89, no. 1 (1978): 76-81.
7. James Rachels, "Why Privacy Is Important," *Philosophy and Public Affairs* 4, no. 4 (1975): 321-33.
8. Ruth Gavison, "Privacy and the Limits of Law," *Yale Law Journal* 89, no. 3 (1980): 421-71.
9. Ibid., p. 440 ff.
10. See Catherine MacKinnon, *Sexual Harassment of Working Women* (New Haven: Yale University Press, 1979); Lin Farley, *Sexual Shakedown: The Sexual Harassment of Women on the Job* (New York: McGraw Hill, 1978); see also Alice Montgomery, "Sexual Harassment in the Work Place," *Golden Gate University Law Review* 10, no. 1 (1980): 879-928; Barbara M. White, "Job-Related Sexual Harassment and Union Women: What Are Their Rights?", *Golden Gate University Law Review* 10, no. 1 (1980): 929-62.
11. Mary Dunlap, "Where the Person Ends, Does the State Begin? An Exploration of Present Controversies Concerning 'The Right to Privacy,' " *Lincoln Law Review* 12, no. 2 (1981): 47-75; Andra M. Pearldaughter and Vivian Schneider, "Women and Welfare: The Cycle of Female Proverty," *Golden Gate University Law Review* 10, no. 1 (1980): 1043-86; J. F. Handler and M. K. Roseheim, "Privacy in Welfare," *Law and Contemporary Problems* 31, no. 31 (1966): 377; J. F. Handler, and E. J. Hollingsworth, "Stigma, Privacy and Other Attitudes of Welfare Recipients," *Stanford Law Review* 22, no. 1 (1969): 1.
12. White, "Sexual Harassment," p. 937.
13. See Andrew Cuomo, "Equal Credit," *Journal of Legislation* 8, no. 4 (1981): 121-39.
14. Montgomery, "Sexual Harassment in the Work Place," p. 889.
15. Barbara S. Bryant, "Sexual Display of Women's Bodies—A Violation of Privacy," *Golden Gate University Law Review* 10, no. 1 (1980): 1211-25.
16. Jean Baker Miller, *Toward a New Psychology of Women* (Boston: Beacon Press, 1976), pp. 94-95.
17. Ibid., p. 18.
18. June A. Eichbaum, "Towards an Autonomy-Based Theory of Constitutional Privacy: Beyond the Ideology of Familial Privacy," *Harvard Civil Rights and Civil Liberties Law Review* 14, no. 2 (1979): 361-84.
19. Millett's comment appears in Elaine Partnow, ed. *The Quotable Woman* (Garden City, N. Y.: Doubleday, 1978), p. 336.
20. Gavison, "Privacy," p. 436.
21. Ibid.
22. Catherine D. Perry, "Right of Privacy Challenges to Prostitution Statutes," *Washington University Law Quarterly* 58, no. 2 (1980): 439-71.

14

A Feminist Analysis of the Universal Declaration of Human Rights

HELEN BEQUAERT HOLMES

The Universal Declaration of Human Rights (UDHR) is a magnificent document.[1] It is a clear testimony that some human beings—represented by the framers of the Declaration—hold within their hearts a deep respect for the personhood of all members of the human species. According to the text of this document, each individual on Earth is equal in dignity to every other person and deserves protection by the law.

On December 21, 1948, at its third session, the General Assembly of the United Nations adopted the UDHR, with 48 nation-states voting in favor.[2] If the UDHR were truly in effect—if, in fact, each and every government in those 48 nations held to each and every Article—the lives of all men *and* all women would be greatly enhanced. Oppression, want, suffering, and injustice would be lessened. But, unfortunately, ours is an imperfect world: since most of those nations pay only lip-service to many of the Articles in the UDHR, its ideals and goals remain to be realized.

Even when nations in good faith do implement the UDHR, women encounter problems in obtaining their human rights. The phraseology of many of the Articles betrays the (I hope) unconscious bias of the framers that women are not actual persons. Indeed, there is evidence that, when certain Articles of the UDHR *have* been implemented by nations (or by global organs such as the World Bank), women in some parts of the world have even lost some of the meager rights they previously had.[3] Subtle bias in language usage may translate into deprivation of rights for as much as 51 percent of humankind.

In the United Nations, the organs and instruments that were brought into being to protect general human rights have failed to defend the human rights of women; furthermore, the special instruments *for* women have been ineffective because of limitations in their terms of reference and in their powers.[4] For example, the Commission on the Status of Women, set up on June 21, 1946, with very limited power, has over the years managed to secure the adoption of a number of international instruments that deal with specific rights of women,[5] but the implementation record is still poor. Disturbed by the continuing oppression and suffering of women throughout the world, this Commission began preparing an inclusive document in 1974. A final version was adopted by the General Assembly on December 18, 1979.[6] This "Convention on the Elimination of All Forms of Discrimination Against Women" (CEAFDAW) calls for equal rights for women in all arenas—political, economic, social, cultural, civil. It went into force officially in September of 1981 after the twentieth nation had ratified it.[7]

In this chapter I point out four problems with the original UDHR, flaws in the text that reveal a general lack of awareness of the condition of women. Certain expressions and words, I maintain, have the potential to continue to limit the human rights of women. It is true that the several U. N. instruments dealing with specific rights of women and the new CEAFDAW have recognized and spoken to some of these concerns, but problems still remain. My analysis will examine some of the current difficulties in implementing human rights and may clarify our vision of the better world we struggle to achieve.

I approach the UDHR as a biologist and as a feminist. The UDHR is a biological statement in that it specifies how we as humans have risen above our biological animalness until we have become creatures who ascribe "rights" to each other. "The uniqueness of humankind comes indeed from its potential ability to escape from the tyranny of its biological heritage."[8] Throughout the centuries and around the world, however, women have generally been defined and delimited by their biology. Thus it is particularly difficult for government agencies and individual administrators to comprehend or even consider that women are to receive the rights specified by a declaration that turns human animals into persons. My criticisms start with Article 16, the one that is most closely concerned with the biological aspects of human nature.

Article 16, Part 3

Article 16 treats the biosocial group, the family. Part 3 states, "The family is the natural and fundamental group unit of society and is

entitled to protection by society and the State."[9] Let us examine
how these seemingly bland assertions may actually jeopardize the
human rights of women and children.

A definition for "family" is the first problem, since each of us has
a personal mental image of this concept. The patriarchs of philosophy have described their visions of the ideal family structure.
Different ethnic groups have different definitions—nuclear, extended, matrilineal, patrilineal, patrilocal, etc. "In a sense, everyone is an expert on the family and has an opinion, deriving from
ultimately unarguable premises of firsthand knowledge."[10] Unfortunately, those with the power to implement Article 16 will implement
it to conform to their own concepts of "family." (In the United
States, for example, the normative family apparently is the two-
parents-with-two-children-under-18 family, which, according to the
1970 census, constituted only 15 percent of American families.)[11] In
short, the first difficulty with Article 16 is that, because some
definition for family must be assumed whenever supporting laws are
enacted, and because we have no guarantee that a wise definition
will be chosen, we risk totalitarian control over people's lives when
laws protecting "families" are enforced.

Indeed, it *is* necessary for relatively helpless, human children to
depend on other humans for care before they are competent to cope
on their own with life-maintenance activities. As *Homo sapiens*
evolved, groups that were the forerunners of what we now call
families served this function and also "required language, planning,
cooperation, self-control, foresight, and cultural learning. [They]
provided the framework for all pre-state society and the fount of its
creativeness."[12] And modern families can serve as interpersonal
support systems, as havens from the competitiveness of the industrial age.

To be sure, some of us *have* experienced a loving and caring
family, with members supporting each other across the generations.
But more of us than would care to admit have seen our only close-up
examples of hate and mistrust in deep and scarring parent-offspring
and husband-wife conflicts. On the one hand, divided and uncohe-
sive families may be the places where youth learn to inflict physical
and verbal harm. On the other hand, intense family cohesion may
feed into tribalism and fail to foster worldwide sisterhood and
brotherhood. Furthermore, since no one has yet achieved a just and
humane world, perhaps there is something faulty with a vision of the
"natural and fundamental group unit" of society. My second difficulty with Article 16, therefore, is that families as they have come to
function in the twentieth century may be a shaky base on which to
build world peace and justice.

But my main contention with Part 3 of Article 16 is the phrase "entitled to protection by society and the State." In practice this phrase seems to be widely interpreted to mean that all legal means are to be used to keep families as families. In certain parts of both Western and Eastern civilizations, for example, divorce—and even separation—are forbidden. My third explicit objection to this part of Article 16 is therefore that protection of the family can harm individuals, depriving them, in many cases, of the rights granted to them by Articles 3, 4, and 5. For example, if a person is being kept imprisoned within the family home by other members of the family and if then the law requires such a person to stay there, then the right to life, liberty and security of that person has been violated.[13] Wives and daughters may be required to perform household and farm chores and to be always available for sexual intercourse. These are forms of slavery—and Article 4 states flatly that "slavery . . . shall be prohibited in all [its] forms."[14] And individual family members are sometimes subjected to torture, or to cruel, inhuman, or degrading treatment, which is in violation of Article 5.[15] Human rights are not served when judges—as they commonly do—send abused children back to the abusing family, nor when police—as *they* commonly do—send battered wives back to their husbands.

Of course, women are the ones who are most likely to have their rights from Articles 3, 4, and 5 violated, and men are the ones who stand to gain from the sexual and housework slavery. This is my fourth concern: the family fosters patriarchy and hierarchy. The state depends on exploiting families as fundamental units in order to protect its own power. Because of labor surplus, wage-earners must be conformists to keep their jobs to support their families.[16] The nuclear family is necessary to capital, an essential core of patriarchy, a micro-unit of the larger society with its own hierarchy.[17] The mother's duty is to prepare her child for the patriarchal system.[18] "The family's existence assumes that a woman will subordinate her individual interests to those of others," thus putting women's equality and the family into conflict.[19]

Note that the "family-heading" role has sometimes turned out to be a two-edged sword for men: while a man wields authority and power over all the members of "his" family, he also incurs a life-long obligation (often an emotionally painful, psychologically debilitating, and/or physically disabling obligation) to provide the financial support for this family.

What should governmental policy be toward families? Just as keeping families together at all costs can be harmful to individual rights, so can the state's usurpation of child-rearing tasks. As demonstrated by the juvenile courts in the United States in the twentieth century and by Soviet communism's initial policy of separating children from their parents, the state is not skilled at raising children, and may even inflict harm.[20] The wise and humane course would seem to be to strengthen the human rights of women and children, who are the potential victims both of abuse within the family and of unwise state intervention. Many decisions of the U. S. Supreme Court in the 1970s have done just this.[21] In the UDHR, Part 2 of Article 25 states: "Motherhood and childhood are entitled to special care and assistance. All children, whether born in or out of wedlock, shall enjoy the same social protection." This should be vigorously implemented.

Unfortunately, even the CEAFDAW has not come to grips with the issue of "family." That document uses "family" in several places where the context indicates that a family—whatever the word may mean—is in fact assumed to be a "fundamental unit." Also the CEAFDAW does not refer in any way to battered wives or abused children, except obliquely by the clause, "in all cases the interests of the children shall be paramount." This caution, this failure to take a radical stance, is understandable. The members of the Commission on the Status of Women come from a spectrum of nations around the globe. In some places, the only hope a woman has for status and for happiness is through the family. For example, in some nations, if a woman produces one or more male children and then survives childbirth and a period of slavery to her mother-in-law, she acquires power within the family, in particular over her own daughters-in-law. There is no other means to fulfillment. In central Africa, the woman who survives genital excision and/or infibulation and then childbirth will after some years acquire the power to perform or to schedule such an operation on her own daughter or granddaughter.[22] Many women in developing countries still conceive of family as an essential framework for their personhood. It may well be that in their unconscious cost-benefit analyses, the power and security they obtain from family structure outweigh the oppression.

Western women, however, are often ready to embrace new definitions and new visions of the family, believing that some changes are essential for a better world. As Kathleen Gough says,

> The past of the family does not limit its future. Although the family probably emerged with humanity, neither the family itself nor particular family forms are genetically determined. The sexual division of labor—until recently, universal—need not, and in my opinion should not, survive in industrial society. . . . The family was essential to the dawn of civilization, allowing a vast qualitative leap forward in cooperation, purposive knowledge, love, and creativeness. But today, rather than enhancing them, the confinement of women in homes

and small families—like their subordination in work—artificially limits these human capacities.[23]

Article 16, Part 1

In my evaluation of the remaining parts of Article 16, I agree completely with Part 2, which states that marriage shall be entered into only with the free and full consent of the intending spouses. I also strongly support the second sentence of Part 1, that men and women are entitled to equal rights as to marriage, during marriage, and at its dissolution. It would indeed be to the great advantage of women if those provisions were in effect throughout the world.

Problems, however, occur with one phrase within the first sentence of Part 1: "Men and women of full age, without any limitation due to race, nationality or religion, have the right to marry and to found a family." The word order in the phrase "right to marry and to found a family" gives a strong implication that marriage is required before procreation. This statement may have been composed for the purpose of stating explicitly the very important right that no state, nor any other authority, should *forbid* a marriage on the basis of a difference between the two persons in their race or in their citizenship or in their religion. The "marry and found" word order at the end of the sentence, however, can be interpreted as a requirement of marriage before parenting, and thus reduce individual rights. It might also subtly decree a lower status to out-of-wedlock children, thus reviving the concept of illegitimacy, the blaming-the-victim concept so out of place in the modern world.[24]

The implications of the phrase, "right . . . to found a family" mirror many of the problems in women's lives in the world today. The phrase reflects an attitude that "founding a family" is a value. It implies that those who procreate are thereby more valuable people, that they deserve privileges in society—or, rather, that those who do not found families ought to be discriminated against. It hints that a woman's life is of no value unless she marries and *then* produces biological children "for" her husband.[25]

One interpretation of this right is that procreation itself is a positive "right." A corollary to such a right is: if all persons have the right to procreate, and if they are biologically unable to procreate, then the state reasonably could presume that it had an obligation or a duty to do everything in its power to make it possible for them to procreate, if they so choose. Indeed, the proponents of in vitro fertilization (test-tube babies) look upon their work as a moral duty, as a means of extending this "right" to more people.[26]

Should public funds then be appropriated to provide in vitro fertilization to everyone who wants it? At the moment, in the USA, only the relatively rich can be candidates for this procedure because of its high cost. Again, since only a few types of infertility can be "treated" by this particular procedure,[27] should not additional public funds be expended to find equivalent solutions for all other types of infertility? In order for procreation to be a positive right, it must be made available to all, both rich and poor, and to those who are infertile for any reason whatsoever. Obviously, this would be a ludicrous expenditure of public moneys when a worldwide population explosion threatens the resources of our planet and when the medically advanced nations consume a disproportionate share of those resources.

Even in the USA, where there are acceptable things other than motherhood for women to do with their lives, status in the local community accrues to any woman who has children (*if* she is wedded to a man, of course, and if there are not too many children!). And sociologists report that teenage pregnancy occurs in some cases not through ignorance of biology, but through a desire for proving oneself a true woman. And even liberated feminists, including lesbians, wish to give birth for entirely different reasons. "Childbirth—the bringing forth of new life energy—is quintessentially a woman's event."[28] It is very tempting to seek procreation as a "right."

Yet, women who are accepted for in vitro fertilization have their bodies and their sex activities monitored closely; they pay large amounts of money; and most attempts end in failure.[29] I believe that such women should not be tempted by suggestions that they might be able to have this procedure granted to them as a "right." Is it not far better for society to find other means for recognizing the worth of women? Accordingly, I recommend that the first sentence of Part 1 of Article 16 be interpreted as follows: "Men and women . . . have the right not to be prevented by the state from marrying or from having children." Such an interpretation protects individual liberties without subtly encouraging pronatalism.

A Missing Right

A third flaw in the UDHR is the failure to make an explicit statement of *the right to one's own body*. Alternatively, this right could be called control over one's body, the right to bodily integrity, or the right to oneself. In 1906 an Illinois appellate court declared that the right to the inviolability of one's person was "a free citizen's first and greatest right . . . the subject of universal acquiescence."[30] It is curious that, since Illinois judges three-quarters of a century ago considered this to be the "first and greatest" right, it somehow was never fully expressed in the Universal Declaration.

The UDHR does, to be sure, contain some hints to this right. Article 3 states that everyone has the right to "security of person." Article 4 forbids slavery, that is, it forbids anyone from legal ownership of another's body. Article 12 states that "no one shall be subjected to arbitrary interference with his privacy."[31] Since many manipulations of one's body come in the "privacy" area, one might stretch the meaning of Article 12 to say that this includes the sole right to the use of one's own body. And, of course, Article 5, which prohibits torture, is meant to protect a person's body as well as a person's mind. But if the right to one's own body *is* the first and greatest right, then surely this right should have been made explicit in the UDHR. When specific rights were first enumerated in Article 3, this should have been stated, either as a second sentence or as a second part in that Article.[32]

This right to one's body would allocate all decision-making power regarding one's body to oneself. A most obvious application, of course, is in medicine. Patients would have the right to the whole truth about their medical problems, the right to privacy and personal dignity, the right to refuse any test, procedure, and treatment, the right to read and copy their own medical records.[33] With the Illinois case mentioned above, the appellate court declared for the patient who had undergone surgery without prior knowledge. An explicit statement of this right is of great importance: such an assertion would validate individual persons; it would open the way toward improving the condition of women.

One's body is the only tangible object that *is* oneself. If this body is treated as something inviolable, then a human being has validity, has recognition. Following the theory of Sara Ann Ketchum,[34] I do not think of a body as being a person's property—instead it *is* the person. This is far different from being something owned *by* the person.

Male behavior often reveals that women's bodies are considered to be the property of men—husbands, lovers, fathers, pimps. A father demands a bride price or loans his daughter's body to an overnight visitor; a husband assumes that marriage gives him unlimited access to his wife's body. Or women's bodies are considered to be common property: the attitude that a woman's body is to be raped; that women co-workers can be fondled; that doctors need not get consent before manipulations to a woman's body; that population planners in developing countries may give wholesale injections to huge numbers of women to render them infertile. The sadomasochistic, flourishing pornography industry thrives on this belief—that women's bodies are not part of their personhood.

The right to one's own body, if it could actually be implemented in full, would thus have profound implications for women. As a primary benefit, women could really decide when *to* and when *not to* have children! Women then would be given information about their bodies and the full range of selection of methods to control fertility. Alice Rossi has said: "Without the means to prevent, and to control the timing of conception, economic and political rights have limited meaning for women. If women cannot plan their pregnancies, they can plan little else in their lives."[35]

Control of population in developing countries is considered to be strategic to U. S. foreign policy; military terminology (such as "target population") is used in these campaigns against the bodies of poor women. One population planner told me that, should women from such "target populations" be allowed to participate in making decisions about population policy and about fertility control, Earth would have a truly gigantic population problem. Such planners really do believe that women, as a whole, want to have one baby after another. Or they believe that poor women do, even if their "own" wives do not. It is only too true that in most parts of the world women do need (and get) extra status from producing off-spring, but they do not necessarily want or get increased status by producing *large* quantities of children. A few living children are enough, as long as some of them are males! And even in countries where large families are official policy and mothers get financial rewards, women in general may fear the dangers of childbirth, and they may worry that their existing children may starve. Husbands and lovers bring excess children into existence: they often refuse to cooperate when a particular method of contraception requires male compliance. Despite their rhetoric, the population controllers really do know this, for their custom is to advocate methods of contraception in women that require absolutely no male cooperation, such as Depo-Provera and IUDs that risk the health of women while permitting men unlimited access to women.[36]

Lucy Stone, in a letter to Antoinette Brown in 1858, said, "The right to vote will yet be swallowed up in the real question, viz., has woman a right to herself? It is very little to me to have the right to vote, to own property, etc., if I may not keep my body, and its uses, in my absolute right."[37]

Some Problems with Wording

To communicate with you I have been using words. But what is the relation of words to reality? Words are a human invention to describe reality—they are not reality and can never be a perfect match for reality. But words can define and limit reality. They do so when they are used to describe an ideal, as in the UDHR. "Language is not neutral—it is not merely a vehicle that carries ideas. It is itself a shaper of ideas."[38]

The UDHR is to be praised for what it has done; we have no way of knowing how much worse the world would be without it. But sometimes it may have come closer to achieving its goals with men than with women; language may have been responsible for this difference.

According to paragraph 5 of the Preamble of the UDHR, "the peoples of the United Nations have . . . reaffirmed their faith . . . in the equal rights of men and women."[39] Furthermore, Article 2 states that "all rights are set forth without distinction of any kind . . . including sex."[40] These statements imply that, should a male-genderized term be used to describe a right in any Article, such usage would be a *generic* use. The masculine form would have been used to stand for both males and females. I object to the frequent use of generic forms in the Declaration; I maintain that the use of the words "man," "mankind," and "he" in 13 Articles has had unfortunate consequences for women. Like Korsmeyer I point out that "language reveals sexist practices—the customary discriminatory treatment of women [and that] linguistic conventions—particularly the generic use of masculine terminology—can be a perpetuator of sexist distinctions, regardless of the intention of the speaker."[41]

Let me speak to some of the claims made by those who believe that the use of such generics is *not* sexist. One such claim is that these terms are widely used and well understood as being generic. Yet considerable experimental evidence has shown that use of the term "man" is accompanied by a mental image of a male. Writers, speakers, and readers who clearly intend to use the generic nevertheless generate a male image.[42]

Let me present two quotations to illustrate this. Erich Fromm wrote, "Man's vital interests are life, food [so far, this seems clearly generic] and access to females."[43] Loren Eisley wrote of man, "his back aches, he ruptures easily, his women have difficulties in childbirth."[44] Thus, "man," "his," etc., are pseudogenerics, we never know when these terms are used generically. A man is sure that he is included; a woman is uncertain.[45]

A second claim is that getting rid of generic forms will result in cumbersome language, such as "he or she," "his or her," "humankind," etc. But the English language provides many simple, unambiguous, nonsexist ways to express the generic. The Universal Declaration uses several of these already: "everyone," "all," "no one."

It has also been claimed that "he" as a generic is "natural" or "correct." Until an 1850 Act of Parliament, however, the plural "they" was customarily used when speakers of English referred to a singular, sex-neutral antecedent. Dale Spender, in her book *Man Made Language,* reviews the history of the generic "he." In 1646, Pool (in Britain) wrote that it was "both natural and proper that male should have 'pride of place' because the male gender is 'worthier.' " In 1746, Kirby formulated 88 grammatical rules. Rule 21 was, "Male gender is more comprehensive than the female." Eventually, in 1850, Parliament stated that legally "he" stands for "she."[46] The grammar "rules" that women are expected to follow are thus the result of a long tradition of male presumption—of men talking to men, of male self-validation.

A fourth claim is that complaints about sexist language are trivial, that such sexist language is innocuous. At this point it is instructive to look at certain articles in the Universal Declaration where the rights proposed are rarely extended to women around the world. Is the failure to be given rights and the sexist language in those instances merely a coincidence?

Article 15—the right to a nationality. Part 2 states: "No one shall be arbitrarily deprived of *his* nationality nor denied the right to change *his* nationality" [italics mine].[47] Perhaps this actually does mean only males. The equal rights of women with regard to nationality are so clearly a problem in so many parts of the world that the "Convention on the Nationality of Married Women" was adopted by the General Assembly of the United Nations in 1957.[48] And Article 9 of the CEAFDAW states (in its second sentence): "[States parties] shall ensure in particular that neither marriage to an alien nor change of nationality by the husband during marriage shall automatically change the nationality of the wife, render her stateless or force upon her the nationality of the husband."[49]

Article 17—the right to own property. Part 2 states, "No one shall be arbitrarily deprived of *his* property."[50] Article 16, Part h, of the CEAFDAW was designed to correct the abuse of this right: "[States parties shall ensure] the same rights for both spouses in respect of the ownership, acquisition, management, administration, enjoyment and disposition of property, whether free of charge or for a valuable consideration." Similar cases can be found in Articles 8, 10, 12, 13, 18, 21, 22, 23, 25, 27, and 29. The right to take part in government, the right to an adequate standard of living—many of these rights have had to be addressed explicitly in the CEAFDAW.

It is obvious that deprivation of nationality, lack of right to own property, and the inability to participate in the government of one's country are not trivial! Is it not likely that the very words in which we then expressed our ideals have hampered the fulfillment of those ideals?

Summary

The text of the Universal Declaration of Human Rights thus contains four problems which, I claim, have hampered the extension of full human rights to women: (1) The phrasing of Part 3 of Article 16 risks legally enforcing the confinement of women and children in situations that may deprive them of liberty or subject them to slavery or degrading treatment. (2) Part 1 of Article 16 prescribes morality, implies that states have obligations to facilitate procreation, and reinforces the notion that baby-production validates women's worth. (3) An explicit statement of the "right to one's own body" should have been included. (4) Masculine nouns and pronouns used in 13 Articles to refer to both sexes may contribute to the perpetuation of sexist distinctions in rights.

Notes

I am grateful to Georgana Foster, Carol Gould, Saralee Hamilton, Fran Hosken, Susan Peterson, Betsy Postow, and especially Francis Holmes, for their encouragement and help in reviewing and discussing previous versions of this paper. I remain responsible, however, for all opinions, interpretations of facts, and prescriptions herein.

1. "Universal Declaration of Human Rights" in United Nations, *Human Rights—A Compilation of International Instruments* (New York: United Nations, 1978), ST/HR/1/Rev.1 Sales no. 78.XIV.2. Also in United Nations, *United Nations Action in the Field of Human Rights* (UNAFHR) (New York: United Nations, 1980), ST/HR/2/Rev.1 Sales no. E.79.XIV.6.

2. UNAFHR, p. 10. No nation voted against; eight abstained.

3. For example, in the implementation of UDHR Article 17. This Article states: "(1) Everyone has the right to own property alone as well as in association with others. (2) No one shall be arbitrarily deprived of his property." Explicit examples of international (World Bank) land "reform" programs that have *removed* ownership of land from women, to the extreme detriment of women's livelihood, are described in Barbara Rogers, "Land Reform: The Solution or the Problem?" *Human Rights Quarterly* 3(1981):96–102; and in Lisa Bennett, "Women, Law and Property in the Developing World: An Overview," *Human Rights Quarterly* 3(1981):88–95.

4. Laura Reanda, "Human Rights and Women's Rights: The United Nations Approach," *Human Rights Quarterly* 3(1981):11–31.

5. UNAFHR, p. 99. Some such instruments are: the Convention on the Political Rights of Women of 1952; the Convention on the Nationality of Married Women of 1957; the Convention against Discrimination in Education of 1960.

6. Catherine Tinker, "Human Rights for Women. The U.N. Convention on the Elimination of All Forms of Discrimination Against Women," *Human Rights Quarterly* 3(1981):32.

7. "Convention on the Elimination of All Forms of Discrimination Against Women" (CEAFDAW). United Nations, document INF/80/4, June 1980 (Official text of draft: A/C.3/34/L.75). See Tinker, ibid., pp. 32–43, for a summary of its provisions.

8. René Dubos, *Beast or Angel? Choices That Make Us Human* (New York: Charles Scribner's Sons, 1974), p. 47.

9. Parts 1 and 2, Article 16, state: "(1) Men and women of full age, without any limitation due to race, nationality or religion, have the right to marry and to found a family. They are entitled to equal rights as to marriage, during marriage, and at its dissolution. (2) Marriage shall be entered into only with the free and full consent of the intending spouses."

10. Barbara Myerhoff and Virginia Tufte, "Introduction," in Myerhoff and Tufte, eds., *Changing Images of the Family* (New Haven: Yale University Press, 1979), p. 15.

11. Judith Hicks Stiehm, "Government and the Family: Justice and Acceptance," in Myerhoff and Tufte, *Changing Images of the Family*, p. 364.

12. Kathleen Gough, "The Origin of the Family," *Journal of Marriage and the Family* 33(1971):369.

13. Article 3, UDHR, states: "Everyone has the right to life, liberty and security of person."

14. Article 4, UDHR, states: "No one shall be held in slavery or servitude; slavery and the slave trade shall be prohibited in all their forms." See also Kathleen Barry, "Female Sexual Slavery: Understanding the International Dimensions of Women's Oppression," *Human Rights Quarterly* 3(1981):48.

15. Article 5, UDHR, states: "No one shall be subjected to torture or to cruel, inhuman or degrading treatment or punishment."

16. Suzanne LaFollette, "Concerning Women," in *The Feminist Papers*, ed. Alice S. Rossi (New York: Bantam Books, 1973), p. 549–50.

17. Carol Gould, "The Woman Question: Philosophy of Liberation and the Liberation of Philosophy," *The Philosophical Forum* 5(1973–74):36; see also references cited in her notes 44, 45, 47, and 48.

18. Adrienne Rich, *Of Woman Born: Motherhood as Experience and Institution* (New York: W. W. Norton, 1976), p. 61.

19. Carl N. Degler, *At Odds: Women and the Family in America from the Revolution to the Present* (New York: Oxford University Press, 1980), p. vii.

20. Stephen J. Morse, "Family Law in Transition: From Traditional Families to Individual Liberty," in *Changing Images of the Family*, ed. Myerhoff and Tufte, p. 348; see also LaFollette, "Concerning Women," p. 561.

21. Morse, "Family Law," pp. 319–60.

22. Genital excision is the removal of the clitoris and the labia minora; in infibulation some of the labia majora are also removed, and the sides of the vulva are fastened together. See Fran Hosken, *Women's International Network News* 2, no. 1 (January 1976):30. For a description of the role of mothers, see Mary Daly, *Gyn/Ecology: The Metaethics of Radical Feminism* (Boston: Beacon Press, 1978), p. 164–65.

23. Gough, "Origin of the Family," p. 770.

24. The U.S. Supreme Court, in a series of cases beginning with *Levy v. Louisiana*, 391 U.S. 68 (1968), struck down as unconstitutional almost every state or federal disability imposed on illegitimate children. See Morse, "Family Law," p. 349; LaFollette, "Concerning Women," p. 555. The Economic and Social Council of the United Nations in Resolution 1679 of June 2, 1972, recommended to Governments of States Members of the United Nations a set of general principles for securing the unmarried mother and her child acceptance on an equal footing with other members of society. See UNAFHR, p. 109.

25. Rich, *Of Woman Born*, chap. 2. See also Norma Swenson, "Childbirth Overview," in *Birth Control and Controlling Birth: Women-Centered Perspectives* ed. Helen B. Holmes, Betty B. Hoskins, and Michael Gross (Clifton, NJ: The Humana Press, 1980), p. 143.

26. Robert Edwards & P. Steptoe, *A Matter of Life* (London: Sphere Books, 1981), p. 110. Dr. Edwards explicitly cites the Universal Declaration of Human Rights. Before there were any test-tube babies, philosopher-geneticist Marc Lappé argued that medical practice has a universal obligation to relieve suffering, and that childlessness is a particularly acute form of suffering. See Lappé, *Hastings Center Report* 2, no. 1:1–2.

27. Lori B. Andrews, "Embryo Technology," *Parents Magazine,* May 1981, pp. 63–70.

28. Byllye Y. Avery and Judith M. Levy, "Contrasts in the Birthing Place: Hospital and Birth Center," in *Birth Control and Controlling Birth,* ed. Holmes, Hoskins, and Gross, p. 238.

29. Douglas Wilson, "Patients and Understanding," *Amherst College Alumni Magazine,* Winter 1981, pp. 11, 32; see also Andrews, "Embryo Technology," p. 65–66.

30. *Pratt v. Davis,* 118 Ill. App. 161,166(1905), *aff'd.* 224 Ill. 300, 79 N.E. 562(1906).

31. Article 12, UDHR, states: "No one shall be subject to arbitrary interference with his privacy, family, home or correspondence, nor to attacks upon his honour and reputation. Everyone has the right to the protection of the law against such interference or attacks."

32. See note 13.

33. George J. Annas, "The Patient Has Rights: How Can We Protect Them?" *Hastings Center Report* 3, no.4(1973)8–9.

34. Sara Ann Ketchum, "Abortion and the Ownership of Bodies," paper presented at the National Project on Philosophy and Engineering Ethics at Troy, New York, August 1978. See also Helen B. Holmes and Susan Rae Peterson, "Rights over One's Own Body: A Woman-Affirming Health Care Policy," *Human Rights Quarterly* 3(1981):75; and Penelope Washbourn, "Body/World: The Religious Dimensions of Sexuality," *Christianity and Crisis* 34(9 December 1974):279.

35. Alice S. Rossi, "The Right to One's Body," in Rossi, ed., *The Feminist Papers,* p. 517.

36. Depo-Provera is a synthetic compound with the effects of the natural hormone progesterone. It is a long-lasting contraceptive, almost 100 percent effective, administered by injection every three months. See Marie M. Cassidy, "Depo-Provera and Sterilization Abuse," in *Birth Control and Controlling Birth,* ed. Holmes, Hoskins, and Gross pp 97–139. An intrauterine device (IUD) is a plastic or metal object placed inside the uterus to prevent implantation of an embryo. See Mark Dowie and Tracy Johnston, "A Case of Corporate Malpractice and the Dalkon Shield," in *Seizing Our Bodies: The Politics of Women's Health,* ed., Claudia Driefus (New York: Random House, 1977), pp. 86–104.

37. Quoted in *Ms.* Magazine 10, no. 5 (November 1981):22.

38. Dale Spender, *Man Made Language* (London: Routledge & Kegan Paul, 1980), p. 139; John B. Carroll, ed., *Language, Thought and Reality; Selected Writings of Benjamin Lee Whorf* (Cambridge, Mass: MIT Press, 1976).

39. Preamble, paragraph 5, UDHR, states: "**Whereas** the peoples of the United Nations have in the Charter reaffirmed their faith in fundamental human rights, in the dignity and worth of the human person and in the equal rights of men and women and have determined to promote social progress and better standards of life in the larger freedom."

40. Article 2, UDHR, states: "Everyone is entitled to all the rights and freedoms set forth in this Declaration, without distinction of any kind, such as race, colour, sex, language, religion, political or other opinion, national or social origin, property, birth or other status."

41. Carolyn Korsmeyer, "The Hidden Joke: Generic Uses of Masculine Terminol-

ogy," in *Feminism and Philosophy,* ed. Mary Vetterling-Braggin, Frederick A. Elliston, and Jane English (Totowa, N. J.: Littlefield, Adams, 1978), p. 140.

42. Spender, *Man Made Language,* p. 151; Elaine Morgan, *The Descent of Woman* (New York: Stein & Day, 1972).

43. Cited in Alma Graham, "The Making of a Non-Sexist Dictionary," in *Language and Sex: Difference and Dominance,* ed Barrie Thorne and Nancy Henley (Rowley, Mass: Newbury House, 1975), p. 62; also Spender, *Man Made Language,* p. 155.

44. Graham, "Non-Sexist Dictionary," p. 62; Spender, *Man Made Language,* p. 155.

45. Other examples of failure to achieve gender neutrality are found in Janice Moulton, "The Myth of the Neutral 'Man,' " in *Feminism and Philosophy,* ed. Vetterling-Braggin, Elliston, and English, pp. 129–36.

46. Spender, *Man Made Language,* pp. 147–48.

47. Article 15, UDHR, states: "(1) Everyone has the right to a nationality. (2) No one shall be arbitrarily deprived of his nationality nor denied the right to change his nationality."

48. UNAFHR, p. 100.

49. Article 9, CEAFDAW, states: "(1) States Parties shall grant women equal rights with men to acquire, change or retain their nationality. They shall ensure in particular that neither marriage to an alien nor change of nationality by the husband during marriage shall automatically change the nationality of the wife, render her stateless or force upon her the nationality of the husband. (2) States Parties shall grant women equal rights with men with respect to the nationality of their children." See also comments in Tinker, "Human Rights for Women," p. 36, note 13.

50. For text of UDHR Article 17, see no. 3.

15

Rights-Conflict, Pregnancy, and Abortion

JANET FARRELL SMITH

A Traditional Formulation of the Abortion Problem

One way many philosophers have formulated the problem of abortion leads to an impasse between the woman's right to choose whether or not to terminate the pregnancy and the fetus's right to life. The rights seem to be in conflict, in the sense that one cannot be granted without withholding the other. These philosophers resolve the conflict by denying or qualifying one or the other of the two rights, or another assumption that makes the two conflict. I shall argue, however, that this formulation of the problem is based on a mistaken parallel between adult life and fetal life. Once we understand how the special circumstances of pregnancy affect a fetus's right to life, we see the problem of abortion in a new light—as a moral issue of care, nurture, and responsibility, rather than a conflict of rights between woman and fetus.

In the traditional formulation of the problem, we assume that the woman has the right to choose whether or not to continue a pregnancy, which includes the right to choose abortion.[1] We also assume that a fetus has a right to life. When we add the assumption that a fetus's right to life implies that the pregnant woman has a duty to the fetus not to destroy it willfully,[2] then the woman's right and the fetus's right are in conflict. Both cannot be granted or recognized. Granting the woman the right to choose means that the fetus's right to life is abridged, and vice versa.

Some philosophers solve the conundrum by making one or the other right paramount. Brody and Noonan, for example, argue that the fetus's right to life is so strong that it outweighs the woman's right to choose.[3] They each maintain that the crucial moral imperative for the situation of pregnancy is the woman's duty to respect the fetus's right to life.

Warren and Tooley, by contrast, deny the assumption of a fetus's right to life. Warren argues that since the fetus is only partially human and does not fulfill the criteria of personhood, the fetus does not have a right to life. That solution leaves the woman's right to choose as the salient moral fact about pregnancy.[4]

Judith Jarvis Thomson presents a third solution in her classic paper "A Defense of Abortion." She argues that even if a fetus has a right to life, a woman does not have the moral duty to lend her bodily resources to that life. It would be beneficent of her to do so, but it is not morally required. In other words, she denies the third assumption that generates the conflict of rights, that the fetus's right to life implies a corresponding duty on the part of the pregnant woman to sustain that life.[5]

Faced with these solutions, still other philosophers have declared the problem insoluble. One way out of the conflict, they argue, is as arbitrary as another. The U.S. Supreme Court, in effect, accepted this formulation of the problem and declared one of the assumptions—a fetus's right to life—beyond its jurisdiction. *Roe v. Wade,* 410 U.S. 113 (1973), argued a woman's right to choose on the basis of the constitutional guarantee of privacy. Yet if some authority beyond its jurisdiction granted the fetus a right to life, the impasse in the conflict of rights might arise once more.

Some philosophers have responded by rejecting the entire framework that leads to the conflict of rights and proposing another in its place.[6] My strategy is different. I question the presuppositions of the traditional framework. When looked at carefully, they can be seen to be based on a mistaken parallel between adult life and fetal life. For one party to have rights against another party, they must be distinct entities. Yet in the special and unique case of pregnancy, the fetus and woman form one interdependent system of life. (Throughout this paper I mean only a pregnancy *in utero* of a pre-viable fetus.)[7] The fetus needs access to life-sustaining conditions that can only be provided by the woman pregnant with that fetus. This calls into question the coherence of assertions of a fetus's right to life as contervailing against a woman's right to choose.

Critique of Traditional Formulation

When we focus on the actual nature of pregnancy, we can see a lack of parallelism between the conditions of life for a fetus and the conditions of life for an adult. A (live, pre-viable) fetus is by definition completely dependent and cannot survive as an independent human being.[8] An adult, by contrast, has the capacity (in general, if not the capability at any given moment) to live as an independent human being. Although the fetus may require assistance from other human beings beside the woman who conceived it, it is completely dependent on that particular woman's bodily system for its life. When an adult is dependent on other human beings, however, he or she can be assisted by various human beings and not just the one with whom he or she has a particular and unique biological connection. An adult has a body separate from other human bodies, while a fetus does not. Finally, a fetus cannot sustain itself through its own bodily resources, while an adult (in general, if not at any given moment) can.

If a right to life is to have any concrete force, it must take into account the conditions for life. For a fetus, the conditions of life are such that one other human being, the pregnant woman, is in a unique position of being able to respond to its alleged right to life. An adult has no such relationship with another adult human being. The question then arises of what it can mean for a being in the peculiar dependent relationship of the fetus to have rights against one other particular human being. In every other case beside pregnancy, when we talk about one being having rights against another, we are talking about beings with the capabilities of adults. A fetus is in a very different kind of relationship with the being against whom it supposedly has a right than is an adult, a fact that the conflict-of-rights formulation of the problem has ignored. Once we take seriously the lack of parallel between the situation of a fetus and the situation of an adult, we see that the meaning of adult "right to life" cannot apply to a fetus.

With an adult, having a right to life would imply that no one should kill that adult. An adult's right to life does not imply that any one person in particular must nurture it, although it may require nurture from some other person in general. For a fetus, having a right to life also implies that no one should kill it. But for a fetus that in turn implies that someone should nurture it, namely the particular woman who conceives it. The woman can respect the fetus's right to life only by nurturing it, a circumstance that does not hold for two adults.*

Thus, an adult's right to life is independent of a particular human being's nurture, while a fetus's is not. The rights-in-conflict formulation of the abortion problem presumes the independent being's right

---

*Nor does it hold for the adult(caretaker)-infant relation, in which a person other than the woman who gave birth to an infant can nurture and support the necessary conditions for life of that infant.

in conflict with the right of another. In that formulation, the woman would have a right to choose independent of any rights the fetus has, and the fetus would have the right to life independent of any rights the woman has. But that implies a distortion of the actual situation of pregnancy. As previously outlined, a fetus's right to life cannot be respected by simple noninterference and general human support, as can adults' right to life. A fetus's right to life requires access to organic support and nurture by the particular woman who conceived it. That is, the fetus's right to life crucially depends on the involvement of the very woman against whom its countervailing "right to life" is asserted.

Unless we accept that a necessary condition of a fetus' "right to life" is the involvement and nurture of the particular woman who conceived it, the right is so extraordinarily abstract that it is hard to see what meaning it could have. When we speak of a fetus's right to life we must also take into account the necessary conditions for the continuance of that life. Asserting that a fetus's "right to life" is in conflict with a woman's right to choose is incoherent when the "right to life" depends on and only makes sense in terms of that very woman's nurture and sustaining of the pregnancy. Serious problems are involved, I am arguing, in imposing a conflict of rights construction on the relation between two such interdependent beings.[9]

Although the pregnant woman and the fetus are interdependent, the relationship is not symmetrical. With interdependence, the well-being of the one is conditional upon the well-being of the other, as in the case of a life-threatening ectopic pregnancy or the fact that good nutrition benefits both. Yet biologically, the fetus needs the woman to survive, while the woman does not need the fetus in order to survive. No other aspect of human life depends on one particular person in this way, which is why many analogies for pregnancy are misleading.

With this asymmetrical relationship in view, rights and duties usually assumed within rights-conflicts appear very odd when ascribed to a woman-fetus relationship. The woman, because of the fetus's right to life, is supposed to have a duty of noninterference toward the life of the fetus, but the fetus cannot have any duties at all toward the woman. While a fetus's "right" requires the woman's care and nurture in order for it to make sense, fetal "duties" make no sense at all. The fetus has no "duty" of noninterference toward the woman, just as trees have no "duty" not to interfere with other plants' need for light or oxygen. Hence, to speak of a *conflict* of rights and duties between the woman and fetus is inaccurate. A conflict of rights presumes independent beings capable of making countervailing claims upon one another.* But woman and fetus form an interdependent system of life-sustenance of which one part has rights and duties, while the other has no duties and exercise of its rights depends on the support of the other. Of course, we could *say* that a fetus has a right to life where there is no woman in a relationship of care and nurture to it, but that situation is so unlike the one where questions of rights actually arise that we have to question whether it even makes sense within the context of rights discourse. This is not to deny that a fetus can have a right to life, only to question whether that right can make sense when asserted against the right to choose of the very woman who is carrying that fetus.[10]

While a fetus cannot do or refrain from doing things which would interfere with a woman's choice to continue or terminate a pregnancy, other adults or social agencies like the state can. A better way of viewing rights-conflict concerning abortion poses such conflict as between women's rights and the rights of other social beings or agencies with the capacity to act to support or restrict her choice. That such conflicts make sense and do occur can readily be seen from a reading of any Supreme Court decision on abortion that discusses states' rights in regulating or intefering with a woman's choice of abortion during her pregnancy. In other words, I suggest that we recast rights-conflict as occurring among social agents in decision-making contexts. Such recasting places fetal interests on a more realistic basis, namely within the interdependent unity of the woman who is pregnant.

In some cases there can occur a conflict of interest between woman and fetus concerning life conditions. That such conflicts do occur and make sense can be seen from cases where medical indications for drug treatment for high blood pressure serve the interest of the woman's health but may injure the fetus. More extreme conflicts of interest occur when a woman decides—for health, psychological, or other reasons—that she is unable to carry a pregnancy to term. But it is questionable how well it clarifies the moral and philosophical issues to regard these as conflicts of *rights*. They are better construed as conflict between the care and nurture required for healthy conditions of life for a fetus which may grow into an infant and the ability of the woman who is pregnant to be responsible for such care.

What do these considerations imply for the traditional rights-

---

*At least, it assumes that it makes sense in terms of some specific social relation to make countervailing claims, as when an agent for a comatose patient sues for damages after an accident. But this relation is justifiably modeled on adult rights (tort law).

conflict formulation of the abortion problem? Although the fetus may be ascribed interests, I have argued that because of the unique relational facts about pregnancy, these are neither sufficient to ground a full-fledged conflict of rights with the pregnant woman nor of such a nature to stand sensibly in opposition to hers. They are not sufficient because they are not distinct from the pregnant woman's interests. (Even in the high blood pressure case the well-being of the fetus and its survival depend on the woman's general health.) They are not of the proper nature because we cannot consider the fetus a being clearly enough individuated from the pregnant woman who sustains it.

When we take these observations seriously we can see that the rights in question in the rights-conflict formulation tacitly presuppose a situation like that between two adults with the fetus right to life modeled on an adult sense of right to life. Because this formulation leaves out the biological and social realities of pregnancy it constructs an opposition between woman and fetus which at worst distorts and at least fails to articulate the complex moral and social dimensions of women's conflicts concerning pregnancies.

Alternative Views

An alternative to the rights-conflict formulation starts out by examining the different types of rights ascribed therein to the woman and fetus. A woman's right to choose whether or not to terminate a pregnancy is a claim against others that they should not interfere with her liberty. Woman's choice in reproductive matters is thus a *liberty-right*. But for the fetus (and here lies the crucial point neglected by most rights-conflict formulations), right to life is primarily a *welfare-right*, a right to well-being that imposes positive duties of care and nurture upon a particular person. It calls for much more than noninterference in the sense of not killing. So the life vs. choice conflict between woman and fetus consists of two different types of rights conflicting with one another. The occurrence of different types of rights in conflict with one another is not in itself problematic. But in the case of the woman-fetus relationship it generates special difficulties.

Because of the special nature of pregnancy, the positive welfare of the fetus presupposes the liberty of the woman to assent or refuse the pregnancy. While it does not always require that a woman deliberately and willfully choose to become pregnant, it requires that the woman be free to decide whether or not to continue the pregnancy. Without this liberty, the well-being and hence survival of the fetus are called into question. The woman who cannot assent but is "forced to live with" an unwanted pregnancy may, even nonconsciously, undermine her health habits to the extent that the fetus is seriously damaged.[11] The content of the rights in conflict therefore do not stand in simple opposition to one another. Yet we need not conclude from these observations that a woman must sacrifice her liberty and compromise her nurturant capacities. Nor need we deny that fetal well-being is ever a genuine concern for pregnant women. We could instead recast abortion questions as conflicts of responsibilities.

Rather than conclude that because of her special relationship to the fetus the woman has a special duty not to abort it, we could conclude that because of her special capacity to reproduce another human being the pregnant woman has a special duty or responsibility to consider whether or not she is capable of bearing it. She has the duty to consider whether or not she is capable of sustaining the continuous process of pregnancy, childbirth, and childrearing, or whether she must interrupt it. The woman should appreciate the moral seriousness of bringing another human being into the world. Yet only the pregnant woman can assess the factors in her situation (her emotional, psychic, and physical capabilities at a particular time) that affect her ability to nurture a pregnancy properly. The right of choice therefore should belong to her rather than to another person or the state.

The pregnant woman's duty of consideration, I would argue, overrides any proposed absolute duty to remain pregnant, since the duty of consideration consists in adjusting the imperative to sustain life to the necessity for care and nurture to be undertaken responsibly. Having the right to choose enables a pregnant woman to uphold that duty of consideration in a responsible way. It does not, of course, guarantee that she will act responsibly. But then rights have never had the moral force of guaranteeing responsible actions. The most that a right can do is hold open the opportunity for choices that will respect the interests and well-being of oneself and of others, in this case of future progeny.[12]

Notes

1. In this discussion of moral rights, right to life and right to choice are taken as claim-rights, following in particular the treatment of Joel Feinberg in "Voluntary Euthanasia and the Right to Life," *Philosophy and Public Affairs* 7, no. 2 (Winter 1978): 96-97, and in *Social Philosophy* (Englewood Cliffs, N.J.: Prentice-Hall 1973), p. 68. It is assumed in the discussion that the rights are absolute in some sense which allows that the fetus's right to life is abrogated when womans right to choice overrides it. For further discussion of the different ways in which right to life may be taken as absolute, see Feinberg, "Voluntary Euthanasia," pp. 98-102.

2. The logical, not moral, correlativity thesis is elaborated in Feinberg, *Social Philosophy*, pp. 61-64.

3. Baruch Brody, *Abortion and the Sanctity of Human Life* (Cambridge, Mass.: MIT Press, 1975); John T. Noonan, "An Almost Absolute Value in History," in Noonan, ed., *The Morality of Abortion* (Cambridge: Harvard University Press, 1970).

4. Michael Tooley, "A Defense of Abortion and Infanticide," in *The Problem of Abortion*, ed. Joel Feinberg (Belmont, Calif: Wadsworth, 1973). Mary Anne Warren, "On the Moral and Legal Status of Abortion," in *Contemporary Issues in Bioethics*, ed. T.L. Beauchamp and L. Walters, (Belmont, Calif: Dickenson, 1978).

5. Judith Jarvis Thomson, "A Defense of Abortion," in Feinberg, *The Problem of Abortion*, p. 130.

6. See Martha Brandt Bolton, "Responsible Women and Abortion Decisions," in *Having Children: Philosophical and Legal Reflections on Parenthood*, ed. Onora O'Neill and William Ruddick (New York: Oxford University Press, 1979); Howard Cohen, "Abortion and the Quality of Life," in *Feminism and Philosophy*, ed. Mary Vetterling-Braggin, Frederick A. Elliston, and Jane English (Totowa, N.J.: Littlefield, Adams, 1977); Kathryn Pyne Parsons, "Moral Revolution," in *The Prism of Sex: Essays in the Sociology of Knowledge*, ed. Julia Sherman and Evelyn T. Beck (Madison: The University of Wisconsin Press, 1977).

7. This essay considers only traditional intrauterine reproductive processes, excluding technological interventions such as embryo transfers, at later stages. Since in vitro fertilizations take place within two to three days following conception and, at present knowledge, no embryo transfers have been made to women who did not produce the original ovum, I suspect that the arguments here still apply to pregnancies generated in vitro. Should the technology of pregnancy change radically in this respect, however, the moral issues considered here might not apply. New philosophical analyses would have to be developed to deal with a new technology of human reproduction. See my "Parenting and Property," in *Mothering: Essays in Feminist Theory*, ed. Joyce Trebilcot (Totowa, N.J.: Rowman & Allanheld, 1983).

8. Confusion between "live" and "a human life" (i.e., "an individuated human life") indicates that a fallacy of equivocation may operate in certain arguments for a fetus's right to life. See Jane English, "Abortion and the Concept of a Person," in Vetterling-Braggin, Elliston, and English, eds., *Feminism and Philosophy*.

9. To say that such a construction involves a semantic failure of reference would be too strong, or more accurately, it would lead the argument in a direction I do not propose. "Fetus" could in fact be taken to denote some segment of tissue. "Right to life" could be taken to denote some set of claims made on behalf of a wide variety of types of things. The problem I am raising here does not lie merely on the semantic level of reference, but on the social and conceptual implications of the denotation, which are still left open to question. What I am claiming is that the social presuppositions of the terms *as they are used in rights discourse* must be read back into the meaningfulness of the terms of that discourse, and that the conditions for life of the beings involved calls these presuppositions into question, thereby calling the rights-conflict formulation into question. In a sense my arguments come in at a pre-moral level of discourse, following through on a suggestion by Joel Feinberg, that conceptual analysis of the woman-fetus relationship must be done before the moral problems are addressed. See "The Rights of Animals and Unborn Generations" in *Rights, Justice and the Bounds of Liberty* (Princeton: Princeton University Press, 1980), p. 180

10. Access to means to fulfill rights may not be available at a given time, and yet it is still significant to claim these rights when we consider cases of the "manifesto sense of right." See Feinberg, *Social Philosophy*, pp. 67, 110. Even if these rights claims concern basic needs, their fulfillment depends on social and political proc-

esses, unlike the basic needs of the fetus, considered here, which concern a necessary biological connection. It would be a different, though quite plausible, sense of right to claim the right to quality maternal and prenatal health care and education, than to claim a fetus's right to life. The former requires an adjustment of social practice in a way that the latter does not.

11. Studies conducted in Sweden have shown that women refused abortion produced offspring both physically and mentally impaired. See K. Hook, "Refused Abortion," in *Acta Psychiatrica Scandinavica* Supplementum 168, 1963. For detailed discussion see Carol Nadelson, "The Emotional Impact of Abortion," in *The Woman Patient, Volume I. Sexual and Reproductive Aspects of Women's Health Care,* ed. Malkah Notman and Carol Nadelson (New York: Plenum Press, 1978).

12. The issues raised in this paper are explored in greater depth in my book manuscript, "Reproductive Rights and Decisions."

16

Sex Preselection: From Here to Fraternity

ROBERTA STEINBACHER

The power of reproduction has been at the core of women's human experience. However devalued, controlled, feared, or exploited women have been, their indispensability to the perpetuation of the human race has remained a stubborn fact, a sine qua non conceded by even the most oppressive of patriarchal societies.

Today, for the first time in human history, the power to negate woman's indispensability to human reproduction—her perceived reason for being—is within the reach of patriarchy. Human eggs can be fertilized in laboratory glassware and cultured until they become embryos of several hundred cells. At the other end of gestation, premature infants are grown for several months in incubators that resemble wombs. Medicine spies on unborn fetuses to determine whether they deserve to be born. What follows is a critical analysis of the current state of the science in but one area of reproductive technology, sex choice technology. Before any analysis, however, some patriarchal postures and myths must be demystified.

Although reproductive technology has provoked a modicum of debate, the discourse has focused on issues such as in vitro fertilization and embryo transplants, both couched in rationales "supportive" of woman's profound power to reproduce. Sex preselection, an area with long-range consequences as unthinkable as femicide (Hanmer and Allen 1981), has developed unfettered by the scientific, religious, and legal cross-examination which could provide critical checks and balances and which finally surfaced, for example, around recombinant DNA research.

Although the myth that science and technology are value-free has long since been exploded, issues of reproductive technology have been obscured by the broad inhibitions of patriarchal imperatives imposed by centuries of male-controlled religion, law, science, and medicine. Commercial exploitation of technology has rarely indulged even in the pretense of being value-free. Consider, for example, why female rather than male methods of birth control have proliferated. Consider the intrauterine contraceptive, the Dalkon shield,[1] and ask who controls the research, who decides to exploit the resulting product commercially, and who are the guinea pigs? Listen critically to British scientist John Postgate (1973) advocating a sex preselection technique, a "man-child pill"—allegedly to ease Third World nations' population explosion. The pill "would ensure . . . that the offspring would be male" (p. 14). Because of cultural male preference, Postgate concludes, "countless millions of people would leap at the opportunity to breed males," and by dramatically reducing the number of females born, population growth would be limited by reducing the number of available uteruses—which is to say, women.

To think the unthinkable, femicide, or women rendered irrelevant to the perpetuation of the human race, requires a tough honesty of mind. It means exposing and seeing through the reversals and double-thinks indigenous to female experience in patriarchy; it may require a willing suspension of disbelief. On the one hand, medical instrument companies have allocated extensive resources to the development and dissemination of artificial laboratory wombs. To the patriarchy this is morally commendable work because it supports the principle of preserving life. In a utilitarian sense, artificial wombs may be thought to promote the general welfare of women by freeing them from the trauma of pregnancy, labor, and childbirth. On the other hand, Postgate's utilitarian argument proposes that providing an opportunity for parents in the Third World nations to choose sons will increase the individual happiness of millions of people (joy at the birth of a boy) and the general welfare (lower population and the consequent higher standard of living). Thus he prescribes the elimination of Third World uteruses, while technicians perfect the capacity to artificially control embryonic development outside the female body. Juxtapose these two morally justifiable technologies and the conclusion—"femicide"—is clear. Ultimately, patriarchy can do without women—except for those few kept for the purpose of producing eggs.

To date, patriarchy's religious, legal, medical, and commercial institutions have controlled women's power of reproduction largely through what can be best described as sublimated legitimization. For example, religion controls by requiring that a child remain in a state of "original" sin until reborn by males in the baptism ritual (Daly 1973). Through Church doctrine, female reproductive power is negated (holy women must be celibate), prescribed ("artificial" birth control and abortion are banned), mystified (sex education is forbidden), sanctified (marriage is a sacrament), and made sinful (adultery is punished). Never is reproductive power treated simply as the natural human process it is.

Similarly, law controls by relegating women to second-class, almost property status. The rights of women to inherit, to hold property, to keep their own citizenship, to receive higher education, for example, are denied over much of the globe.[2] Bride prices still exist; in India women pass from being the property of their fathers to being the property of their mothers-in-law. Law also pronounces children birthed by females to be "legitimate" or "illegitimate," depending on the female's state-defined relationship to a male. American law, which long classified women as property, is now toying with the issue of whether the state has a compelling interest to prevent the birth of "unhealthy" fetuses. "Wrongful life" suits are a reality; damages can be recovered on the grounds that a fetus with genetic defects was "permitted" to be born. It is not inconceivable that enterprising lawyers will soon see fit to initiate "wrongful sex" suits, either on behalf of parents who used sex selection technologies that failed, or "in the best interests of" the unloved child herself.

Medicine controls by tirelessly imposing itself as indispensable to the reproductive process by intervening in woman's natural conception and birthing process, surgically and pharmacologically, with complex monitoring devices and with multi-stage hospitalization. In 1980 the Quebec Order of Pharmacologists declared that human sperm is medicine.

Commerce, on the other hand, profits from, rather than directly controls, female reproductive power. Consider the commercial appropriation of female lactation through infant formulae distribution which (with U. S. government acquiescence) continues unabated to produce staggering number of infant deaths throughout Third World countries. Consider the medical equipment manufacturers' push to get electronic fetal monitors into every delivery room in America.[3] And consider the pharmaceutical houses' monopoly on contraception.

These few examples, boosted by an acute female consciousness of evidence such as that carried in the bodies of our DES daughters,[4] should provoke an uncluttered assessment of the real implications of sex preselection technology in the context of the male quest to control human reproduction. In addition, research in this area continues to be almost entirely in the hands of men; government and private agencies which fund this research are controlled by men; and the pharmaceutical companies that commercially produce, merchandise, and sell the products are run by men (Cowan 1980). Of deeper concern, however, is a powerful unacknowledged ingredient: the fact of male and female preference throughout the world for giving birth to sons (Clarke and Kiser, 1951; Freedman and Takeshita 1969: Markle and Wait 1976; May and Heer 1968; Morrison 1975; Pebley and Westoff 1982; Pohlman and Roa 1969; Stinner and Mader 1975; Westoff and Rindfuss 1974; Wood and Bean 1977).

That women as well as men prefer male offspring may not be surprising. Social and economic forces have conditioned women to accept the perceived greater rewards accruing to themselves and to their family units when a son is born. Millions have experienced vicarious or first-hand disappointment, sorrow, or penalty resulting from the birth of a daughter. From the mountains of Lebanon to the villages of Africa to the modern maternity wards, crying midwives, dejected family faces, and even infanticide have been known to accompany the birth of a daughter. The consequences of this societally conditioned male preference coupled with the potential wide-spread commercial availability of sex preselection techniques are staggering.

Historically, humankind has attempted to select the sex of offspring *before* conception. Aristotle with no knowledge of sex determination or of the function of egg and sperm, expounded theories in Chapter 1, Book IV, of *The Generation of Animals,* which were believed for centuries. His and other preconception theories have suggested herbs, diet, direction of the wind, douches, position of the body during intercourse, or the presence or absence of female orgasm. Folk wisdom that correlates sex determination with the timing of intercourse in the menstrual cycle persists in both lay and medical literature and may indeed have some substance. Susan Harlap's (1979) careful study of orthodox Jewish women in Israel seems to show that male babies have a somewhat higher than 50% chance of being conceived two days before *or* two days after ovulation. And in recent years diet theories have been revived as physicians and veterinarians report evidence that diets high in sodium and potassium increase the probability of conceiving male progeny; those high in calcium and magnesium, female progeny (e.g. Langendoen and Proctor 1982; Stolkowski and Choukroun 1981).

A more-sophisticated method is the use of sperm separation technique followed by artificial insemination with the desired X- or Y-bearing sperm (Dmowski, Gaynor, Rao, Lawrence, and Scommegna 1979; Ericsson 1977).[5] Ericsson's method has been developed reportedly for the purpose of aiding male fertility (Glass 1977) and isolates, thus far, only the Y-bearing sperm for reproduction. Seven locations in the United States have embarked on the commercialization of son preference using this sperm isolation procedure. They are advertised as "Centers for Sex Selection (Male) and Male Infertility." Pills and gels to destroy one type of sperm or the other are also under investigation. A diaphragm permitting only one type of sperm to pass, predictably the smaller or male-producing sperm, has been discussed as a potential selection technique.

With the advent of prenatal diagnosis, initiated by the development of amniocentesis in the 1950s, the possibility for *postconception* sex choice arose. The option of abortion on the basis of sex alone is today a reality. The original questionable goal of ridding society of genetic defects made the knowledge of the sex of the fetus accessible. The extent to which abortion is used as a means to select sex is not empirically known. Other fetal detection methods under development permit sex information at an even earlier stage of gestation than does amniocentesis (which can now be perfomed at 16 to 20 weeks). Attempts to find safe and efficient methods of determining sex in the first trimester include the examination of maternal blood for male sex hormones (Glass and Klein 1981) or for the presence of fetal cells (Herzenberg, Bianchi, Schroeder, Cann, and Iverson 1979; Newberger and Latt 1979; Porreco, Sarkar, and Jones 1980) and the analysis of fetal chorionic villi cells. In this last technique, developed by the Chinese (Tietung Hospital 1975), cells from the chorion of the fetus are removed by aspiration through the cervix of the mother and are examined for sex chromatin. Reportedly the sex of the fetus can be detected as early as 47 days after conception. Of the 99 cases reported in 1975, 29 of the 46 predicted females were aborted; one of 53 predicted males was aborted. The method is being refined considerably in Great Britain. One chorionic villus is removed by an endoscope while the process is carefully monitored by real-time ultrasound; then in a procedure taking 3 to 4 days DNA from the cells removed is analysed for Y-chromosome specific DNA (Gosden, Mitchell, Gosden, Rodeck, and Morsman 1982).

Also continuing are investigations to refine methods of fetal sex detection in the latter half of pregnancy. For example: the sampling of amniotic fluid for male sex hormones (e.g. Ansaldi, Voglino, Coppo, and Massobrio 1981); analyses of male hormones in the mother's saliva (e.g. Held, Bruck, and Koske-Westphal 1981); and the identification of external genitalia through ultrasonic scans of the fetus (e.g. Juhel and Pourcelot 1981).

When it is convenient and inexpensive to select the sex of offspring, the commerical tide cannot be reversed. Family planning becomes simple and straightforward: everything we know indicates that a vast majority will choose to have a first-born son. Daughters, to the extent that they are chosen at all, will be later born.

Studies of the effects of birth order and the societal advantages of being first-born (Belmont and Marolla 1973; Breland 1973; Dalton 1976; Eysenck and Cookson 1970; Maccoby, Doering, Jacklin, and Kraemer 1979; and Zajonc and Markus 1975) clearly indicate that the results (even in "balanced" selections) are critical for women, collectively and individually. First-borns are found in disproportionate numbers in positions of power and privilege. Today, even with a 50/50 chance of being first-born, women are not found in powerful, privileged positions in proportion to their numbers in society. Individually, the psychological ramifications subsequent to the discovery that one was chosen-to-be-second are unmeasurable but predictably negative. Inferiority, now societally dictated for women as a class, would be further internalized and externalized as "big brother, little sister" became institutionalized in family relationships. A dramatic alteration in the natural sex ratio and an increase in number of male first-borns through widespread sex selection could not only sharply reduce the number of females born, but could relegate those born to powerlessness (Fidell, Hoffman and Keith-Spiegel 1979; Steinbacher 1980, 1981).

Sex preselection technology and its commerical development proceed at a rapid pace, cloaked in the protective silence of laboratories and boardrooms. Women must closely examine why these particular technologies, unrelated to generally accepted concepts of disease and genetic or social engineering, are advancing. Furthermore, women must look with unblurred vision at the morality of the mindset that would select the sex of children. Powledge (1981) has called these technologies "the original sexist sin . . . they make the most basic judgment about the worth of a human being rest first and foremost on its sex" (p. 197).

The task women face is almost insuperable; it makes unprecedented demands on our human responsibility. As we spend our energies struggling for fundamental rights for ourselves and our daughters in the present, we are constantly thwarted because a technological future awaits us for which we are ill-prepared. As Zimmerman (1982) cautions:

> For all their potential value, reproductive technologies, like those of computers, telecommunications, and energy, offer women glitter without goal achievement. Unless women gain control of these technologies, they will find they have created new lives for themselves today, only to have forfeited the future—an empty womb indeed [p. 365].

What can be done? Women must break the silence, must force the full facts and implications of sex preselection technology into the open, and generate the critical checks and balances of vigorous public debate. Women must raise the moral consciousness of men and unconvinced women so that they realize the invidiousness of assigning value to persons on the basis of their sex. But a strong word of caution is also necessary. Legislation to prohibit any of these technologies would in itself be dangerous: any regulation of human reproductive risks cutting away women's reprodutive rights in general (Powledge 1981). Therefore, moral suasion remains the ethically acceptable tool—and it can be powerful. We must make it powerful. We need more education about the perniciousness of sexism. We need, once and for all, to separate the myths from the truth about those factors (e.g., math "anxiety," limited access, career counseling, etc.) that inhibit us from choosing careers in science and consequently prevent us from having a voice in its application. We need to help all women to realize the primacy of their life-affirming relationships with other women. We need to create more opportunities for women to participate as valued decision-makers in society.

Whether or not viewed as a concomitant of women's historic power to reproduce, species preservation can be characterized as a female force in the world; males have historically been the authors and kingpins of destruction, enslavement, and war. Perhaps the final irony in patriarchy's attempts to control reproduction would be if male cooptation of women's power to reproduce worked to inhibit the pervasive patriarchal need to destroy.

Notes

1. The Dalkon shield is an intrauterine device (IUD) that has led to several deaths and sterilizations of women in whom it was inserted. See Mark Dowie and Tracy Johnston, "A Case of Corporate Malpractice and the Dalkon Shield," in *Seizing Our Bodies: The Politics of Women's Health,* ed. Olaudia Driefus (New York: Random House, 1977), pp. 86–104.

2. See Helen B. Holmes, "A Feminist Analysis of the Universal Declaration of Human Rights," Chap. 14, this volume.

3. Once a hospital obtains an electronic fetal monitor (EFM), it must use the device even in low-risk births to make the purchase cost-effective; the EFM requires that a woman be in an unsuitable position for normal labor; EFM readings often lead to unnecessary cesareans. See Helen B. Holmes, "Reproductive Technologies: The Birth of a Woman-Centered Analysis," in *Birth Control and Controlling Birth,* ed. Holmes, Hoskins, and Gross, pp. 3–20, esp. p. 6; and David Banta, "Benefits and Risks of Electronic Fetal Monitoring," in the same volume, pp. 183–91.

4. Diethylstilbestrol (DES) was a synthetic estrogen given in the 1950s to many women who were at risk for miscarriages. Some of their daughters have developed a form of vaginal cancer, some have reproductive tract abnormalities, and some have difficulty carrying pregnancies to term.

5. Y-bearing-male-determining; X-bearing-female-determining.

References

Ansaldi, E., G. Voglino, F. Coppo, and M. Massobrio. 1981. "Amniotic Fluid Testosterone and Fetal Sex Determination." *Ricerca in Clinica e in Laboratoria* 22: 349–54.

Belmont, L., and F.A. Marolla. 1973. "Birth Order, Family Size, and Intelligence." *Science* 182: 1096–1101.

Breland, H.M. 1973. "Birth Order Effects: A Reply to Schooler." *Psychological Bulletin* 10, no. 3: 86–92.

Clare, J.E., and C.V. Kiser. 1951. "Preference for Children of Given Sex in Relation to Fertility." *Milbank Memorial Fund Quarterly* 29: 440–92.

Cowan, B. 1980. "Ethical Problems in Government-Funded Contraceptive Research." In *Birth Control and Controlling Birth: Women-Centered Perspectives,* edited by H.B. Holmes, B.B. Hoskins, and M. Gross. Clifton, N.J.: Humana Press, Pages 37–46.

Dalton, K. 1976. "Prenatal Progesterone and Educational Attainments." *British Journal of Psychiatry* 129: 438–42.

Daly, M. 1973. *Beyond God the Father: Toward a Philosophy of Women's Liberation.* Boston: Beacon Press.

Dmowski, W.P., L. Gaynor, R. Rao, M. Lawrence, and A. Scommegna. 1979. "Use of Albumin Gradients for X and Y Sperm Separation and Clinical Experience with Male Sex Preselection." *Fertility and Sterility* 31, no. 1: 52–57.

Ericsson, R.J. 1977. "Isolation and Storage of Progressively Motile Human Sperm." *Andrologia* 9, no. 1: 111–14.

Eysenck, H.J., and D. Cookson. 1970. "Personality in Primary School Children. Part 3: Family Background." *British Journal of Educational Psychology* 40: 117–31.

Fidell, L.S., D. Hoffman, and P. Keith-Spiegel. 1979. "Some Social Implications of Sex-Choice Technology." *Psychology of Women Quarterly* 4, no. 1: 32–41.

Freedman, R., and J. Takeshita. 1969. *Family Planning in Taiwan: An Experiment in Social Change.* Princeton: Princeton University Press.

Gosden, J.R., A.R. Mitchell, C.M. Gosden, C.H. Rodeck, and J.M. Morsman, 1982. "Direct Vision Chorion Biopsy and Chromosome-Specific DNA Probes for Determination of Fetal Sex in First-Trimester Prenatal Diagnosis." *The Lancet* 2: 1416–19.

Hanmer, J., and P. Allen. 1981. "Reproductive Engineering—The Final Solution?" In *Alice Through the Microscope: The Power of Science over Women's Lives,* edited by Brighton Women and Science Group. London: Virago Press.

Harlap, S. 1979. "Gender of Infants Conveived on Different Days of the Menstrual Cycle." *New England Journal of Medicine* 300: 1445–48.

Held, K.R., U. Burck, and Th. Koske-Westphal. 1981. "Pränatale Geschlechtsbestimmung durch den GBN-Speicheltest. Ein Vergleich mit den Ergebnissen der Pränatalen Chromosomendiagnostik." *Geburtshilfe und Frauenheilkunde* 41: 619–21.

Herzenberg, L.A., D.W. Bianchi, J. Schroeder, H.M. Conn, and G.M. Iverson. 1979. "Fetal Cells in the Blood of Pregnant Women: Detection and Enrichment by Fluorescence-Activated Cell Sorting." *Proceedings of the National Academy of Science* 79: 1453—55.

Juhel, Ph., and L. Pourcelot. 1981. "Détermination Echographique de Sexe Foetal." *La Nouvelle Presses Médicale* 10:705–7.

Langendoen, S., and W. Proctor. 1982. *The Preconception Gender Diet.* New York: Evans, M & Co.

Maccoby, E.E., C.H. Doering, C.N. Jacklin, and H. Kraemer. 1979. "Concentrations of Sex Hormones in Umbilical-Cord Blood: Their Relation to Sex and Birth Order of Infants." *Child Development* 56: 632–42.

Markle, G.E., and R.F. Wait. 1976. "The Development of Family Size and Sex Composition Norms among United States Children." In *Papers of the East-West Population Institute*, No. 39. Honolulu: East-West Center.

May, D.A., and D.M. Heer, 1968. "Son Survivorship Motivation and Family Size in India: A Computer Simulation." *Population Studies* 22: 199–210.

Morrison, W.A. 1975. "Attitudes of Females Toward Family Planning in a Maharashtrian Village." *Milbank Memorial Fund Quarterly* 35: 67–81.

Newberger, P.E., and S.A. Latt. 1979. "Improved Fluorescent Staining of Interphase Nuclei for Prenatal Diagnosis." *Lancet* 8126, no. 1: 1144.

Pebley, A.R., and C.F. Westoff. 1982. "Women's Sex Preference in the United States: 1970 to 1975." *Demography* 19, no. 2: 177–89.

Pohlman, E., and K. Roa. 1969. "Why Boy Babies Are Preferred for Adoption and Procreation." *Journal of Family Welfare* 15: 45–62.

Porreco, R.P., S. Sarkar, and O.W. Jones. 1980. "Something New for Prenatal Diagnosis: Fluorescent Cell Sorting." *Contemporary OB/GYN* 16: 15–23.

Postgate, John. 1973. "Bat's Chance in Hell." *New Scientist,* April 5, Pages 13–16.

Powledge, T. 1981. "Unnatural Selection: On Choosing Children's Sex." In *The Custom-Made Child? Women-Centered Perspectives,* ed. H.B. Holmes, B.B. Hoskins, and M. Gross. Clifton, N.J.: Humana Press. Pages 193–99.

Steinbacher, Roberta. 1980. "Preselection of Sex: The Social Consequences of Choice." *The Sciences* 20, no. 4: 6–9, 28.

———. 1981. "Futuristic Implications of Sex Preselection." In Holmes, Hoskins, and Gross, eds., *The Custom-Made Child?* Pages 187–91.

Stinner, W.F., and P.D. Mader. 1975. "Sons, Daughters, or Both. An Analysis of Family Sex Composition Preference in the Philippines." *Demography* 12: 67–80.

Stolkowski, J., and J. Choukroun. 1981. "Preconception Selection of Sex in Man." *Israel Journal of Medical Sciences* 17: 1061–67.

Tietung Hospital (Department of Obstetrics and Gynecology). "Fetal Sex Prediction by Sex Chromatin of Chorionic Villi Cells During Early Pregnancy." *Chinese Medical Journal* 1: 117.

Westoff, C.F., and R.R. Rindfuss. 1974. "Sex Preselection in the United States: Some Implications." *Science* 184: 633–38.

Wood, C.H., and F.D. Bean. 1977. "Offspring Gender and Family Size: Implications from a Comparison of Mexican Americans and Anglo Americans." *Journal of Marriage and the Family* 39: 129–39.

Zajonc, R.B., and G.B. Markus. 1975. "Birth Order and Intellectual Development." *Psychological Review* 82: 74–88.

Zimmerman, J. 1981. "Technology and the Future of Women: Haven't We Met Somewhere Before?" *Women's Studies International Quarterly* 4, no. 3: 355–67.

17

Contemporary Feminist Perspectives on Women and Higher Education

GERALDINE PERREAULT

Introduction

... our brother who has been educated at schools and universities.
Do we wish to join that procession, or don't we? On what terms shall
we join that procession? Above all, where is it leading us, the
procession of educated men?

Virginia Woolf, Three Guineas

Where is the procession of educated men leading? Do women want
to join that procession? If so, on what terms? Woolf's questions
provide this chapter with the basic framework and organizing theme
for exploring the nature of the feminist debate about higher education. The essay presents three contemporary responses to Woolf's
questions in the form of three feminist perspectives. These perspectives reflect fundamental differences regarding the goals and purposes of higher education, the analysis of the problem of women's
subordinate position in higher education, and recommendations for
change.

While others in the first half of the 20th century sought to join the
procession of educated men, Woolf raised fundamental concerns
about the procession itself, the procession of men who had been
educated in colleges and universities. In her estimation, the procession was leading to war. The political and social system, she
believed, generated competitiveness, tyranny, possessiveness, in-
vidious distinction, and violence (Carroll 1978). Woolf viewed educated men as part of that system, and she did not want women to

become men's counterparts. In her long essay *Three Guineas,* when a man from a peace society asks a woman for help in preventing war, her response is: "We can best help you to prevent war by not repeating your words and following your methods but by finding new words and creating new methods" (p. 143). Woolf's questions remain relevant for examining contemporary feminism vis-à-vis higher education. Are today's feminists seeking to join the procession as it is, to transform it, or to ignore it and create their own?

Three Feminist Perspectives

Equality. Liberation. Integrity. Although it is always a precarious task to summarize anything with one word, and even more so, fluid ideas within a social movement, these words summarize the central focus of three feminist perspectives on women and higher education: liberal feminist, left feminist, and radical feminist. These feminists share a common concern about the subordinate position of women in higher education and in society, but they differ in their goals, analyses of the problem, and recommendations for change. Liberal feminists focus on equality of educational opportunity and the preparation of women for positions in public and professional careers. Left feminists focus on liberation and transformation of higher education and society. Radical feminists focus on integrity and countering the patriarchal university and society.

The three perspectives might best be considered ideal types, constructed from the complexity of reality.[1] In any construction of types, ideas naturally become simplified and distorted; the ideas of each feminist perspective or type presented here, therefore, exist more completely in an ideal form than in the reality of a single author or article. The feminist types are constituted not as descriptions with a one-to-one correspondence to reality, but as analytical aids. By accentuating certain views within the feminist movement, the presentation of the perspectives provides a means to explicate and to further understand feminist debates concerning higher education.

The three perspectives are presented below in terms of the following categories: (a) *goals of higher education*—the broad outcomes feminists seek for women and higher education in general; (b) *justification or rationale*—the reasons for which feminists think education important; (c) *analysis of the problem* of women's subordinate position—the definition of the problem and its specified cause; and (d) *recommendations for change*—the proposals for change which grow out of each perspective's goals and analysis of the problem.

In the discussion which follows, goals and justification are discussed together, as are analysis of the problem and recommendations for change.

GOALS AND JUSTIFICATION

Equality, liberation, and integrity respectively express the central goal for each of the three perspectives. The goal liberal feminists seek is equality:

> We need to show high school girls that they can go to the universities on the same basis as men, that they have a chance for an intellectual life within the university or working life in private industry. . . . Women throughout society (should) have the same choice about their roles that men have. That really has to be the focus—equality [*AAUW* (American Association of University Women) *Journal,* November 1970].

Specifically, the goal is equality of educational *opportunity* as opposed to equality of *result or outcome.* This opportunity is to be based on ability and qualifications; for example, Fitzpatrick (1976), argues for "equal opportunity for the equally qualified" (p. vi). Liberal feminists focus on public and professional life and want to assimilate women into all the levels of higher education and societal structures occupied by men. They seek the opportunity for women to compete for positions without being blocked by sex discrimination, and see higher education as the way for women to obtain the skills and credentials necessary for career success. The justification liberal feminists give for the education of women is based heavily on arguments of social utility (for example, material productivity) and freedom of choice for individuals.

The goal left feminists seek is liberation; they want not equality *with* but liberation *from* structures they consider oppressive. Left feminists reject the idea of equality of opportunity and the goal of simply adding and assimilating women into present institutions. In their view, achieving that goal would equalize the sex ratios at all levels but would not change the oppressive and alienating nature of the institutions. Foster (1973), for example, explains:

> Thus our greatest resources for a new Weltenschauung are members of the minority groups and women as a cultural group. But if these groups are absorbed into the patriarchal system of education at the cost of giving up their cultural identity, their value as change-agents will be lost. For this reason, women say, "Not equality, but liberation" [p. 13].

Increasing women's participation, then, is to be seen not as an end in itself or an avenue to assimilation, but as a means to transform educational and societal institutions.

Left feminists do not spend as much time justifying education for women as liberal feminists do, and focus instead on criticizing higher education. When they do argue for educating women, the rationale is to prepare women as change agents. Also, when they focus on women (as opposed to both women and men) such discussion is frequently justified by placing it in the "larger" context of transforming class society. Some left feminists are reluctant to discuss women apart from human or social liberation.

The goals of radical feminists are to reclaim integrity and to counter the patriarchy.[2] Daly (1978) explains:

> Radical Feminism is not reconciliation with the father. Rather it is affirming our original birth, our original source, movement, surge of living. The finding of our original integrity is re-membering our Selves [p. 39].

Radical feminists seek integrity in the sense of wholeness of self. "Re-membering our Selves" refers to the need to help women become whole and return to an original unity that existed prior to the fragmentation and dichotomization imposed by patriarchy.[3] Heide (1979b), like Daly, defines integrity as "a state of being whole, entire, undiminished" (p. 29).

Radical feminists, like left feminists, reject an emphasis on equality of educational opportunity. Unlike left feminists, however, radical feminists make their primary commitment to women and feminism. They share the left feminist goal of transforming higher education and society, but differ in that their focus is patriarchy rather than both capitalism and patriarchy. In addition, their relationship to higher education is more peripheral, "on the boundary," as Daly (1978) would describe it.

Radical feminists, like left feminists, do not spend much energy justifying education for women. They focus on warning women about its intellectual, psychological, and physical dangers. (Left feminists are also concerned about the dangers of education, but their focus is the assimilation of women and the cooptation of women's potential as change agents.) When radical feminists do justify education, often the basis is the need for an education per se, rather than the need to transform society and class relations (left feminists) or to contribute to society and material productivity (liberal feminists). Radical feminist goals of countering patriarchy and reclaiming integrity can, however, also be considered justifications for education.

ANALYSIS OF THE PROBLEM/RECOMMENDATIONS FOR CHANGE

The analysis of the problem and the recommendations for change emerge from different goals. Liberal feminists define the problem in terms of women's lack of equal educational opportunity and their unequal status. They criticize the relegation of women to lower and marginal educational ranks (such as civil service, part-time, and temporary positions) and to positions as instructors and assistant professors, rather than full professors and administrators. They also criticize the way education tracks women into stereotypic roles and careers such as teaching and nursing. The causes of the problem specified by liberal feminists are sex discrimination, sex-role socialization, and women themselves (for example, women's unwillingness to seek high-level administrative positions).

Liberal feminist recommendations for change emphasize eliminating barriers to equality of opportunity and changing women's unequal status. The basis of the recommendations is the desire to add women to all levels and positions in higher education and society, especially those which are non-traditional, that is, male-dominated and stereotyped as masculine. Central to obtaining such equality is the elimination of sex discrimination through the establishment of legal protection and fair procedures. Churgin's (1978) comments represent such a view:

> Women have most to gain in the construction of a truly meritocratic order, for in the final analysis, it is not compensatory measures that will guarantee them a permanent place under the academic sun but a change in procedures that solidifies equal opportunity as the immutable standard [p. 221].

To counter sex-biased socialization, liberal feminists recommend that counseling be provided to encourage women to think about nontraditional career areas as well as how to combine family and career responsibilities.

Left feminists do not share the liberal feminist definition of the problem. Since they reject the idea of equality in a system they consider inhumane and oppressive, they also reject a definition of the problem as lack of equal educational opportunity. Rather, they see the problem as exploitation, alienation, and oppression of all women and men at the university, including civil service staff. The university is perceived as an institution that trains people for oppressive roles: for positions of dominance and subordination in society, for maintenance of the ideological system, and for alienating slots in technical and ideological structures (Mitchell 1973; Shor 1973; Smith 1975, 1979). As part of the training for oppressive roles, women are relegated to lower levels and subordinate positions. "Ideology"

here means the "forms of thought"—images, ideas, and symbols—
which order and control people's experiences, consciousness, and
behavior (Smith 1975, pp. 354, 356) or, similarly, "a set of ideas that
help mystify reality" (Eisenstein 1981, p. 10). Education mystifies
people, creates a "bifurcation of consciousness," a split between
people's experience of their everyday world and the "forms of
thought" available to explain it (Smith 1974, 1979).

Left feminists attribute the causes of the problem to capitalist/
corporate/bureaucratic society, its institutionalized roles of dominance and subordination, and the patriarchy. They explain women's
position in higher education in terms of the needs of both capitalism
and patriarchy. Their main focus, however, tends to be on capitalism and bureaucratic/corporate structures, rather than on patriarchy
and capitalism equally. Left feminists, for example, criticize the
close relationship between male supremacy and the "academic
establishment," but they define male supremacy in terms of material
reality and the material rewards men receive. The same is true for
the term "patriarchy."[4]

Left feminist recommendations for change focus on educating
women to be change agents and to transform society. They do not
wish to educate women only for success in obtaining career positions and consider such positions oppressive and reinforcing of roles
of dominance and subordination. Their views are, of course, at odds
with liberal feminists, who want to help women move into such
positions. Left feminists do not, however, object to women obtaining these positions if the positions are viewed as a means to an end—
social change—rather than an end in itself.

For radical feminists, analysis of the problem centers on dichotomies and fragmentation and on androcentrism and masculine subjectivity (Daly 1978; Heide 1979b; Rich 1975). Pervasive in radical
feminist discussion is criticism of the numerous splittings and
fragmentations—of world view, knowledge and disciplines, and
self—that are said to originate in patriarchy. (Refer back to their
goal of integrity.) Because the university is a patriarchal institution it
is androcentric (male-centered) and grounded in masculine subjectivity. As a result, women are invisible and their experiences
throughout history are omitted.

Radical feminists cite other effects of patriarchy. At the university, women experience rape in various forms—intellectual, psychological, physical. Education performs the function of "mindbinding," comparable to Chinese foot-binding, and mystifies women
about their experience of the world (Daly 1978; Heide 1979b). The
structure of the university is a patriarchal hierarchy in which wom-
en's positions are structured in relation to men just as they are in the

patriarchal family. In addition, for some radical feminists the invisibility of lesbians and "compulsory heterosexuality" is integral to the definition of the problem, and women's studies and feminist scholarship are not exempt from this criticism (Frye 1980; Rich 1980).

Radical feminists differ from left feminists in their analysis of the cause of the problem. Although both discuss patriarchy and mystification processes, the context differs. For a left feminist, the origins of these processes are economic and material, based on needs of a capitalist and bureaucratic society. For a radical feminist, the origins are biological and psychological, based on needs of men.

Radical feminist recommendations for change emphasize reclaiming women's integrity and countering the patriarchy. Specific recommendations include transcending dichotomies and fragmentations, "naming" the lies of patriarchy, creating anew women's selves and places to exist; and remaining "on the boundary" of patriarchy (Daly 1978). Radical feminists also want to change the university's patriarchal hierarchy as well as create a "female counter-force" to patriarchy through a woman-centered university (Rich 1975). Inclusion of lesbian experience and analysis of compulsory heterosexuality are also integral to some recommendations (Frye 1980b; Rich 1980).

Curriculum and Pedagogy. The three perspectives have different views on curriculum and pedagogy. Liberal feminists give these little attention, compared to the attention they give educational access and career success. When they do discuss curriculum, they criticize the omission of women, sex-role-stereotyping, the lack of role models of successful women, and sex bias in classroom interaction (for example, not calling on women students). Their recommendations for change address those criticisms.

Left feminist analyses include the sex-biased concerns of liberal feminists, but focus on the ways curriculum and pedagogy support capitalist society and reinforce roles of dominance and subordination. "Banking education," a core concept of Freire's pedagogy (1970, 1974), is used as the basis for much of their discussion (Schram 1975, 1976; Hague 1978). In this model, which is said to characterize all education, the teacher is considered the source of knowledge and truth to whom students must go for answers, just as customers go to a bank for money. In addition, the teacher-student relationship is authoritarian and alienating and provides training for such roles in society.

Left feminist recommendations emphasize developing curriculum and pedagogy to counter banking education, training students to be change agents, and providing an education that is emancipatory and liberating. This "dialogic" model (again based on Freire's work) allows more interactive and less authoritarian processes between student and teacher. It advocates inclusion of student experience as content and as the basis for problem-solving and seeks to motivate and help students acquire the skills to take action in transforming their lives, institutions, and society.

While liberal feminists discuss the importance of role models of successful career women, left feminists do not discuss role models per se. Implicit in their writings, however, is the need for models of liberators, strugglers for social justice, and women engaged in collective (as opposed to individual) action.

Radical feminist recommendations differ from those of liberal feminists in going beyond discussion of sex bias in curriculum, and from those of left feminists in giving primacy to issues related to women and the patriarchy. They discuss curriculum and pedagogy in relation to the problems cited earlier (androcentrism, mindbinding, and intellectual rape) as well as the invisibility of women's experience, the silence and passivity of women students, and the enforcement of heterosexuality. In addressing those problems, radical feminist recommendations center on making women's experience visible, taking women students seriously, pointing out patriarchal lies and distortions, facilitating an interactive learning process, and including lesbian experience and an analysis of institutionalized heterosexuality.

In addition, radical feminists recommend the inclusion of women's experience and intuition as knowledge and content in the classroom. The value radical feminists place on experience and intuition differentiates them from left feminists, who do not mention intuition and who give student experience a role but caution that it must not be given a "privileged epistemological status" (Elshtain 1978). If this chapter had not been limited to feminists who write about higher education, the difference between left feminists and radical feminists regarding experience and, especially, intuition would probably have been even more pronounced, for radical feminists such as Gearhart (1979) value women's intuition and psychic powers as modes of learning.

Like left feminists, radical feminists do not discuss role models per se, yet implicit in their works is discussion of the need for models of independent women, lesbians, women bonding with each other, and women as survivors.

Knowledge and Scholarship. The greatest difference on knowledge and scholarship is between liberal feminists and the other two perspectives. Liberal feminists seek to add women as subject matter to research studies, probe why women's educational and career aspirations are so low, increase women's participation and productivity as researchers, and document discrimination (Carnegie Commission 1973; Astin 1978; Churgin 1978; Gappa and Uehling 1979). Left feminists and radical feminists share some of those concerns but place their central emphases elsewhere. Both criticize the presumed political neutrality and objectivity of the university's research (Gordon 1975; Smith 1975; Rich 1977; Heide 1979b). They challenge the university's belief that it is a neutral and disinterested observer, as well as its social science norm which assumes subject and object can be separated. But they differ in the *origins* they identify for the university's lack of neutrality and objectivity. Left feminists attribute it to the researcher's class membership and ideological and bureaucratic positions. Since men are dominant in these positions, their perspectives and interests prevail without the fact that they do so being apparent. As Smith (1975) points out, "The perspective of men is not apparent as such for it has become institutionalized as the 'field' or the 'discipline' " (p. 367). Radical feminists, on the other hand, see the lack of neutrality and objectivity stemming more directly from men themselves and from the patriarchal position of the researcher. Radical feminists do not emphasize economic class or bureaucratic position, although some share such concerns with left feminists. Others, however, think economics is irrelevant.

Left feminists and radical feminists share other criticisms of knowledge and scholarship. Both discuss the problem of methodological and conceptual tools, which disallow women's experience as valid data and prevent women from being able to perceive and name their own experiences. Left feminists, however, discuss "bifurcation of consciousness" (Smith 1974, 1979), and radical feminists discuss "methodolatry" (Daly 1973, 1978). Both also criticize treatment of women as objects of research, increased specialization and fragmentation of the disciplines, and artificial dichotomies. Radical feminists emphasize the dichotomies and splittings of world views and knowledge. Left feminists focus more often on the split between the public and private realms of life. Again, radical feminists and left feminists differ in their perception of the causes of these problems. Also, radical feminists view heterosexual bias as a scholarship problem, whereas left feminists hardly ever mention it.

Left feminists and radical feminists make a number of similar recommendations: for example, acknowledging the limits to achieving neutrality and objectivity, developing a method of conducting research that places women at the center, and using an interdisciplinary perspective that redresses fragmented and dichotomous views. In addition, both emphasize the need for women to become subjects (meaning agents or originators) of inquiry, rather than to remain objectives of inquiry. But they also have important differences along lines previously outlined. In addition, radical feminists differ from left feminists in emphasizing the need for women scholars to do the following: reclaim integrity of self, recognize that knowledge is indivisible and knowing is interconnected, include intuition as a process of knowing, acknowledge the importance of women working with women, and analyze institutionalized heterosexuality.

The purposes of research differ. Most liberal feminists do not propose an activist role for scholarship; the university's norms of political neutrality and epistemological objectivity are generally accepted. Some liberal feminists, however, are concerned about the need to document discrimination and barriers to equal opportunity (e.g., Sadker and Sadker1980). Left feminists and radical feminists have a more-activist perspective and consider their primary allegiance to be to the community, not to the university, disciplines, or professions. The left feminist goal is liberation; they want "studies toward a future of freedom," studies of how women have fought and have overcome male oppression (Foster 1973; DuBois 1980). They want research directed toward personal and societal change and toward enabling women to participate in a "common world" of women and men (Smith 1978, p. 282). For radical feminists, the purposes of research are integrity and countering the patriarchy. They want studies to reclaim women's experience and integrity or wholeness and to assist in building a "common world" of women (Rich 1977, p. xviii). Radical feminists also emphasize the need to research women's experiences and their interactions with each other. They believe the left feminist emphasis on studying how women overcome male oppression continues men's studies and devalues women's strengths.[5]

Women's Studies. Women's studies as curriculum and scholarship is viewed and valued differently by each perspective. Liberal feminists give women's studies little attention compared to their concerns about equal educational opportunity and career success. They discuss it as compensatory and remedial, and necessary as a transitional measure until women are integrated as subject matter in the disciplines. Some liberal feminists view it as a potential danger in contributing to divisiveness between women and men (e.g., Rose 1975).

Left feminists hold a range of views but generally consider women's studies compensatory and remedial, yet important. Women's studies is seen to play important roles in changing consciousness; in radicalizing students, faculty, and administrators; and in asking new questions. In addition, women's studies is interdisciplinary and, as such, counteracts the fragmentation and specialization of disciplines and produces "new social understandings" (Gordon 1975, p. 563). Left feminists, however, do fear that women's studies will become an end in itself and dilute a needed emphasis on organizing civil service staff and changing the institution as a whole (Kolodny 1978, p. 24). Left feminists also object to the definition of women's studies as revolutionary and want the term "revolutionary" restricted to mass movements that occur outside universities and in which scholars can participate by uniting with these larger groups (Gordon 1975).

Radical feminists consider women's studies critically important, revolutionary, and central to achieving their goals. In addition, since women's experiences do not fit traditional disciplinary perspectives, women's studies requires an interdisciplinary perspective and approach and a reconceptualization of disciplines. Although left feminists also discuss women's studies in terms of an interdisciplinary approach, they differ from radical feminists in frequently placing their discussion in the context of producing "new social understandings" and understanding male experience better. For radical feminists, understanding women's experience per se is itself sufficient justification.

Radical feminists do express some fears. They worry lest women's studies become an illusion of power. And they are concerned that students might receive messages that women's studies is faddish and that any knowledge worth knowing is men's studies. Radical feminists do not, however, share the liberal feminist concern over women's studies' potential to divide women and men. In fact, some would applaud such division as a necessary step in the process for women to reclaim self.

This concludes the description of three contemporary feminist perspectives. In addition, since the higher education literature does not tap the full range of feminist movement perspectives and since perspectives continually develop and change, I will briefly mention other perspectives that may be emerging. One is a lesbian feminist perspective that would present the goals, analysis of the problem, and recommendations for change in higher education within the context of a primary focus on lesbianism and institutionalized heterosexuality. Examples of works reflecting such a perspective are Frye's (1980a, 1980b) articles on the heterosexual bias of women's studies programs and Cavins (1979) article on "lesbian origins sex ratio theory."

A psychoanalytic perspective could develop, based on the works of Dinnerstein (1977) and Chodorow (1978, 1980). These authors have not applied their ideas to higher education, but Grumet (1979) provides a linkage in her discussion of the different epistemologies of females and males and how these differences relate to learning and research in higher education. The psychoanalytic perspective has a number of problems (see West 1979; Bart 1981; Lorber et al. 1981), including a heterosexist bias, but is worth considering as another explanation for different epistemological approaches to the disciplines and scholarship.

Another perspective on higher education may emerge among black feminists. Whether or not they will develop a perspective which would present goals, analysis, and recommendations within the context of a primary focus on blacks and institutionalized racism is difficult to determine. At present, Harris (1974) writes from a liberal feminist perspective, and Russell (1975, 1977), from a left feminist one.

Last, French feminist thinking has recently become available in this country. Their work has been presented at the Barnard College Conference on "The Scholar and the Feminist" (see West 1979) and at the Second Sex Anniversary Conference in New York in 1979 (see Douglas 1979; Wittig 1979); *New French Feminisms: An Anthology* by Marks and deCourtivron was published in 1980; it was reviewed by Bartkowski (1981) and Burke (1981); and a French feminist journal, *Questions Féministes (Feminist Issues),* is being distributed in this country and has been publicized by the American Council on Education's Project on the Status and Education of Women. While these works were not available for inclusion in this essay, reviews in feminist journals indicate that their theories and concepts may well have important contributions to feminist theory.

Assessment of the Three Perspectives

The three feminist perspectives on women and higher education have been described but generally have not been assessed, although a degree of assessment is always embedded within description. While an in-depth, critical evaluation is beyond the purposes of this chapter, a limited assessment will be made based on criteria which include the following: (a) the complexity with which the position of women in higher education is described and analyzed; (b) the comprehensiveness with which all women in higher education are considered, including civil service staff; (c) the valuation of women's experiences and perspectives; and (d) a concern about social inequality.

LIBERAL FEMINISTS

Liberal feminists have a number of important strengths. One is the extensive sociological and statistical descriptions of the current position of women in higher education and of the specific ways sex discrimination and sex-biased socialization processes are perpetuated. Books by the Carnegie Commission (1973), Rossi and Calderwood (1973), and Furniss and Graham (1974) are prime examples of such work. Second, their mainstream framework of equality of opportunity makes their arguments for change the most easily understandable and acceptable of the three perspectives. In addition, the arguments based on social utility and freedom of choice are relatively noncontroversial, and the emphasis on individual merit and competence fits higher education's espoused selection criteria. Third, their affirmative action recommendations outline clear and precise procedures for facilitating women's inclusion as students, faculty, and administrators in higher education. The combination, then, of all of the above is a powerful force toward increasing women's participation in higher education.

The liberal feminist perspective has a number of limitations, however. Perhaps the greatest is that liberal feminists seek to increase women's participation in higher education and society but, in general, do not fundamentally challenge the values and structures in which they seek integration. For example, the emphasis is equality of opportunity rather than social equality; and the outcome from such an emphasis, assuming it would be effective, would be a general equalization of the distribution of the sexes from the top to the bottom of the hierarcy. Basic social inequality would, however, remain; it would just be distributed differently. Bowen's (1977) general discussion of the limits of equal opportunity applies here:

> equality of opportunity in the sense of non-discrimination in the competition for places on the totem pole will not reduce inequality of social position. It will only rearrange the relative positions of individuals and classes [p. 333].

The liberal feminist perspective does not challenge social inequality per se but asks that it not be based on factors such as sex or race.[6]

Second is the limited analysis of the causes of the problem. "Discrimination" implies generally acceptable standards and structures which are not available to all. A related weakness is the tendency toward "blaming the victim," that is, emphasizing that women are the cause of their problems (for example, women's lack of confidence, career commitment, and preparation for higher education). Such an orientation also includes a tendency to discount women's achievements and values. The consequence of focusing on women themselves as the problem, rather than patriarchal structures and values, is that the burden for change is placed on women rather than on the patriarchy.[7] I do not mean to imply that these foci are either-or choices, only that it makes a difference if one is emphasized over the other. Third, liberal feminists focus on educated and professional (or career) women. Some attention is given to women of color, but working-class women, lesbian students and employees, and civil service staff are rarely included.[8] Last, liberal feminists do not indicate any awareness of perspectives other than their own. They rarely cite left feminists and radical feminists in their writings, and their own assumptions appear to be taken as the way the world has been and is.[9] This narrowness of vision limits the range of alternative criticisms and directions open to them and to higher education in general, since their perspective is predominant in mainstream higher education literature.

LEFT FEMINISTS

It is not surprising that left feminists have strengths that differ from liberal feminists and counter some of their limitations. They question higher education's structures and values, and point out the inadequacies of an equal educational opportunity approach, which may change the distribution of women and men from top to bottom in higher education and in society but preserve basic inequality. Second, in specifying the causes of women's subordinate position in higher education, they go beyond an analysis of discrimination and socialization and focus on the relationship between educational structures/ideology/curriculum and societal structures/ideology, especially economic ones. Their analysis includes attention to the ways the content and process of education reinforce roles of dominance and submission. They also present specific strategies for both students and faculty to use in countering these practices.

Third, they are persistent in calling attention to the need to recognize class and race differences among women students, faculty, administrators, and staff. Working-class and Third World women and men are central concerns. Such concerns are especially important in a society largely unaware of class differences and as a counter to the idealistic views of some feminists who believe being a feminist automatically eliminates differences among women. Left feminists, therefore, function as a conscience for others regarding women of different races and classes. Fourth, they bring new perspectives to knowledge and scholarship. They challenge the presumed objectivity of knowledge and scholarship and emphasize the ways in which one's historical, class, and political positions affect one's research. In addition, they argue for scholarship which is *for* women rather than *about* women, and they discuss ways to conduct research from an interdisciplinary and more holistic perspective.

Left feminists have limitations, which of course differ from those of liberal feminists. One is the tendency to set aside women's issues for the "larger cause" or to see women only in the service of a "larger cause." Historically, women have been asked to put their own needs last, whether in higher education, in a family, or in a social movement. This has meant, for example, that socialist revolutions from which women's freedom was expected to follow automatically have had little effect on the patriarchy of the particular country; patriarchal values and women's oppression continued unabated.

Second, in their efforts to avoid dividing working-class women and men, they risk the danger of a premature focus on human liberation. They also tend to overemphasize "organizational processes," sometimes to the seeming dismissal of the fact that people (mostly men) hold these high-level, decision-making positions. This approach can prevent self-analysis and acknowledgment of one's own androcentric perspectives and behaviors. In working for change, at least two foci need to be addressed: (a) organizational processes that tend to have a life of their own in perpetuating discrimination and oppression and (b) the role of specific people who maintain those processes by actively working to keep them or, passively, by doing nothing to change them. Third, they too quickly discount liberal feminist reforms as being worthless. This dismissal is more evident in general feminist movement literature than in feminist higher education writings, but one can assume that similar views operate in both areas. Left feminist views on reforms are changing, however, toward a recognition of their importance to the change process; see, for example, Harding (1976) and Eisenstein (1981). Fourth, their focus tends to be working-class and Third World women and men. Women administrators, career-oriented women, and lesbians are not of much concern.

RADICAL FEMINISTS

Perhaps the most important strength of radical feminists is the persistence with which they call attention to the need to end the dichotomization of worldviews, knowledge and scholarship, and self and to the need to seek connections and integrity (wholeness). Their perspective (and to some extent the left feminist perspective) forms the basis for a more-complex and interdisciplinary approach to knowledge and scholarship and for a fundamental paradigm shift from fragmentation and unrelatedness to interconnectedness and interdependence. In another article I have argued that such a shift is sorely needed by society and the planet.[10] A second strength is the important centrality with which radical feminists focus on women.

They implicitly and explicitly argue that for once women must not be set aside or in relation to someone else (a man, a child) or a cause. Women's experiences, thoughts, and problems are considered valid in their own right. Third, in pointing out the dangers of cooptation, radical feminists function as a conscience against "selling out." Daly's (1978) discussion of the token is a good example of this kind of analysis; she argues that the token's role in higher education is to perpetuate patriarchy (p. 334). The recommendation to "live on the boundaries" of patriarchy is also relevant here. Yet the practical question—just what is meant by remaining on the institutional boundaries of higher education—remains. University women's studies courses and women's centers are given as examples of boundary living. Are there other ways to "live on the boundary," and/or is the concept more useful as an admonition, a warning to maintain vigilance against the "mindbinding" dangers of the patriarchal university? Perhaps the concept is most useful for feminists in higher education as a "concrete" metaphor that serves as a reminder that feminists must be careful not to be coopted. A fourth strength is the complexity and depth with which radical feminists call attention to the integral relationship of patriarchal education and scholarship to worldwide manifestations of patriarchy. Radical feminists especially address myth and culture, which includes not just the fine arts, but a broader definition encompassing institutions, values, language, and underlying worldviews. In doing this, they sharpen the ability to question taken-for-granted assumptions and beliefs. For example, Truman (1974), a liberal feminist, discusses women and higher education and asserts that a society can live with injustice "as long as it is in some sense socially useful" (p. 57). The radical feminist asks "useful to whom?"

A fifth strength is the new thinking left feminists bring to knowledge and scholarship. They not only challenge its androcentric orientation, but also consider women's experiences and interactions with each other as worthy of study, and try to reduce the multiple fragmentations and dichotomies of knowledge through interdisciplinary perspectives and methods. In addition, they present a challenge to epistemological assumptions that assume the knower is separate from the known and that exclude experience, intuition, and imagination as ways of knowing.

A sixth strength is that they call attention to lesbians as students, faculty, and administrators and to the ways in which compulsory and institutionalized heterosexuality function as yet another means for the subordination of all women. Lesbians and compulsory heterosexuality are rarely mentioned in the other perspectives.

The limitations of the radical feminist perspective differ depending on which radical feminist work one is reading, but some generalizations can be made. First, their overreliance on the power of ideas to change patriarchy is a danger. Although it is important to "name lies" and to challenge language and thought in order to "reclaim" one's own self and to change society, other structures of society can easily continue to operate unless they are also challenged.[11]

Second, some radical feminists are blind to economic and racial differences among women and fail to recognize oppression based on such differences. An example of blindness to racism is Daly's book *Gyn/Ecology*; material she criticized for its misogyny should have also been cited for its racism. Not all radical feminists evidence inattention to racial differences; Rich (1980/1981) and Heide (1979b), for example, include women of color in their work. And some radical feminists are concerned about racism in feminist and lesbian feminist writings (for example, Bulkin 1980).

Third, like left feminists, radical feminists too easily dismiss liberal feminists reforms. Fourth, "living on the boundary" can be necessary for survival and integrity but can encourage a ghetto mentality in which living with and interacting with a women's community becomes so comforting that little is done to change institutuions. Both Brooke (1980) and Daly (1978, p. xv; 1979b) recognize such dangers.

A fifth limitation of many radical feminist views, Heide and Rich being exceptions, is the lack of concern paid to working-class and Third World women and, for some radical feminists, even non-lesbian women.

Sixth, the emphasis by some radical feminists on women's innate superiority may become a two-edged sword. Although radical feminists use such an argument to improve women's lives, others may use the argument to support policies that maintain women in a subordinate position.

ADDITIONAL COMMENTS

Like the proverbial story of the elephant in which each observer sees only a part,[12] each perspective presents only a partial and inadequate view, but together they contribute to a comprehensive picture of the situation of women in higher education. Combined, they present multiple analyses on the causes of women's subordinate position; discuss the lives and concerns of all women; contribute to development of a range of alternatives and goals for changes in higher education; and challenge, redefine, and present new views on knowledge and scholarship.

A comment needs to be made about liberal feminism, since this perspective has been presented as the most conservative of the three. One should note that it is a radical perspective, compared to the full range of views on women held by people in higher education and society in general. The goals of liberal feminists could not be achieved without making important changes in many areas of higher education. Further, what has not been addressed is the question whether or not the addition of women to higher education and other societal structures by itself might fundamentally change those structures. What Yates (1975) said of the liberal feminist perspective in her study also applies to the liberal feminist view on higher education: "How much it is radical will depend on whether it is true that women *are* different from men and will do things differently, even in this case, despite espousal of values similar to men."

It is distressing that one must read widely in order to become aware of all three perspectives. Mainstream education journals generally cover only the perspectives of liberal feminists, yet even their views and concerns are not much represented. Also distressing is the extent to which feminists in each perspective rely almost entirely on works by feminists from their own perspective. This is most true for the liberal feminist, since feminists in the other two perspectives do cite liberal feminist works, if only to reject their ideas and analyses. Communication and interaction are needed across and within all perspectives. That statement is, of course, based on an assumption that such dialogue will produce a better understanding of the problems women face, new synthesis among the perspectives (see, for example, Kelly 1979), and new insights regarding the scope of the values and issues involved. This work is intended to facilitate such dialogue.

Implications for Higher Education

While a number of implications for higher education are probably apparent, I will highlight two.

POLITICAL LEGITIMATION OF HIGHER EDUCATION

All three perspectives are consistent with the trend toward the "political legitimation" of higher education described by Brubacher in *On the Philosophy of Higher Education* (1977). Reviewing the history of higher education, he identifies two legitimations: an "epistemological" justification, which considers knowledge an end in itself, and a "political" justification, which considers knowledge a resource or a means to an end, and emphasizes its significance to "the body politic" (p. 13) Trow (1970) makes a similar distinction about the functions of higher education, classifying them as "auton-omous" vs. "popular" (cited in Clecak 1977, p. 412). "Autono-mous" includes transmission of high culture, pure research, and development of intellectual elites; "popular" includes service to larger social institutions, and education of everyone to her or his limits.

Brubacher (1977) describes how the two legitimations have changed over time. The political was dominant in the early period of higher education but was superceded in the 19th century by the epistemological, when the research emphasis of German universi-ties influenced American higher education. In the 20th century the political again became dominant as higher education took on public service functions (pp. 15-25). He concludes:

> In spite of the attractive logic of a value-free epistemology for higher education modeled on that of the German research university, history seems clearly to favor the political legitimation of the higher learning [p. 25].

Although the nature of the political legitimation for higher educa-tion differs in each perspective, all three feminist perspectives would effect a further increase in the political legitimation of higher education. Each assumes, either implicitly or explicitly, a close relationship between higher education and society. Liberal feminists do not explicitly state a close relationship between higher education and the world outside: their general stance is that they are con-cerned with the development of individual talent and are not part of a political movement, from which, they believe, a university must remain neutral and separate (see, Truman 1974). Liberal feminist do, however, see higher education in the role of educating women for careers and for mobility to top positions in its own institutions and in society, and more-activist liberal feminists see research as a re-source in documenting discrimination.[13]

In contrast, left feminists have an activist stance and explicitly state a close relationship between higher education and society. They want higher education to be involved in the liberation of individuals and institutions from oppressive beliefs and practices of capitalist/bureaucratic/patriarchal society. They criticize liberal feminists for their relationship to society not because of the relation-ship itself, but because they consider it the wrong relationship—career success for individuals rather than social transformation of society. They also criticize liberal feminists for considering their position to be a neutral one; left feminists consider education for careers in society's institutions to be political, not neutral. The left feminist goal is to change society, not to add women who might then contribute to maintaining society's oppressive features.

Like left feminists, radical feminists see an activist and political role for themselves and want higher education to be involved in countering patriarchy within its own institutions and in society. They also share the left feminist criticism of liberal feminists who consider education of women for career positions an end to itself. Radical feminists, however, maintain a closer relationship to women and the feminist movement. For example, in criticizing liberal feminists, they place more emphasis on the patriarchal nature of the positions liberal feminists seek, whereas left feminists emphasize the corporate/capitalist/bureaucratic nature of the positions. In addition, they emphasize the need to create new spaces and institutions for women and the need to counter patriarchal institutions.

Both left feminists and radical feminists believe universities should work on problems that need solving in the community and should be a resource for the community and the feminist movement. Universities should also learn from the community. They differ, however, in the communities which are their reference group. Left feminists focus more on Third World and working-class women and, frequently, men also. Radical feminists focus more on women in general, including lesbians.

The three perspectives, then, extend the trend toward political legitimation of higher education. But they go beyond the political legitimation as discussed by Brubacher to include both a critical evaluation function and a social change one.

KNOWLEDGE AND SCHOLARSHIP

The three perspectives have important implications for knowledge and scholarship and present challenges to their most basic assumptions and beliefs. First, all three perspectives present a convincing case that the university represents mankind, not humankind. The feminist perspectives present compelling arguments that the university is indeed, as Heide (1979b) defines it, a "semi-versity," not a university. The university is grounded in androcentrism and masculine subjectivity. Women's thoughts, interests, and experiences are generally excluded, and the predominant subject matter for scholars and students is men's thoughts, interests, and achievements. Further, this androcentrism is institutionalized; as was pointed out earlier, the men's perspectives are not apparent, for these have been "institutionalized as the 'field' or the 'discipline' " (Smith 1975, p. 367). Moreover, scholarship not only generally excludes women and assumes the study of man represents women, but also participates in justifying women's subordination and oppression. The presentations by the three perspectives, then, provide an answer to the question

"Now that you have women's studies, when will we have men's studies?" The focus for the university's curriculum, knowledge, and scholarship is men's studies, the study of men. The university's claims to neutrality and objectivity are, therefore, undermined.

Second, an even greater challenge confronts its ontological and epistemological assumptions. Radical feminists and some left feminists argue that scholarship must recognize the centrality of the human being in all knowing and the unity or interconnectedness of reality and of all knowing. In this view, the human being is not separate from the world nor is the observer separate from the observed. Noteworthy is the striking similarity of such views to the worldviews underlying modern physics (Perreault 1980). In addition, left feminists and radical feminists argue for inclusion of intuition and imagination in this process.

Third, the perspectives themselves demonstrate the necessity for scholars to be conscious of the basic assumptions that form the context for their own work. Comparison of the three perspectives confirms a statement by Elshtain (1978) that facts "move within theories and may be assimilated within a number of competing explanatory frameworks" (p. 312). Facts do not exist independently, but are viewed quite differently depending on the particular theory or framework within which they are embedded. For example, feminists in all three perspectives agree that women as employees are concentrated in the lower ranks and that women as students are concentrated in relatively few fields. But they differ significantly on the context (definition of the problem, analysis, recommendations for change) within which they place these facts. Liberal feminists interpret the facts in terms of discrimination and sex bias; left feminists in terms of exploitation, capitalism, and patriarchy; and radical feminists in terms of androcentrism and patriarchy. These differences highlight the importance of recognizing that descriptions of a problem are not neutral. As Jaggar and Struhl (1978) observe in their discussion of feminist frameworks in general:

> even apparently straighforward *descriptions* of a social situation also make presuppositions. These are presuppositions regarding the choice of categories or concepts which will be the most useful in bringing out those features of the situation which deserve emphasis. For example, to say that women suffer from job discrimination is to presuppose (among other things) that certain procedures for assigning jobs are appropriate and that others are inappropriate; to say that women are exploited is (usually) to presuppose some version of Marxian economic theory; to say that women are oppressed is to presuppose a certain view of justice and equality. Many philosophers argue that all descriptions of reality are, in this way, "theory-laden" [p. x.]

These observations are applicable to all scholarship, of course, not just to feminist scholarship. Scholars need to be sensitive to the differing contexts and the explicit and implicit assumptions and values within which research and scholarship are grounded, including their own work.

Woolf's 1983 Questions Revisited

In concluding this chapter, I return to Woolf's questions regarding "the procession of educated men." The three perspectives demonstrate that feminists today provide different responses to these questions. Some feminists seek to join and assist men in their procession, while others focus on transforming higher education and the procession of educated men. Liberal feminists direct their efforts toward having women join the procession and become assimilated, and they seek modifications necessary to make joining possible. The basic structures and purposes of the procession as well as criteria for joining it are unquestioned, except that the criteria for exclusion must be based on merit, not sex or race. Woolf's questions are, for the most part, not asked; the assumption is that women need to join the procession and do not need to address the question of terms or conditions. Woolf's image of a procession is appropriate, for procession implies linear and continued progress, a view consistent with the liberal perspective on history.

In contrast, left feminists question the very nature and purpose of the procession and oppose women joining a procession they consider oppressive. They focus their efforts on changing the procession's capitalist, bureaucratic, and patriarchal structure. The image appropriate for their view is not a procession at all, but a dialectical process. They see the history of women not as linear progress, but as a dialectical struggle between people who are oppressed and the system which oppresses them.

Radical feminists also question the very nature and purpose of the procession, and take two approaches. One seeks to alter radically the procession's patriarchal nature; the other generally seeks to ignore it, remain on its boundary, and create alternatives to the procession. In neither of these approaches is the linear image of a procession appropriate. The images used by radical feminists, spinning a spiral or web and weaving cosmic tapestries, represent the radical feminist's emphasis on wholeness, interconnectedness, and process.

Both left feminists and radical feminists, then, share Woolf's concern about where the procession has led and is leading. Woolf saw the procession perpetuating competition and tyranny and leading to war. Left feminists see it leading to exploitation, alienation, death, and destruction. Radical feminists increasingly see it threatening planetary survival with nuclear destruction. Many of today's feminists, then, would agree that Woolf's questions are still relevant, especially since higher education has become increasingly interconnected with society, and they would stress the critical importance of continuing to ask Woolf's questions.

As critics of higher education, contemporary feminists have a significant role. Clecak (1977) comments on the importance of higher education's critics: "the critical debate itself complexly affects outcomes. . . . Insofar as critics help to shape the range of desired goals, they affect judgments of actual outcomes" (p. 426). In presenting the different perspectives of feminist critics of higher education, I have intended this chapter to be a contribution toward helping to "shape the range of desired goals."

Notes

1. Representative writings analzyed for the three feminist perspectives included those of the following feminists: *Liberal Feminists:* Carnegie Commission (1973), Rossi and Calderwood (1973), Truman (1974), Astin and Hirsch (1978), Churgin (1978), Gordon and Kerr (1978), and Gappa and Uehling (1979). *Left Feminists:* Foster (1973), Webb (1973), Gordon (1975), Schram (1975, 1976), Smith (1975), Elshtain (1978), Hague (1978) and DuBois (1980). *Radical Feminists:* Daly (1973, 1978), Rich (1975, 1980), Heide (1979a, b), and Smith-Rosenberg (1980).

Radical feminists writings on higher education were difficult to find. Therefore, Daly, Heide, and Rich, but especially Daly, were relied on fairly heavily for presentation of the radical feminist view.

2. As will become clear, the term "patriarchy" is used differently by feminists from the three perspectives. When the term is not used in the context of one of the three, however, its definition will be as follows: a worldview which assumes females inferior and males superior; the multiple ways in which that worldview is institutionalized; and the characteristic ways of viewing and relating to the world, most frequently associated with stereotypic masculinity, e.g., rational, agentic, inexpressive.

3. Daly's use of integrity is similar to Raymond's (1975), who discusses integrity as an integral whole, not in the sense of addition of parts but "an original unity from which no part may be taken" (p. 64). This integrity "is an 'original' state of be-ing before the 'fall' of patriarchy, an original state that does not reside in a static historical past . . . , but which resides rather in the intuitive wanderings of a mytho-historical past which has the potentiality of generating for all of us a future vision of becoming, beyond a gender-defined society" (p. 64).

4. Note the emphasis on a material base in this definition of patriarchy by Hartmann (1979): "I define patriarchy as a set of social relations which has a material base and in which there are hierarchical relations between men, and solidarity among them, which enable them to control women. Patriarchy is thus the system of male oppression of women" (p. 232).

5. See debate between Smith-Rosenberg and DuBois in *Feminist Studies,* Spring 1980. DuBois emphasizes the need to study men's oppression of women, and Smith-Rosenberg disagrees with this focus. She explains that while in the past she had

"explored male ideology," she came "to realize that such an exclusive emphasis on male oppression of women had transformed me into a historian of men" (pp. 60-61). Instead, she argues for the study of the female world (p. 62) and of women's interactions with each other (p. 59). Only then, Smith-Rosenberg says, can historians "begin to untangle the intricate relation between the female world and the economic and institutional power structure of the 'external world' " (p. 59).

6. Whether or not women could be included as students and employees in equal numbers with men in higher education without fundamentally challenging underlying values and structures, including social inequality, raises different issues and questions.

7. Refer to note 2 for use of the term "patriarchy."

8. Omission of a concern for the physically disabled is apparent in the writings from all the perspectives. Consciousness of the disabled is too new to criticize any perspective for thus far having excluded them, however.

9. See a similar view of liberal feminists expressed by Eisenstein (1981) in her book on liberal feminism.

10. The article compared the world views of physics and feminism (Perreault 1980), argued the need for a paradigm shift to interconnectedness and interdependence, and outlined the contributions of feminism and physics to such a shift.

11. I am not here arguing that every feminist must work on every issue, since that is impossible. I am saying that one should consider and note in one's writing the importance of these other areas. For example, for various reasons, education has been the focus of most of my feminist work so far, but in speaking on education I always preface my speech with comments about the interrelationship of all the areas and that we each make choices about where we put our energy.

12. I recognize that this analogy has its limitations. The different parts of an elephant are compatible with each other, whereas the different feminist views are not. Nevertheless, the analogy is useful in communicating both the usefulness and limitations of the different views.

13. Liberal feminists within higher education in contrast to those outside may differ on the question of neutrality versus activism and may see a more-activist role for feminists within higher education as well as for higher education in general. The present essay did not, however, seek to answer this question.

References

Astin, Helen S. 1978. "Factors Affecting Women's Scholarly Productivity." In *The Higher Education of Women,* edited by Helen S. Astin and Werner Z. Hirsch. New York: Praeger Publishers.

Bart, Pauline. 1981. "The Reproduction of Mothering." *Off Our Backs* 11, no. 1 (January): 19-23.

Bartkowski, Fran. 1981. "Since the Second Sex." *New Women's Times Feminist Review* 15 (April): 8-9.

Bowen, Howard R. 1977. *Investment in Learning.* San Francisco: Jossey-Bass.

Brooke. 1980. "The Chador of Women's Liberation. Cultural Feminism and the Movement Press." *Women: A Journal of Liberation* 3, no. 1: 70-74.

Brubacher, John S. 1977. *On the Philosophy of Higher Education.* San Francisco: Jossey-Bass.

Bulkin, Elly. 1980. "Racism and Writing: Some Implications for White Lesbian Critics." *Sinister Wisdom* 13 (Spring): 3-22.

Burke, Carolyn. 1981. "Book Review: *New French Feminisms.*" *Signs* 6, no. 3 (Spring): 515-17.

Carnegie Commission on Higher Education. 1973. *Opportunities for Women in*

Higher Education: Their Current Participation, Prospects for the Future, and Recommendations for Action. New York: McGraw-Hill.

Carroll, Berenice A. 1978. " 'To Crush Him in Our Own Country'. The Political Thought of Virginia Woolf." *Feminist Studies* 4, no. 1 (February): 99-131.

Cavin, Susan. 1979. "Lesbian Origins Sex Ratio Theory." *Sinister Wisdom* 9 (Spring): 14-19.

Chodorow, Nancy. 1978. "Mothering, Object-Relations, and the Female Oedipal Configuration." *Feminist Studies* 4, no. 1 (February): 137-58.

———. 1980. *The Reproduction of Mothering.* Berkeley: University of California Press.

Churgin, Jonah R. 1978. *The New Woman and the Old Academe: Sexism and Higher Education.* Roslyn Heights, N.Y.: Libra Publishers.

Clecak, Peter. 1977. "Views of Social Critics." In Bowen, ed., *Investment in Learning.* Pages 388-427.

Daly, Mary. 1973. *Beyond God the Father.* Boston: Beacon Press.

———. 1978. *Gyn-Ecology: The Metaethics of Radical Feminism.* Boston: Beacon Press.

———. 1979. "Interview: Mary Daly Speaks and Sparks." *Off Our Backs* 11, no. 5 (May): 22-23.

Dinnerstein, Dorothy. 1977. *The Mermaid and the Minotaur: Sexual Arrangements and Human Malaise.* New York: Harper Colophon Books.

Douglas, Carol Anne. 1979. "The Second Sex—Thirty Years Later: A Commemorative Conference." *Off Our Backs* 11, no. 11 (December): 4-5, 24-26.

DuBois, Ellen. 1980. "Politics and Culture in Women's History: A Symposium." *Feminist Studies* 6, no. 1 (Spring): 28-36.

Eisenstein, Zillah. 1981. *The Radical Future of Liberal Feminism.* New York: Longman.

Elshtain, Jean Bethke. 1978. "The Social Relations of the Classroom: A Moral and Political Perspective." In *Studies in Socialist Pedagogy,* edited by Theodore Mills Norton and Bertell Ollman. New York: Monthly Review Press. Pages 291-318. Originally published 1976 in *Telos* (Spring): 97-110.

Fitzpatrick, Blanche. 1976. *Women's Inferior Education: An Economic Analysis.* New York: Praeger Publishers.

Foster, Ginny. 1973. "Women as Liberators." In *Female Studies VI: Closer to the Ground; Women's Classes, Criticism, Programs—1972.* 2nd ed. New York: The Feminist Press. Pages 6-35.

Freire, Paulo. 1970. *Pedagogy of the Oppressed.* New York: Seabury Press.

———. 1974. *Education for Critical Consciousness.* New York: Seabury Press.

Frye, Marilyn. 1980a. "On Second Thought . . ." *Radical Teacher* 17 (November): 37-38 (issue on women's studies).

———. 1980b. "Lesbian Perspectives on Women's Studies." Paper presented at the annual meeting of the National Women's Studies Association, Bloomington, Indiana.

Furniss, W. Todd, and Patricia Albjerg Graham, eds. 1974. *Women in Higher Education.* Washington, DC: American Council on Education.

Gappa, Judith M., and Barbara S. Uehling. 1979. *Women in Academe: Steps to Greater Equality.* AAHE-ERIC/Higher Education Research Report No. 1. Washington, DC: American Association for Higher Education.

Gearhart, Sally Miller. 1979. *The Wanderground: Stories of the Hill Women.* Watertown, Mass.: Persephone Press.

Gordon, Linda. 1975. "A Socialist View of Women's Studies: A Reply to the Editorial." *Signs* 1, no. 2 (Winter): 559-66.

Gordon, Margaret, and Clark Kerr. 1978. "University Behavior and Policies: Where Are the Women and Why?" In Astin and Hirsch, eds., *The Higher Education of Women.* Pages 113-32.

Grumet, Madeleine R. 1979. "Conception, Contradiction and Curriculum." Paper presented at the annual meeting of the American Educational Research Association, Boston, Mass.

Hague, Patricia Lynne. 1978. "Toward a Feminist Pedagogy: Use of Paulo Freire's Pedagogy of the Oppressed in Women's Studies Classes." Master's thesis, George Washington University.

Harding, Sandra. 1976. "Feminism: Reform or Revolution." In *Women and Philosophy: Toward a Theory of Liberation*, edited by Carol C. Gould and Marx W. Wartofsky. New York: G. P. Putnam's Sons. Pages 271-84.

Harris, Patricia Roberts. 1974. "Problems and Solutions in Achieving Equality for Women." In Furniss and Graham, eds., *Women in Higher Education*. Pages 11-26.

Hartmann, Heide. 1979. "Capitalism, Patriarchy, and Job Segregation by Sex." In *Capitalist Patriarchy and the Case for Socialist Feminism*, edited by Zillah Eisenstein. New York: Monthly Review Press. Pages 206-47.

Heide, Wilma Scott. 1979a. "Scholarship/Action: In the Human Interest." *Signs* 5, no. 1 (Autumn): 189-91.

———. 1979b. "The Quest for Humanity via Higher Education." In *Learning Tomorrows: Comments on the Future of Higher Education*, edited by Peter H. Wagschal. New York: Praeger Publishers. Pages 27-40.

Jaggar, Alison M., and Paula Rothenberg Struhl. 1978. *Feminist Frameworks: Alternative Theoretical Accounts of the Relations Between Women and Men*. New York: McGraw-Hill.

Kelly, Joan. 1979. "The Doubled Vision of Feminist Theory: A Postscript to the 'Women and Power' Conference." *Feminist Studies* 5, no. 1 (Spring): 216-27.

Kolodny, Annette. 1978. "Can Women Organize on Campus?" *Politics and Education*, Summer, pages 22-25.

Lorber, Judith, Rose Laub Coser, Alice S. Rossi, and Nancy Chodorow. 1981. "Book Review: *On the Reproduction of Mothering:* A Methodological Debate." *Signs* 6, no. 3 (Spring): 482-514.

Marks, Elaine, and Isabelle deCourtivron, eds. 1980. *New French Feminisms: An Anthology*. Boston: University of Massachusetts Press.

Mitchell, Juliet. 1973. *Woman's Estate*. New York: Vintage Books/Random House.

Perreault, Gerri. 1979. "Futuristic World Views: Modern Physics and Feminism, and Some Implications for Teaching/Learning in Colleges and Universities." Presented at the annual conference of the World Future Society—Education Section, October, and at the annual conference of the National Women's Studies Association, May 24, and 1980. Reprinted 1980 in *Sourcebook II Education: A Time for Decisions*, edited by Kathleen Redd and Arthur Harkins. Washington, DC: World Future Society. Pages 168-90.

Raymond, Janice. 1975. "The Illusion of Androgyny." *Quest* 11, no. 1 (Summer): 57-66.

Rich, Adrienne. 1975. "Toward a Women-Centered University." In *Women and the Power to Change*, edited by Florence Howe. Berkeley, Calif.: Carnegie Commission. Pages 15-46.

———. 1977. "Foreword." In *Conditions for Work: The Common World of Women*, edited by Sara Ruddick and Pamela Daniels. New York: Pantheon Books. Pages xiii-xxiv.

———. 1979. *On Lies, Secrets and Silence*. New York: W. W. Norton.

———. 1980. "Compulsory Heterosexuality and Lesbian Existence." *Signs* 5, no. 4 (Summer): 631-60.

———. 1980/1981. "Wholeness Is No Trifling Matter: Some Fiction by Black Women." *New Women's Times Feminist Review*. December/January, p. 10-13.

Rose, Clare, issue ed. 1975. *New Directions for Higher Education: Meeting Women's Educational Needs* 111, no. 3 (Autumn).

Rossi, Alice S., and Ann Calderwood, eds. 1973. *Academic Women on the Move*. New York: Russell Sage Foundation.

Russell, Michele. 1975. Speech given at National Conference on Socialist Feminism. Reprinted in *Socialist Revolution* 26 (5, no. 4) (October/December): 100-106.

———. 1977. "An Open Letter to the Academy." *Quest* 3 (Spring): 70-80.

Sadker, Myra Pollack, and David Miller Sadker. 1980. "Sexism in Teacher-Education Texts." *Harvard Educational Review* 50, no. 1 (February): 36-46.

Schram, Barbara A. 1975. "What's the Aim of Womens Studies?" *Journal of Teacher Education* 26, no. 4 (Winter): 352-53.

———. 1976. "Women's Studies as Humanist Education: Some Concepts, Activities and Curriculum." *The Humanist Educator* 14, no. 4 (June): 157-69.

Shor, Ira. 1973. "Anne Sexton's 'For My Lover . . .': Feminism in the Classroom." *Female Studies III: Closer to the Ground*. New York: Feminism Press. Pages 57-67.

Smith, Dorothy E. 1974. "Women's Perspective as a Radical Critique of Sociology." *Sociological Inquiry* 44, no. 1: 7-13.

———. 1975. "An Analysis of Ideological Structures and How Women Are Excluded: Considerations for Academic Women." *Canadian Review of Sociology and Anthropology* 12, no. 4 (Part 1): 353-69.

———. 1978. "A Peculiar Eclipsing: Women's Exclusion from Man's Culture." *Women's Studies International Quarterly* 1, no. 4: 281-95.

———. 1979. "A Sociology for Women". In *The Prism of Sex: Essays in the Sociology of Knowledge*, edited by Julia Sheman and Evelyn Beck. Madison: University of Wisconsin Press. Pages 135-87.

Smith-Rosenberg, Carroll. 1980. "Politics and Culture in Women's History: A Symposium." *Feminist Studies* 6, no. 1 (Spring): 55-64.

Trow, M. 1970. "Reflections on the Transition from Mass to Universal Higher Education." *Daedalus,* Winter, pp. 1-42. Cited 1977 by Clecak, "Views of Social Critics."

Truman, David B. 1974. "The Women's Movement and the Women's College." In Todd and Furniss, eds., *Women in Higher Education*. Pages 56-60.

Webb, Marilyn. 1973. "A Radical Perspective on Women's Studies." *Women: A Journal of Liberation* 3, no. 2: 36-37.

West, Lois. 1979. "French Feminist Theorists and Psychoanalytic Theory." *Off Our Backs* 9, no. 7 (July): 4-5, 23.

Wittig, Monique. 1979. "One Is Not Born a Woman." In *The Second Sex—Thirty Years Later: A Commemorative Conference on Feminist Theory*. New York: The New York Institute for the Humanities. Pages 70-75.

Woolf, Virginia. 1938. *Three Guineas*. New York: Harcourt, Brace & World.

Yates, Gayle Graham. 1975. *What Women Want: The Ideas of the Movement*. Cambridge: Harvard University Press.

Index

Notes on Contributors

CAROL GOULD, editor, is an Associate Professor of Philosophy in the Department of Humanities at Stevens Institute of Technology, and has also taught at S.U.N.Y. at New Paltz, Lehman College of C.U.N.Y., Swarthmore College, and the University of Pittsburgh. The author of *Marx's Social Ontology: Individuality and Community in Marx's Theory of Social Reality* and the coeditor of *Women and Philosophy: Toward a Theory of Liberation,* she has published numerous articles in social and political philosophy and is currently completing a book on democratic theory.

ALISON M. JAGGAR is Professor of Philosophy at the University of Cincinnati. She is interested in social and political theory, epistemology and metaphysics, the relations between these fields, and especially in feminist challenges to some of their traditional presuppositions. She is coeditor (with Paula Rothenberg) of *Feminist Frameworks* and author of *Feminist Politics and Human Nature* (Rowman & Allanheld, 1983).

SANDRA HARDING is Associate Professor of Philosophy at the University of Delaware. She is the author of many essays on issues in feminist theory and the philosophy of the natural and social sciences, the editor of three collections of essays, and the coeditor, with Merrill Hantikka, of *Discovering Reality: Feminist Perspectives on Epistemology, Metaphysics, Methodology and Philosophy of Science.* Her next book will be on feminism and science.

CAROLINE WHITBECK is NSF Visiting Professor at the Center for Policy Alternatives, M.I.T., and Associate Professor, Massachusetts General Hospital Institute. She has written several articles on feminist philosophy and the philosophy of medicine, and was guest editor of the issue on Women and Medicine of *The Journal of Medicine and Philosophy.* Her research projects at the Center for Policy Alternatives concern the role of values in decisions regarding technology and science.

ANNE DONCHIN is Assistant Professor of Philosophy and coordinator of the Women's Studies Program at Indiana University at Indianapolis, where she teaches courses in women and philosophy, and in bioethics. She writes on topics in philosophical psychology, moral theory, and clinical medical ethics.

ROSEMARY RADFORD RUETHER, whose Ph.D. degree is in Classics and Patristics, has taught at Howard University School of Religion and the Yale and Harvard Divinity Schools, and is currently the Georgia Harkness Professor of Theology at Garrett Theological Seminary and a member of the Graduate Faculty of Northwestern University. She is the author of 17 books on theology and social justice, of which the most recent is *Sexism and God-talk: Toward a Feminist Theology.*

HILDE HEIN, who teaches philosophy at Holy Cross College, is the author of a number of articles dealing with the absence of women's perspective from philosophy, science, and morality, as traditionally practiced. Other interests include aesthetics, philosophy of law, and philosophy of biology. She is currently at work on a study of the Exploratorium, San Francisco Museum of Science and Art.

EVA FEDER KITTAY is Assistant Professor of Philosophy at the State University of New York at Stony Brook, and previously taught at the University of Maryland and at several branches of the City University of New York. She has published articles on the philosophy of language and on feminist and ethical issues, and is writing a book on metaphor, which will include a study of woman as metaphor.

MITCHELL ABOULAFIA is Associate Professor of Philosophy and the Humanities at the University of Houston at Clear Lake City. He is the author of *The Self-Winding Circle: A Study of Hegel's System* and is currently pursuing research on social theories of the self.

JANICE MOULTON teaches at Smith and Mount Holyoke colleges. She has written a book in linguistics (with G. M. Robinson) entitled *The Organization of Language* and is currently at work on a book on ethical problems in higher education.

FRANCINE RAINONE has taught philosophy at the University of Colorado and at Colby Sawyer College, where she was also head of Women's Studies. She currently practices polarity theory and acupuncture in Boston.

PAULA ROTHENBERG teaches philosophy and women's studies at William Paterson College. She writes and lectures on Marxist feminism and is coeditor of a number of anthologies, including *Philosophy Now* and *Feminist Frameworks.* She is active in the Mid-Atlantic Regional Association of the National Women's Studies Association; she is currently serving as Coordinator of the Mid-Atlantic region. She is currently involved in integrating the study of racism and sexism at the college level.

LINDA NICHOLSON is Associate Professor in the department of Educational and Social Thought and adjunct Associate Professor in Women's Studies at the State University of New York at Albany. Her forthcoming book will be on feminist theory and political philosophy.

ANITA ALLEN has taught at Carnegie-Mellon University and has served as a Program Officer at the National Endowment for the Humanities. She is presently completing law school at Harvard University, where she is also a Teaching Fellow in philosophy. She plans to practice law in New York City. Her *Women and Privacy* will be published by Rowman & Allanheld in the New Feminist Perspective Series.

HELEN BEQUAERT HOLMES is a geneticist/bioethicist and works as a consultant and writer. She was most recently Visiting Scholar in the

Philosophy Department at Spelman College, Atlanta, and has taught in the biology departments of Eisenhower College and Tufts University. She is coeditor of *Birth Control and Controlling Birth: Women-Centered Perspectives* and of *The Custom-Made Child? Women-Centered Perspectives,* and is interested in ethical issues in reproductive medicine, such as sex pre-selection and in vitro fertilization.

ROBERTA STEINBACHER is Administrator of the Ohio Bureau of Employment Services, the first woman in the state's history to hold this post. She is also Professor in the Department of Urban Studies at Cleveland State University and was the department's first chairperson.

GERALDINE PERREAULT works in the administration of the College of Liberal Arts at the University of Minnesota. She has served as co-chair of Minnesota Women in Higher Education and is a member of the Education Council of the state of Minnesota and a board member of the Minnesota Women's Consortium Steering Committee. Her scholarly interests include feminist perspectives on higher education and on science.